THE HANDGAME OF THE
KIOWA,
COMANCHE,
AND
APACHE

SWAIM-PAUP SPORTS SERIES
Sponsored by
James C. '74 & Debra Parchman Swaim
and
T. Edgar '74 & Nancy Paup

THE HANDGAME OF THE

KIOWA, COMANCHE, AND APACHE

SPIRITED COMPETITION ON THE SOUTHERN PLAINS

WILLIAM C. MEADOWS

TEXAS A&M UNIVERSITY PRESS

College Station

Copyright © 2025 by William C. Meadows
All rights reserved

First edition
∞ This paper meets the requirements of ANSI/NISO
Z39.48-1992 (Permanence of Paper).
Binding materials have been chosen for durability.

Library of Congress Cataloging-in-Publication Data

Names: Meadows, William C., 1966– author.
Title: The handgame of the Kiowa, Comanche, and Apache : spirited
competition on the southern plains / William C. Meadows.
Other titles: Swaim-Paup sports series.
Description: First edition. | College Station : Texas A&M University Press,
[2025] | Series: Swaim-Paup sports series | Includes bibliographical
references and index.
Identifiers: LCCN 2024057803 (print) | LCCN 2024057804 (ebook)
| ISBN 9781648432958 (hardcover) | ISBN 9781648432965 (ebook)
Subjects: LCSH: Indians of North America—Games—Oklahoma. | Indians
of North America—Oklahoma—Music. | Kiowa Apache Indians—Games.
| Comanche Indians—Games. | Apache Indians—Games. | Hand
games—Competitions—Social aspects—Oklahoma.
Classification: LCC E98.G2 M43 2025 (print) | LCC E98.G2 (ebook)
| DDC 976.6004/97—dc23/eng/20250210
LC record available at https://lccn.loc.gov/2024057803
LC ebook record available at https://lccn.loc.gov/2024057804

Cover: *Kiowa Hand Game* (2007) by Sherman Chaddlesone (Kiowa,
1947–2013) used with support and permission by the Kiowa Tribe.

FOR

Jack "Asau" Yellowhair
(November 11, 1926–June 22, 2005)

AND

Bill M. "Tuke" Koomsa Jr.
(September 8, 1937–May 8, 2013)

who taught me how to play handgame

However simple this game appears, it causes much excitement and
deep attention in the players. The singing, the gesticulation, and the dark,
flashing eyes as if they would pierce through the body of him
that has the tooth, their long hair and muscular, naked bodies,
their excited, yet controlled countenances, seen by no other light
than a small fire, would form a fine scene for an artist.

—*David Thompson, circa 1800*

This is the most exciting game I have ever seen played by Indians,
and apparently the most fascinating to them.

—*Richard Irving Dodge, 1882*

Coming into the winter camp at night, it was very pleasant to
hear Indians singing in this way, as there would almost always
be a hand game going on in some tipi.

—*James Mooney, 1911*

CONTENTS

Acknowledgments   xi

Introduction 1

CHAPTER 1: The Origins and Background of the Native American
Handgame 11

CHAPTER 2: The Traditional Handgame of the Kiowa, Comanche,
and Apache 54

CHAPTER 3: The Modern Kiowa, Comanche, and Apache Handgame 120

CHAPTER 4: The Kiowa-Crow Association and the Handgame 185

CHAPTER 5: The Kiowa, Comanche, and Apache Handgame Today 241

CHAPTER 6: Conclusions 319

Glossary: Western Oklahoma Handgame Terminology 335

Notes 337

Reference List 359

Index 373

ACKNOWLEDGMENTS

WHEN I BEGAN playing handgame, one of the first things Jack Yellowhair told me was that "handgame people" are extremely friendly, more so, he said, then people in some other social circles. He was right. Above all else, handgame people come to play and have a good time. And they do. During my research I have been blessed with meeting some wonderful people of all ages and making some wonderful friendships and relatives. This time was much more than research; it was about making friends, experiencing fellowship, and learning a new set of traditions. Sometimes my research was so much fun that it was difficult to think of it as fieldwork. The relaxed atmosphere of handgames aided in performing the participant-observation necessary to gain an in-depth understanding of the game and its traditions. Most importantly I learned to appreciate how the Kiowa, Comanche, and Naishan Apache (KCA) of Southwest Oklahoma view the game and its importance. The emic view emphasized that above all else handgame is about having fun. It is, after all, a game. But it is also much more—a traditional activity, a social network, a community, and, for those most active in it, a distinct component in a contemporary Native way of life.

There are many people I would like to acknowledge in the Kiowa, Comanche, Apache, and Cheyenne communities of southwestern Oklahoma. The people known by several names through time—Naishá, Naishan Apache, Naishan Dene, Kiowa-Apache, Plains Apache—will be referred to as Apache or Plains Apache unless otherwise specified. Whether briefly visiting with me about varied aspects and history of the game, conducting recorded interviews, allowing me to photograph and film handgames they hosted, or inviting me to play on their teams, all made important contributions to this work. I offer my sincere thanks to Bill Koomsa Jr., Jack Yellowhair, Gregory Haumpy Sr., Adam Kaulaity, Parker P. McKenzie, Ina Paddlety Chalepah, Phil "Joe Fish" Dupoint, Sherman Chaddlesone, Ace Yellowhair, Jackie Ray Yellowhair, Major Yellowhair, Joanna Yellowhair, Leland Yellowhair, Lela Jo Yellowhair, Brandon Yellowhair, Jeremy Yellowhair, Adawnya Geionety Yellowhair, Alan Yeahquo, Louis Cozad, Tim Tsoodle, Collier Oyebi, Delores Toyebo Harragarra, Ernestine Kauahquo Kauley, Vanessa Jennings, and Genevieve Chanate Old Bear (Kiowa); Alfred Chalepah Sr., Alonzo Chalepah, Augustine Methvin, Bertha Soontay (Plains Apache); Carl Atauvich, Carla Tahah Atauvich, Marie Yokesuite Haumpy, Jed Querdibitty, Vernon Atauvich, Oris Chasenah, Lanny Asepermy, Shelley Klinekole-Asepermy, Donnell Atauvich, Del Wermy, Eleanor Atauvich McDaniels, Lydia Meat Yellowhair, and Robert Old Bear (Comanche); Ed "Buck Day" Little Light (aka Mr. Handgame), Bob Little Light, Allen Little Light, Raymond White Man Runs Him, Virgil Williamson, and Jeremy Shield (Crow); Willie Bearshield, Pete Bearshield, and Mary Bearshield Beaver (Cheyenne); and Eddie Longhat (Delaware). Many of the elders are no longer with us, and in 2021 Pete Bearshield left us too soon. They are appreciated and missed, and I hope that the inclusion of their voices in this work will allow them to continue to teach us as we fondly remember them.

I offer a special thank you to Bill Koomsa Jr. and to Jack Asau Yellowhair and the Yellowhair family. Mr. Koomsa introduced me to the game and provided me with much material on the content, history, and development of the game. He took a great deal of time to inform and coach me on aspects of the game and its traditions during matches and tournaments I attended. Central to anthropological fieldwork, participation was essential to fully experiencing, understanding, and enjoying the handgame. Soon after I began playing, Mr. Yellowhair invited me to be a regular member of his family team. He gave me the opportunity to experience each type of handgame and nearly all facets of the game including hiding, guessing, drumming and singing, and serving as a referee, scorekeeper, and team medicine man. In 1998 Mr. Yellowhair made a handgame drum and a drum-beater for me. The Yellowhairs are a true handgame family. Mr. Yellowhair often had his children and grandchildren over to play handgames between themselves. It was enjoyable and a good way for family members to learn the songs and gain experience playing. I am always

ACKNOWLEDGMENTS

grateful to my brothers Ace, Jackie, Jeff, and Leland Yellowhair, who have always included me in activities and continue to teach me. Àhô (thank you), for the meals, visits, interviews, church meetings, sweat lodges, and good times on South Buzzard Creek. My thanks also to Phil "Joe Fish" Dupoint (Kiowa), Mary Bearshield Beaver (Cheyenne), and Jeremy Shield (Crow) who have long welcomed me at handgames, run tournaments, and provided valuable material on the game. These opportunities were critical to experiencing and learning about the handgame of Southwest Oklahoma.

My thanks also to the western Oklahoma handgame teams, the Crow Tribe of Montana, and Mr. Ed Little Light for welcoming me to handgames, and to my former student Steve and Ginny Main of Fort Collins, Colorado, for sharing their home as I traveled to and from Crow Agency, Montana, in 1998. A very special thank you to Carl and Vanessa Jennings, my host family on Mopope Hill near Redstone, Oklahoma, for providing me with a home during much of my work. My thanks to Jackie Ray Yellowhair, Mary Beaver, and Jeremy Shield for reading drafts of the manuscript and providing useful commentary. Finally, my sincere thanks to Dr. Dan Gelo (University of Texas, Austin, emeritus dean) and Dr. Matthew Despain (Rose State College) for thorough and thoughtful readings and comments, Dr. Jay Dew and Thom Lemmons at Texas A&M Press, and copy editor Chris Dodge for their support and help with the manuscript.

THE HANDGAME OF THE
KIOWA, COMANCHE, AND APACHE

Introduction

LONG AGO ON cold winter nights, members of Plains Indian tribes gathered inside firelit tipis to play a traditional winter game—known today as hand-game.[1] Accompanied by rawhide hand drums and songs with an exhilarating, often entrancing tempo, individuals placed bets against one another and then alternated guessing which hand their opponents hid specially marked gaming implements in. Swaying in time to the music, individuals employed a host of upper body, arm, and hand movements and feints to inhibit their opponents' concentration and confuse them. Combining sleight of hand, keen observation of body language, numerical odds, psychology, and magic, players competed in a form that combined chance and skill. Shaking their hands at one another with confusing and magical gestures, and in spirited competition, play continued, often late into the night. The sounds emanating from the lodges and the shadows produced by the low-lit fires must have made an enticing audiovisual spectacle.

Handgame is the most widely played Native gambling game in North America. This work focuses on the Kiowa, Comanche, and Plains Apache handgame of western Oklahoma. The game is often described as combining singing, drumming on hand drums or tapping wooden rods on a pole, intense competition, luck, skilled observation, and intuition. Sometimes called a "simple game of intuition," it is much more. The southern plains handgame is a fast-moving guessing game that can quickly produce spirited and infectious

2 INTRODUCTION

singing, drumming, gestures, and competition. With relatively few rules, the hand and head movements, loud and intense music, shaking of rattles, cheering, and hollering can appear confusing—even intimidating—to the unfamiliar. The game, which allows all ages to play, is extremely contagious, and many quickly get the handgame bug soon after being introduced to it.

Over time the game has changed. Canvas arbors and multipurpose buildings have replaced tipis, some groups now play the game year-round, and many of the rules, associated gambling, equipment, and singing styles have changed. Yet the handgame continues with as much or more spirit than ever and remains the most widespread surviving traditional Plains Indian recreational form after powwows.

ACADEMIC STUDIES OF SPORT

Compared to many topics, games and sports have long been understudied in the social sciences including anthropology. As sports anthropologists Kendall Blanchard (1981, 14, 23; 1995, 9–24); John Hargreaves (1982, 30–33, 54–55) and Jeremy MacClancy (1996, 1, 18) have noted, little anthropological attention was given to sports and games in its first one hundred years. Even by the late twentieth century most sociologists, social historians, and archaeologists, and many anthropologists, had neglected sport as a worthwhile and fruitful subject of study, seeing it as a fun, playful, or mindless activity but unworthy of systematic study. Following important works like Roberts, Arth, and Bush's 1959 "Games in Culture," anthropological attention to sports increased. The formation of the Association for the Anthropological Study of Sport in 1974 began addressing this dearth of focus, resulting in several important works in the 1970s. Yet by the early 1980s only a small cadre of social science scholars approached sports with an analytical focus. This is particularly ironic in light of the role English-speaking countries have held in the development of anthropology, organized amateur and professional sports, and the role of sports in Western popular culture and economics. Sports are usually passed over or, where studied, of a largely descriptive focus, rarely theoretical, and often neglect their association to important cultural foci such as power and cultural retention (Hargreaves 1982, 30–31, 34).

Containing deep levels of symbolism and meaning, sports are integrally linked to and often reflect the larger cultural values and premises (Blanchard 1981, 81) or ethos of their respective group. In many countries the economic importance of professional sports alone merits its importance for study as leisure and tourism has at times represented the third-largest global industry, outranked in income production only by oil and cars. Competition to

INTRODUCTION

host the Olympics represents a major economic stimulus, and even amateur sports through high school levels involve significant participation and cost. As MacClancy (1996, 2) adds, "Sport is a central activity in our societies, one embodying social values and as such, as deserving of systematic investigation as any other. Sport may be fun. That does not mean it should be disregarded by academics." Although culture change varies widely, Blanchard (1995, 211) notes, "In the process of assimilation, most of the customs of subordinate cultures, including its sports and games, are simply lost." While Native peoples in western Oklahoma maintain many cultural forms, the handgame has been the primary traditional game to survive. Anthropological studies on Native American sports and games have increased since the mid-1970s (Blanchard 1979, 1981, 1995; Boyd 1979; Fisher 2002; Vennum 1994, 2007; Zogry 2010), but there is still much work to do, including study of the handgame.

Conceptual classifications of "play," "game," and "sport" represent another obstacle in understanding cultural forms. Early works tend to gloss over such distinctions in the descriptions of other cultures, terms are not agreed on by all social scientists, and they sometimes contain a Western and European bias, as not all cultures conceive and classify their activities, even by larger classifications of "recreation" or "leisure," the same (Blanchard 1995, 29–31). Efforts to present the Native views of the handgame are emphasized herein.

Such distinctions depend on the nature of the individual, event, intent, and effort, which can vary with the purpose of the event. As Blanchard (1995, 48, 50) described in his quadrant model of sport typology, "Specifically, sport can be viewed as assuming several different forms, each reflecting varying combinations of work, leisure, play, and not-play." As with different types of baseball, football, and Native American stickball Blanchard's different types of handgames (1995, 50–51) occur 1) in family homes after dinner with no entry fee or prize money, 2) at free-for-alls, matches, or tournaments with multiple teams, tribes, entry fees, betting, and prize money, and 3) as paid or pro bono cultural demonstrations at public schools. Blanchard (1995, 51) surmises, "In general, games are competitive activities that involve physical skills, strategy, and chance, or a combination of these elements. In addition, any game may exhibit variable amounts of constriction (i.e., rules or predetermined patterns) and can be classified as more or less playful or worklike in actual manifestation."

As its English name suggests, the handgame is best classified as a game played by amateurs. Hargreaves (1982, 36) distinguishes games from play, "in that they are said to be, in contrast, rule-bound and organized, and sport is then classified as a type of game, usually physical in nature, and involving a

4 INTRODUCTION

contest between players, and regulated by formal rules." As far more people participate in amateur than professional sports, the presence or absence of a paycheck should not determine whether sports are studied or not.

The English concept of game closely correlates with the Kiowa names for the handgame (*jòáugà*—tipi game), awl game (*chǫ́áugà*—awl game), and baseball (*cômǎugà*—friendship game). The Kiowa do not appear to have originally distinguished between forms of play and games, regardless of the presence or absence of betting, and they and neighboring tribes discussed in this work had no professional or full-time sports in pre-reservation times. Kiowa elder and tribal linguist Parker McKenzie (1991) explains that the Kiowa noun *áugà* denotes "any form of game or way of playing; as gambling, soccer, baseball, Kiowa handgame." Not every word for a form of play or game contains *áugà* as a suffix, however.

"Athletic" and "non-athletic sport" are distinguished largely by the amount of physical exertion, such as football and golf (Sack 1977, 194). One of the first systematic anthropological attempts to delineate the constant features of games (J. Roberts, Arth, and Bush 1959, 597) defined them as "a recreational activity characterized by; (1) organized play, (2) competition, (3) two or more sides, (4) criteria for determining the winner, and (5) agreed upon rules," with a categorization of games as entailing 1) physical skill, 2) strategy, and 3) chance. Sack (1977, 144) later defined "game" as "any form of competition, staged for the enjoyment of either participants or spectators, whose outcome is determined by physical skill, strategy, or chance employed singly or in combination." Most western Oklahoma handgames contain all these features and, though played while seated, require considerable physical skill in singing and drumming.

Certain aspects of the handgame also correlate with Huizinga's (1949, 13) definition of "play" with the exception of being an "activity connected with no material interest, and no profit . . . gained from it." Although small handgames with no betting are sometimes played in homes for enjoyment and practice, larger games always involve betting. Sports and games such as chess and tennis require two people at a minimum, whereas handgames typically involve larger groups of players, often larger than professional basketball teams.

Sports can fulfill many functions, including defining existing moral and political boundaries, maintaining or creating social identities, expressing and reflecting on certain social values, defining and changing gender roles, and as acting as contested space as recreation or between rival groups. Sports also relate to larger political events and regularly appear in news and popular media. Mergers, contracts, team relocations, hiring and firings, and both the beneficent and illegal behavior of players and staff are common. Films

INTRODUCTION

addressing the Cold War (*Rocky III*, *Pawn Sacrifice*), race relations (*Remember the Titans*; *Ali*; *42*), apartheid (*Invictus*), incarceration (*The Longest Yard*), beating the odds (*Major League*, *Rudy*, *Invincible*, *The Replacements*), and many others focus on sports. In 2015 the University of Missouri football team refused to play until campus race issues were addressed, and in 2016 debates over National Football League players in the United States kneeling during the national anthem appeared.

Western Oklahoma handgames involve aspects of recreation, economics, social status, ethnic identity, gender, kinship, political power, conflict, media, and artistic performance. They are integrally linked to many other social structures in their respective Native communities. For Native Americans, the handgame is one tradition that helps maintain a distinct ethnic identity in contemporary America.

ETHNOGRAPHY

My reasons for undertaking this work are ethnographic, theoretical, and personal. Although Culin's monumental 1907 *Games of the North American Indians*, based on a survey of 225 tribes, has long been the broadest ethnographic work on handgames, little work has been undertaken on the Plains Cultural Area. Aside from brief sketches of material culture and basic rules of play (Culin 1907), scholars have published virtually nothing on the southern plains handgame. The few related works either focus on the handgame and its association with the Ghost Dance (Lesser 1933; Slotkin 1975:18–21), the stickgame among people in Plateau and Subarctic Culture Areas (Helm, Lurie, and Kurath 1966; Brunton 1974), or broader topics of tribal gambling and music in the northern plains and northwestern United States (Flannery and Cooper 1946; Desmond 1952; Stuart 1972; Maranda 1984) and are over fifty years old. Lawrence Johnson's 2001 documentary film *Hand Game*, focusing on tribes of the northern plains and the Plateau, is an important source on the handgame and contemporary Native American life, while Kernan's 2016 film *Crow Stories* includes a segment on the Crow handgame. Although handgames and brief sources of information occur on the internet, scholarly work on the game continues to lag.

There has long been a need for a definitive treatment on the southern plains handgame. In contrast to Lesser's (1933) and Slotkin's (1975, 18–21) research, this work focuses on the non–Ghost Dance form of the handgame among the southern plains groups of western Oklahoma. Focusing on the Kiowa, Comanche, and Naishan Dene or Plains Apache (often referred to as "KCA" by members of the three tribes, other Indians, and non-Indians from the combined Kiowa-Comanche-Apache Reservation), this ethnography represents

6 INTRODUCTION

a new and major source on the handgame. The handgame is similar among the KCA and constitutes the "southern" or "Oklahoma style" of play. Due to the role that western Oklahoma tribes have played in developing the southern style of handgame, several other tribes have adapted this style of play. Consequently, the KCA handgame offers both a case study for regional analysis and the most influential form of the game in the southern plains. As many Oklahoma Native people, including the KCA, use the term "Indian," both it and "Native American" are used throughout this work.

The KCA regularly play handgame with the Southern Cheyenne and Arapaho in Oklahoma and the Crow in Montana. The Kiowa have maintained annual reciprocal visits to play handgame with the Crow since the 1950s, and significant influences have come from the Crow. More recently southern plains groups have traveled to play tribes of the Great Basin (Ute) and Plateau Culture Areas. Some material relating to these groups is included, primarily as it relates to the southern plains style of handgame.

Theoretically, this work addresses two areas. First, the Plains Indian handgame has been classified solely as a game of pure chance (Dorsey 1901a, 363; Culin 1907, 31; J. Roberts, Arth, and Bush 1959, 597–98; Cheska 1979, 229). Because more complex strategic games such as chess, checkers, and tic-tac-toe were absent in North America, earlier ethnographers assumed that games of strategy were absent. However, as will be shown for the western plains tribes of Oklahoma and others, skill, strategy, and chance are all significant parts of the contemporary handgame and consciously recognized by these populations. While true sleight of hand has been all but eliminated from contemporary play, keen observation of human behavior, psychology, mathematics, and belief in the use of magic (or "medicine" or "power") remain integral parts of the handgame.

Second, this work addresses many of the objectives of the anthropology of sport as defined by Blanchard (1995, 22–23). Beyond focusing on non-Western cultures, this work includes sections relating to the definition, description, and classification of the handgame in ethnography and the anthropological study of sport, and its relation to archaeology and oral history. It examines the relation of sport to other areas of culture, including sport language, gender roles, and economics. This work also explores the increase of sport in ethnic and multicultural educational environments and its impact in Native cultural maintenance and change. Today venues ranging from Native culture camps to colleges include handgame to foster cross-cultural understanding of the game and its associated cultures.

The handgame constitutes its own arena of social activity in tribal communities and is just as important, traditional, and adaptive as powwows,

INTRODUCTION

Gourd Dances, military societies, Indian Christian churches, sweat lodges, Sun Dances, bingo, stickball, and Indian softball and basketball leagues. For handgame players it is a distinct focused activity in Indian life. Important in maintaining Indian culture and ethnicity, each handgame community maintains a distinct genre of ethnic practice and continuity that reflects tribal and pan-Indian distinctions. In addition, I will provide the reader with a sense of how the handgame has evolved, what people feel about it, and what it means to them. Reporter Roger Clawson of the *Billings Gazette* (Bryan 1996, 79) described the handgame in Montana as "part poker psychology, part ritual and medicine-making, part pep rally and totally sociable." These traits apply to western Oklahoma handgames as well.

Because the Kiowa, Comanche, and Apache have shared a similar form of handgame since at least the mid-1800s, a comparative approach is necessary to elicit individual tribal and broader regional patterns. This approach facilitates comprehending the social and cultural dynamics of each group and of the neighboring populations with whom they continue to share a generally similar historical experience. Like distinct ethnic communities, individual handgame teams play against teams from their own tribe and others. This is especially relevant when examining the diffusion of recent handgame traits among teams and communities playing the same form of game. While this work focuses on the Kiowa, Comanche, and Apache, to discuss the handgame of only one—or of these three without contrast and comparison with the others they regularly play—would distort the cultural dynamics of their historical experiences, which include intertribal diffusion and innovation.

In many respects the Kiowa, Comanche, and Apache define and reinforce their identity in reference to one another much as Fowler (1987) describes for the Gros Ventre and Assiniboine, and Meadows (1999, 2010) has described for KCA military societies. As with several cultural forms, numerous KCA similarities allow for an in-depth comparison of the handgame among multiple neighboring ethnic groups—the boundaries for an excellent controlled regional analysis and ethnohistorical comparison.

The handgame is another public forum through which contemporary Native American cultures maintain, integrate, and even introduce new cultural forms (Meadows 1999). Although involving a smaller crowd, handgames facilitate enculturation for Native cultures within the larger United States. The continued maintenance of kinship, communal gatherings, meals, reciprocity (sharing), redistribution (giveaways), songs, and teamwork, helps maintain a sense of a distinct ethnicity as members of a focused activity (handgame players) on team, tribal, intertribal, and Native levels.

8 INTRODUCTION

For many tribes today, the handgame has become a traditional form of social gathering. Following allotment, which demographically shifted many tribes from band encampments to more scattered locations across reservations, periodic large-scale gatherings were needed to maintain face-to-face social interaction. Handgames, on the increase since the 1950s, provide one such occasion for gathering. As an enjoyable form of play with low-stakes gambling, centered in music as with many Native American activities, and increasingly incorporating all genders and ages, handgames provide an important social event.

DATA COLLECTION

Having observed a few previous games, I was formally introduced to the handgame in 1993 by noted Kiowa singer and long-time handgame player Bill Koomsa Jr. (1937–2013). After relating a little about the game to me at a dance, Mr. Koomsa invited me to attend an evening of games he was hosting against members of the Crow Tribe from Montana at Carnegie, Oklahoma, on November 12, 1993, and allowed me to videotape the match. I soon began occasionally attending KCA handgames, conducting interviews, and collecting information on the game. I spent October 1997 to May 1998 in Southwest Oklahoma conducting ethnographic fieldwork, much of it devoted to the handgame. During this time several Kiowa, Apache, Comanche, and Cheyenne handgame players described Mr. Koomsa as "Mr. Handgame," noting that he was the most knowledgeable individual about the game, an exceptional singer among the southern plains tribes, and knowledgeable of songs, their composers, and who owned them. His father, Bill Koomsa Sr. (1909–1990), was also known by this name for his extensive knowledge of the game and his role in creating the modern style of play in the 1960s. Koomsa Jr. carried on his father's contributions.

On New Year's Day 1998, Bill Koomsa Jr. and Alan Yeahquo invited me to play with their team, and I began to regularly play in handgames. One weekend when Mr. Koomsa's team did not attend to play, I was introduced to Jack Yellowhair Sr. (Kiowa) at a tournament in Carnegie, Oklahoma. He told me that they enjoyed seeing new faces around the game and welcomed me to learn. Mr. Yellowhair invited me to play with their family team that day, and I accepted. We placed second that day. After visiting with me he went out of his way to introduce me as Dr. Meadows, saying that I was a professor and that I liked to play handgame. Jack apparently took a shine to me, as the next weekend he told Mr. Koomsa that I was now on the Yellowhair team! Everyone had a good laugh, and Mr. Koomsa said it was fine. I continued to play with the Yellowhairs after that time and became a regular member of their family handgame team. Mr. Yellowhair later took me as a son. I also continued to interview and learn from Mr. Koomsa and others who mentored me on many aspects of the game.

A survey of existing literature and unpublished archival data produced a small but very rich quantity of data on the handgame of the Kiowa, Comanche, and Apache. I learned a tremendous amount about the game through participant-observation, playing and visiting at handgames every weekend. Because most Oklahoma handgames are round-robin tournaments, where teams alternate playing one another, only two teams play at a time. As teams may have two or three games off until they are scheduled to play again, these opportunities provided excellent opportunities to watch games and visit at length with individuals on aspects of the game. The style of handgame played in western Oklahoma today is a modified form of the traditional style played by the Kiowa, Comanche, and Apache tribes and is the form now also played by members of other neighboring tribes (Cheyenne, Arapaho, Wichita, Caddo, Delaware, and Fort Sill Apache), whose handgames are similar in some aspects. The Wichita and Caddo also retain their own version of handgame during certain tribal gatherings.

This study is based on fieldwork conducted in Oklahoma between 1993 and 2023 and in Montana in 1998. I interviewed and visited with Kiowa, Comanche, Plains Apache, Cheyenne, Arapaho, Crow, Ponca, Wichita, Delaware, and Fort Sill Apache of varied ages, including several elder team leaders. My observations in Montana involved playing with the Kiowa team during the 1998 Senior Crow Handgame Tournament (April 29–May 3) in Crow Agency, Montana, watching the other tournament games, and conducting conversations and interviews with both Kiowa and Crow handgame players. Mr. Ed Little Light made a spot for me to film the games, allowing me to study many hours of play at length. Since 1997 I have continued to play in handgames whenever in Oklahoma.

This long period of ethnographic research has allowed me to examine change and consistency in the game over the past thirty years. The fieldwork for this project was extremely enjoyable and relatively easy to access as a secular topic. As one elder explained, "There are no ceremonial aspects to handgame, and I can talk openly about it." On a personal level I have long enjoyed the game, whether playing or watching. Although I greatly enjoy playing, I claim no talent or skill in the handgame. Sometimes I have been able to score a series of points and make a series of correct guesses, other times I have not been so fortunate—but such is the nature of the game. My goal has been to learn the game and its traditions and to provide a solid ethnography of the game and those who play it. That I was able to make many friends, some relatives, and enjoy the game in doing so only added to my experiences and the quality of this work. The opportunity to play, research, and document handgame has been important to me. If I can convey to the reader a little of the traditions, spirit, sense of community, humor, and antics that so permeate the game, then I will have achieved what Plains Indian peoples have emphasized to me.

FORMAT

This work is primarily ethnographic and ethnohistorical, emphasizing ethnographic fieldwork, participant-observation, and archival research. To understand its development, a diachronic approach is used to show how the handgame has evolved. I seek to produce a solid ethnography of the handgame in western Oklahoma, emphasizing a balance of anthropological concepts, handgame vocabulary, a diachronic concern for change and process, and Native voice and perspective. A heavy use of descriptive material and Native voice from tape-recorded interviews provides depth into the subject and an appreciation for the human experience in the game and its traditions, and this allows individuals to convey significant data in their own words. While many consultants are named, discussion of sensitive topics such as hiding and guessing strategies, medicine, or opinions about others remain anonymous.

This work is organized into six chapters. Chapter 1 introduces the handgame in Native American cultures, discussing the game's origins, distribution, historical longevity, and relationship to Native forms of gambling. Because little has been written on the handgame, this chapter offers a general survey of what is known of the game across the Great Plains and Plateau and briefly surveys the recorded ethnography on the handgame and stickgame. Chapter 2 reconstructs the KCA handgame from tribal origin stories and ethnographic data from the mid- to late nineteenth century through the 1950s. Chapter 3 focuses on the modern form of the KCA handgame that has developed from the late 1950s to the present, demonstrating that while the handgame has long been classified solely as a game of chance or guessing game (Culin 1907, 31; Cheska 1979, 229), strategy is undeniably present and merits reassessment. Chapter 4 examines the historical Kiowa-Crow relationship, the Crow handgame, and its impact on the southern plains handgame. Chapter 5 examines social, gender, legal, and monetary aspects of the current western Oklahoma handgame, beliefs in medicine, and anthropological analyses of magic in gambling. Chapter 6 concludes by discussing the game's current importance in western Oklahoma Native communities.

CHAPTER

1

The Origins and Background of the Native American Handgame

NATIVE AMERICANS HAVE a long history and extensive range of recreations including toys, games of skill and chance, athletic competitions, songs, dances, graphic arts, ceremonies and festivals, clowns, oral history and storytelling, and more. Several scholars have classified Native American games. Stewart Culin (1907, 31) divided Native games into two general classes: 1) games of chance (guessing games) and 2) games of dexterity (games of athletic skill). Roberts, Arth, and Bush (1959, 597–98) classified games based on physical skill, strategy, and chance. As they write, "games of chance are so defined that chance must be present and both physical skill and strategy must be absent," and they include "the moccasin games," which would include handgames.

Cheska (1979, 228–29) reclassified Native games into four categories: 1) games of kinetic competence, using physical skills; 2) games of chance, using random selection; 3) games of representation employing replicate actions and attributes of people or things; and 4) games of strategy in which rational choices are made from among possible courses of action. Combinations of these categories may exist in a single game with secondary and tertiary factors (J. Roberts, Arth, and Bush 1959, 597; Cheska 1979, 228–229). Cheska subdivided the first three categories: Games of kinetic competence were divided into 1) body handling, such as foot races or wrestling and 2) object handling, such as ball games and hoop and pole games. Games of chance were divided into 1) hidden ball games and handgames, and 2) dice games, such as dish and bowl games. Games of representation were divided into games of mimicry including 1) imitation, such as the use of miniatures and toys, and 2) iteration, such as games reenacting animal hunting and representational string figures or noise-making devices (Cheska 1979, 229).

While the handgame has been classified as a game of chance or a guessing game (Culin 1907, 31; 1979, 229), this work will demonstrate that strategy is also undeniably present in the Plains Indian handgame and calls for a reassessment of its categorization. As Cheska (1979, 229) discusses of the alleged absence of strategy in Native American games, "This does not imply that the concept of strategy was not employed in kinetic and mimicry games." To categorize game forms as "pure skill" is also inaccurate in that every game involves some degree of chance. Games of "pure skill" such as chess also involve elements of chance in that a player may not make the best possible move at any given time.

Native American games of chance or guessing games fall into two categories: 1) games in which implements such as dice are randomly thrown to determine a numerical count that is kept by means of sticks, pebbles, or an abacus, counting board, or circuit, and 2) games in which one or more players guess two or more places in which a specially marked object is concealed, with scoring recorded by gaining or losing counters (Culin 1907:31).

Culin classified four types of North American guessing games: stickgames, handgames, the four-stick game, and the hidden-ball game. However, Lesser (1933, 125, 127–28) found significant variations in the two types of hidden-ball game, varied forms of stickgames, and the two major types of handgame. Variants of a single game often differ enough to be considered as different from one another (as with the two major types of hidden-ball games and handgames), as they are from other major game forms (as with the handgame and the hidden-ball games). According to Lesser (1933, 129), no American Indian population originally played all four types of guessing game. Four tribes play three games. The Klamath, Achomawi, and Washo play the four-stick game, stickgame, and handgame, while the Plains Cree play the stickgame, handgame and moccasin game. With these exceptions, most American Indian populations with guessing games played two of the four forms. In the eastern woodlands and northern plains, the moccasin and stickgames overlapped. In the Great Plains, either the moccasin and stickgames or the stick and handgames overlapped. Generally, the hand and moccasin games overlapped only when Plains tribes, whose native game was the handgame, played against tribes more accustomed to the moccasin game (generally western Great Lakes groups). While groups generally play the style of the host, groups in peripheral areas became intimately familiar with both forms. Both handgames and

The Origins and Background

stickgames were common in the Northwest Coast, Plateau, and California Culture Areas (Lesser 1933, 129). The moccasin game and handgame occurred throughout the northern plains including the Lakota (Powers 1973:184). The Lakota version of both games, known as "Hiding a Stick" (Densmore 1918, 485, 489–91), and the southern plains handgame are similar in structure, rules, and guessing signs.

The western Oklahoma handgame can be classified as a traditional sport of "Level II Band" political organization, earlier associated with the term "tribe" (Blanchard 1995, 154–55, 248). In contrast to the professional, commercial, political, and media-driven aspects of modern sports, Blanchard (1995, 248) defines traditional sport as "those forms of sport activities which are tied directly to particular ethnic or folk cultures. It is competitive, it is physical, and it has play and game-like elements, but it has limited or no professional variants, tends to be more local in its expression, and has stronger ritual overtones than does so-called modern sport. Traditional sport can also be referred to as ethnic or folk sport. Such sport is important in that it functions to preserve traditional values, develop the skills of concentration and self-discipline in its participants, and helps to connect the present with the past." As Renson and Smulders (qtd. in Blanchard 1995, 249) similarly define, "Folk games are traditional, local, active games of a recreational character, requiring specific physical skills, strategy or chance, or a combination of these three elements."

The western Oklahoma handgame also correlates with the characteristics Blanchard (1995, 257–58) associated with traditional games. First, traditional sport is not tied to political ideology but rather to ethnic and cultural heritage: "It is not a statement about national interests but rather about the meaning of shared symbols and the identity afforded by culture." Second, traditional sport is more about performance than competition, more about the experience, feeling good about oneself, and achieving flow that allows one to transcend oneself. Competition is present but more as an exhibition than as an Olympic-type event. Third, philosophically, traditional sports recognize both the universality of sports and the diversity of that experience. This duality facilitates mutual respect, admiration, and cooperation across ethnic and national lines. Fourth, traditional sport focuses more on inner life than the externalities of performances, material rewards, and public victories. It is more of an end in itself than modern sport participation and can relate to other parts of life not associated with sport. Fifth, traditional sport tends to glorify the ideal of youth less than modern sport, placing greater emphasis on experience and mastery than pure physical athleticism. Sixth, traditional sport can contribute to consolidating the identity, mutual understanding, and peaceful coexistence of multiple ethnicities (Salamone 2012). As with sports in general, traditional

14   CHAPTER 1

sports are an important part of understanding cultures and thus a valuable part of the ethnographic record (Blanchard 1995, 258).

Conspicuously popular among many tribes were dice games and various forms of a game equivalent to the Anglo "Button, Button, Who's Got the Button," known among most Plains tribes today as the "handgame" or "stickgame." The name "handgame" is a generic, non-tribally specific, descriptive Anglo term referring to the hiding of playing objects in the hands to be guessed during the game. The game is also referred to in English as bone game, stickgame (or "stick game"), grass game, and gambling game. Native names varied from tribe to tribe including Slahal, Peon, Tep-Weh, Tep-wi, Ch'enlahi, and others (Rathbun 1999, 249). Among the Kaibab Southern Paiute the handgame was called Ne Ang-puki or "Kill the Bone" (Culin 1907, 312).

Native American groups east of the Continental Divide generally play handgame, while those to the west play stickgame (Boyd 1979, 216). As Lesser (1933, 127) describes, "The hand games proper are those which employ the hands as places in which an object to be guessed for is concealed." Although the game often varies in detail from tribe to tribe, the basics are usually similar. Because of the great distribution and variation in play throughout North America (Culin 1907, 267–327), only the game's general aspects are described here.

In addition to recreation and gambling, handgames were sometimes used to settle disputes in land use and ownership without going to war, for healing, and, according to some accounts, to determine female companionship (AAANA 2012; Tsong 2010). The game was normally a winter-time recreation played in varied forms of tipis, lodges, and permanent or temporary shelters determined largely by the cultural ecology of western North America, in particular the factors affecting seasonal weather, subsistence acquisition, and communal aggregations. For most Plains and Plateau populations, winter was a period of reduced mobility and subsistence activities, relative group dispersal, and increased sedentism, much of which centered upon the repair and manufacture of material culture for the following year. Aside from occasional cultural rites associated with councils, births, deaths, doctoring, and naming ceremonies, indoor recreations such as storytelling and games provided a break in the potentially dull and monotonous winter period (Desmond 1952, 29). As with seasonal taboos on winter storytelling and flute playing, some groups believed that to talk about or play the hand or moccasin game in the summer would bring snakebite, prolonged itching, or other maladies to the

Ne Ang-puki: "The Game of Kill the Bone." Kaibab Southern Paiute. Photo by John K. Hillers, 1873. Bureau of American Ethnology photo 1624-R, Smithsonian Institution. National Anthropological Archives. INV.00194300 OPPS NEG.BAE 1624.

16   CHAPTER 1

transgressor. For the Navajo (Gabriel 1986, 25), "Such a transgression invited 'lightning disease,' or snakebite for the teller, their families, and their stock."

However, non-winter play of the game is documented among some pre-reservation populations. Among the Blackfeet (also known as Blackfoot), Ewers (1958, 155) reports, "In the old days this was one of a series of games played between men's societies during the summer tribal encampment." Desmond (1952, 9) later attended Yakama handgames at their Fourth of July and fall encampments in 1944. Non-winter handgames in parts of the northern plains may have once been more extensive than now realized, while increased intertribal proximity on reservations likely fostered play over more of the year.

Intersex play varied highly. Some accounts report all-male and all-female handgames. Among some tribes only men could fully play the game, with females limited to assisting in singing, cheering, and hiding. In some groups in the 1800s a strict division by sex existed in which women could only play with other women. Although some cases of games involving both sexes exist, most early sources report that the handgame was usually played separately, with men and women holding separate games in separate lodges. In a work first published in 1848, George Ruxton (1951, 101) describes, "Large bets are often wagered on the result of this favourite game, which is also often played by the squaws, the men standing round encouraging them to bet, and laughing loudly at their grotesque excitement."

James Mooney (1896, 1008), who conducted fieldwork among the Kiowa from 1891 to 1918, describes, "It is played by both men and women, but never by the two sexes together. . . . Frequently there will be a party of twenty to thirty men gaming in one tipi, and singing so that their voices can be heard far out from the camp, while from another tipi a few rods away comes a shrill chorus from a group of women engaged in another game of the same kind." By the mid-twentieth century both men and women were participating as hiders and guessers (Garcia 1996, 229–30).

Among the Gros Ventre, women and children could bet and sing in games played by men but could not be guessers, hiders, or tally keepers. However, in women's games women could perform all these roles (Flannery and Cooper 1946, 409). Two teams of any number of members sat facing one another in linear fashion to play. Bets were normally placed between the two opposing lines before starting to play. In some tribes, anyone could bet on a game.

Varied small items were used as hiding implements, including bone or wooden chips or cylinders, small squared sticks, strings of beads, bullets, shells, large single beads, elk teeth, bear claws, wild plum or cherry seeds, and other items. The most common form consisted of bone cylinders—either solid bones 2–4 inches long or slender hollow tubes such as hair pipes, elongated tubes of various sizes up to 4 or 4.5 inches in length and usually 1/4 to 3/8 inch wide used in the construction of breastplates, chokers, and other dress items common in powwow regalia. John Wesley Powell collected several sets of Numa bi-pointed handgame bones made by carving solid bones into the previously mentioned size with pointed ends (Fowler and Matler 1979, 70, 159). Objects to be hidden could be a single item or a pair of identical items, with one distinguished from the other by some form of marking, usually around the center. Markings could be a residual bark ring or the addition of a buckskin thong, strip of otter skin, thread, or paint, usually of a dark color. In addition to the central marking, many tribes etched or incised markings on one of the hiding items to differentiate them (Dorsey 1901b).

Numerous forms of the handgame exist through North America, with differences in types and numbers of hiding implements, players (number of hiders ranging from one to eight), score sticks, hand signs, music, and forms of betting. Although tracing the diffusion of the game is difficult, tribes likely introduced their own adaptations to others over time. Multiple guessing forms for more than two hiders are common among Arctic Drainage Athapascans. The Dogrib have the largest recorded number of players guessed simultaneously (eight) and thus the largest and most elaborate series of hand signals (Helm, Lurie, and Kurath 1966, 91, 96).

In the past the two-hand (one person hiding one item or a pair of differentiated objects in their hands) and four-hand (two people each hiding one item or a pair of differentiated objects in their hands) forms of play were the most common Plains form, although the Crow played a four-hider form (with the option of designating one to four guesses at a time). Depending on the tribe, the unmarked or marked item was sought in guessing a pair of hiding objects. Despite team size, in single-hider play only one person per team hid at a time. This widespread form was used in play between two individuals or in team play. In some historical forms, an individual on each team took turn hiding the game pieces for one hide per round or exchange, whether guessed correctly or missed. A correct guess gained the guesser's side a point, while a miss gains the hider's side one point. After each guess, a member of the opposition hid the bone. The process was repeated until the number of points needed to win was reached (Culin 1907).

In traditional play, the hiding objects were hidden by one or more members of one side who, depending on the form of play, either hid them themselves or sometimes tried to secretly pass them to another team member to begin the offense. Hiders often went through a large and varied repertoire of graceful

18   CHAPTER 1

and intricate hand, arm, and body movements, swaying in time to the music. Teammates sang, drummed on hand drums or wooden logs, and elicited calls and hollering to distract and confuse the opposing guesser while encouraging their team's hiders. Hand drums were typically small, round, double or single rawhide-headed surfaces secured with thongs stretched across the backside or edges.

In most documented forms, the primary object of the game was for a member of the defense to guess which hand the offense hid the specified object in. In games using one hiding implement per hider, the hand containing the object was sought; in games using two hiding objects per hider (and for either one or two hiders), the specified hiding implement for each hider (marked or unmarked depending on the region and tribe) was sought. In early accounts, most groups focused on guessing the hand of the unmarked object. Regional patterns exist, as California, Oklahoma, and Dakota groups tend to guess for the marked object, whereas the Crow and most other tribes guess for the unmarked object. Male and female distinctions in the marking of gaming pieces are recorded for some groups and types of games (handgame, dice, and disc) (Dorsey 1901a; Maranda 1984).

The guesser indicated their choice by swiftly extending their arm and signaling with the hand, indicating one of two (for one hider) or one of four (for two hiders) possible selections according to the position and motion of their thumb or finger position. Correctly guessing all the other side's hiding implements generally resulted in the bones going to the other side to begin their offense. In some forms of play one or more points were scored for a correct guess in addition to obtaining the bones and thus the offense, while, in other forms of play, points were scored only when possessing the bones and being incorrectly guessed by the opposition. Mooney (1998, 1009) describes this form of play among the Arapaho. The score was kept by moving a series of wooden sticks placed between the two teams. The hiding items used in the handgame were often highly valued, believed to hold great luck, and considered by their owners to transfer their luck to the individual who acquired them (Culin 1907, 267).

According to Culin (1907) and Lesser (1933, 128), other major variations were local developments and probable specializations of handgame forms. Californian peoples often played against one another with four member teams, however, the guessing consisted of individual player against opposing individual player as they sat. This pattern also applied to opposing individuals betting against one another, even in collective team play. Intermediate forms between the two and four hand forms of the handgame sometimes occurred. Among the Pomo, two players hid counters, and the opposing guesser had the

The Origins and Background 19

option of guessing one or both hiders at a time. In some forms (Achomawi, Haida, and others), one counter was used, and the opposition guessed in which hand (usually of four) it was located. Among some populations a single counter was passed along a usually unspecified number of players of the same side, and opponents had to determine which player and hand it was located in. Among Yuman peoples, each member of a side (usually four) concealed a counter, and the guesser tried for the entire distribution, continuing only for those incorrectly guessed (Lesser 1933, 128). This style closely resembles the modern form played by the Crow.

ABORIGINAL DISTRIBUTION

Native American guessing games have a geographically contiguous and chronologically continuous distribution throughout central North America. The handgame extended throughout the western two-thirds of North America, including the Plains, Great Basin, California, Plateau, Northwest Coast, Subarctic, and Southwest Culture Areas, and in the eastern woodlands from between the Great Lakes and St. Lawrence regions southward to the northern border of the Southeast. Handgames are absent east of the lower Mississippi River, among the Puebloan and Athapascan Peoples of the Southwest, and among most Algonquian populations who play the moccasin game or stickgame. The central area of distribution of North American handgames was and still remains the Plains and Great Basin regions (Lesser 1933, 124–30).

Peacock (1955, 5) reported the handgame as the "most popular and widespread Indian gambling game on the Plains—indeed, on most of the continent." Guessing games were traditionally absent throughout much of the northern arctic and subarctic regions of the continent, including the Eskimo (Inuit), the Athapascan populations of Alaska and northwestern Canada, and the Algonquians of northeastern Canada, the Hudson Bay region, Maine, and much of the southeastern United States (Lesser 1933, 124–25).

By 1900 the handgame remained the most commonly played Native American guessing and gambling game from Oklahoma to Alaska (Dorsey 1901a, 364). Culin (1907, 267–327) described varieties of the handgame among eighty-one tribes from twenty-eight linguistic groups in the Plains, Great Basin, California, Plateau, Northwest Coast, and parts of the Subarctic Culture Areas. The game remains common from Oklahoma to Alberta and from parts of the Cross Timbers of the eastern plains to California and into the Northwest Coast and Canada. Today varieties of the game are particularly common in Oklahoma, Montana, Idaho, Utah, California, Oregon, Washington, and parts of British Columbia and Alberta.

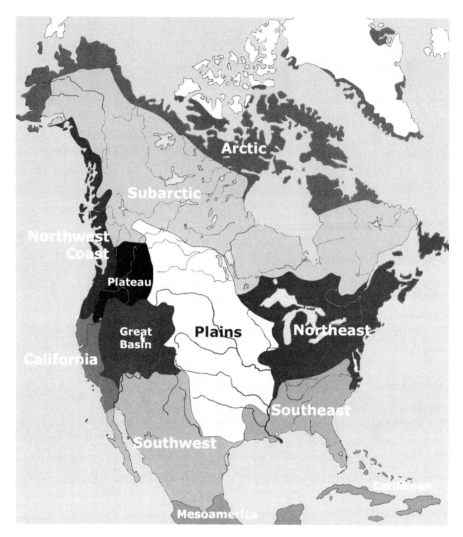

North American ethnic regions. Classification of indigenous peoples of North America according to Alfred Kroeber. Wikimedia Commons, 2019.

Those strongly involved in the Ghost Dance, primarily those who received the dance through the Arapaho, developed a ceremonial form of handgame integrally linked to the ceremony. Concerning an Arapaho Ghost Dance song, Mooney (1896, 1008) reports, "In a trance vision the author of this song entered a tipi and found it filled with a circle of his old friends playing the *ga'qutit*, or 'hunt the button' game." Dorsey (1901a) witnessed a Wichita Ghost Dance in a traditional grass lodge north of Anadarko, Oklahoma. The

The Origins and Background 21

next day a handgame was held at the same location. His description of the sedate, solemn, and dignified performance of the Wichita game, in contrast to the loud, boisterous, secular style of others, reflects the deep religious significance among those groups that associated the handgame with the Ghost Dance (Dorsey 1901a, 369–70). Densmore (1929; 1936, 68–69, 72) found great similarity in the words and customs contained in Ghost Dance and handgame songs among the Pawnee, Cheyenne, and Arapaho. During intervals at handgames, the Pawnee are known to have sung and danced to Ghost Dance songs, while the Cheyenne and Arapaho sang and danced to Rabbit, Forty-nine, and other social dance songs (Densmore 1936, 70). Among the Ponca, the Ghost Dance handgame, which superseded the traditional Ponca moccasin game and handgame, was still held several times a year in the mid-1960s (Howard 1965, 109).

Except for those tribes that developed Ghost Dance ceremonial handgames—the Arapaho between 1892 and 1899, the Oto by 1894, the Pawnee and Wichita before 1901, possibly the Cheyenne before 1906, probably the Assiniboine by 1907, and the Southern Ponca (acquired from the Pawnee) from circa 1900 to 1914–15—the game was played as a secular gambling game (Lesser 1933, 127, 322–26; Howard 1965, 109; Fowler 1987, 58–59).[1] Handgames are the only guessing game played by the Caddoan peoples, the Kiowa, several Plains Algonquian and Siouan populations, all Shoshonean peoples (except the Pyramid Lake Paiute, who share the four-stick game with the Washo), the Hopi (who play the reed game like other Puebloans), and by the Kootenai and all Shahaptian populations except the Klickitat (Lesser 1933, 127). On the Great Plains and adjacent areas, the handgame is recorded among nearly every tribe, including the Arapaho, Arikara, Assiniboine, Bannock, Blackfeet, Blood, Cheyenne, Comanche, Cree, Crow, Gros Ventre (or Atsina), Hidatsa, Kiowa, Kiowa-Apache, Kootenai, Lakota, Nez Perce, Omaha, Osage, Otoe, Pawnee, Piegan, Ponca, Sarci, Shoshone, Ute, Wichita, and Yanktonai (Culin 1907, 267–327; Densmore 1918, 489–90; Lesser 1933, 149, 154).[2]

SIGN LANGUAGE

The handgame is played with sign language. Guessing games between groups with different languages almost always involved the use of signs rather than words. Whether involving inter- or intra-tribal play, the vigorous drumming, singing, shaking of rattles, and shouting during play make verbal communication difficult if not almost impossible. The fast pace, generally hectic atmosphere of play, and the fact that while playing rarely can one see all of either team's hiders, often result in all players not being able to keep track of the game at some moments.[3]

22   CHAPTER 1

Sign language allowed groups otherwise unable to communicate to play against one another. Although three forms of Plains Indian Sign Language (PISL) are noted, good signers could understand each dialect (Meadows 2015, 11–13, 23), and the few signs needed to play handgame were fairly obvious and thus universal. As Culin (1907, 267) describes, "The extensive distribution may be partially accounted for by the fact that, as it was played entirely by gesture, the game could be carried on between individuals who had only the sign language in common." Several early observers report the game played entirely by gestures (Oxendine 1988, 154). Sign language use is also noted in the Northwest (Stuart 1972, 5). Albers (1993) identifies many of the factors involved in the formation and maintenance of historic Plains Indian intertribal relationships through the processes involved in symbiosis, merger, and war, and in the subsequent diffusion and growth of major socio-ceremonial forms, including the Sun Dance, military and doctoring societies, the Omaha or War Dance, the Ghost Dance, and the Native American Church. For Plains and adjacent populations (who had the most widespread and intensive use of sign language), political alliances, trade networks, intermarriage, extensive hosting and visitation, the diffusion of larger religious and military society ceremonial forms, extensive tribal and intertribal sibling adoption, and extensive gift exchange fostered the spread and popularity of social and ceremonial forms throughout the region (Albers 1993; Meadows 1999), including the handgame.

Native Americans often exhibit a great affinity and relationship with widespread variations of a single game form. Similar relationships are found for several gaming traditions, with the same game often played among populations of varied and unrelated linguistic stocks. In general, gaming variations do not correlate solely with linguistic differences. Lesser (1933, 125) states that two primary criteria point to the aboriginal development of the American Indian guessing games and to historical relations between those groups exhibiting such games: 1) the contiguous distribution of the presence and absence of guessing games in North America, and 2) the lack of such major development of guessing games in other similar populations worldwide.

As Lesser (1933, 125) notes, this does not mean that the game had to have a single origin and subsequent diffusion, since any guessing game involves a complex combination of elements that are not necessarily or inherently related. Guessing games entail considerable variation, including widespread differences in objectives, forms of play, scoring methods, paraphernalia, methods of concealment, presence and form of accompanying music, and associated ritualism. Greater variation is generally found in the materials employed in the games than in the object or method of play (Culin 1907, 31). Only a detailed

The Origins and Background 23

consideration of these independent themes, their distinct distributions, and the integration and adaptation they have undergone in varied cultures could elicit the exact historical understanding of the development of guessing games (Lesser 1933, 124, 125). To date, inquiry of this depth and breadth has not been attempted.

ORIGINS AND HISTORICAL LONGEVITY

Many Native American games date to prehistoric and mythological times, including lacrosse, stick ball, kickball races, and double ball (Culin 1903, 63; Cheska 1974, 26; Cheska 1979, 231; Vennum 1994, 27–32). The handgame is a very old and popular hiding and guessing game among the Native American populations of the Plains and Northwest. References to the handgame exist in many tribal oral histories. Citing Hopi and Zuni ceremonies, Dorsey (1901a, 363, 364) and Culin (1907:32–35) suggest that all guessing games may have derived from processes of divination and that a widespread relationship may exist between various Native American gaming traditions, ceremonies, associated paraphernalia, and myth. Roberts, Arth, and Bush (1959, 599, 601) note the association of games of chance with religious activities. "[The] relationship between games of chance and divining (ultimately a religious activity) is well known," they write, and it may be more clearly demonstrated in ancestral forms of present games.

While the exact origin of the handgame is unknown, like the moccasin game it is undoubtedly old. Some tribes maintain it has been played since "time immemorial." A Kiowa pointed out that it is older than many other Kiowa religious traditions, including the Sun Dance. The game predates recorded history as its accoutrements appear in archaeological sites and a well-established body of oral history extending into folklore and mythology at the time of first recorded ethnography. Archaeological findings of bone, shell, and wood gaming dice and related pieces date back to circa 5700 BP with some earlier estimates. An 1896 excavation in Pueblo Bonito included "hundreds of wood and bone gaming sticks and dice chips" (Gabriel 1996, 93, 117). On the western edge of the Great Salt Desert in western Utah, two forms of gaming materials were recovered from level V of Danger Cave: bone dice and gaming sticks. A bundle of six painted and one unpainted wooden gaming sticks (24.2 to 26.0 cm long), made from serviceberry wrapped in cliff rose fiber, dates to between 4000 BC and AD 20 (Jennings 1957; 1974, 157–58, 163; Aikens and Madsen 1986, 158).[4] Aikens and Madsen (1986:158) state, "The nature of the game is unknown, but it can be assumed that it has parallels in the stickgames recorded for Basin ethnographic groups."

24   CHAPTER 1

In the American Midwest, bone gaming pieces have been recovered in Late Archaic Riverton Culture (ca. 1600 BC to 1000 BC) sites along the Wabash River on the Illinois-Indiana border (Winters 1969, 84) and from Late Woodland–Early Mississippian Period Fort Ancient Culture (ca. AD 1100 to 1750) sites in southeastern Ohio (Hanson 1966). As Winters (1969, 84) describes, "Like the Riverton Culture specimens, the Fort Ancient Culture gaming pieces seem to have had a rather casual disposition, since of the 113 examples, 71% came from the general midden, 12% from features that might be considered refuse pits, and 17% from burial associations. Most of the other scattered records of gaming equipment from Middle and Late Woodland sites seem to indicate similar casual disposition. Perhaps, gaming equipment tended to be viewed throughout its history in the Midwest primarily as items of secular equipment, no matter what other relationships may have pertained between gaming and other spheres of activity."

In the late 1980s a set of thirteen rod-shaped bones, two much shorter than the others, were recovered with Clovis artifacts from a site in Douglas County, Washington. Dating to circa 13,800 years ago, their purpose has been debated by tribal members and archaeologists. Snoqualmie tribal members interpret the bones as representing the five score sticks for each side, the kick stick, and the two shorter hiding pieces of a Slahal (stickgame) set.[5]

The game's association with other historical and ethnographic cultural forms and its many ethnic and regional variations also point to a lengthy temporal existence. Bone gaming pieces of several varieties found in houses and burials are especially distinctive of Pacific-period sites dating from 2050 BC to AD 1769 in California (Chartkoff 1998, 310–11). That the historic Great Basin, Plateau, and Plains Culture Areas contain the most widespread geographic distribution of stickgames and handgames suggests that these gaming traditions are of great antiquity. These findings suggest a long-term secular disposition toward gaming forms and their equipment that has continued to the present.

Oral Traditions

References to games and gambling, including the moccasin game and handgame, are common in the mythology of North American tribes (Culin 1907; Oxendine 1988, 151). Oral traditions of the handgame's origins are widespread, often referencing how people learned the game from animals. One of Howard's (1965, 129) Ponca consultants indicated that the handgame developed from the older moccasin game. Culin (1907, 32) states, "References to games are of common occurrence in the origin myths of various tribes. They usually consist of a description of a series of contests in which the demiurge,

The Origins and Background   25

the first man, the culture hero, overcomes some opponent, a foe of the human race, by exercise of superior cunning, skill, or magic." Culin (1907, 809) also notes that North American Indian games, "as they now exist . . . are either instruments of rites or have descended from several observances of a religious character."

Gambling holds a sacred place in the origins and mythologies of many ancient cultures and their religions. Gabriel (1996, 27) reports collecting over one hundred Native American gambling myths. In most of these cultures, gambling myths are associated with the sacred, often involving a culture hero–like epic gambler who is involved with the early origins and cultural formation of the people. Although the gambler motif is especially ubiquitous and well developed in Mexican and southwestern Native American mythology, it is so common that it inhibits suggesting that any given area produced an archetypal model from which it spread (Gabriel 1996, 25–27). The grandiose, shape-shifting trickster Coyote often appears as a gambler in early tribal myths.

Johnson (2000) provides a Coeur d'Alene story of the origin of death in the stickgame:

> Every time Coyote would get killed, his wife would come and jump over him, back and forth, and he's become alive again. And then there was Owl . . . "It's not fair. Every time you die, you can come back. Every time one of us dies, we stay dead. It's not fair to the people." And so they talked and talked, and they couldn't come up with a fair answer. So then Coyote thought and says, "Well, let's play a game . . . I have this stick right here" . . . And Owl said, "Well, how do we guess?" . . . And Coyote looked around. "There's the campfire, and right next to the campfire is a couple of bones. . . . Okay, whoever guesses the good bone, wins." [After Owl had won twenty-one sticks] Coyote says, "You won. Owl, you won." Owl stood up, says, "Okay. Everyone's gonna die when it's their time. That's it." And so that's how we got life and death, and that's how we got the stick game.

Snoqualmie tribal member Michelle Kempf described the game in one of their origin stories. "Michelle tells it like this: Animals and humans were fighting it out, and running out of food. The creator gave humans and animals a game to play—sla-hal—and decreed that whoever won the game could eat the other from then on. But humans were losing, down to their last stick, and beseeched the creator to take pity on them, Michelle said. So the spirit let humans win the game, and also gave them four laws—to turn away from greed, lust, hate, and jealousy. 'The spirit gave us a gift, to show the people who we are,' she said."[6]

26 CHAPTER 1

Other references to handgames and stickgames are found in mythological accounts of the Blackfoot (Wissler and Duval 1908, 132–33), Crow (Lowie 1922, 234–36; 1983, 99; 1993, 25–28), Gros Ventre (Flannery and Cooper 1946, 418), Ponca (Howard 1965, 128–29), Wichita (Dorsey 1995, 102–6), Naishan Apache (McAllister 1949, 17–22; Bittle 1964, 8–9; Beatty 1999), Okanagan (Commons 1938), and in the origin of Assiniboine handgame bundles (Fowler 1987, 211). Among the Okanagan (Commons 1938 186), the stickgame was "the only pastime other than foot racing that was mentioned for the mythical period." Other accounts attribute the origin of the game to more recent historical processes of intertribal visitation.[7]

All Apachean groups have an origin story involving a handgame between good and evil animals at the beginning of time to determine whether the universe would remain in eternal darkness or have light (Schweinfurth 2002, 25–26). Their prevalence may indicate a northwestern origin for the game. Eubank (1945, 138) provides a similar Navajo legend describing the origin of the moccasin game and its play when the gods were making the world.

Howard (1965, 128–29) provides an origin account for the Ponca handgame involving a dream and ghosts:

> A Ponca war party of about 20 warriors left to raid an enemy tribe. Months passed, but no word of the departed men reached their anxious relatives. Finally they were presumed to have been ambushed and were given up for dead.
>
> A year or two later a young Ponca was hunting in the region where the war party had disappeared. Night fell and he wrapped himself up in his robe and went to sleep. In his sleep he began to dream. A wolf howled four times, each time coming closer. Finally it was only a few feet from him. The wolf spoke to the young hunter, telling him that the missing war party was nearby. The wolf then taught the young man a medicine song and vanished.
>
> The young man rose and walked in the direction the wolf had indicated. He saw a light in the distance, and as he came nearer he noticed that it came from a fire burning in a large grass lodge. Indians were playing some sort of game inside, near the fire. It was the hand game. They sang as they played and seemed to be having a wonderful time. The young hunter recognized the players as the members of the lost war party. He spoke to several of them but they ignored him, absorbed in their gambling. He stayed with the group most of the night, watching the game and learning the songs used to accompany it. Just before dawn he left and returned to the main camp of the Ponca.
>
> He informed the head chief that he had located the missing warriors. The chief and his Buffalo-police went to investigate. When they arrived

The Origins and Background 27

at the spot which the young men had described they found only the ashes
of a campfire and various scattered human bones. When the young man
was informed of this he realized that he had been watching ghosts play the
hand game. From that time on the Ponca played the game as their own.[8]

Two accounts involve the eventual betting of one's scalp. Wissler and Duvall (1908, 132–33) recorded the Blackfoot story "The Meeting in the Cave,"
involving a stickgame between a Piegan and a Snake (Shoshone) Indian.

Once a Snake and a Piegan went out into the same country to hunt buffalo. Their camps were far apart. In this country there was a kind of cave
in which scouts and hunters often spent the night. The Snake and the
Piegan were in the habit of sleeping there, but neither had met the other.
One winter evening the Snake arrived at the cave and put up for the night.
After a while the Piegan came along and began to grope his way into the
cave, for it was now dark. The Snake was asleep. As the Piegan was grop-
ing around, he felt a person. He took the hand of the stranger and began to
shake it. Then the Snake asked him to what tribe he belonged. The Piegan
took the hand of the Snake in his own, and moved it around on his cheek
in a small circle. [This is the sign for Piegan, or the people with small
robes.] Then the Snake took the hand of the Piegan and made the sign for
Snake. [The sign is to move the pointing finger as if drawing a waving
trail in the dust.] Then the Piegan took the hand of the stranger again and
told him by signs that to-morrow they would play the stick-game. To this
the Snake replied, "Yes." When morning came, they played the sick-game,
and the Piegan was the winner. First he won the weapons of the Snake,
and then all his clothes. Then the Snake wagered his hair; and the Piegan
won this also. "Now," said the Snake, "'we will stop." So he tied a string
around his head across the forehead. The Piegan said; "I shall cut the hair
close." The Snake said, "No you won in this game; you must scalp me." So
the Piegan took his scalp. The Snake bled a great deal and became very
weak. The Piegan left him and started home. As he approached his camp,
he came over the hills singing.
    After a time, the Snake in the cave revived and went home to his people.
He explained to them what had happened, telling them that he had lost his
scalp in a game. Ever since that time the people often speak of gambling
as fighting.[9]

In 1847 Ruxton (1951, 101–2) recorded a story involving a handgame between a Brule Lakota and a Crow.

A Burnt-wood ["Brulé"] Sioux, Tah-tunganisha, one of the bravest
chiefs of his tribe, was out, when a young man, on a solitary war expedition against the Crows. One evening he drew near a certain "medicine"
spring, where, to his astonishment, he encountered a Crow warrior in the

28   CHAPTER 1

act of quenching his thirst. He was on the point of drawing his bow upon him when he remembered the sacred nature of the spot, and making the sign of peace, he fearlessly drew near his foe, and proceeded likewise to slake his thirst. A pipe of kinnik-kinnik being produced, it was proposed to pass away the early part of the night in a game of "hand." They accordingly sat down beside the spring, and commenced the game.

Fortune favored the Crow. He won arrow after arrow from the Burnt-wood brave; then his bow, club, his knife, his robe, all followed, and the Sioux sat naked on the plain. Still he proposed another stake against the other's winnings—his scalp. He played, and lost; and bending forward his head, the Crow warrior drew his knife and quickly removed the bleeding prize. Without a murmur the luckless Sioux rose to depart, but first exacted a promise from his antagonist that he would meet him once more at the same spot, and engage in another trial of skill.

On the day appointed, the Burnt-wood sought the spot, with a new equipment, and again the Crow made his appearance, and they sat down to play. This time fortune changed sides, and the Sioux won back his former losses, and in turn the Crow was stripped to his skin.

Scalp against scalp was now the stake, and this time the Crow submitted his head to the victorious Burnt-wood's knife; and both warriors stood scalpless on the plain.

And now the Crow had but one single stake of value to offer, and the offer of it he did not hesitate to make. He staked his life against the other's winnings. They played; and fortune still being adverse, he lost. He offered his breast to his adversary. The Burnt-wood plunged his knife into his heart to the very hilt; and, laden with his spoils, returned to his village, and to this day wears suspended from his ears, his own and enemy's scalp.

While I collected some Kiowa and Plains Apache oral history accounts of handgames in early myths (chapter 3), few detailed ethnographic accounts exist. Lesser (1933, 330–31) and Helm, Lurie, and Kurath (1966, 84–85) note that traditions can transform back and forth over time from more formal religious rites or rites with elements of supernaturality to more secular social events.

Historic Accounts

Brief descriptions, frequently appearing in trappers' firsthand accounts of playing in games with Native Americans, also attest to the longevity of the handgame. In the north, Thompson (1916, xv, 359–60) reports the playing of arrow throwing, the bowl and dice game, and the handgame among the Piegan Blackfeet between 1784 to 1807, while Thompson (1916, 360–61) and Ewers (1958, 155–56) report of the game's popularity among the Blackfeet for over a century and a half.[10] Lewis and Clark described the handgame among the Nez

The Origins and Background 29

Perce and other Plateau tribes in 1805–6, noting a generally similar regional pattern (Coues 1893, 3:1008; Moulton 1991, 6:118–20, 7:137–42, 154, 249). Alexander Ross (Thwaites 1966, 7:129–30, 291–93) noted handgames among the Columbia River tribes throughout the summer at The Dalles or Long Narrows during his travels between 1810 and 1813. Nathaniel J. Wyeth (1899, 192), described the handgame in the 1830s, as did Benjamin L. E. Bonneville from two visits to the Nez Perce between October 1832 and March 1833 (Irving 1961, 331–32; Todd 1982, 277–78) and among Plateau and Columbia River tribes (Parker 1838; Thwaites 1966, 27:171–73).

Guessing games were common among northern plains tribes in the 1830s. Maximilian, Prince of Wied (Thwaites 1966, 22:392), reported a variant of the handgame among the Assiniboine near Fort Union in late June through early July 1833: "Many games are in use among these Indians; one of these is a round game, in which one holds in his hand some small stones, of which the others must guess the number, or pay a forfeit. This game is known also to the Blackfeet." Maximilian also (Thwaites 1906, 23:112) recorded a variant of handgame among the Blackfeet near Fort McKenzie in August–September 1833: "They have invented many games for their amusement. At one of them they sit in a circle, and several little heaps of beads, or other things, are piled up, for which they play. One takes some pebbles in his hand, moving it backwards and forwards in measured time, and singing; while another endeavors to guess the number of pebbles. In this manner considerable sums are lost and won." Maximilian also described the use of legerdemain and medicine in gambling. In describing a Cree medicine man, Maximilian mentioned, "Many of these Indian jugglers are very dexterous in sleight of hand" (Thwaites 1906, 23:201). He also reported (Thwaites 1906, 23:375), "The Manitaries [Hidatsa] . . . have as much faith in their medicines, or charms, as the Mandans." He noted the case of a man who was believed killed and buried—but revived and lived on for years: "A white man had given him . . . a paper, by means of which he was enabled to return to his own village on earth. . . . After this, when he played at what they call billiards, he rubbed his hands with the talisman, and nobody could ever win a game from him." Hayden (1863, 408, 430–31) noted a wide range of recreations and gambling among the Mandan and several language terms for games and gambling among the Crow, while George Catlin (1973, 1:132) reported the related moccasin game among the Mandan and others in the 1830s.[11]

Farther south, the handgame was recorded among the Comanche in 1828 (Berlandier 1969, 60–61), the Osage in 1839–40 (McDermott and Salvan 1968, 181), and the Shoshone in 1839 (Wislizenus 1912, 86–88). George Ruxton

30   CHAPTER 1

(1951, 101) described how Lakota, Dakota, Cheyenne, and Pawnee trading on the Platte River in 1847 commonly engaged in horse racing, ball play, and gambling, of which the handgame was a major part, until trade commenced. Dorsey and Kroeber (1903, 269–72) recount the Arapaho story "Split-Feather," in which Star Society members were once invited to the headman's tipi for an evening of handgames.

Handgames might be played between members of a single band or larger community aggregations. Among the Blackfoot, Piegan, and Crow military societies often played one another, each singing their respective society songs (Wissler 1911, 59–60; Ewers 1958, 155; Lowie 1983, 98; Powers 1973, 185). Piegan military societies served as social police during handgames to prevent any conflict from escalating. As Thompson (1916, 359) describes for the Piegan, "But the great business of the Soldiers is with the Gamblers, for like all people who have too much time on their hands, they are almost to a man, more or less given to gambling day and night. All these soldiers watch with attention, and as soon as they perceive any dispute arise, toss the gambling materials to the right and left, and kick the stakes in the same manner; to which the parties say nothing, but collect everything and begin again." Handgames between warrior societies exhibited the good-natured rivalries that existed between them, each trying to outdo the others, seeking the bets wagered on games and the social notoriety of their success.

Playing against one's own close relatives was apparently avoided and would have complicated social norms regarding the sharing of daily goods. Some Gros Ventre accounts (Flannery and Cooper 1946, 416–17) state that gambling between relatives was generally disdained because of the bad feelings or fighting it might lead to. Excessive or high-stakes gamblers were looked down on, lost the respect of people, were not likely to be chosen as chiefs, and could not be chosen as sacred pipe keepers. However, economic considerations generally appear of minor importance since most resources were easily replaced and kin were obligated to share with one another. They recorded no instances of individuals lacking basic necessities due to gambling losses.

Thompson (1916, 361), describes the popularity and intensity of play among the Piegan between 1784 and 1807: "However simple this game appears, it causes much excitement and deep attention in the players. The singing, the gesticulation, and the dark flashing eyes as if they would pierce through the body of him that has the tooth, their long hair, and muscular naked bodies, their excited, yet controlled countenances, seen by no other light than a small fire, would form a fine scene for an Artist." While noting separate play by sex, Mooney (1898, 348–49) describes the popularity of the game among the

The Origins and Background

Kiowa: "So the game goes on far into the night, until the contest is decided and the stakes won by one side or the other. It is a most animated and interesting game, of which they are very fond, and frequently at night in the winter camp the song chorus may be heard from several games in progress simultaneously, the high-pitched voices of the women in one tipi making a pleasing contrast to the deeper tones of the men in another."

Gambling was sometimes used to settle disputes, preventing outright hostilities and further injuries. Ford (1979, 717) reports that most southwestern tribes preferred trade and other forms of exchange such as gambling instead of "raiding and the expensive and unpredictable results of warfare." While other political reasons were possibly involved, Gabriel (1986, 136, 225nn29–30) reports that the moccasin game was played to settle a dispute at Keres Pueblo between the Kachina Society chief and the Moki Society chief, the latter who was painting and dancing like the Kachina Society. The Moki chief stated that they would paint and dance as they wished. In the end the Moki won, and the Kachina chief conceded to their use of the contested paint style and dance.

Games were common between friendly tribes and during temporary reprieves between tribes with long historical or ongoing hostilities. The Kiowa are known to have played against the Naishan Apache, Comanche, Cheyenne, Osage, and Pawnee.[12] The Skiri Pawnee report playing handgames against the Osage, Ponca, Omaha, Oto, Arapaho, and Kiowa, and the moccasin game against the Sac and Fox from the pre-reservation period into the 1930s (Lesser 1933, 149). Shimkin (1986, 323) reports frequent intertribal games between Shoshone and Bannock during pre-reservation summer encampments, while Desmond (1952, 45–47) reports considerable intertribal play between Yakama, Klikitat, Wishram, and various Plateau tribes traversing the Columbia River trade route. Mooney (1898, 347–49) and McAllister (1949, 10; 1970, 31, 54–55) tell of historical intra-tribal games among the Kiowa, and intertribal games between the Kiowa and Apache in the late 1880s, and the Apache and Comanche in 1933–1934. Wissler (1913, 447–50) reports the Blackfoot acquired the Stickgame Dance from the Gros Ventre in the winter of 1910–1911. Flannery and Cooper (1946, 408) describe a game between the Gros Ventre and Flathead (Salish) held between 1873 and 1875. A detailed pre-reservation Pawnee account of an evening of handgames with the Kiowa is also recorded. A Pawnee hunting party under Bowchief met up with a Kiowa hunting party under Big Bow in December, in present-day Oklahoma, probably before 1880. After the two parties visited one another's camps, some Pawnee initiated a second visit and the challenge of a handgame that resulted in three games being played that evening (Lesser 1933, 149).

32 CHAPTER 1

In Oklahoma, widespread intertribal play continued well into the 1930s. On May 31, 1935, Frances Densmore attended a Cheyenne and Arapaho hand-game north of El Reno, Oklahoma, held in a large tent in a government camp that housed Indian families employed on "relief projects." Densmore (1936, 69) reported that games were held weekly, most likely on weekends. Literature from several tribal communities demonstrates that handgames declined in frequency and participation throughout the first half of the twentieth century from economic and governmental Indian agency factors but increased with the widespread revival of Native American cultural forms in the 1950s and 1960s. Handgames, known as "stickgames" by the northern and northwestern tribes, continue in most Plains and Plateau communities.[13]

THE BONE GAME OR STICKGAME

Closely related to the handgame, the bone game or stickgame merits brief discussion. In the northwestern US plains, the Plateau Culture Area, and adjacent parts of Canada, some tribes refer to the game as the "bone game" from the hiding implements, while others refer to it as "stickgame" in reference to the tally sticks. In this form, sticks are tapped on a log placed in front of each team, or a single log or plank between them, for percussion while singing. Others use a number of hand drums. In some Northwest forms, ten tally sticks are equally divided between the two teams at the start of each game. A representative from each team, often the team leader, begins a preliminary round of guessing to decide who will start the game with the first offense. The two individuals, each using one set of bones, begins guessing and hiding in turn until one defeats the other in a round of reciprocal hiding and guessing. That is, they guess in reciprocal rounds until one individual correctly guesses his opponent and is missed in turn. Several ties may occur between the two individuals until the first point is finally won. The loser tosses his bones to the side of the winner, who receives the eleventh "kick" or "king stick," and their team begins their offense.[14]

Helm, Lurie, and Kurath's (1966) work on the Dogrib and Maranda's (1984) work on the Coast Salish handgame, or Slahal, provide the most in-depth studies of the handgame or stickgame. Maranda (1984, 61) describes a variety of concealment methods while hiding or "mixing" the bones among the Coast Salish. When a hider is guessed correctly, they must give the bones over to the other side. Each hide that is missed results in a stick from the guessing side. When both sets of bones are guessed correctly, the offense shifts sides and the other side begins singing, drumming, and hiding. In some forms a double score (two points) results in the bones being given to the other side to begin hiding. Play continues until one side has all of the sticks. The kick stick is

The Origins and Background 33

typically the last stick to be given up. Many northern tribes allow fake guessing gestures before signaling their actual guess to try and get hiders to give themselves away. Bets are typically double or nothing, include larger "game bets" placed before the game starts, and "round bets" held up as a challenge to someone to match and placed on individual rounds during the game (Stuart 1972, 1–5).[15]

Stuart (1972, 8) describes songs with ridiculing and taunting lyrics and several tactics used to confuse, distract, and rile opponents while hiding. These include shouting verbal taunts such as "You're blind," individuals who move around a great deal, and an attractive "well-built" female. As Helm, Lurie, and Kurath (1966, 78) describe, "The excitement, the psychological tensions, and the pleasures of a Dogrib handgame session are difficult to portray in words."

By the 1920s, songs with words were becoming rare. Of 194 songs Stuart recorded in 1969–1971, none contained lyrics. Most Coast Salish Slahal songs are pentatonic, although frequent inversions of that scale are used, as is duple meter. Stuart recorded only three songs of triple meter. While some songs have an undulating contour, most are descending in form, but some demonstrate considerable rise in pitch. The excitement and intensity of the game may add to the increasing rise in pitch as a team continues to score points or nears the last stick, repeating the song again and again (Stuart 1972, 8–9, 102a, 105). Stuart (1972, 9) reports rapid and frequent change in Coast Salish Slahal songs, including variations of songs and the replacement of songs with new compositions. Most Coast Salish do not consider Slahal songs to be individually owned or to contain private or spiritual associations, as with "spirit" songs sung at more private gatherings (Stuart 1972, 12–13).

Helm, Lurie, and Kurath (1966, 77) characterize the Dogrib handgame as "one of intellectual skill and judgment tempered by luck": "Ethically, 'you've got to play honest'; there is no sleight of hand in the game, only the skillful outwitting of opponents." They note (1966, 85) that some players had power in the past:, but they add: "This supernaturality is not ceremonial or ritual in nature and purpose, however. It lies simply in the recognition that in the recent past, when men had strong 'medicine' . . . some men had great power for performance in the hand game." While consultants reported that eight men with shamanistic power remained, no living men claimed to have handgame medicine.

Helm, Lurie, and Kurath (1966, 77–78) also recognize the strategy of hiders and guessers scrambling their patterns and of the guessers "to exploit successfully [their] memory, judgment, and skillful observation of opponents." They describe the ability of skilled Dogrib guessers to memorize the patterns of hiding. "Some gamblers can remember from long before." Regional

34   CHAPTER 1

band-based teams typically played against other regional groups. However, only a small percent of the male population typically played handgame year after year. "It is therefore possible for a captain to build a mental file through the years regarding the idiosyncrasies and patterns of Idzi-hiding of at least his more frequent opponents. Of course, some of the 'old-pros' of the hand game may be too clever to allow any distinctive idiosyncrasy of play to type them." Indeed spouses, siblings, and others have told me the tendencies of their friends and relatives that they regularly play against or with.

Densmore (1943, 65) states that "skill depends largely on a study of averages and probabilities." While particularly true regarding the location of the bones, other skill is involved in the guesser's ability to observe and remember the habits of hiders. These are two closely related but different forms of skill. Maranda (1984, 44–46) notes the presence of skill in Coast Salish handgames, including physical skill in forms of cheating.

For the Dogrib and Coast Salish, Helm, Lurie, and Kurathe (1966, 81) and Maranda (1984, 86) describe the handgame as a communal festive event that serves as both a form of inter-group competition and a means of maintaining or reinforcing intra-group identification, while establishing and endorsing individual status, a sense of personal achievement in contributing to a successful group action, and a means of reaffirming Indian identity. Other regional scholars support these assessments (Commons 1938; Densmore 1943; Barnett 1955; Merriam 1955; Stuart 1972).

Several forms of cheating have been reported, including 1) throwing the bones after being guessed, 2) slipping a band of sinew over the unmarked bone, which worked only if showing one bone when guessed, and 3) using a third or "cheating" bone, typically blank on one side and marked on the other so either could be shown as needed (Maranda 1984, 45). Documented among numerous cultures, the one-device form of the handgame made switching the hiding implement easier (cf. Culin 1907; Maranda 1984, 47). According to Barnett (1955, 262), excessive cheating among the Coast Salish resulted in replacing the one-device with a two-device style.

For Coast Salish in Washington and British Columbia, gambling games served as "an expression of man's power affiliation," while the handgame served as a forum for supernatural power (Maranda 1984, 87, 118). Power is viewed as the difference between winning and losing, the element determining the outcome of each gambling event, "an endorsement of power favour," and thus "examples of power in action." Suttles (1955, 6) asserts, "[Power is] evidently sometimes conceived as an entity, but more often the term seems to mean simply 'strength' or 'ability' in a physical as well as a spiritual sense and possibly derived from several sources." It was also believed that once

The Origins and Background 35

obtained, power "could ensure outstanding success in practically any field" (Duff 1952, 97). Individuals could become skilled or even professional gamblers with or without power. One consultant described handgame power as the ability to read a person's mind and said that one's guessing choices were made by the power, not the person (Maranda 1984, 114–15). Maranda (1984, 116–17) reports that although some people were still believed to possess handgame power, belief in the power concept and its relevance in the game was rapidly declining. A Squamish consultant spoke of the teams to the west as using and depending on power to win in the handgame: "[They] depend on luck . . . and some players are just luckier than others." However, Maranda aptly noted that skill and strategy in the game through one's being able to study an opponent and assess their patterns in hiding or guessing contradicts the idea of "pure luck," in that luck implies that the forces that bring about events and cause things to happen are beyond the control and influence of individuals.

Pre-reservation (pre-1859) Yakama had two large annual "big time" celebrations of a week or more around the first of June and the first of August. Although the host group harvested food resources for all who camped at both gatherings, a ritual and celebratory feast or "first fruits" rite was normally held only at the June encampment. Following this feast, the remainder of the time was spent visiting, renewing friendships, and exchanging news, jokes, and stories (Desmond 1952, 36). These events were held at locations where valuable roots, especially camas roots, were ready for harvesting and permitted large-scale, extended aggregations of Yakama and sometimes neighboring tribes. Formal feasts, athletic competitions, horse racing, bone games, trading, and socialization occurred. Traders and "professional" gamblers from nearby tribes frequently attended. While the range of activities varied from year to year, horse races and bone games were always held the day after the ritual feast. Reflecting the scale and formal importance of these gatherings, bets during the "big times" were of greater value and quantity than any other time of the year. Formal declarations were sometimes declared prohibiting the use of sleight of hand to change the bones after a guess was made and certain positioning of the arms and hands to facilitate such changes. Violators, if caught, were removed from the proceedings. The application of individual power was often applied to one's hand and the game bones during the hiding of the bones (Desmond 1952, 42). However, faking one's guessing motions to trick hiders into giving their selves away occurred, as did the opportunity to demonstrate one's power in an acceptable public format. "The bone game sessions at the 'big time' was the supreme occasion for skillful manipulators to show off their prowess to the best advantage" (Desmond 1952, 41).

36   CHAPTER 1

During September and October, Plateau groups traveling back and forth through the Yakama area to the Wishram and other Columbia River villages commonly stopped to visit and gamble. With permanent winter residences established by October, bone and other gambling games occurred in greater frequency than at any other time of the year (Desmond 1952).

During the period (1860–1944) described by Desmond, the Yakama quickly modified their traditional ceremonial schedule to include three major celebrations. The three-day Fourth of July celebration contained a parade with Yakama in traditional dress, an Indian village of canvas tipis, and a series of bone and card games. Stemming from the earlier "big time" celebrations, two three-day festivals were also held simultaneously at several locations around the first of June and the middle of August. These modified celebrations continued to focus around the modern conception of the first-fruits rite. Whereas individuals formerly went to dig roots and gather berries after the daytime feast, dances in the long house and gambling games, predominated by card games by the 1940s, became the post-feast norm (Desmond 1952, 9–10).

In the twentieth century, northwestern tribes regularly held handgames at hop-picking camps in the Fraser Valley of Canada, fish canneries where members of many tribes worked, and on weekends at public festivals in local reservation communities. Today stickgames comprise an integral part of most powwows, tribal fairs, or other major encampments, and they are, of course, the focus of stickgame tournaments sponsored by individual tribes or Indian organizations. In much of the Northwest, tribes associate sex to the bones. Some identify the unmarked bone as female and the marked bone as male, while the Coast Salish and others practice the opposite (Stuart 1972, 1–3).[16]

At powwows and other large cultural events in the northern plains and the Plateau, Northwest Coast, Great Basin, and California Culture Areas, gambling remains popular. Although wall tents located near concession areas often draw card players, the handgame andstickgame remain the premier forms of traditional gambling. Many northern plains powwow grounds contain special areas for the stickgame, usually open-sided arbors or enclosed buildings. Players sit in opposing rows singing their respective songs while playing hand drums or tapping long wooden poles. With many teams playing simultaneously, the drumming and clacking sounds of the stickgame often continue day and night (Roberts 1992, 45, 93).

Like those who travel the powwow circuit, some individuals travel nearly every weekend to play handgame. Northern plains and Plateau tribes, including the Shoshone-Bannock at Fort Hall, Idaho, the Chippewa-Cree at Rocky Boy, Montana, and the Flathead Indian Reservation powwow at Arlee,

The Origins and Background   37

Montana, host large stickgame tournaments at their annual celebrations. The handgame circuits allow players to travel, see new areas, and make friends from other Indian communities. Seeing individuals that one knows is an important part of stickgame.

THE ROLE OF GAMBLING

Prior to play, wagers were regularly made on the outcome of most Native American games and sports of skill or chance (Lowie 1954, 128, Wissler 1955, 239). Gambling on games of chance and skill was practiced by both sexes, most all ages, and both players and spectators. Varied items were bet in Plains Indian handgames, including toys, beads, brass thimbles and tubes, bows, arrows, guns, horses, mules, bison robes, blankets and serapes, saddles, personal ornaments, bridles, clothing, money, and any property one might wish to wager.[17] Yakama could wager almost any possessions except food, objects associated with magico-religious beliefs, canoes, shelters, major fishing equipment, personal effects such as breechclouts and fighting clubs, and basic work and subsistence tools common to all (Desmond 1952, 17–23).

Dodge (1882, 326) describes the betting he saw in Plains Indian handgames:

> The betting is not confined to the players, almost every looker-on, man or woman, choosing sides, and backing his opinion with whatever he feels like risking. All the articles wagered are laid out on one side of the blanket, and a most heterogeneous agglomeration is sometimes presented.
>
> A fine silver-mounted Mexican saddle is wagered against a warbonnet of eagles' feathers, a shield against a bow and quiver full of arrows, a pair of moccasins against an old hat, or a dollar against a white shirt. The women bet their necklaces, leg ornaments, bead-work of every kind. Nothing is too costly or too worthless to minister to this appetite.

Betting was typically dyadic, where one individual matched the wager of another. Although many items used as bets were not identical, unlike money, they were considered equal enough in value between the two individuals betting. Each individual tried to match their wager against something a little more valuable. Consequently, a great deal of time was sometimes expended in matching bets before play could begin (Dodge 1882, 327). In Gros Ventre handgames the use-value of a bet was sometimes considered more important than the actual or store value (Flannery and Cooper 1946, 393). Most bets appear to have been individual rather than team bets and were placed between their respective sides. In Kiowa games, when a member of one side made a bet, it was called for and matched by a member of the other team. As Lesser

38   CHAPTER 1

(1933, 152) describes of a Kiowa and Pawnee game, "Each man bets against one of the other side; the two things are tied together; the bundles are heaped at the west before the leaders."

Reports of wagering in Native American handgames appear in nearly all early explorers' accounts (Thompson 1916, 358–61; Moulton 1991, 7:137, 140, 154; Parker 1838; Dodge 1882, 325–33; Dodge 1989, 281; Irving 1961, 119; Irving 1964, 336; Thwaites 1966; Berlandier 1969, 60–61) and in many tribal ethnographies (cf. Ewers 1958, 155–56). Wissler (1955, 239) mentions Blackfoot boys betting their wooden tops and arrows, with bets increasing with adulthood and the acquisition of more valuable possessions. The stories, songs, and ceremonies of numerous tribes suggest that while excess should be prudently avoided, it often occurred. Early American accounts often describe what they perceived as "high" or excessive betting (Parker 1838; Boller 1868, 16; Thompson 1916, 360; Denig 1930, 567–69; Irving 1961, 119; Berlandier 1969, 60–61; Moulton 1991, 6:199, 7:154).

David Thompson (1916, 360) wrote, "[Handgame is] the Game to which all the Indians of the Plains are most addicted, and which they most enjoy." In describing gambling among Piegan men circa 1800, Thompson (1916, 361) stated, "The stakes are Bison Robes, clothing, their tents, horses, and Arms; until they have nothing to cover them but some old robe fit for saddle cloths. They have some things which are never gambled, as all that belongs to their wives and children, and in this the tent is frequently included; and always the Kettle, as it cooks the meat of [for] the children, and the Axe as it cuts wood to warm them. The dogs and horses of the women are also exempt."

Thompson (1916:358) described how two lodges of Piegan, between 1784 and 1807, had gambled away all of their possessions even down to their dried provisions, forcing them to break an existing ban on non-communal bison hunting, for which they were caught and punished by the appointed soldier society. Gambling at Plateau stickgames was so prevalent that Parker (1838) surmised it as a "ruling passion." Of Mandan-Hidatsa hoop and pole games around 1860, Boller (1868, 160) reported, "I have frequently seen Indians play until they have lost everything." Among the Blackfoot, Wissler (1911, 60) reported, "The amount of property exchanging hands in such gambling was truly astonishing, whole bands and societies sometimes being reduced to absolute poverty and nakedness." A visiting Yakama player (Desmond 1952, 26–27) once "sang a song with tears running down his face, which told how he was a wild boy in his youth who refused to obey his father and lost everything playing the bone game, and . . . he wanted a few gifts . . . so he could play the bone game." In a Hopi myth (Malotki 1978, 207–8) everyone in the village

The Origins and Background 39

of Pivanyokhapi became so addicted to the game of Sosotukwpi, a guessing game using four wooden cups and a hiding item, that the chief arranged for the village to be destroyed through fire to purify the dissolute community.

Some individuals were apparently habitual gamblers, sometimes losing most or all they owned and requiring them to replace sufficient wealth to continue play. This was often achieved through raiding for horses and other goods. Among the Upper Missouri tribes who regularly bets horses, Denig (1930, 567) describes, "There are some who invariable lose and are poor all of their lives." For the Blackfoot, Wissler (1955, 239) states, "Some young men were . . . inveterate gamblers, who lost all their horses and were forced to return again and again to enemy camps to recoup their losses. Their love of gambling kept them poor and at the same time kept them active as horse raiders." Dodge (1882, 328) reports similar instances among the Comanche in the 1840s: "The unlucky gambler, having lost wives, children, and property, yielded all to the winner and started alone for Mexico to recuperate his fallen fortunes by stealing. This was not in those days so very unusual an occurrence." Some accounts report that men sometimes bet their own wives (Dodge 1882, 281, 328; Lowie 1954, 131; Irving 1964, 336; Berlandier 1969, 60–61). A Kiowa elder told me of a man who once allegedly bet his wife in a handgame.[18]

Despite some residual grumbling—and Thompson's (1916, 369) reference to Piegan military societies ensuring that disputes did not escalate—a relative high degree of sportsmanship appears to have characterized pre-reservation Plains Indian handgames and gambling in general. Under the entry for "Bet" in his study of sign language, William Clark (1885, 66) notes, "The passion for gambling is strong in the Indian heart. The two most noticeable characteristics are the high stakes for which they will play and the calm, serene grace with which they will lose all they have in the world." Dodge (1882, 327) likewise describes, "I have never seen any quarreling, . . . and they win or lose 'like gentlemen' with unvarying good humor." These accounts suggest that Native American views toward betting and losing may be more accepted than in some other cultures, with losers matter-of-factly regrouping to replace their losses. Ross (Thwaites 1966, 7:293) provides another example among the Oakinacken.

Accounts of excessive betting abound. Dodge (1882, 328) reports, "Indians are possessed of true gambling passion, and will, if in bad luck, lose blankets, robes, lodge, arms, ponies, wives, and even children (although this is extremely rare)."[19] Dodge (1989, 281; 1882, 325) also describes two Arapaho chiefs wagering $120 on a single hand of cards, attributing this "excessively developed" passion for gambling in part to the relative confinement and inactivity of the winter season. Based on the 1810–1813 journals of the Astor Expedition to Oregon, Washington Irving (1964, 336) says in his 1836 account about Indians of the region, "They have a great passion for play, and a variety of games. To such a pitch of excitement are they sometimes roused, that they gamble away everything they possess, even to their wives and children." Lowie (1954, 131) describes, "Adults were addicted to games of chance, at which a man might gamble away all of his property—if legends are to be believed, even his wife and his own body." He also noted (1954, 134), "At times two or three horses were the prized stake." Berlandier (1969, 60–61) recounts an individual betting his own freedom and a Tahuacano (Towakoni) man betting and losing his two wives and his mother.

Numerous traders described extensive gambling among the tribes of the Columbian Plateau in the first half of the nineteenth century, often labeling it as "addictive." In 1843 Father Pierre-Jean De Smet (Thwaites 1966, 27:171–73) described betting among Columbia River tribes in which a man might bet his own person, limb by limb, and finally his head. If he lost, he and his wife and children became slaves to the winner for life, as no mention of dismemberment is known and would have been counterproductive to winning. Traders also expressed their disdain for what they viewed as an excessive amount of time and wealth spent by Indians gambling (Vibert 1997, 140–44). However, these accounts are based on the values and goals of Euro-American fur traders and consider neither the Native views toward these activities nor the social and economic importance of gambling among these populations, such as the role of gambling as a common mode of economic exchange in this region. Generosity and the distribution of wealth were forms of ideal social behavior and principal means of achieving social status. Gambling was one venue to both acquire and redistribute disposable wealth. As Vibert (1997, 141) notes, "Clearly, gambling and these other pursuits [that redistributed wealth] were perceived as competition for the fur trade. Gambling in particular was construed as 'losing time' or 'doing very little'—that is, very little of use to the traders."

When asked if he knew of people that almost always lost but still keep on playing, Cecil Horse (Kiowa) remarked, "Well, it's that way with every game. I guess there's lots of people that they get used to it, that even if they lose, they keep playing. That's gambling today, you know. That's the same way." Jenny Horse, born in 1895, also stated, "Yeah. I heard of these. They like the game so much, they don't care if they lose. Sometimes they'd win. I guess."[20]

Wallace and Hoebel (1952, 117–18) recorded a Comanche account in which Breaks Something won all of another man's possessions in a dice game.

The Origins and Background 41

Continuing, the man wagered his two horses, his wife's tipi, twelve hides his wife had yet to tan, and finally his sister. Breaks Something initially declined the offer, stating it was too much, but after encouragement accepted and won everything. The next day Breaks Something took pity on them, taking only the blanket worn by his opponent.

Sometimes a winner returned a small portion of his winnings to allow the loser to continue to play against additional opponents. From games observed among Lakota, Assiniboine, Yankton, Cheyenne, and Pawnee on the Platte River in 1847, Ruxton (1951, 101) describes, "When playing at the usual game of '*hand*,' the stakes, comprising all the valuables the players possess, are piled in two heaps close at hand, the winner at the conclusion of the game sweeping the goods towards him, and often returning a small portion 'on the prairie,' with which the loser may again commence operations with another player."

Although games could end in a matter of minutes, the unpredictability of play often resulted in games lasting several hours. Sometimes the momentum of a game swayed back and forth, and neither team could win. Usually if a game went until morning and neither side had won, a draw was declared if all agreed. Each individual gathered their original bet and then dispersed. Ethnographic sources are full of accounts of long games. As Thompson (1916, 361) described among the Piegan in 1784–1807, an ongoing game might be called for the night, to be finished the following night: "Thus the game continues with varied success until they are tired, or one party cannot produce another stake; in this case the losing party either give up the stakes they have lost to the winners or direct the Umpire to keep [them] for the renewal of the game the next night."

However, the desire to compete sometimes enticed individuals and groups to play on until a win was secured. Among the Oregon Oakinackens from 1810 to 1813, Alexander Ross (Thwaites 1966, 7:293) observed, "It sometimes happens, that after some days and nights are spent in the same game, neither party gains: in that case, the rules of the game provide that the number of players be either increased or diminished; or, if all parties be agreed, the game is relinquished, each party taking up what it put down: but so intent are they on this favorite mode of passing their time, that it seldom happens that they separate before the game is finished; and while it is in progress every other consideration is sacrificed to it; and some there are who devote all their time and means solely to gambling; and when all is lost, which is often the case, the loser seldom gives way to grief. They are a happy people, never repining at what cannot be remedied."

42   CHAPTER 1

Controlled Wagering

When considering the extent of wagering in Native American games, it is important to examine the subject from an emic or Native and not just Euro-American view. First of all, Native peoples did not categorize gambling as something associated with the Anglo concept of a "vice" but rather as a social activity. Children and adults could play and or place wagers on handgames. Games were announced and played in public, participation involved a significant portion of the resident population as players, singers and drummers, or spectators, and everyone knew who was winning and who was not. As Dodge (1989, 281) describes from his years among Plains tribes, "There is no secrecy about the gambling. A blanket, spread on the ground in the open air in good weather, on the floor of the lodge in bad serve as table. Spectators crowd around, and if a man is losing heavily the whole camp soon knows it." The drumming, singing, and cheering of the participants resonated throughout the camp, often until dawn. In short, there was neither secrecy nor any real stigma associated with gambling.

It is also important to note that Native Americans recognized the detrimental effects of compulsive gambling and took measures to limit its growth and effects. Accounts vary on the extent a married individual could wager a couple's possessions. Thompson (1916, 361) indicates that Blackfeet men were prohibited from wagering possessions of their wives and children. However, Wallace and Hoebel (1952, 117) state, "Husbands and wives were free to gamble each other's goods, and each was supposed to pay up the other's debts." After consulting with his wife, a Yakama man might risk jointly owned property (Desmond 1952, 52).

Dodge reports (1882, 329) that when a man began losing heavily, his wife or wives might intercede and stop play before his losses became enough for concern, often producing domestic verbal disputes and (1989, 281) other forms of spousal pressure when a man began to lose heavily: "In such case his wives generally put in an appearance, before things have proceeded to extremities, and break up the game, either by bullying the husband or by informing the winner that they will not live with him if won." Gene Weltfish (1965, 397) describes how the Pawnee were cognizant of compulsive gambling and its detrimental effects: "Gambling was a main recreation for some Pawnees and an occasional one for others. It was recognized that habitual gambling was a compulsion that should be avoided as a psychologically destructive trait, and Old-Man-That-Chief could often be heard to give advice on how to regulate one's conduct to keep this impulse under control. He especially exhorted the chiefs to set a good example to the rest of the people."

The Origins and Background 43

As in many cultures, some individuals bet and lost what was considered excess in that respective culture. However, gambling was not seen as immoral as in many Western cultures. Wallace and Hoebel (1952, 117) provide an insightful observation regarding Comanche views of gambling: "The Comanches, like other Indians, had no moral inhibitions against gambling, so they went all out in their betting. After all, it was only an exchange of property between friends, and generous gift giving was the custom anyhow."

The Navajo name for Pueblo Alto, "Home of the one that wins (you) by Gambling," is associated with where the Great Gambler played, and several Navajo individuals had personal names related to gambling. Navajo chantways and origin myths indicate that gambling is an acceptable, and in some instances even sacred, activity during the intermission of long ceremonials when singers are resting. Indeed, gambling may be seen as an indicator of well-being: since it does not satisfy immediate biologically based survival needs, it suggests that a group has sufficient excess for recreation (Gabriel 1996, 97–98, 154–55).

Many Native Americans raise and redistribute capital through gambling. As Ford (1979, 716) notes, "Gambling and games of skill were informal and voluntary mechanisms by means of which possessions circulated through a community and often allowed booty or newly acquired trade goods to pass to new owners." Several widespread social patterns placed limitations on the amount of property that could be won or lost, ensuring the maintenance of a group's social fabric. First, wagers generally consisted of surplus property. Yakama wagering involved items that were more secondary than primary in daily necessities, and that, if lost, did not endanger an individual's ability to maintain shelter, minimum clothing, food, and the tools to procure these basic necessities (Desmond 1952). Wealthy individuals were expected to wager and essentially risk redistributing larger amounts than others, and heroic gamblers who lost most of all they owned were admired and compensated through increased social status. Regarding wagering jointly owned property, Desmond (1952, 52) writes, "As a rule, the wife not only agreed to this but apparently urged her husband to gamble by suggesting that he might win. If goods wagered by either husband or wife were lost, there were no recriminations. Thus, the use of goods for gambling was not inimical to family harmony, and while gambling losses might leave the family short in some articles, the members were never left in absolute want. Therefore, gambling losses could be sustained without affecting the basic physical requirements of life."

Second, because bets were even, no odds, pools, prizes, or means by which a large amount of wealth could be won with a smaller wager existed. A winner could only double his wager, often with a similar item. When a large amount

44   CHAPTER 1

was won, it was distributed among the individuals wagering of the winning side. When visiting another village, one had to estimate in advance how much one could take along and wager because all bets had to be physically present (vouchers or markers were not accepted), limiting the amount of wealth wagered. Anyone who bet a single item per game was considered a moderate better by Yakama standards (Desmond (1952, 53). Individual games were relatively long, normally allowing for six or less in an evening, which also helped limit wagers.

Third, it was understood that individuals, even those with recognized power, could not live by gambling alone, and few, if any, actually became rich. The widespread emphasis on generosity ensured the redistribution of any large winnings. Fourth, a highly developed sense of community, interdependence, generosity, and the constant flow of goods and services throughout the community prevented an individual from remaining in a precarious position for very long. Accounts of camps impoverished from enemy raids or natural disasters and being reprovisioned with basic necessities by neighboring camps or military societies are numerous. Aside from charity, which would not have been a reliable strategy for repeated loses, individuals had three primary forms through which they could recover their losses: 1) additional play, which was risky and could increase indebtedness, 2) individual economic initiative (work), or 3) acquiring supernatural power through visions to aid in future play.

If suddenly destitute from gambling losses, a man could concentrate his efforts on hunting, trapping, and raiding to replace his collateral. Losses through gambling provided one factor stimulating the larger raiding complex for the Comanche (Dodge 1882, 328) and Blackfoot (Wissler 1955, 239). Lowie (1922, 235; 1983, 99) reports Crow accounts of individuals who, following heavy losses in handgames, undertook vision quests and acquired supernatural power. Afterward these individuals recovered all that they lost and were reportedly very hard to beat. In this light, gambling can be viewed in anthropological terms as a leveling mechanism that, like giveaways at numerous Plains Indian socioreligious activities, served to further distribute the already fluid exchange of wealth throughout highly cooperative kin-based communities.

Family, band, and tribal structures generally supported one another in games against external social units. Intervillage or intertribal games allowed for the strengthening of in-group solidarity by means of out-group competition. As the seriousness of the competition could accelerate with more-distant (and thus less-related) social groups one played, adequate social controls existed to ensure fair play, sportsmanship, and harmony. These controls were exhibited in the supervisory roles and social influence of the host (who ensured fair play and anticipated incipient disagreements), game announcers or criers (who helped to smooth the progression through the games), and the careful handling, custodianship, and redistribution of bets. Desmond (1952, 53) describes something about Yakama gambling that likely existed in other Plateau and Plains communities: "It helped to cement in-group solidarity without causing out-group rivalry of such dimensions as to threaten harmonious relations." Desmond also notes (1952, 56), "Although out-group rivalry was keen, and expressed itself characteristically in gambling, it was so controlled that the harmonious relations among all the people of the region—based as it was on intermarriage, frequent contacts for trading, common exploitation of some resources, and the like—were not unduly disturbed." Enjoyment of play seems to have outweighed the bets involved. According to Helm, Lurie, and Kurath (1966, 81) financial losses at Dogrib handgames in the 1960s were small, emphasizing the pleasure derived from play and the value in which the game was held.

Recorded Ethnography

The recorded ethnography for Native American gaming traditions is considerable but largely dispersed and rarely comprehensive. Although tribal ethnographies briefly mention a few gaming traditions, most works on Native games are one of five major types: pan-Indian works on games in general (Culin 1907; MacFarlan 1958; Baldwin 1969; Oxendine 1988); general works on the games of a particular tribe (Hough 1888; Beauchamp 1896; Stevenson 1903); tribally specific accounts of a particular game (Mooney 1890; Daniel 1892; Lesser 1933; Flaskerd 1961; Peavy and Smith 2014; Bassett 2024); works on the distribution of a particular gaming tradition (Nabokov 1981; Cheska 1982; Vennum 1994); or accounts of individual Native American athletes (Wheeler 1979; Lucas 1983). Culin's voluminous *Games of North American Indians* (1907) was the first work to classify and illustrate most American Indian games involving gaming implements, with a nearly exhaustive literature review. Most sources for Native American gaming traditions are found in the bibliographies of Culin (1907), Dockstader (1957), MacFarlan (1958), Baldwin (1969), Nabokov (1981), MacFarlan and MacFarlan (1985), Oxendine (1988), Vennum (1994) and Blanchard (1981, 1995). Ethnography on Native American hand- and stickgames offers few in-depth works (cf. Dorsey 1901a; Lesser 1933; Helm, Lurie, and Kurath 1966; Brunton 1974, 1998). American Indian lacrosse and stickball have received far more ethnographic attention (Mooney

46   CHAPTER 1

1890; Swanton 1946, 674–80; Fogelson 1962; Blanchard 1981; Vennum 1994, 2007; Fisher 2002; Zogry 2010; Downey 2018; Bassett 2024).

Early accounts of handgames appear in the journals and accounts of explorers, military personnel, travelers, Indian agents, missionaries, and ethnographers for many North American tribes. Most briefly mention recreational traditions as a whole, usually conveying little beyond the most basic components of the game in one or two pages, with largely biased conclusions concerning the socioeconomic role of the game and associated betting. Little attention is given to the variables, details, and local classifications and rules of the game, inhibiting widespread comparisons. These scattered accounts make up most of what Culin (1907, 267–327) compiled and, as the most comprehensive body of handgame information, form the basis of most subsequent sources. Culin's work was largely prompted through an invitation to prepare and oversee an exhibit illustrating the games of the world for the 1892 Columbian Exposition in Chicago (Culin 1907, 29).

The great variability in Culin's descriptions of American Indian guessing games suggest uneven coverage, errors and misunderstandings of the early traveler's accounts he relied on for some regions. In some cases, modern information supersedes early accounts, while in other now extinct cultures the accounts remain unclear. Lesser (1933, 124) called for a "new treatment and reclassification of American Indian games . . . amplifying and correcting Culin." As Lesser (1933, 127) pointed out, Culin's early material failed to distinguish the two primary types of handgame play, single hider and dual hider, even though the forms were differentiated in the data he collected.

Culin emphasized the two-hand or single-hider form, especially among the Northwest Coast, which Franz Boas confirmed. However, subsequent Plains, Great Basin, California, and Plateau data from scholars including Kroeber, Lowie, Wissler, Spier, Gunther, Dorsey, and Powers suggest that the four-hand or dual-hider form of play was extremely widespread. As Lesser (1933, 128–29) noted, "Probably both forms of play occur side by side in many more tribes than we have on record, the former for individual play, the later for team play. . . . It is probable that the Plains method of play for the four-hand form, in which, if the guesser locates the counter of one opponent only, his side loses one tally and he continues to guess only for the counter not found, would prove more widespread if better information were available." Of early descriptions, Lesser continued, "This form, being more complicated, undoubtedly confused the casual observer of earlier days. As a result, we cannot be sure of independent distributions of the two forms, or the distribution of their coexistence. What Gunther states for the Klallam, ' . . . they play with two bones, guessing for the marked one. Occasionally in a big game four bones are put into play, being held by two people,' is likely to be an option much more widespread in the Plains, California, the Basin, and the Plateau than our records show."

Most hiding bones collected by Culin are sets of four bones, consisting of two sets of similar bones as used in the four-hand or dual-hider form of play. The presence of two-bone sets does not rule out the possibility of the four-hand or dual-hider form of handgame, if one bone were given to each hider. However, as two-bone sets collected by Culin are generally marked differently to distinguish them, these are two-bone sets for single hiders.

Interest in Native American gaming traditions in the late 1800s resulted in increased ethnographic inquiry by several scholars. Between 1892 and 1907 a greater emphasis was placed on the systematic collection of gaming implements (Culin 1907, 29). In surveying the handgame among eighty-one populations in some sixty-one pages, Culin's work is useful for a limited comparison of geographical distribution, material culture, and basic rules. But because of the inconsistent quantity and quality of data collected and the massive scope of the project Culin undertook, he did not document the game in depth for many populations. His accounts are extremely sparse for some and range from one or two sentences to several pages per group. Following Culin's work, little research on Native American handgames occurred.[21]

THE PAWNEE GHOST DANCE HANDGAME

Of all subsequent works, Lesser produced the most in-depth study of a tribal handgame tradition with *The Pawnee Ghost Dance Hand Game* (1933). Lesser shows how the Pawnee revitalized several rituals, including the handgame, in the Ghost Dance religious doctrine of 1890. The popular gambling game was transformed into a social arena whereby many tenets of Pawnee belief and worldview became embedded in a social ritual. The secular game became as much of an expression of Pawnee belief as it was a set of elaborate rituals. As the game became intertwined with Ghost Dance ideology and the belief that the ghosts of deceased Pawnee ancestors could appear to individuals and instruct them in the practices of the true religion—the religion of their ancestors, it became more ritualized and holy because it was viewed as a gift from Pawnee who had become spirits. The handgame was but one element of a reconstituted and revitalized Pawnee culture. Lesser's work demonstrates ethnic persistence with adaptation or modification as a strategy for the survival of a small and encapsulated ethnic community undergoing significant forced acculturation (Kehoe 1996).[22]

48 CHAPTER 1

The developments of the handgame in the 1890s among the Pawnee are unique. Originally only men played the handgame. No drum was used, but players clapped their hands as they sang handgame songs. Pawnee games were closely linked to their origin stories, mythology, and religious bundles. A formal gaming myth was recited on the third day of the Chawi White Beaver Ceremony, focusing on the revival of hibernating animals, and, similar to gambling, this contained heavy elements of rejuvenation. Rites for spring, war, gambling, and buffalo hunting were not mutually exclusive. According to James Murie, the Kitkahaki Creation Bundle was the keeper of all games. In Plains Indian cultures, gambling and war held parallels with the fluctuation of victory and defeat. In spring, Pawnee prepared supplies for warfare and began playing games as the war societies performed dances prior to men setting off to make war. The Pawnee viewed and played the handgame as a warpath, with challenges between boys, between Pawnee bands, and even against other tribes (Lesser 1933, 139–54; Gabriel 1996, 72–73), proclaiming "We've come on the warpath for the hand game" when approaching another group or tribe to play (Lesser 1933, 141). Other metaphors between war and the handgame are found in imitating animals, concealment of the warrior's trail, scouting for the enemy's trail, counting of coup (touching or striking an enemy in battle) by the winners, and later the war drum. Other rituals included war-pipe ceremonies, an elongated fire, player orientation related to entrance to a camp, and the performance of war society dances and songs. In one game, Knifechief rose to sprinkle ashes to hide tracks. Then the Kiowa guesser searched for the trail. Much of this faded after entering the reservation (Lesser 1933, 139–54; Gabriel 1996, 73, 78, 82).

By 1892 many Pawnee religious ceremonies, societies, and material culture forms had ceased. The Ghost Dance came to the Pawnee in the fall of 1891 through Frank White, simultaneous to agency efforts to implement allotment on the Pawnee Reservation. When pressures against the dance mounted, Joseph Carrion (Arapaho), a close friend, brother-in-law, and fellow dancer, went to an Arapaho dance seeking direction. During the dance he fell into a trance and dreamt. The next day it was decided to stop the Ghost Dance and to play a handgame for four days. Carrion fasted during these four days and saw several images in the sun, including a bison (an important symbol of spring renewal), crow, eagle, designs, and Jesus standing with his hand extended toward him. The Arapaho later interpreted his vision as a gift of the handgame by Jesus to Carrion, who took the vision to the Pawnee, who then began conducting their own visions, leading to more sanctions of the handgame (and additions to it) from Christ. This allowed the Ghost Dance handgame to surpass White's form, and—because it was now vision-based, came from an Arapaho, and was not owned and sanctioned by priests in the traditional Pawnee fashion—it could evolve into a new cultural form. Carrion's vision also mandated the inclusion of the handgame in the Ghost Dance. This new form merged the old gaming ritual and myth with the burgeoning Ghost Dance to create the Ghost Dance handgame ceremony as a means of reviving various components of Pawnee heritage. Bundle materials and rituals, religious societies, and games were combined with visionary mandates and inspirations to revive the old ceremony and play, renew and re-create old ritual paraphernalia, and transform earlier symbols and concepts into new ones. Men played hoop and pole, hand, and moccasin games; women played the plum-seed dice game, shinny, and double ball game. The Pawnee Ghost Dance handgame was based on the old game, with variations based on visions and older bundle ritual symbolism. Unlike the original handgame, the Ghost Dance handgame evolved into a ceremony involving no gambling. Winning and losing were now interpreted as omens of luck directly related to the dance. Luck through winning was linked to the Ghost Dance's blessing and probably helped in coping with the trauma of the reservation experience. Although one still needed luck from visions to ensure communication with the spiritual realm, the Ghost Dance handgame doctrine promised luck in the next life. The ceremony continued until the end of the century (Lesser 1933, 155–57; Gabriel 1996, 67–72, 75–78).

According to Lesser (1933, 318), Pawnee compared handgame competition to warfare. With the rise of the Ghost Dance, the warfare metaphor was dropped and the game was used for more ceremonial purposes. Lesser maintains that the earlier emphasis on power for success in the game was reconfigured in meaning as it shifted to ceremony. Instead of representing the acquisition of spoils through war in the form of the bets associated with the game, an emphasis on demonstrating power in play developed. Victory represented the presence of supernatural aid and power (Lesser 1933, 156).

Much of the basic structure of the Pawnee handgame has remained intact, while other significant changes have occurred. In contrast to past highly religious association, games today are secular events, often for birthdays, to raise funds through raffles and donations for social clubs, or to honor a veteran. Games are no longer sponsored to offer prayers, and pipe offerings are no longer used to begin each game. Evening play beginning with a supper has replaced afternoon play, to accommodate work schedules. An individual drum for each side has been replaced by a single drum that is alternately shared, and Round Dance songs sung between sets of handgames have replaced Ghost

50   CHAPTER 1

Dance songs. Lively songs provide plenty of opportunity for joking. Most sets of handgame sticks are owned by service clubs, and singers are fed and paid by the host group for their services. The main religious elements are the opening prayer and a prayer at mealtime. Although the Ghost Dance elements of the game are largely gone, it continues as a social event similar to that among other north-central Oklahoma tribes (Kehoe 1996, xvii).

Yet a ritual order remains in formal games, and a distinct belief that luck can be affected by prayer, spiritual exercises, and the use of personal amulets continues. Some Pawnee find handgame more enjoyable than bingo, slot machines, and blackjack because of the social nature of the play and because the players cultivate real skill. An enjoyable recreation, the handgame also contributes to ethnic maintenance. Kehoe (1996, xvii) describes: "Playing the hand game is a fun way to assert the persistence of the Pawnee nation and its culture." Although tribes have slightly different traditions, material culture, and songs, and a distinct sociocultural arena for demonstrating and maintaining ethnic identity, general similarity allows intertribal handgame play.

MUSIC

Little work has been produced on handgame music. Herzog (1935, 6–7) briefly discusses the distinctive style of handgame songs and American Indian gambling music, and Flannery and Cooper (1946, 391–419) provide a basic account of the handgame in examining the relationship of gambling and Gros Ventre social structure. Most early graduate student publications on Native American gaming traditions are general works with little or no attention to the handgame (Dockstader 1957).

Following Lesser, only a few in-depth studies on Plateau and Subarctic gaming traditions focus on the handgame. Desmond's 1952 work on Yakama gambling from 1860 to 1880 and Helm, Lurie, and Kurath's 1966 work on the Dogrib handgame offer rare in-depth examinations of the game for a single tribe. Stuart's 1972 account of the Coast Salish handgame (Slahal) of Washington State and British Columbia focuses on the range of play and accompanying music, while Maranda (1984) examined the history, structure, and customs of Coast Salish gambling games, the handgame being one of three principal forms, and their association with supernatural power.

Studies of Plateau hand- and stickgames include Bruntun's (1974, 1998) detailed accounts of the role of the stickgame in Kootenai culture and Plateau populations in general. Boyd (1979) briefly discusses the relationship between expressions of identity in hand- and stickgames among Montana tribes, suggesting a geographical and cultural distinction between the Great Basin stickgame and Plains handgame. These data demonstrate how groups

The Origins and Background 51

in each geographical region use gaming traditions as a means of expressing and maintaining ethnic identity and social proximity or distance with other Indian populations and non-Indians.[23] Thomas Green (1979) reports the use of the handgame by some American Indian Movement members as a form of political activism and symbolic of larger struggles on a macrocosmic level.[24]

Peacock (1955, 6) describes popular and ceremonial versions of the handgame among the Cree. In the ceremonial version, sometimes played by elders and medicine men, a special group of "Holy Hand-Game Songs" are sung. While improvised groups of sticks and bones can be used, elaborately carved sets of bones and sticks, some of ivory and viewed as family heirlooms, are used in Holy Games. Additional literature includes brief accounts on handgames and music of the Wichita (Dorsey 1901a), Omaha (Howard 1950), Shoshone (Randle 1953), Flathead (Merriam (1955), and Blackfoot (Nettl 1967, 149–150; Nettl and Blum 1968, 15–19). Indian House Records (Isaacs 1968) provides live recordings and a brief account of the Kiowa, Comanche, and Apache handgame, while Canyon Records has released several albums of stickgame songs.

Cheska (1979) has examined how traditional game participation, including guessing and dice games, assures social maintenance among North American Indian tribes. She demonstrates how games serve as strategies reinforcing the social processes of sex role differentiation, group identity, decision-making models, and symbolic identification as indirect contributors to social maintenance. Despite changes, participation continues to promote these social processes. Overall, little interpretive research has been undertaken with Native American forms of gaming.

PLAINS STUDIES

Recent studies on Plains Indians have largely neglected the game and its importance as an ongoing, significant traditional focus of tribal activity and ethnic maintenance of considerable historical duration. Only Blaine (1982, 126–28) for the Pawnee and Wichita, Fowler (1987, 211–12, 58–60) for the Gros Ventre and Assiniboine, and Kracht (1989, 733–37) for reservation-era Kiowa, briefly mention the game. Works on the Northern Arapaho (Fowler 1982), Comanche (Gelo 1986; Foster 1991), Cheyenne (Moore 1996), and Naishan Apache (Lasko 1997) lack any significant mention of the handgame.[25]

Works concerning southern plains tribal ethnicity and ethnic expression follow this pattern. Gelo's (1986, 74) work on Comanche religion briefly mentions the continuation of the handgame and discusses the impacts of the brief Comanche oil boom of the early 1980s (1986, 68–72) but not their correlation. In his work on Comanche maintenance of social face and forms of focused

52 CHAPTER 1

community interaction, Foster (1991, 81, 92, 122) mentions the gambling forms of monte and horse racing but little on the handgame. He states (1991, 92), "There is no record of agency gatherings being used as occasions for focused public activities other than gambling and horse racing." Foster (1991, 122) quotes Comanche elder Leonard Riddles on the presence of handgames and other forms of gambling at encampments near Walters, Oklahoma, during the post-allotment period: "They used to have that hand game, too, at nights. Maybe this bunch at Walters would take on another bunch . . . They'd bet on the hand game. Most of 'em put up a kind of jackpot." Unfortunately, Foster does not include the handgame and other formats of gambling as important social gatherings or "focused public activity," stating (1991, 196n111), "The gaming aspects of winter encampments were simply a continuation of Comanches' enjoyment of gambling from the prereservation and reservation periods. A certain carnival atmosphere had become attached to that segment of the encampments, with card games played in tents during the day." However, handgames continued throughout the pre- and post-allotment periods among the Comanche and neighboring tribes and were common at agency grass lease and annuity payment encampments.

Lasko (1997) examines persistent identity systems and the relationships between the Plains Apache tribe, the historical depth of community identity, transmission of cultural forms to younger generations, and the foci of the Apache connection to their past. Although the Apache language, Blackfeet Society, and Native American Church are discussed, the handgame is absent.

In the 1990s Bill Rathbun published a work titled *Handgame!* (1992) followed by *Whatever Happened to Professor Coyote? A Journey to the Heart of the Handgame* (1999), a novel set around an anthropology professor, his brother, and the handgame. The books are based on his personal experiences over twenty-five years of playing handgame with California and Nevada tribes and ethnographic data on the Maidu of Northern California (Rathbun 1999, 248). Young and Gooding (2001, 1024–25) provide a brief overview of Plains handgames.

More recently Johnson (2001) made the first documentary video on the subject, *Hand Game: The Native North American Game of Power and Chance*, which summarizes the game's origins, historical developments, and contemporary forms. Emphasizing the Plateau, *Hand Game* uses material obtained from over seventy-five hours of recording and visits over six years to seven northern Great Plains, Plateau, Great Basin, and southern Northwest Coast tribes (the Blackfeet, Crow, and Flathead of Montana, Coeur d'Alene of Idaho, Makah and Spokane of Washington, and Walker River Paiute of Nevada).

Johnson shows games during the annual Flathead powwow in Arlee, Montana, a Paiute Pine Nut Festival in Nevada, and the annual Crow tournament. Eloquently blending folklore, live play, historical imagery, and consultant testimony, the documentary uniquely explores the cultural significance of the game, linked through segments of Coyote's storytelling, and participant statements rather than an academic narrator or specific theoretical approach. It also examines the game as an example of increased economic sovereignty through its inclusion in the Indian Gaming Regulatory Act of 1988. Testimony from Yakama and First Nations players enriches the film. The nuanced conversation and spontaneous responses from avid players provide significant insight into the game, its meaning for participants, and much of what constitutes life and current problems in these Indian communities. Frey (2001) provides a positive and insightful review of Johnson's film. For several years, video recordings of hand and stickgames have been regularly posted on YouTube and other internet sites.

CHAPTER

2

The Traditional Handgame of the Kiowa, Comanche, and Apache

ORIGINS

A FEW MYTHOLOGICAL and historical accounts of the Kiowa handgame have survived. According to Bill Koomsa Sr., elder Kiowa stated that the handgame has been around "since the time animals could talk."[1] Sherman Chaddlesone related an account of the origin of the Kiowa handgame he learned from his father, John. The account explains not only how the Kiowa obtained the game from their trickster Séndé but also why it was restricted to certain parts of the year, namely the fall through early spring.

> The last thing that Saynday did was—I got this from my father—the last thing that he did was when he was getting ready to leave our world: he told the Kiowas, "I'm gonna give you something, leave something with you to help you get through the long winter months." You know, to live in tipis and confined to tipis and all that. And he said, "I'm gonna teach you how to play a game," and so he did. He started teaching the handgame to these Kiowas, and he brought them all together, all the leaders of the tribe, in one tipi, and then he was sitting there explaining to them how to structure the teams, sides, and all that, and originally it was just like play between . . . just two people and usually either band leaders or chiefs or whatever. Nowadays you know there's teams all lined up, and they'll pass these bones back and forth between each other. But originally it was only two people. One would hide the bones, and the other would guess, and they would go

The Traditional Handgame 55

back and forth like that. That's how he taught it, but, while he was doing that, he was sitting by the door of the tipi, and . . . every once in a while [he would] lean over and . . . stick his arm outside the tipi. And then they . . . started learning the game. They got into it, they started playing it, and then he was guiding them along, teaching them the songs and all that, and then he'd keep doing that, sticking his arm out the tipi door.

Finally somebody got curious and asked him why he kept doing that, sticking his arm out. . . "Well, when the environment is just right," he said, "I'm going to leave you"—which was winter. And so he was doing that and, one time he stuck his arm out like that, and all of a sudden he disappeared while they were playing this game, and then they all jumped up and ran outside, and they went looking for him, and they couldn't see him around anywhere. Somebody yelled, "Look up, look up in the sky!" It was at nighttime. Oh, he said he was gonna leave a sign. He said, "When you see that sign it's the only time you play this game." And so he disappeared, and they went out looking for him. Somebody noticed something in the sky. They looked up, and they saw this new constellation of stars shaped like his arm, and it's the constellation—its name is Orion's Belt. But it wasn't there before, and so now, you know, the only time it's visible is in the—it comes out in the fall time and goes away again in the springtime. So that's why the Kiowas didn't play in certain times of the year. The constellation wasn't available [visible].[2]

Parsons (1929, 64–66) recorded an account from Edgar Keahbone in 1927 involving a young man, the handgame, and a battle between the buffalo and white bear:

There was a camp. At this camp they had the ceremony of hand game (towa) [jòǎugà] every night. One night there came a young man from another camp to attend their hand game. There was a young man in the camp who was gazing closely at what the visitor had on him. He noticed the visitor had around his neck a necklace of bear claws, very beautiful and different from other bear claws. They were red and shining. The young man wished for a set for himself. When the game ended the young man approached the visitor and asked how he could obtain a necklace like his. He answered that one had to be daring before he could get a necklace like that. "If you want one, I will give you instructions how to reach the place, and how to kill a certain kind of bear. Arm yourself with a lot of arrows, kill a deer, take it to the river nearby, look for a good size tree, lay your deer under the tree, climb the tree, sit there and wait until a bear comes to feast on the deer. If the bear first to come is black, shoot him; but if a white bear comes first, I advise you not to shoot him. His claws are different. In case he notices you, you can get away by jumping into the river." After the young man heard this, he killed the deer, and took it where he thought it would be a good place to kill the bear. He prepared his game under the tree and climbed up the tree. He sat and waited until he saw the first bear approach. He noticed it was the kind of bear he had been instructed not to shoot. As this bear began to eat the deer, the young man noticed he had beautiful claws. He had made up his mind to kill the bear for the claws. He longed for them as they were different from what he had seen. He began to shoot at the bear, but the arrows glanced off. Finally the bear noticed the young man shooting at him. He growled and raised up on his hind legs. He started to climb. The young man saw the bear coming for him, he leaped into the river. The bear followed. The young man dove under the water and came up on the surface at another place. The bear also dove, following him at every dive. The young man dove at a different angle until he was out of sight of the bear. He crawled on to the bank of the river and got away, and found a hollow log into which he crept. The bear tracked him until he came to where he was. The bear grabbed the log and carried it some distance and threw it into the river. The bear rode the log until he thought he had drowned the young man. While the bear was rolling the log around in the river, the young man crawled out, from one end, and dove as far as his breath lasted. He peeped cautiously out of the water to see how far he was from the bear. He dove again, he came out of the river and ran. While he was running he looked back and saw the white bear and a number of other bears on his trail. As the bears drew near, the young man cried for help, as he knew he would be killed by the bears. He had noticed in the distance four buffalo and he thought he would run by them so they could hear him. The buffalo began to stand up, they began to talk and asked why he was running. He told them that the bears were after him. One of the buffalo told the fastest buffalo, the yearling, to carry the young man on his back to where there was another group of buffalo, while they stayed there and fought with the bears. The bears killed all the buffalo and took after the young man and the yearling. As they approached them they came to where was the second group of buffalo, where another buffalo carried the young man on to a third group while the other buffalo in the group fought against the bears. The bears killed all the buffalo and began to pursue the young man and the buffalo with him. After they reached the third group of buffalo he was carried by one to the fourth group, the big herd, while the third group fought against the bears and were killed. The bears pursued the young man and his buffalo. After the young man reached the last group, he told them the bears were after him. So one of the buffalos ordered the others to fight with the bears, while he made medicine (doybapai, magic power [sic]) [possibly dáuibàp̣ài or magic powder/dust] by rolling on the ground and heaping dust on his back to form a whirlwind. When he stood up after that, he was a different buffalo, his horns were of flint. He noticed that the bears had killed nearly all of the buffalo. By this time the buffalo had killed all the bears except the white bear. The white bear and the leader buffalo began to fight, it was magic against magic. They fought until one had to be killed. Now the buffalo killed the white bear. The young man began to collect all the claws from the bears the buffalos killed, including those of the white bear. The leader buffalo appointed seven of his buffalo to carry the boy back to his home, and he instructed the young man to be cautious of one thing, never to smell the odor of burning dung. "Whatever you do, be on guard against this. It would mean your death.' The young man told him that he would follow his instruction. The young man started his journey by riding on of the buffalos until the buffalo gave out, and so on he rode each in turn until he arrived home. The young man had already fixed the claws before he reached camp so he could wear them to the next hand game. A few days later he went to where they were playing the game. He joined it. The other young man had noticed the bear claws on the young man. He went and asked how he had been so daring to wear the claws of the white bear. He asked how he had killed a white bear. He told him that the buffalo had helped him kill the bear. A few days later he forgot the instructions of the buffalo, he did not notice that some boys were playing at a distance, burning dung. The wind blew from them to him. When he breathed the smoke, he fell dead. The necklace was kept sacred by the people.

The handgame appears in another story recorded from Kiowa elder Frank Given in 1935:

There was a lake next to a hill where people went for power but could never stay because something in the lake frightened them. One man was going there and was not afraid. He lay down on the hill and the water-monster had pity on him and took him under the water and gave him power to cure all diseases and his family gave him up. He stayed there, learning, and when he knew what to do he came out. In the meantime his people had moved. The monster told him to sit on the bank and the wild geese, his servants, would carry him. He must keep his eyes shut from the time they lifted him till they landed. So he waited and the geese came, one on each side and he put his arms round their necks and hung there till they were in sight of the camp. People were playing the hand game and a young man looked up and called his brother's attention to the geese. They saw them land and set down the man. People came out to see him. He told them to have a tipi put up for him and then he would come home. They fixed it for him and he came. They respected him. He cured and used his power for good. The monster had told him he had given him all but one thing. When he had been there some time they heard smallpox was coming. He could not heal this. He wanted everyone to move but they refused and tried to make him stay. Finally he agreed to. That night he and his family moved away. He was going back under the water. In the morning they trailed him to the lake and saw the tracks going into water and that's the last anyone heard of him.[3]

58   CHAPTER 2

The underwater monster and immersion into a lake relate to when the Kiowa resided near "Medicine Lake" in the northern plains in the 1700s, often believed to be Spear Lake or Lake DeSmet in Wyoming (Mooney 1898, 239; Meadows 2008, 116–17).

Gregory Haumpy Sr. learned a version of the game's origins in a story from his parents, in which the Kiowa had no handgame but met another tribe that did. Soon the Kiowa learned how to play and made songs of their own. His parents stated that the Kiowa obtained the game from the Cheyenne and Arapaho.[4]

The handgame also appears in Kiowa artwork. Zo-tom produced a ledger drawing of a Kiowa handgame while a prisoner at Fort Marion, Florida, in 1877. The image was titled "Gambling with hair pipe," by Mrs. Eva Feñyes, who commissioned the work (Zo-Tom 1969, plate 5). Painted by Parker Boyiddle, the third of the ten Kiowa murals in the Kiowa Tribal Museum depicts the Half-Boys, the Kiowa culture heroes, one of whom is walking into Spear Lake and the other who is cutting himself into ten pieces with a knife, symbolizing the basis of the Kiowa Ten Medicine Bundles. On the right side of this mural are two parallel lines of ten arrows stuck into the ground across from each other. Between them are two bone hair pipes—one marked, the other unmarked (Denton and Maudlin 1989, 71). Sherman Chaddlesone painted a ledger-style depiction of a Kiowa handgame, closely resembling that by Zo-tom, now in the Kiowa Red River Casino Hotel at Devol, Oklahoma. Jeff Yellowhair made a painting of his father Jack singing and playing a hand drum, with spirit-like handgame players in traditional Kiowa dress playing behind him, that is now in the family home.

The Naishan Apache

In 1933–1934, Gilbert McAllister (1949, 17–22) recorded two Plains Apache stories involving the handgame during the mythological period. In the first (McAllister 1949, 17–20), the primary Apache creation story, a handgame played between the animals in the beginning of time constitutes a central part of the story. This story tells of a time of darkness, the formation of the earth and people, the basis of varied animals' phenotype, and how the animals got rid of Nistcre, a human-like form of Stone Monsters.[5]

In the Beginning

In the beginning when the earth was put here it was soft. It was like walking on soft rubber. At this time everything was in darkness; there was no day. Out west in the Panhandle of Texas there was a big bluff, over which

The Traditional Handgame

water was running, making a river. Since the earth was soft as quicksand it was washing away rapidly. That was how it began.

Gradually the earth began getting hard and grass started to grow. Then trees began to spread out from the rivers. There was more moisture then, so everything grew bigger than now. Plants were similar to the ones we have today, except sage. It grew as big as trees then.

In the springtime everything looked green; it looked pretty and around the creeks something smelled sweet. In the fall everything dried up.

It was dark then, since there was no day, but big stars gave a little light. In this dim light the creeks looked white and the sage looked white.

Somebody was molding mud in the shape of humans. Many were being so formed: men, women, young ones—all kinds. These forms were told to speak and right there the Apaches learned to talk. All these people talked differently and couldn't understand each other.

In this time of continued night when they had snow, the people put sticks under their feet so they could walk on the snow. The Apaches didn't know very much then.

There was one place that looked as if smoke was coming from it. The people went over there and found deer. They killed them and had to dig them out of the ice.

The people were accustomed to living in the dark and didn't mind it. They didn't know about light. It was like living in the nighttime with only starlight.

They talked about playing a game. On one side there was Nistcre, Elk, Deer, Squirrel, Rabbit. On the other side there was Buffalo, Bear, Bobcat, Mountain Lion, Swift-Hawk, and some others. They were going to play the hand game. Since Swift-Hawk was such a good guesser, they took the poker from the fire and hit him in the face, and that is why he has a black stripe across his face. All this time it was still night.

Coyote was the umpire. He kept the sticks and sat on the west side. He helped both sides and once in a while would holler, "Wau, wau, wau." It was night then and he still howls in the night.

Dragonfly was on Buffalo's side, as was Turkey. They told the latter to sing, but all he could do was say, "Gobble, gobble, gobble." He forgot his song. Bobcat was dancing around the fire dragging his tail. He got so excited he came too close to the fire and burned his tail. That is why it is short and black.

Nistcre was a good guesser. When he would hide the bean behind his back, Dragonfly would be there watching. He would run back and say, "He hid it on the right," or, "He hid it on the left." When they guessed right they would all holler, "Nistcre, Nistcre, Nistcre." They wanted to win quickly, so Dragonfly kept looking. He was peeping through a hole. He could keep looking and never close his eyes. The side that was losing said, "Somebody must be telling on us." They looked around and saw the hole.

60 CHAPTER 2

They got a stick and punched Dragonfly's eye, but he didn't even wink. He stayed real still never closing his eye. "No, that isn't anybody," they said.

Nistcre was losing. He just had a few more sticks. It was Turtle's time to hide the bean. He sang his song, which was a good one. He had paint on the side of his face, and still has today.

Buffalo's side was lucky. The other side would have been, too, except Dragonfly was giving them away. It was Magpie's time and he sang a good song. He was a lucky one, for they couldn't guess him.

Nistcre had just one more stick. It was Bobcat's time. Dragonfly went around and told him where the bean was. Right there Nistcre lost. Rabbit and Squirrel, who were on Nistcre's side, had bet their fat and lost. That is why they haven't any now, except a little between the shoulders. That is what was left when they pulled the other fat off.

During the game there were many side bets. Possum bet his wooly tail, and having lost, he hasn't any fur on his tail. Skunk also lost, and since he bet his back, you can still see the white scar. Buffalo bet his upper teeth and lost them, and Horse bet his side teeth. Coyote bet his night's sleep, and if the sun comes up and finds him asleep, that means he is going to die.

After the game had ended and the animals had paid their bets, they took Nistcre to that high bluff out west and pushed him off. All that is left of him now are the big rocks lying at the bottom of the cliff.

That is how they played a hand game in the beginning of time. The old folks told this story. If they lied, we lie too.

The second Apache story (McAllister 1949, 20–22), narrated by Big Lobo Wolf (Apache Ben Chaletsin) and translated by Harold Sunrise, tells of the handgame between the animals and Nistcre. While some aspects of this story duplicate the former, others differ significantly. This story tells of how the battle for control of the earth between the herb-eating animals and Nistcre was settled in a handgame, the origins of daylight, how Coyote gave directions to the different animals, and how, through Crow's jealousy, mortality came to the people.

The Hand Game between the Animals and Nistcre

This is a story about the time when there was no day. Then it was always dark. People were lined up on two sides to play a hand game. On the north side were the herb-eating animals, on the south side were the Nistcre. Coyote was the scorekeeper, sitting on the west side in charge of the sticks. Chaparral or Road Runner was sitting next to the door. He had charge of the day, or light. The Nistcre laid the bet: "If we win there will be no more people. Even if you propagate, we will kill your children. If you of the north win, we will be here on earth no more."

The game was started. They kept playing and playing and playing. The sticks kept changing from one side to the other. Back and forth the sticks moved. Coyote would encourage and back the side which had the most sticks. When the Nistcre had the most Coyote would support the old men; if most sticks went to the herb-eating people, Coyote would back them. The game lasted a very long time. They played and played and the sticks moved back and forth. Neither side was able to win, nor does anyone know how much time elapsed. Road Runner, who had charge of light, would occasionally start to raise his wings, and day would begin to dawn, but the others would go over and make him cover up and it would get dark again. Whenever, Chaparral raised his wings, the Nistcre would holler, "Nistcre, Nistcre, Nistcre."

There came a time when Nistcre had only one stick and Coyote was encouraging the north side. Finally the north side won. Road Runner held up his wings and day began to dawn.

The winners took the Nistcre to a high bank, a bluff, and placed them on the edge of it. But these Nistcre took some rosin and rubbed it on the bottom of their feet. They were on the edge of the cliff and the people pushed them over, but they would spring back up because of the sticky stuff on the bottom of their feet. The people did this twice, only to have the Nistcre come back in place. Then Coyote said, "Wait, I'm going back after my necklace."

After traveling some time he came to Snapping Turtle in the water. "Lend me your necklace, we have something great over there," Coyote said. Turtle answered, "No you are crazy, you might press it too hard and if you do I'll float out of the water." Coyote asked for the necklace again. Turtle refused, "If you press it too hard the creeks will get very high and I'll not float." Coyote said, "No, I'll press very easy." Finally Turtle gave the necklace to Coyote and he ran back.

Coyote brought the necklace to where the Nistcre had been placed on the bluff. He put it behind them on the ground and each end hung off the cliff. Coyote pressed hard on the necklace and much water ran out. The water began washing the dirt out from behind the Nistcre. Then Coyote began to press even harder and more water ran out. The rivers below got full of water. Finally the bank caved off into the stream with the Nistcre.

Then Coyote told the animals to go to different parts of the world. "You will live to be old," he said to the animals. To the Nistcre he said, "You are all dead now. People who come will sharpen their knives on you." To the grass-eating animals he said, "You go out to the plains and when people come they will eat you and live off of you." Then he said to the birds, "Get together and have a meeting and make a blue eagle."

The birds then got together and selected one bird. They fixed him up to look like an eagle and then set him up and looked at him. He didn't look right, so they pulled the eagle clothes off of him. They tried bird after bird, but none of them looked like blue eagle and the clothes didn't fit. There were just two birds left, one of which was Crow. They fixed Crow up to look like an eagle and put him up and looked at him. He also failed and they pulled him down. Only one bird was left and they dressed him up. He looked good in eagle feathers, so they made him Eagle.

After Coyote had given directions to the different animals, he grabbed up some pithy wood and said, "You watch this. I'm going to throw it in the water and if it sinks and does not come back up, there will be no resurrection. It if comes back up people will come to life after death." He threw the stick in the water and it came back up.

Crow was still mad that they had not made him Eagle. He picked up a rock and said, "If this comes up there will be no death, but if it sinks there will be death." The rock sank and there is death today.

Beatty (1999) provides a variation of these stories and a brief account of the Apache handgame. Typical of much mythology, these accounts offer explanations for why things are as they are, including the physical attributes of many animals. In one version, Turkey appears in the final episode of the game and after the animals and humans are separated from the monsters places the handgame sticks in his boots. As the Apache explain, the sticks became the small "extra" leg bones of the turkey.[6] Skunk bet his back (or back hair, depending on the version), and, after his side lost, his black hair was clipped from the back of his head to his tail. When it grew back it became white. These accounts are of great historical significance not because they simply appear in mythological form but because they suggest that the origin of the handgame is of considerable temporal length to have become interwoven with their mythology and, in particular, their origin story. Descriptions of some of the rules for hiding, guessing, scoring, and the presence of bets and side bets suggest a long tradition, as these elements of the game continue to the present.

HISTORIC AND ETHNOGRAPHIC ACCOUNTS

Historic and ethnographic documentation indicate that the handgame is an old game among the Kiowa, Comanche, and Apache. Neighbors (1852, 133), Dodge (1882, 329), and Bancroft (1886, 516) provide early, brief accounts of Comanche handgames, while Battey (1875, 319, 326), in reference to the KCA, describes the Kiowa handgame. Using archival and fieldwork data, this section reconstructs the handgame among the Kiowa, Comanche, and Apache before entering a reservation in 1875 to its modern innovation in the 1950s.

The Kiowa

The Kiowa call the handgame jŏáugà (tipi game), from jŏ̀ (tipi, house, indoor abode, etc.) and áugà (any form of game or way of playing or gambling), from its originally being played inside a tipi at night during long, cold, winter evenings when members of a band gathered in their winter encampments.[7]

The Traditional Handgame

While stationed at Fort Sill from 1889 to 1897, Hugh L. Scott recorded several volumes of ethnographic and linguistic material through Plains Indian Sign Language. One entry (Meadows 2015, 449) describes the Kiowa handgame:

Moccasin Game [Handgame]

The young men have a game for winter nights. It is played inside of a lodge. They choose sides and each side has a leader. They make bets on it. They have a certain number of counters which are divided in half between the two sides. One leader has a bean or a pebble in his hand. He crosses his hands at the wrists and moves them back and forth in time to different songs to deceive the opposite side. He sometimes pretends to pass the pebble on to other members of his side. The attention of the other side is distracted by the motion of the hands in unison. They hop up and down [move in place?] as they are sitting on the ground. Suddenly a member on the opposite side who thinks he knows where the pebble is claps his hands and extends the right with the thumb extended (fingers closed) to the right or left according as he desires him to open the right or left hand. If the pebble is in that hand his side gets the pebble and takes a stick from the other side that lost the pebble. This goes on from side to side until all the sticks are won and lost. Expert leaders have many ways of deceiving the other side and are well known and sought after on important occasions.

This is called by Kiowas Doo-au = Moccasin Game.[8] The [sign language] sign for it is crossing wrists alternately right in front, then left, as is done in the game to distract the attention of opponents.[9] This game is played by all the southern tribes.

Handgames were traditionally limited to the winter months. As Bill Koomsa Jr. related, the Kiowa watched the migratory patterns of geese to determine the handgame season. When geese began flying south in the fall, it soon became cold and was time to start playing. When the geese began returning northward in the spring (about mid- to late March in western Oklahoma) the weather became warmer, and it was time to stop playing for the year.[10] Battey (1875, 326) writes, "The young men and warriors have many games of chance, which they play, accompanied by singing and sometimes drumming; these are often continued throughout the entire night. Indeed, in large camps of from one hundred lodges, seldom a night passes without the sound of the drum, continued until long after sunrise." As with Séndé stories, handgames were traditionally limited to winter play and were associated with a taboo. According to Mrs. Horse (Po-e-to-mah or Fíjómà [Food Keeper]), children were told that if they played handgame in the summer "the worms [would] get on them" or that they "would catch the itch."[11]

64   CHAPTER 2

TEAMS AND PLAYERS

Among most southern plains tribes, handgames were traditionally played both inside a tipi and out in the open. When inside a tipi, a fire was maintained for heat and light. Mrs. Horse stated that women and men played handgame, sometimes together and sometimes separately, but only in the winter.[12] Some games were relatively small, with only a few men per side sitting in a line across from each other on the north and south sides of a lodge with the fire between them. Women sat behind the men on the side they supported. Often the crowd was so large that all could not fit inside a large tipi, whereupon the sides were rolled up so that spectators could watch, or two or three tipis might be joined together to make a larger composite lodge to hold more people. Composite tipis were common among Plains groups, including those at Kiowa Sun Dance encampments to facilitate large military society meetings of up to sixty men. In other instances, depending on the weather, a game might be held outside around a large fire. As a Pawnee account (Lesser 1933, 152) of a pre-reservation game in a Kiowa camp describes, "The tent was big, but the crowd was so large that there was not enough room inside for all, so the bottom of the tent cover was rolled up all around, and those who couldn't get in settled themselves around outside. Many had to sit outside this way in the cold. If such a large crowd had been anticipated, the hand game would have been played in the open around a big fire, but it was too late to gather enough wood to build such a fire. . . . In the excitement of the game, the cold is forgotten, even by those who must squat outside."[13]

Cecil Horse also reported the use of elongated composite lodges: "They get over there and then they have their tipi all set up. And it's got to be built long so they don't sit in a circle, they sit on one side like that, you see." After eating dinner, and singing four songs, the people began to play.[14]

A camp crier would call out in the evening: "Where are we going to have a big handgame tonight?" The camp chief would respond "In my tipi!" and there in the camp chief's tipi all would later meet (Parsons 1929, 121). According to Parsons players divided into two teams of ten men sitting on the north and south sides of a tipi respectively. Typical of Plains hospitality, visiting teams were fed by the hosts (Lesser 1933, 150–54).

In intertribal games, tribes sat on the side of their home territories, the one residing north of the other on the north side and the more southern tribe to the south. In pre-reservation times, visitors occasionally approached an encampment of another tribe from a direction other than that of their home territory, then assumed the opposite side during the handgames (Lesser 1933, 152–54). When the Crow come from Montana to play the Kiowa in Oklahoma, they

The Traditional Handgame 65

sit on the north side, while the Kiowa and other Oklahoma tribes sit on the south.[15]

Whether playing against members of one's own tribe or another tribe, any number of players exceeding two could play. The number of players did not have to be equal. Frizzlehead II (aka E-mau-ta, Èmáuthâa̱, or Arising Crying) stated that Kiowa teams consisted of four to ten men, each having a leader, and, although teams were not organized, some "men rallied to a leader—a man who has a reputation for hand game skill."[16] During his youth, Cecil Horse (born 1891) reported that when contingents from two communities gathered to play against one another, such as Anadarko and Hobart, the guest community usually traveled by horses and buggies. Sometimes individuals were free to sit, play, and bet on either side, a form likely more common among intra-village games.[17] Teams sat in horizontal lines facing one another. In some early games, individual matches between two people were sometimes held using only one set of hiding implements. A diagram made by the 1935 Santa Fe Laboratory of Anthropology Field School (fig. 3) illustrates the layout of a Kiowa handgame in a tipi.

EQUIPMENT

In earlier times a single hiding object small enough to conceal in a single closed hand was used by each hider. Ethnographic accounts of Kiowa hand-games report the use of elk teeth, bison teeth, small bones, beads, rings, and coins. Later two pairs of hiding objects, usually four elk teeth or four bone hair pipes, were used, with one item of each set of hiding objects marked. McAllister (1970, 54–55) reports the use of a bean (probably a mescal bean) in pre-reservation games between the Kiowa and Apache against the Comanche, and between the Kiowa and Apache against the Cheyenne.[18] Marriott records the use of two bone buttons.[19]

Each team had a set of score sticks. According to one account I recorded, arrows were originally used in the game both as counters and to wager. In discussing the Kiowa murals in the Kiowa Tribal Museum, Sherman Chaddlesone, one of three artists who painted them, explained, "It's a part of the murals over there, if you saw that portion that Parker [Boyiddle] did where the arrows are standing up in the ground. That's why that's a part of the murals over there. . . . The arrows were used as the gambling, the stakes in the gambling. Whoever won, one guess would get an arrow from the other side, you know, until somebody ended up with all the arrows, and then it evolved from there."[20]

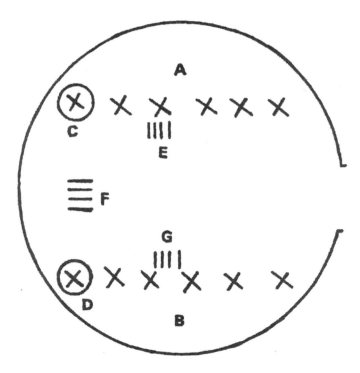

Kiowa handgame positions in a tipi. Adapted from the Santa Fe Laboratory of Anthropology Kiowa Field School Notes, 1935. National Anthropological Archives.

Arrows were a valued commodity in historic times and were frequently traded. Their linear shape made them ideal as tallies or counters and as bets in the handgame. Zo-tom's 1877 ledger drawing (Zo-Tom 1969, plate 5), titled "Gambling with hair pipe," depicts a game between two groups of men sitting across from one another—one team of nine men playing against a team of ten men, with a row of arrows stuck in the ground between them (fig. 4). All are lavishly dressed, and each side has a feathered bonnet on a pole behind them. Two opposing players are shown making hand gestures associated with the game, one making a guessing motion with a somewhat closed hand and the other displaying an open and upraised hand. Based on the clothing worn by these men, this may include both Kiowa and Cheyenne (including Cheyenne-style beaded blanket strips) and may be a game that occurred at Fort Marion. The team on the left has bows and arrows held or planted erect beside them, while the team on the right has straight sticks of similar length containing eagle feather pendants and other decorations. Despite the presence of beaded

"Gambling with hair pipe." Ledger drawing by Zo-tam (Kiowa), Fort Marion, Florida, 1877 (Zo-Tom 1969, plate 5).

blanket strips on each side—possibly depicting a game with mixed teams of Kiowa and Cheyenne on both sides—the fact that these upright linear sticks closely resemble Cheyenne-style pointing sticks used in their version of the handgame, and the triangular beaded designs on their moccasins, suggest that this drawing depicts a game between Kiowa on the left and Cheyenne on the right. The drawing shows the use of nine arrows stuck into the ground in a row between the two teams as scoring sticks and possibly as bets. Eventually the use of arrows seems to have been replaced with wooden score sticks in the shape of dowels. The need for arrows began to decline once tribes entered the reservation in 1875.

In other historical accounts, as depicted above, twelve wooden score sticks were used. Each team had four score sticks placed in front of their team. Four neutral sticks to the west of and between them were used to count successful hides and to determine when a team's score stick moved to the other side.

HAND DRUMS AND BEATERS

Hand drums were used in handgames. The small drums, usually about fourteen to sixteen inches in diameter, were single or double sided. A single-sided hand drum had the hide stretched over only one side, with the lacings tied together in the middle of the other or back side that were also used to hold

CHAPTER 2

the drum by while playing. A two-headed hand drum had a hide stretched across each side and was laced together on the side or edges of the drum. This type of drum usually had an attached thong on the side, to hold it by while playing and to hang the drum up. One or more individuals played a hand drum with a single drum beater made of short lengths of wood with a small padded buckskin head sewn around one end.[21]

OFFICIALS

In earlier times there were no referees or judges, as everyone present watched the play to ensure everyone followed the rules and to discourage cheating. In later times, *Pítdǫ́gàdé* (Standing Inside Ermine Pendants [and Feathers], aka Mrs. Emily Bosin) (Parsons 1929, 121) reports four judges who sat on the west side of the lodge behind the four neutral counter sticks. Each team had a leader or captain who sat at the west end of his team, appointed the hiders and guessers for his team, and in some cases did all of the guessing. Several elders mentioned that teams in the past had a single male guesser. The leader maintained this authority unless passing it to another. In earlier times a person was often delegated to hold their team's score sticks.[22] In 1969 Cecil Horse reported teams of twelve to fifteen players, with a guesser for each team sitting together on one end of each line with the four neutral counter sticks and a drummer and each side's four counter sticks at the other end of each line. Relating to seasons, directions, stages of life, and other ritual aspects, the number four is a widely used sacred number in Native American cultures. Horse noted a man serving as a "counter" between the two sides at one end of each line (with four neutral sticks in front of him), who may also have kept watch over the bets placed in the middle. Horse also reported that each team chose a "head man" who sat on the ends of their team's line, on opposite ends from one another, to watch the bets. This individual decided who he would hand out the hiding objects to.[23]

FIRST OFFENSE AND POINT

To start a game and determine who hid first, each team appointed one person to represent their team in a two-man preliminary match. During this part of the play each side sang the Starting Song in unison to encourage their team member. Using one pair of bones, the two players took turns hiding the bones, usually behind their back, then brought their closed fists forward in front of them. The two players took turns hiding and guessing until one guessed correctly and the other guessed incorrectly in the same round or exchange of hiding. The visitor traditionally hid first, and the host player guessed. When the host made his guess, the visitor revealed the bones to determine whether it was correct or not. The host player then hid the bones, and the visitor guessed. If

The Traditional Handgame

both players were correct, or both incorrect, another round followed until one was successful and the other unsuccessful. The Starting Song was continued by both teams until one of the preliminary players won. The successful hider's team received two of the four scoring sticks from the four in the middle and continued hiding to begin the offense. The team of the unsuccessful guesser, now on defense, prepared to guess.[24]

HIDING

The leader of the team hiding chose two individuals, each of whom were given one set of bones to hide. According to Frizzlehead II, the hiding was generally left to the more skillful members of the team. Not every individual present participated as a hider during a game, as some men only took part in the singing and betting. Both hiders hid the bones simultaneously, with no communication or discussion between them. Hiders could hide the bones behind their back, behind another person's back, under their blanket or an item of clothing, or in their hands cupped together in front of them but had to bring their hands forward and separated. Once hidden, the hider brought his closed hands forward into plain view of the opposition, with one item in each. Secreting the hiding item or items anywhere than in one's hands was considered cheating and would result in the loss of the game and that side's bets. Hiders could not change their hiding position until after a guess was made by the opposing side or a new guesser was appointed when the hider was allowed to "go down" and hide again. Facing the team hiding, there were four possible combinations for where the two marked hiding objects might be (see fig. 3): in the adjacent hands between the two hiders (inside), in their outside hands (outside), in their right hands (to the guesser's left), or in their left hands (to the guesser's right).[25]

Pítdǫ́gàdę́ (Parsons 1929, 121) reported that with two lines of ten men each facing one another, the game began with a man in the center of one line hiding and the man opposite him in the opposite line guessing him. Unfortunately, her account does not describe the further progression of hiders and guessers. Cecil Horse reported a style of play in which each side took turns hiding (and thus being guessed) four times, which the other side then did. Each time that one side won the four center sticks they moved one of the other team's sticks to their side.[26]

LEGERDEMAIN AND CHEATING

Cheating through sleight of hand was not uncommon among those with sufficient dexterity and speed to get away with it. Elder Kiowa report that originally only one hiding item was used by each hider, usually an elk tooth or a bead. The small size of the hiding objects and the low lighting inside tipis during cold winter nights undoubtedly aided those with skill in legerdemain or sleight of hand in switching the item. Doctors or shamans, who often used such techniques in their curing rituals, were especially adept at sleight of hand. In the mid-1900s, two objects were introduced to deter switching. As Mrs. Horse and George Hunt reported in 1935, "There are tricks of throwing the button from one hand to another, but a man caught doing it is beaten with a brand from the fire and his side losses. The winning side sang, 'Go back to the hills and pray and fast till some spirit has mercy on you and gives you power and then come back and we will play again.'"[27]

In 1969 Cecil Horse, who played handgame before becoming a Methodist minister, described the use of medicine in the game, including legerdemain, hypnotism, and secreting the hiding object in their mouth and ears. "They throw it from hand to hand. Like this, see. You go to guessing, you start to make your motion and you go to guessing and you say, on the right and I throw it over here, you see. And then you go on, maybe you say on the left and I throw it over here."[28] Cecil and Jenny Horse, the son and daughter-in-law of Mrs. Horse, described the prevalence of throwing the hiding object in the game to cheat, using both one's hand and mouth. Cecil Horse told of one man that appeared to have been using some form of thin rubber band attached to both ends of a ring used as the hiding object, "They throw that. There's lots of tricks to that. You throw it, you know. Throw that way, you see. They throw it. . . . Yeah, they throw it just so you don't see it. . . . Oh, trick! I saw a man at Anadarko who had a ring. You see, when he put it in here [his hand]—then he's got a rubber, this little thin rubber [rubber band]. He's got two on there and then when he goes to throw his hand back there, then they make a guess, he let go of that rubber and it jumps in one hand like that. Never could catch him for a long time. Then sometimes they throw it in their mouth. They throw it in their mouth. They go like that—how they do it. They're perfect in gambling that way."[29]

After hiding in their mouth, a hider would blow it out as needed after the guess was made. Plains Indian shamans commonly hid and coughed up objects—known as "blowing"— while doctoring individuals, or "shot" individuals in rituals of witchcraft (magically shot something into an individual). This form of legerdemain is possible with smaller items such as a bead or elk tooth and could be aided by rapid hand motions and low levels of firelight in tipis. As Cecil Horse described, "They blow it out, see. And that fellow make a guess on the right hand, he blow it on the left. So that's tricky." Both men and women sometimes cheated by switching the hiding item after a guess had been made. As Cecil Horse noted, "Some women do this way. They do that and then they trick it. They throw it, they fool you, you know. They throw it from hand to hand."[30] One Kiowa woman told me of Kiowa men even hiding the object in their long braids at one time.

Players were occasionally caught throwing the hiding object. When asked what happened when someone was caught cheating, Cecil Horse reported that the other side took a stick out of the fire and began to beat them. "They catch them—they got fire in the, not in the center, but they have a stick. They have a burning fire and they whip you with that burning stick. They have a burning fire and they whip you with that burning wood there. And that's your punishment if they catch you cheating in that game."[31] The punishment was meted out by the leader of the opposing team: "The man that's boss. He does that, you know. It's just kind of a little—you know. You try to cheat and they hit you with that stick with the fire on it. Set your clothes on fire."[32]

When disputes involving cheating arose, the goods won were sometimes returned, or the game started over again to settle the issue. Cecil Horse reported, "Both sides, sometimes they have a squabble. They say, 'That man's cheating.' And this man says, 'No.' So on and they get to squabbling. Sometimes they just gather up their stuff because they're cheating over there and they play over again."[33] During a game between the Pawnee and Cheyenne scouts, the Pawnee had lost several horses until discovering that the Cheyenne hider was cheating by secreting the hiding implement in his robe instead of in either hand. At one point a Pawnee exposed the ruse by grabbing the Cheyenne's wrists before he could drop the bone into either hand. The incident was peacefully resolved by the Cheyenne returning all of the horses they had won (Grinnell 1908, 28).

In addition to legerdemain, Kiowa and neighboring tribes also believed in the use of supernatural power or magic, generally called "medicine," in handgames. Cecil Horse described the frequent use of magic by "witches" in the handgame, in particular emphasizing the use of hypnotism and legerdemain, most likely by doctors or shaman:

> But the Kiowas, they kind of have a ceremony that they use in playing that, you see, because there was lots of witches in these games and they take that. . . . They take that elk teeth and they use that and take and put it in their hand. This witch is bad. He witch you. They play it that way. This fellow, he hypnotize you . . . and then he'll win the game every time. If he's a witch some take it out of their head. You know, them big. They trick in big shows. They pull a big old chicken out of their mouth or rabbit in their hat. Well, that's just the way. I don't know how they do it.[34]

72 CHAPTER 2

Jenny Horse continued:

> They used to bet in a big way with horses, saddle, or gun, things like that.
> That's why they really try hard to win. Sometimes the witch man—we got
> right ear and left ear and right hand and left hand. That fellow, he'll say,
> "That's right, that's left, that's center." If he says center, and then you have
> to have in both, in outside hand. Well, he's a witch and this fellow make
> a guess and say well, you got it on the left. He pull it out of his ear, the
> witches. Sometimes them witches get together and play their own game—
> trying to witch among their own selves. I don't like them. They trick you.
> They'll beat you. I used to play. I used to throw it. See. I'd make out like—
> I sit this way and I get all the extension and all I can and then—he'll go
> this way and I ain't got it, it's gone. It's right here or maybe I throwed it
> here. I got here and I got here. . . . Lots of them used their mouths—lots of
> them. Blow it. Sometimes . . . they have sticks in the fire and they got coal,
> fire on them. And if they catch you cheating they just beat you with that.[35]

Of particular interest are Jenny Horse's comments that being tricked by
witches in the game was somehow unfair or cheating, although she admits to
throwing the hiding item herself to cheat.

GUESSING

A team began hiding (offense) with two hiders, while the defense began by
guessing the two hiders. The leader of the opposing team selected a member
to begin guessing (defense). After examining the hiders from his side of the
playing area, the guesser gave a quick shout of "Ho!" and indicated his guess
with one of four hand signals.

These positions are described from the point of view of the guesser, since
it is from this position that guessing occurs. As the game is still played today,
a guesser faces the hiders; the hiders' left is on the guesser's right side, their
right is on guesser's left side. Determined by the hand signs signaled by the
guesser, these guesses are known as "inside," "outside," "right," and "left."
Inside guess: If the guesser believes the two hiders have both hidden the
marked bone in their inside hands (the two hands between the two hiders), the
guesser signals an inside guess by positioning his hand down the middle, palm
vertical, fingers open, extended forward. *Outside guess*: If the hider believes
the two objects are in the hiders' two outside hands, he signals for an outside
guess by holding their hand palm down horizontally, back of the hand facing
upward, with the fingers together and thumb separated and extended forward.
Right side guess: If the guesser believes the two hiding objects are both in
the left hands of the two hiders (to the guesser's right side), he signals for a
right side guess by holding his fingers closed in a fist, back of his hand facing

The Traditional Handgame 73

downward, with his thumb extended to his right (the hiders' left hands). *Left side guess*: If the hider believes the two hiding objects are both in the right hands of the two hiders (to the guesser's left side), he signals for a left side guess by holding his fingers closed in a fist, back of his hand facing upward, with his thumb extended to his left (the hider's right hands). The latter two types of guesses were and are sometimes referred to as "east" and "west," referring to their pointing toward either the door (east) or the back (west) of the tipi.[36]

After a guess is made, hiders must open their hands to reveal the bone's locations to determine whether the guess was correct or not. Guessers often try to fake the hiders into giving their position away by feigning a series of guesses without committing. Thus, a guess is not official unless preceded and signified by the shout "Ho!" If the shout does not accompany the guess, the guess does not count, and the hiders are permitted to hide again if they wish.

If one hider is guessed and one missed, the offense scores one stick and the remaining hider hides again. When guessing a single hider, a guesser signals either left or right. If correct the offense shifts to his side. If he misses the remaining hider, another stick is scored, the other hider becomes active again, and the guesser is back to guessing two hiders on the next hide. To acquire the offense (hiding), the guesser must guess both hiders correctly within a single guess or in two consecutive guesses. Otherwise, the offense continues to score points and continues hiding. Thus, three possibilities can result on the initial guess of two hiders: 1) incorrectly guessing both hiders 2) correctly guessing both hiders, or 3) correctly guessing one hider and missing the other.

As described by Marriott's sources, for each hider missed by the guesser, one of the four counter sticks from the middle pile was brought over to the side then hiding (as in the game played today, only in the preliminary match to determine which team hid first did one pair of bones win two counter sticks from the neutral pile).[37] When the four center sticks were acquired, the offense took one stick from the other side's four sticks, the four center sticks were returned to the center, and play continued. When one side had all twelve sticks, they won the game. [38]

Mrs. Horse (Po-e-to-mah or Fíjómà), and George Hunt described the start of a handgame to Alice Marriott in 1935:

> Two bone buttons are used. The bets are placed. U[mpire] hands a button
> to each L[eader]. Singing begins. The L[eader] rolls the button in his hands
> and gives it his power. Button is given to the next player. The button is
> held in the hands behind the body to hide it. The index finger extended,
> thumbs against them and arms swung in front of the body, or arms folded

74 CHAPTER 2

Table 1 : Handgame Guessing Signs

	TWO HIDERS				
	Possible Hiding Positions				Guessing Signs and Hand Positions
	Hider A		Hider B		
1.		X	X		Hand down the middle, palm vertical, fingers open, extended forward (inside guess) (*t'aida* [*thã́-dâu*]— "between two objects")
2.	X			X	Palm down horizontally, fingers open, extended forward (outside guess) (*apkana*—outside)*
3.		X		X	Fingers closed in fist, back of hand facing downward, thumb extended to the right (right side guess, hiders' left hands)
4.	X		X		Fingers closed in fist, back of hand facing upward, thumb extended to the left (left side guess, hiders' right hands)
	ONE HIDER				
	Possible Hiding Positions				Guessing Signs and Hand Positions
5.		X			Palm up, fingers closed, thumb extended to the right (right side guess)
6.		X			Palm down, fingers closed, thumb to the left (left side guess)

* Elders that I interviewed no longer recognized the term *apkana*, using only the English "outside." An examination of McKenzie's *Kiowa Disyllables* (1991, 33) produced only one term that may be related: *áup-càu* ("those who" or "which," said of persons or things, sometime pronounced "áut-càu"). In guessing, this term may suggest a usage of "those [outside hands]."

and fists tightly closed. Each side repeats the motion of the holder. L[eader] warms a hand and presses over his eyes, arm extended, thumb pointing right and left, several [times] to get holder to give away which side [he is hiding it on]. Same on the other side. If equal [both either guessed or not guessed in the same round], the game goes on. When the button is not found, the side holding it gets one stick from U[mpire]'s pile and the other button. L[eader] calls the two buttons in and whirls in front of the fire and redistributes the buttons to his own side, which is singing. Originally no drums [were used].[39]

This account richly illustrates the battle for the offense and first stick, the role of the medicine men or "leaders" in working magic on the hiding bones and attempting to force the opposing hider to give away the location of the

The Traditional Handgame 75

hidden bone, and of the support of each side's team through singing and hand motions. In some cases, the team captain might relieve the medicine man and hand out the bones himself.

THE MEDICINE MAN

Elders report that originally a single man served as the head or team captain, guesser, and distributed the hiding objects to whomever he wanted to hide. Today this individual is like a team captain in that he directs the offense and defense of his team by choosing who will hide and guess, and he is known as the "medicine man," a term some report was introduced by the Crow in the mid to late twentieth century.

In earlier times, men served as medicine men in all-male games and in games with men and women. However, in all-women's games a woman likely performed this role. In larger teams, the medicine man would not sing and drum but walked around his team handing out and collecting the hiding implements, choosing guessers, and, when necessary, choosing replacements when someone was hiding or guessing unsuccessfully. When a guesser began making more than two or three consecutive unsuccessful guesses, he was usually replaced. Likewise, if two hiders were guessed and one was missed, and the remaining hider was missed on the second guess, making both hiders active again, the medicine man might replace the individual who was correctly guessed for the next round of hiding. Gregory Haumpy described the position of medicine man:

> That's what [they] call medicine man. So we pick somebody out, like they pick me, and I don't sit with the men up there in the front row. I just get them bones, and when it's our time to hide the bones, well, I go on out and give them to someone that I think his luck is [good] and let them play. And if one of them gets out, gets caught, and the other stays, I go over there and get it [the bones] and give it to somebody else. The medicine man has the right to do that. . . . The medicine man also picks the guesser for their team. And the guesser, if he misses one or two times, he can change [pick] the next guesser."

"He can go over there and give him horns," Haumpy said. And he can take away the horns: "You're dehorned, sit down," he says, laughing. "When you 'put horns' on the guesser, he is the boss. It means he's the boss in guessing. On guessing, nobody interferes with him.[40]

THE GUESSER

Based on an old Kiowa custom of associating the guesser in a handgame with a chief, some elders report that guessers once wore horned bonnets. On Gregory Haumpy's team the guesser once had a hood with a set of attached

76   CHAPTER 2

steer horns. As Bill Koomsa Jr. described, "Back then the guesser was identified by wearing buffalo horns on his head. Today we still say, 'you take the horns' when we change guessers."[41] When a guesser decided to pass the position to another, he signaled the exchange by making the sign language sign for "bison" (i.e., horns) by holding his hands beside his head, index fingers extended and curved like bison horns, then motioned with both hands towards that individual. Symbolizing the association of chiefs wearing horned bonnets, this motion conveyed passing leadership to the new guesser. The new guesser often reciprocated by making the same sign of having horns beside his head to acknowledge the transfer prior to arising to guess.[42] As Gregory Haumpy described, making the sign, "He put horns on him and told him to go ahead and guess."[43] Some Kiowa still make the sign language sign for "bison" in passing the position of guesser to another person, commonly called "putting horns on him" or "giving them the horns."

As long as a guesser is successful, they continue to guess, even into the next game. If the guesser became ineffective, he could voluntarily pass the position to another or be replaced by the medicine man, who interceded and chose a new guesser. Often a guesser gave up his position after missing four or more points. When a team successfully hid from the opponent's guesser, often resulting in their replacement with a new guesser, this was, and still is, known as "Breaking His Horns."[44]

SCORING

In guessing two hiders, three possible scoring circumstances exist: 1) If both hiders are incorrectly guessed, two scoring sticks are taken from the neutral center pile and placed on the hiding team's side. Both hiders then hide again, and the process is repeated. 2) If the guesser correctly guesses both hiders on the first guess, no points are scored, and the offense switches to the other team. 3) If one hider is correctly guessed and the other missed, one counter is taken from the center pile and placed on the hiding team's side. The correctly guessed hider is out, while the incorrectly guessed or missed hider is allowed to hide again. At this point the hider must decide whether to hide the marked item in the same hand again, called "staying home," or switch to the other hand, known as "jumping." The guesser then guesses the remaining hider. If correctly guessing on the second guess (making two out of three correct selections in two guesses), the offense shifts to their side, and they begin to sing and hide. If the remaining hider is missed, another scoring stick is taken from the neutral pile, the other hider becomes active again, and both hiders hide again.[45] As long as both hiders are not guessed correctly within a single guess or two consecutive guesses, a team continues to score points. If a guesser misses four guesses, losing all four counters in the middle, resulting in the loss of one of his side's four counters, he usually passes the position of guesser to another teammate.

CHANCE PRINCIPLE

In any form of the handgame, the object is to guess the marked objects as quickly as possible and regain the offense, or, if hiding, to make the other side miss guessing you. The principles of chance are important in understanding the game. Two levels of chance exist: a one in two or 50 percent chance with a single hider (left or right) or a one in four or 25 percent chance with two hiders (inside, outside, left, or right).[46] Lesser (1933, 124) suggests that the principle of chance found in handgames may have been basic to those in other forms of North American guessing games.[47]

The game is won when one side has all eight scoring sticks, their own four sticks and the four from the opposing side. Thus, a team must minimally win sixteen points, winning the neutral sticks four times over to obtain the four scoring sticks of the opposing team, again suggesting the ritual association of the number four. As the score could fluctuate back and forth, a game could take a few minutes to two or three hours to win. Sometimes a single game lasted all night long, with no winner.

SINGING

Following the Starting Song, singing to the accompaniment of one or more hand drums continues alternately throughout the game by the team on offense. As soon as one team acquired the offense, the players on the hiding team began to play their hand drums and change from the Starting Song to another song. Teammates often wave their arms and hands to distract and discourage the opposing guesser and team. At one time the Kiowa continued singing the same song until a score stick (won upon acquiring the four counter sticks) was won or until both hiders were correctly guessed and they lost the offense. If a score stick was won, they immediately began a new song, which was continued until gaining another score stick or losing the offense. When one team lost the offense, the other side immediately began drumming and singing and continued in the same manner. As James Mooney (1911, 54) describes, "While playing the Indians sang songs to keep time with the movements of their hands; and they put their whole spirit into the game. Some of the songs had a meaning and some had no meaning, being sung simply to occupy the attention of the other side while the singers [side] were hiding the button."

78   CHAPTER 2

Singing and percussion styles varied among tribes. Often, while several members of each side might sing, only one hand drum was used per team. As Mark Evarts, a Pawnee, described of a pre-reservation game he attended against the Kiowa (Lesser 1933, 152), "When they hide the bones, the Kiowa sing old handgame songs accompanied by the beating of one hand drum. When the Pawnee have their bones; they sing their old handgame songs. They clap their hands; they do not beat a drum." Apache and Comanche elders also report the use of only one hand drum in earlier times.[48] In 1935 Frizzlehead II (Kiowa) reported, "There were about ten handgame songs."[49] As Isaacs (1969) notes, the tradition of singing one song for each score stick makes it possible to follow the movement of the game and scoring in audio recordings.[50]

Direct analogies between competition in the handgame and warfare, coup recitations and military societies existed in pre-reservation games. These principals were demonstrated in the singing of a military society song as a victory song and the dancing of the accompanying military society dance by the winner after each game won. In games between the Kiowa and Pawnee, after each game was won the Pawnee performed their Crazy Dog Military Society song and dance as a victory song. This was followed by a personal warfare coup recitation made by their leader (Lesser 1933, 152–53). Frizzlehead II reported that a victory song was sung by the winning team, with Jáifègàu Military Society songs being the favorite among the Kiowa.[51]

ADDITIONAL GAMES

In the second and succeeding games of a set or match, the Starting Song and preliminary match were not performed. The winners of the previous game were automatically allowed to hide first and began with a song of their choice. However, they did not receive a two-counter-stick credit as in the first game; everyone began with the four counter sticks in the neutral position between the two teams. A game set or match can consist of any number of games agreed on by the two teams. According to Kiowa data, when a game was over, the winners decided if they want to play another. The losers, however, initiated the bets on the second game, allowing subsequent games to continue by preventing the winners from betting more than the losing team's remaining funds.[52]

Mooney (1898, 348–49) indicates that multiple games were sometimes simultaneously held: "The song chorus may be heard from several games in progress simultaneously." He also described, "It is played by both sexes, but never together. . . . the high pitched voices of the women in one tipi making a pleasing contrast to the deeper tones of the men in another." This suggests that male and female games were simultaneously but independently held. Guy Quoetone also noted that multiple games occurred simultaneously in a single encampment.[53] As Mooney's fieldwork among the Kiowa ended in 1918, this pattern appears to have changed by the time of Parson's fieldwork in 1927, as she reports (1929, 121) mixed games in which women sat behind the men and played and same-sex games in which women played handgame together. Marriott also recorded in 1935, "Women as well as men played this, sometimes together and sometimes separately."[54]

Gregory Haumpy recalled playing handgames as a youth during the weekdays. Watching his parents and grandparents play handgame as a child, he remembered seeing women bet shawls, dry goods, dresses, moccasins, and shoes, and men betting rings, pocket watches, and even a horse or beef. At one game he saw a steer staked out in an encampment, which was put up as a prize for the team that won two of three games. Winning the steer, the Kiowa butchered and cooked it after the match. Another time a calf was played for in similar fashion. Although a wide variety of items were bet at this time, money was not the principal item. As Mr. Haumpy recalled, "You know, during that time I didn't hardly see any money. There wasn't hardly any cash, it was just a few dollars that they put out."[55]

Jenny Horse once used one of her mother's purses to bet in a handgame without her knowing: "I play some of them kid games. I was young, but I thought it was a lot of fun. I played, and I bet against this young girl. My mother didn't know I sneaked away and played. And I bet them a jewel purse—it belong[ed] to my mother—against a young lady, and we won. So I got what I bet. I didn't tell mother. I knew I couldn't tell her. When I brought those things in that I won, I told mother. She said, 'Don't do that next time.'"[56]

The Comanche

Several accounts of Comanche handgames recorded between the 1820s and 1930s provide a good understanding of the organization and structure of the game. In 1933 Herman Asenap reported the Comanche name for the handgame as *nahiwetʉ*.[57] Robison and Armagost (1990, 63) give *na?yʉwetʉ* as a verb for "play hand games." The *Revised Comanche Dictionary* (CLCPC 2010, 34, 129) gives *na?yʉwitʉ* as the Comanche name for "handgames." This name seems to consist of na- (reciprocal or reflexive prefix "with each other together"), yʉwi ("down, out of sight"), and –tʉ (a nominative suffix). These forms may be a dialect variation or alternate transcription for *nahiwetʉ*.[58]

Jean Louis Berlandier (1969, 60–61) provides what may be the earliest description of a Comanche handgame, in 1828.

> The Comanches are very fond of a game the settlers call *palitos*, or little sticks, because it is played with small bits of wood. I have seen them stake

their bows, their arrows, their clothes, their women, and even sometimes
their freedom on games of chance, despite their love of independence. In
Bexar they have seen a Tahuacano stake his horses, two wives, and his
mother, and lose them all in a couple of minutes. I myself, while traveling
with the Comanches, have seen them lose their weapons this way. When
the natives come to the garrison towns to trade they spend the whole night
gambling in their tents.

This reference to "little sticks" likely refers to the use of wooden counter
sticks in the handgame.

In 1852 Neighbors (1852, 133) reported, "Their principal game is the same
as all the northern bands, called 'bullet,' 'button,' etc., which consists in
changing a bullet rapidly from one hand to the other, accompanied by a song
to which they keep time with the motion of their arms, and the opposite
party guessing which hand it is in. They sometimes stake all they possess
on a single game." Dodge (1882, 329) provides a more in-depth account of
the Comanche handgame, comparing it to the related moccasin game of the
North and Northeast.

The Comanches have a game somewhat like "hide the slipper," in which
an almost unlimited number may take part. Two individuals will choose
sides, by alternate selection among those who wish to play, men or women.
All ten seat themselves in the parallel lines about 8 feet apart, facing each
other. The articles wagered are piled between the lines. All being ready,
the leader of one side rising to his knees holds up the gambling bone, so
that all may see it. He then closes it in the two hands, manipulating it so
dexterously that it is impossible to see in which hand it is.

After a minute or more of rapid motion he suddenly thrusts one or generally both hands, into the outstretched hands of the person on the right
and left. This marks the real commencement of the game, no guess of the
other watching-side being permitted until after this movement. He may
pass the bone to one or the other, or he may retain it himself. In either
case, he continues his motions as if he had received it: passing or pretending to pass it on and on to the right and left, until every arm is waving,
every hand apparently passing the bone and every player in a whirl of excitement. All this while, the other line is watching with craned necks and
strained eyes for the slightest bungle in the manipulation, which will indicate where the bone is. Finally someone believes he sees it and suddenly
points to a hand, which must be instantly thrust out and opened palm up.
If the bone is in it the watching party wins one point, if not it loses. The
other side then takes the bone and goes through the same performance.
If during the manipulations the bone should be accidentally dropped,
the other side takes a point and the bone. The game is usually 24 points,
though the players may determine on any number.

The Traditional Handgame 81

In this account only one hiding bone was used, multiple hiders might be employed, teams took turns in making a single hide, and the dropping of the hiding bone resulted in one point and the offense to the other team.

In 1933 Richardson (1996, 16) also described a Comanche game closely resembling the handgame:

> The Comanches were fun-loving and fond of games. A favorite contest was a guessing game in which two opposing sides participated. The leader of one side took a small bone in his hand and passed it or pretended to pass it on to one or two others. Each of these, in turn, pretended to have the bone and went through the motion of passing it on, everyone being careful to keep his hands closed so that it was impossible or difficult to determine which one of the several players had it. Then one of the opposing players, who thought he had detected who really had the bone, made his designation. If he was correct, his side won a point; if he was in error, his side lost a point. The other side took the bone in turn and went through the same performance. The Indians bet heavily on this game and there was much excitement.

The most extensive data on the Comanche handgame are three entries in the notes of the 1933 Santa Fe Laboratory of Anthropology Field School among the Comanche; edited and published by Thomas Kavanagh (2008). Herman Asenap described the basic rules of the game, which closely correlate with the version played well into the 1950s: "Games: Hand game maxweit. The hand game was played with four game sticks. Any number of players could play. There were two sides, each with four sticks. One side conceals a stick in one player's hands, while the other side guesses. If he guesses wrong, they lose one stick of its four. Each side has chants and song leaders who used drums. Each side gambled on the outcome. When one side has all the other's sticks, they are returned and a stick was taken from the scorekeeper. When all of the scorekeeper's sticks are gone the game ended."[59]

This entry describes a reverse order of scoring regarding the movement of the game counters in other accounts. In later games, all four counter sticks (kept by a scorekeeper) had to be won by one side prior to receiving one of the other team's four sticks. Upon acquiring each score stick of the other team, the four counter sticks were returned to the middle, and play resumed.

Howard White Wolf described many of the game's characteristics—fall and winter play, play during larger-scale tribal encampments, nighttime play, rules, betting, periodic rotation of guesser and hider positions, and terminology—and noted that pre-reservation handgames could be interrupted by enemy raids:

82   CHAPTER 2

Maxweit is the hand game. The game was announced a day before hand.
Heavy bets were placed. It was played when different bands came together.
A special large tipi was erected; generally in the fall or winter. They gathered a lot of wood because the game usually lasted through the night; each
side had a number of men, as follows: 1 guesser, *wauati'kawayp,'* who, if
he were unlucky could turn the job over to another man. The men of each
band might bet blanket, leggings, *karohko* [bone or shell bead breast-
plates], etc., against the men of the other band. Two men came out from
one side; everyone sings, and they advance toward the guesser, chanting.
Each of the two men had a bone cube, *takia,* in one hand. They held their
hands behind them, then put them forward. If the guesser missed one of
two hands, he tried again. If he missed the bone again, both had the right
to play again.

There were 8 tally sticks. When the guesser missed both hands, that side
got 2 sticks. When they missed one, they got one stick, and the guesser
had another chance at [the] person who got by. If he missed again both
had the right to resume play. If he guessed both right, the bone went to the
other side. When one side had all sticks, the first bets were paid off and
new bets were made [thus starting a new game].

The *dwaitsiawayaa* was the scorer on each side. A side might win 3 or 4
sticks, but when they lost the bone, the sticks were replaced and they had
to start over again the next time.

They would spit on one hand, rub hands together, then point to where
he thought the bone was hidden in each of the two players hands. If one
of [the] players who is trying to hide the bone is consistently guessed out,
one of his friends has the right to take his place, as in the case of a poor
guesser.

The spectators [and] players all sing a chant, and clap hands, especially
when one side wins all the sticks. They yell and clap their hands repeatedly
against the mouth as [a] sign of victory. No drums or rattles were used.

A Pawnee war party once came down for devilment during a hand
game. Some of [the] warriors went and looked into the gambling tipi.
One Pawnee came up, laid [his] hand on a Comanche man in a friendly
way and looked in, but [the] other Comanches recognized him as an enemy, and killed him; the other Pawnees got away.[60]

The word *maxweit* may be intended to represent *na?yʉnwetʉ,* although *ma*
denotes "with the hand." Kavanagh (2008, 338) transcribes *wauati'kawayp'*
as *wuhtekwawapI,* from the term *tekwawapI* or "talker" for the guesser, and
dwaitsiawayaa as *teritsiwapI,* possibly based on *tʉbitsi* ("true") and the agen-
tive suffix *–wapI,* for the scorekeeper. Of significance is the scoring method:
"A side might win 3 or 4 sticks, but when they lost the bone, the sticks were
replaced and they had to start over again the next time." In KCA games in

The Traditional Handgame

1968, Isaacs (1969) reported, the sticks remained where they were when a team lost the offense.

Frank Chekovi stated that in earlier times the game was played only during the nighttime and only by men, which contemporary Comanche elders confirm. This source also suggests that opposing teams began alternately sharing the drums (probably hand drums) used in singing handgame songs, which continues today. "In later days, women became participants in handgames, and the drum was used by each side. It's played in the daytime now."[61]

From the 1933 Santa Fe Laboratory of Anthropology field notes and other published works, Wallace and Hoebel (1952, 116) briefly describe the Comanche handgame. They report that games could be of any agreed upon number but were usually twenty-one points. While singing, time was kept by beating with a stick on the ground, a parfleche, or a small drum, or by motion of their arms. Variations included passing or pretending to pass the hiding object from one player to another. If the hiding object was dropped while hiding, the offense passed to the other side along with a score stick, in effect a penalty.

Born in 1933, Carl Atauvich (Comanche) learned to play handgame at Cache, Oklahoma, as a child of seven or eight years of age. Games were commonly held across the road at Camp 7, at Roy Wocmetooah's across the creek, and west of his home at his aunt May Tenequer's home. Carl and Moon Atauvich, Billy Joe and Bernard Wermy, Virgil and Kenneth Pocowatchit, and Micky and Ray Tahdooahnippah held games in the woods. As Atauvich recalled, "As kids we used to go down to the creek in the timbers. We'd clear out a good place, . . . clubhouse-like, and there would be about seven or eight of us . . . we would choose sides, and we would play handgames as kids. We'd tear up magazines for money you know, like we were playing for money, and we broke sticks and everything you know to use. . . . We used to imitate those playing at the house, the older folks. We used to have a lot of fun. . . . Back then they played the old way, the original way."[62]

Money was not always the primary item in betting. Carla Atauvich, the wife of Carl Atauvich, remembered playing the old style in her youth: two hiders on each side, with one hiding object (a small bone, a button, or even a bear claw), and with four sticks on each side and four in the middle. When the offense changed, the sticks stayed where they lay. The seesaw nature of play resulted in some games lasting all night. She remembered people betting and playing for fruit that was placed in a basket. When the game ended, the winner received the basket, took some of the fruit, and then shared the rest with the losing team. Lanny Asepermy remembered how his grandfather George Asepermy Sr. in the 1950s had a red line painted down the side of his

84   CHAPTER 2

basement walls and across the floor to serve as the centerline for handgames held at his home 1.5 miles west of Apache, Oklahoma. People who came to play did not bet with money but instead with baskets of fruit, which the winning side received.[63]

Handgames continued during Comanche winter encampments into the 1930s. As Marie Looking Glass Haumpy recalled,

> When I was a little girl my folks went also, and they used to have what they call Christmas handgames. And they have . . . a big tent up . . . made out of what . . . is like arbors, like those willow arbor things. They have it like that, and they put the canvas up, played [in] wintertime. And they used to have a big ol' washtub, it was plum full of fruits. That was the first game. The winners take that, they take the fruit, and there was such things as, [in] them days, you know bubble gum . . . penny apiece, and suckers were a penny, and the fruits: bananas, apples, oranges, and grapefruits, and just all kinds of fruits and gum and . . . candy bars. I've seen that played. That was the first game, the winner took that, and then after that they bet one another.[64]

The Naishan Apache

The Naishan or Plains Apache refer to the handgame as *say-its-say-leh* (pulled back and forth) in reference to the hand motions used in hiding the guessing object during play. I have also been given the name *sah-tah-klit-sah-eh*, referring to the hiding sticks called *tséé* (rock).[65] Following Gilbert McAllister's (1949, 1970) accounts, William Bittle recorded data on the Plains Apache handgame during his fieldwork in the 1950s and 1960s. As described in the following account, the origin of the handgame appears in one of the Apache creation stories (Bittle 1964, 8–9).

> In the beginning, all of these people and animals spoke one language. They all understood each other. There were monsters and other people. The other people were animals and human beings both. The monsters were going to take over the whole world, but the other people didn't want them to. They decided to have a hand game, and the monsters played against the other people. They decided that whoever won the hand game would take over the world. They began to play, and the people were losing the game. They just couldn't beat the monsters. Finally the people had just four sticks left. They gave the beads to Turtle. He had a special song that he sang, and he hid the beads. But the monsters guessed where they were. Then they gave the beads to Jackrabbit. He also had a special song that he sang, and he hid the beads. The monsters again guessed where they were. Then they gave the beads to Frog, and he sang his special song. But the monsters guessed again. Finally, when they had only one stick left, they

The Traditional Handgame 85

wanted to give it to Coyote. But Coyote didn't want to play against the monsters if he was going to lose. Coyote just couldn't be a loser. So Coyote ran off up the river bank. The game was being played on a bluff over a river, and the monsters were sitting right on the edge of the bluff. Coyote met Beaver and said, "Say brother, we're about defeated by the monsters." Beaver asked why, and Coyote told him what was happening and asked for his help. Beaver said, "Take some moss and make it into two ropes like braids. Put it around your neck, and when you go back to the game, start singing your song. When you come to a certain point in the song, squeeze the moss braids, and water will spill out, fall over the cliff, and make the river below choppy. Waves will wash up against the bluff, and cut it away." Coyote went back to the game. The people had only one stick left. Coyote sat down and began to play. At a certain point in his song, he squeezed the moss, and water spilled over the edge. Waves began to wash up against the cliff. Coyote did this again and again, and finally all of the cliff gave way, and the monsters fell in and drowned. Then Coyote looked over the edge of the bank and said, "Now you monsters aren't going to be on earth anymore. You are all dead. The only way people will ever know you existed is by your bones which they will find," And that is where the bones we find come from. Those bones are from these prehistoric monsters . . . something like dinosaurs.[66]

Bittle's field notes contain other unpublished entries on the Plains Apache handgame. Louise Saddleblanket recounted a shorter version of the game's origin:

There were these big rock like things that goes around. You can't shoot it or anything. We said let's have hand game. He met cow and bigger animals—all big animals on his side, cow, dog, I forgot other animals. Smaller animals, rabbit and whole bunch of smaller ones, turtle also. When they start playing hand game, rock monster say if you little animals win push me off [the] river bank into [the] river. Cow bet his upper teeth. Rabbit jump up and joined big animals because he thought they would win. For long time smaller animals won. Rock monster got on cliff and they (small animals) pushed them off. Rock monster broke all to pieces when he hit the bottom. Today when you see clear crystals of rocks in creek or river. They say those are rock monster bones. Rabbit bet his fat— he lost his fat. Turtle lost his run fast (speed)—he can't run fast anymore. Cow lost his upper teeth. I think owl lost—he can't see in daytime.[67]

Ray Blackbear reported to William Bittle in 1964: "Dinosaurs and other animals, including humans, had a hand game to decide who would take over— We won by cheating—we [are] here because we cheated you might say."[68] Similar to taboos in other Plains tribes, boisterous, irreverent, or unconventional behavior was not allowed near the four Apache tribal medicine bundles.

86   CHAPTER 2

To do so would show disrespect to the bundles and cause bad luck. Activities prohibited near lodges containing the bundles included the throwing of balls or anything that might strike the lodge, arguing, whistling, stirring things with a knife, and any form of gambling, including playing handgames (Brant 1969, 79; Schweinfurth 2002, 61).

Ray Blackbear provided a general overview of the Apache handgame to William Bittle in 1961:

> There is a special song that is sung to open the hand game. If you win all of the counters, you also sing a special song, the victory song. There are four elks teeth, tied together in pairs, that are hidden. Each team is given one pair at the start of play. The first hiding and guessing is done by the captains or leaders of the two teams. One leader hides one pair first, then the other leader tries to guess which hand it is in. The hands are kept in motion in time to the songs after the sticks have been held. Hands are moved back and forth in front of a person, laterally. If the guesser guesses the teeth, then both teeth (the pair) are given to the other side, which now has both pair. One pair is given to a player, the other pair retained by the captain. There are twelve counters, four on each side and four in the middle. The guessing is done with the hands. An opponent will point thumbs to the left to indicate he guesses the hider's left hand; to the right for the right hand. Palm and hand open, palm to the left, hand vertical means both pair are in the "inner" hands; palm down, hand horizontal means both pair are in the "outer" hands.
>
> Counting operates as follows: Team A has both pair of teeth, and Team B fails to guess either correctly. Two counters from the middle are taken by Team A. If another incorrect guess is made, two more counters are taken from the center. When all of the middle sticks are taken, another incorrect guess costs the losing team one of its own counters, and the four middle counters are replaced. Hence, a team's counter is worth four middle counters. When the four center counters have been taken, new songs are sung.
>
> According to the Apache, the hand game can only be played in the winter. You can't play it when the grass is green. They say you'll get the seven year itch if you play the hand game at the wrong time of year. In summer, we go dancing, that's the time for dancing.[69]

Rose Chalepah Chaletsin provided another account to William Bittle that offers further insights into the Apache version of the handgame:

> The hand game is just like that stick game. Got two sides, got a man sitting in front; sticks and drum. These tribes got different games of this hand game (version). There's 12 sticks all together. Four sticks on each side and four sticks where the leader sits. These men they sit down got

The Traditional Handgame

shell, elk teeth or bones. They play with two elk teeth tied together in the past. Always have one drum and if party of both sides wants it they have own drum—otherwise they pass it back and forth. Well they have these bones (elk teeth tied together). They pick it up on one side and make signs for (hold both hands to side of head and crooks forefingers like horns), he [to] be chief of bones. If my side going to guess those bones he hits the ground or makes any kind of sign that makes you laugh. This man he going to make medicine get on ground and make everyone laugh and throw (bones) into the air then gets it in his hand and the other fellow will guess it. Sometimes miss and sometimes guess. The chief gives it (bones) to anybody in the crowd. We miss (guess) then they get stick. Back and forth them sticks go. If we put four sticks together (those that are by the leader) we get one of their sticks. If we miss guess, they take a stick away from us. One game sometimes lasts 5 or 6 hours. They play all night until daylight sometimes. Women they got to tough it out, we love it. If we get all four of their sticks we beat them. Them old days they have their babies behind them. They get dusty. Their faces get dirty but they wrapped in buffalo hide. They don't bet nothing. Just have a good time. They still play in wintertime. They play down at Boone [Oklahoma] today in winter. The Comanches say if you play in summer snake going to get you, bite you. We say if you play game in summer your dog going to bite you. They start playing game Thanksgiving. Some northern tribes play it at fair. Apaches say it bring bad weather if you start playing in summertime. The Kiowa play it anytime. They don't believe in nothing. Anything to get money. They have night dances for money. When I played the game it's cold sometimes. I clap my hands and sing. They got lots of songs. They don't use them old songs today, just use those new songs now. If my side wins we dance for the losers. I get up and dance for them and they all leave otherwise they got to give me something. We dance for them and shake our handkerchief at them.[70]

Of particular interest are the concluding statements Bittle recorded from Ray Blackbear in an account regarding the Apache origin of the handgame and cheating. As Blackbear explained,

While the game is going on, the hands are moved back and forth, laterally. If you dropped the pair, you lost the game. The Apaches were good at shifting the pairs of teeth back and forth [and] were like "con" men. Was not really fair, but if you could get away with it, you went ahead and did it. You can also change the pair of teeth from hand to hand after the guess has been made, if you can get away with it. But that is still cheating. The first hand game was won by cheating. That accounts for the present belief that there is cheating everywhere. There was no cheating before that first time, that's what we believe."[71]

The end of Blackbear's earlier account and this one are of particular interest as the Apache attribute winning the original game by cheating. As discussed in chapters 3 and 5, suspicion and accusations of cheating remain common in the contemporary southern plains Indian handgame.

I had the good fortune to work closely with Alfred Chalepah for several years. Born in 1910, he was the eldest member of the tribe, a wealth of information on Apache culture and history, and was active in handgames from the 1920s into the 1960s. Chalepah reported that, like the Kiowa, the Apache maintain that if one told "Coyote stories," generally reserved for nighttime settings in the winter, at the wrong time, they would get the "itch." Chalepah stated that originally two sets of elk teeth (*dah-say-sah-bee-gwoo*), each consisting of two teeth tied together, were used as hiding implements in the game. Each of the two hiders hid a set of the elk teeth in one of their hands. The guessing signs and rules were the same as those of the Kiowa and Comanche.[72] In later times a straight bone (*it-sehn-ee*) was used. Chalepah thought this might have occurred in the 1920s. Although a variety of hiding items have been recorded in handgame play, the depopulation of elk, scarcity of their teeth, and the increased availability of bone hair pipes from traders by this time likely contributed to changes in hiding items. For several decades now, a bone with a black mark or tape on it has been used. Scoring sticks were known as *chay-ith* (score). Only men sat on the front row of each team, with women and others sitting in rows behind them. Women could hide if chosen. Once a hider brought their hands forward they could not switch the bone, and, if caught switching, or if one dropped the hiding implement, the game was forfeited. In his youth, the handgame season was typically November to around the end of February, and bets often included horses and cattle. Chalepah remarked that tipis "were too small" to play handgame in at this time.[73] This suggests that either more Apache were now playing and attending handgames, or that they had ceased combining multiple overlapping tipis to form larger composite lodges to facilitate larger crowds as was sometimes done for group activities.

Chalepah remembered Apache playing handgames two or three times a month during the winter, and at several locales around Apache and Fort Cobb, Oklahoma, including Old Lady Bela's allotment north of Apache, Hank Kozuta's home and the Mithlo's home just west of Apache, and Misupcut's home just south of Apache.[74] Just west of Boone, Oklahoma, a nearly year-round aggregation of Apaches camped on the allotment of Chalepah's uncle Henry Archilta. Numerous councils, meetings, powwows, peyote meetings, and handgames were held there. On the east side of Archilta's house near the

The Traditional Handgame 89

creek, handgames were held in a large canvas-covered bungalow. Two box stoves and fifty-five-gallon drums converted into wood stoves were often used to provide heat inside. If the weather was warm, games were held outside, usually under a canvas shade with no sides on it. Chalepah recalled that his maternal grandfather Archilta kept a pair of handgame bones. Apaches also held games at Apache Jay's camp, two miles east and one-half mile north of Rainy Mountain. The allotment belonged to Apache Jay's wife or her deceased husband, in the Kiowa section of the reservation. Chalepah, who had been raised during part of his youth by Apache Jay, knew him well and played at games there. Apaches also held handgames at the Red Bone Dance Ground southwest of Fort Cobb, Oklahoma, where games between the Cache Creek and Washita Apache communities were held.[75]

Chalepah recalled that Kiowa and Apache often sat on the north side against the Comanche on the south. Games sometimes went to 4:00 or 5:00 a.m., resulting in a draw, whereupon the game was stopped and bets were returned. Efforts were made not to schedule overlapping events, such as awl games, peyote meetings, or powwows. Due to the Apache tribe's small size this helped ensure attendance and a successful event. As a youth Chalepah remembered traveling by team and wagon to visit relatives and play at handgames, which his parents and grandparents enjoyed. Later he remembered driving his grandfather to play at handgames, often not returning until early in the morning. As he described, "To play other tribes, to me it was wonderful. It makes you feel everybody got love for one another. And they got a lot of respect for one another."[76]

Older players state that in the early 1900s the team captain was often also the primary guesser and in charge of handing the hiding objects for their side, the position today called "medicine man." As Chalepah described, "The guesser is in charge of the bones. After the kill [the term used for correctly guessing the other side], he gets the bones, and that's up to the guesser to give the bones to the person that he thinks might win for us, you know, that might be a good hider." The same emphasis on efficacy applied to the guesser: "Sometime they rely on somebody that's good at that. . . Through them maybe you win. If you're poor at it, you know you lose." In his youth, Chalepah remembered, the primary Apache guessers were Major Pewenofkit, near Fort Cobb, and Captain Kosope, Sam Klinekole, and Henry Archilta at Boone. According to Chalepah the guesser did not have to be old, just effective. He recalled that Major Pewenofkit was the "number one" guesser and often relied on, in part because he was an effective "hustler."[77]

90   CHAPTER 2

Chalepah recalled significant changes in Apache handgames. Around 1925 the Apaches began using lanterns and gas lamps to play at night in the willow-framed canvas arbors of the period. Another change involved the use of handgames for benefit causes. Around 1928 to 1930, Chalepah remembered, younger Apache started to play handgame. In the late 1920s the practice of selling or auctioning off box suppers at social events began at Apache handgames. Individuals would buy food, prepare the suppers, and then sell them at handgames to raise funds to help individuals with an illness or to help sponsor an upcoming Native American Church meeting. Chalepah remembered beginning to sell them around 1928–1929 and eventually selling them at Apache, Kiowa, and Comanche events. Prior to World War II only a very few powwows and occasional handgames were held. Afterward powwows for outgoing and incoming servicemen increased markedly.[78]

Table 2 provides handgame terminology for the Kiowa, Apache, and Comanche. Comanche terms are from the 1933 Santa Fe Laboratory of Anthropology Fieldnotes (Kavanagh 2008).

MEDICINE AND THE HANDGAME

Perhaps the most interesting aspect of the handgame is the belief in and uses of "medicine" or magic in the game. Some players with exceptional skill and or luck in hiding and guessing are alleged to have possessed handgame "power" or "medicine," and many tribes believed supernatural power or medicine was commonly used in the game. These allegations commonly appear in historical and ethnographic accounts and continue to the present. The use of magic in the handgame appears to have been a well-established pre-reservation practice associated with other common forms of power acquisition, such as the vision quest and fasting. In 1927 Emily Bosin reported the use of medicine from vision quests in the Kiowa handgame (Parsons 1929, 121): "Hand game is the one game they used medicine for, medicine to keep the other side from finding the bone when you have it. They use some animal, a deer or eagle. They go to a high mountain, hide by a big rock, let no man or eagle see. (An eagle would carry you away.) Stay four days, fasting without food or water." Her account references the undertaking of a vision quest to obtain supernatural power and a spirit helper.

Belief in the use of magic in the handgame may be of great longevity based on a Kiowa account Mooney (1898, 276) collected about the summer of 1841. A party of Arapaho met and surrounded a group of Pawnee near White Bluff along the upper South Canadian River close to the present-day Texas–New Mexico state line. Although the Pawnee threw up defensive earthen

The Traditional Handgame 91

Table 2: Kiowa, Comanche, and Apache Handgame Terminology

	Kiowa	Apache	Comanche
1. Handgame	*jò-ău-gà* (tipi game)	*say-its-say-leh* (pulled back and forth)	*nahiwet℧*; *noch-gway* (hand swinging); *toe-quay* (gambling)
2. Hiding object	*qĭ-bàu* (to throw)	*dah-say-sah-bee-gwoo* (elk teeth)	*takia* (bone cube)
a. bead	*fǫ́-gàut* (s) *fǫ́-gà* (d/t)	- - - -	- - - -
b. elk teeth	*qó-cáui-zǫ̀*	see above	- - - -
c. bone	*tǫ́-sè-gàu* (s) *tǫ́-sè* (d/t)	- - - -	*takia* (bone cube)
3. Scoring sticks	- - - -	*chay-ith* (score)	*too-hoo*; *tuu huupi* (black wood)
4. Scorer	- - - -	- - - -	*dwaitsiawayaa*
5. Medicine man (captain)	*Dắu-há-qĭ* (One Who Is Power)	- - - -	- - - -
6. Handgame player	*jò-ău-qĭ* (male); *jò-ău-mằ* (female)	- - - -	*na?yuwetu* (to play handgame)
7. Hide	- - - -	- - - -	*namabimaru watsi̱ habiit℧*(lost–lie down); *watsit℧kit℧*
8. Hider	*thóm-xò-qĭ*; *thóm-xò-mằ*	- - - -	*kee-yah*

Table 2: Kiowa, Comanche, and Apache Handgame Terminology continued

	Kiowa	Apache	Comanche
9. Guess	- - - -	- - - -	*nunipukaru*
10. Guesser	- - - -	- - - -	*wauati'kawayp'* or *twuh-pah-ee-tuh* (they're hitting)
11. Handgame song	*jò-áu-dàu-gà* (tipi game song)	- - - -	*hubiya?* (song)
12. Drum	*fául-kàu-gàu* (s) *fául-kàu* (d/t)	- - - -	*pihkaru*
13. Drumbeater	*fául-kàu-tòi* (s) *fául-kàu-tò* (d/t)	- - - -	- - - -
14. Bets	*kàu-xé-gàu* (s) *kàu-xé* (d/t)	- - - -	*narubahkaru* (lit. reciprocity; make a payment)

s = singular
d/t = dual and triplural

breastworks, "an Arapaho medicine-man who knew the proper medicine song sat down facing the breastworks and sang the song, moving his hands as in the handgame, and thus 'drove them out,' when they were killed in line one after another as they ran." Although occurring in a warfare context, this account references a connection to magic and conjuring commonly found in the handgame.

Like other forms of power or medicine, handgame power appears to have often been used by doctors or shamans, individuals with medicinal or curing abilities who often possessed exceptional ability in legerdemain or sleight of hand. How many players relied on chance and skill, including sleight of hand by more manually adept individuals, rather than beliefs in supernatural power or aid for success in the handgame, is unknown. Some exceptional players were believed to have had and used medicine in the game. In the KCA handgame, accompanying drumming and singing were not associated with any magical or religious qualities. Certain individuals possessing keen powers of observation from practice and experience were particularly adept at hiding, guessing, or both. Often this small number of individuals served as the primary hiders and guessers for a team. Whether a talented individual's play was attributed to luck, observational skill, or medicine depends on the criteria used in determining these categories. Exceptional players were generally believed to have "medicine." Both men and women could have medicine. Older Kiowa women related how women also wore amulets or forms of medicine during play.[79]

Among the Yakama (Desmond 1952, 30–31), power was closely associated with the handgame and "professional" gamblers "who were markedly successful in the bone game and horse racing." These individuals were usually wealthy enough to accept all challenges and absorb any losses, and they usually claimed to have specific power for gambling obtained through vision questing. Such power was seen as similar to that used in curing a specific disease or injuries, in hunting and salmon fishing, and in craftwork but of a lower class than that held by shamans, who could cause illness or death by their powers and also cure illnesses caused by their own powers or that of a weaker shaman (Desmond 1952, 31).

Flannery and Cooper (1946, 407–9) report similar associations with power in Gros Ventre handgames. Gambling power was of a lower level and taken less seriously that that obtained from fasting on mountains and hilltops. It could not be, or at least was not, transferred to another, and it limited one to gambling mostly against members of other tribes. Although bringing a certain amount of prestige, possession was associated with ailments and a shortened life, making it viewed as more of a liability than a benefit. Flannery and Cooper provide examples of premature illness, death, extended luck, and fellow tribal members ceasing to play against them.[80]

Medicine was used for both offensive and defensive purposes—while hiding the bones to prevent an opponent from correctly guessing them, and when guessing an opponent. Discussions of the use of medicine or magic in the handgame remain lively to the present.

Plains Indian medicine men prided themselves in their magical abilities and powers, sometimes actually competing with one another in public to demonstrate their powers. With the passing of warfare in 1875, bison by the 1880s, the Kiowa Sun Dance in 1890, and much of the old way of life, and with the new hardships of the reservation system, many individuals struggled to adapt to this period. As the Kiowa, Comanche, and Apache adjusted to life on the reservation (1875–1901), significant changes developed in most aspects of life.

94   CHAPTER 2

While major religious structures such as the Sun Dance (held by the Kiowa only four times during the 1880s) and its traditional relationship to bison, the sun, and warfare declined, new sources of supernatural power or medicine were explored. Supernatural power or medicine are known respectively as *dǎudǎu* (Kiowa), *puha* (Comanche), and *tijieh* or *tizze* (Apache).[81]

During the 1880s, two Kiowa medicine men claiming to be "prophets" attempted to use their *dǎudǎu* to reestablish the old life in 1882 and 1888 (Mooney 1898, 349–60). Both were unsuccessful. This period was also marked by the development of vivid power contests and competition between medicine men in two primary public arenas: early peyote meetings and handgames (Kracht 1989, 733, 738). Many medicine men combined their supernatural powers with peyote doctoring. According to Haumpy, Gregory Haumpy Sr.'s paternal grandfather, doctors sometimes performed magic when they doctored for several reasons: to give confidence to their patients, to demonstrate their power, or to compete with one another, including in handgame contests.[82]

During the reservation period, intertribal visiting helped to spread new Native socioreligious forms, including Peyotism, Christianity, the Omaha or War Dance, and the Ghost Dance and Ghost-Dance Handgame (Lesser 1933; Slotkin 1975; Gage 2020). Intertribal visiting also facilitated the revival and continuation of earlier forms of entertainment, including dances, giveaways, and the handgame, which has been classified as both a Native and syncretic religious movement (Slotkin 1975, 17–20). The KCA practiced the more secular, non–Ghost Dance form of handgame.

Hiding games containing the use of supernatural power, including medicine in handgames, involved the use of one's powers to magically see where the marked hiding object was hidden, thus involving shamanic power (Harner 1982, 132). I have recorded past and contemporary allegations of the use of power in handgames among the Kiowa, Comanche, Apache, Cheyenne, Crow, and Wichita. The Kiowa refer to such power as *áudàui*, a collective noun for alleged "gambling medicine" or power.[83] This widespread ability was noted by many early American fur traders. Saum (1965, 130) wrote, "Various men of the trade recorded their wonder at the Indians' feats of sleight-of-hand. Some of these performances impressed the traders so much that they were certain only of their skepticism in confirming the dexterous and denying the occult."

Depending on what one believed, an individual could possess supernatural power, exceptional skill in legerdemain, or both, but these were often hard to distinguish. As Frizzlehead II (Kiowa) reported to Donald Collier in 1935, "Some men use medicine power in the hand game. Te/pde.a [Tape-deah or Tépdéą̀, Standing Sweathouse] was called Do'wdwdw (hand game medicine man) [Jòáudầudẫu]. He was not a medicine man but was so skillful at sleight of hand that it was supposed that he had some special power. When Fh [Frizzle-head II] was a boy there was a hand game in which all the participants were medicine men trying to best each other. This hand game was called dwDo'w [dẫujòáu] (medicine hand game)."[84]

Other noted players are acknowledged to have had handgame medicine or power. Daveko (Recognizes [or Knows] His Enemies), the noted Naishan Apache medicine man who was widely believed to possess considerable pow-ers for divining, doctoring, and witchcraft, was one such player (Mooney 1898, 347–48; McAllister 1970). Elder Apache report that Daveko could make things disappear and was one of the last Apache to have power. Reflecting the popularity of intertribal handgame playing and power contests of the 1880s, a great handgame was played during the winter of 1881–1882 under the auspices of two rival leaders, each claiming greater power for the game. The Kiowa were led by Pẫujépjè (Bison Bull Coming Out, also known as Jẫudèkẫu or Retained His Name a Long Time), while the Apache were led by Daveko, known among the Kiowa by the name Jòáudầuqì or Handgame Medicine Man (McAllister 1970: 31, 54). The game was played in the Kiowa winter camp near the mouth of Hog Creek along the Washita River, west of present-day Anadarko, Oklahoma. It was of such importance that it became the principal event depicted for the winter of 1881–1882 on the Kiowa tribal calendar of Set'tan and was known as Émdẫujóẫudèsài or "Winter when they played the medicine tipi-game" (Mooney 1898, 347).

Mooney (1898, 348) describes the match between the two noted shaman:

> The Kiowa leader was recognized distinctively as having "medicine" for this game, and it was said that he could do wonderful things with the "button," making it pass invisibly from one hand to another while he held his hands outstretched and far apart, and even to throw it up into the air and cause it to remain there suspended invisibly until he was ready to put out his hand again and catch it; in other words, he was probably an ex-pert sleight-of-hand performer. His Apache rival Daveko was known as a medicine man and as a chief, and was held in considerable dread, as it was believed that he could kill by shooting invisible darts from a distance into the body of an enemy. On this occasion he had boasted that his medicine was superior for the dó-á [jò-ẫu] game, which did not prove to be the case, however, and as the Kiowa medicine-man won the victory for his party, large stakes were wagered on the result and were won by the Kiowa. It is said that this was a part of Pa-tepte's effort to revive the old customs and amusements on a large scale.[85]

Kiowa calendar depiction of the 1881 handgame between Jáudèkáu (Kiowa) and Daveko (Plains Apache). From Mooney (1898, 348).

In 1934 McAllister (1970, 54–55) recorded another account of Daveko's legendary handgame power, an instance when the Kiowa were playing the Cheyenne and sent for Daveko to play on their side:

> The Kiowas were playing the hand game with the Cheyenne and losing every time. They were losing all their goods. Daveko's brother said, "My brother is good, you can't guess him. He knows about the hand game." The Kiowas took the pipe to Daveko, who thought they were coming to

The Traditional Handgame   97

get him to doctor somebody. After they had smoked, Daveko said, "What do you want? Is somebody sick?" "No," the head Kiowa told him, "I'm getting beat every time at the hand game. We want you to play for us." "All right," said Daveko, "I'll be there." They had a big tipi and there were many Cheyenne there. The Cheyenne leader was good. He took a buffalo rib and put it in front of him. Some of the Kiowa men said, "About the middle of the game we'll let Daveko have the bean." The head man who brought the pipe to Daveko said, "You be quiet. We will give it to Daveko at the beginning." They let the Cheyenne man who had the rib before him begin the game. They began singing and the Cheyenne leader made the motions with his hands that go with the rhythm. The Kiowas tried to guess which hand the bean was in, but there was nothing there. He was so good nobody could guess him. Daveko told the Kiowas to get a black handkerchief and tie knots in it. The Cheyenne man had something white, maybe the teeth of something, or perhaps ribs. When Daveko got the bean they could not guess him either. Both sides tried, but neither side could guess the other. The game ran a long time. Some women, the wild type, made a lot of noise. Toward midnight these women got sleepy and slipped away. Everything got quiet. They stopped singing, and were just guessing. The Cheyenne man said to Daveko, "Go ahead and do something with that bean." Daveko was going to show them. He rolled his sleeves way up, so his arms were bare. They thought he had the bean in his hand, but he shook hands with them and there was nothing there. He shook hands again and the bean was there. The Kiowas told the Cheyenne that if they failed they would take their goods. The Cheyenne tried to guess Daveko again, but he did not have it. He reached in the fire and pulled the bean out. The Kiowas told the Cheyenne to do something like that, but the Cheyenne man said he could not do anything like that. The Kiowas then claimed that the Cheyenne had failed, but the Cheyenne would not give up their goods. They quit the game. They never beat Daveko. Only sometimes did he use these powers.

In the 1950s, Brant (1969, 114–16) recorded a variation of the previous account, again emphasizing Daveko's power in the handgame but between the Apache and Cheyenne.

One time before the country opened [pre-allotment], the Apaches were camping east of Two Hatchet Creek. Some Cheyenne camped just to the east of there. After several nights, the Cheyenne came over and said they wanted to play the Apaches a handgame. The Apaches got everything ready.

The next day the Cheyenne had everything ready and knew what they were going to bet. The Apaches were good at switching the bone from one hand to the other without anyone being able to see it. That is why they could beat everybody in the hand game.

Daveko (Recognizes Enemies), Plains Apache. James Mooney, 1893–94. Photo Lot 74, James Mooney photographs, Smithsonian Institution. National Anthropological Archives. NEG. BAE GN 02588 B.

In the evening the Cheyenne came to the Apache camp. They were singing. When all of them got there they sat down. Everything was ready. There were four sticks in the middle and four on each side. One of the Cheyenne who was noted as a good player brought a rib and put it down on the ground in front of himself. Then they began betting. Everything

The Traditional Handgame 99

was put up—horses, blankets, saddles and bridles. They agreed they were going to play just one game.

One old Apache man said, "We are betting a lot of things. We have played this game many times. But this Cheyenne man here must know something, the way he has placed that rib there. You had better go get Daveko to help us."

The fellows who went after Daveko told him, "We are playing those Cheyenne and betting heavily. You better come over and help us out."

Daveko said, "Yes I already know about it." He went with them and sat right opposite the Cheyenne who had put the rib down on the ground.

They got started. They began singing the hand game songs. The Cheyenne man said, "You go ahead and hide it first and I will guess."

Daveko said, "No you hide it first and I will guess." So the Cheyenne man hid the bone first. Daveko said, "I can tell which hand he has it in. I can see it." But when he guessed, the Cheyenne had it in the other hand and Daveko lost that time.

Then Daveko hid the bone and the Cheyenne missed when he guessed. Right then both of them knew that each was using some kind of power against the other.

It was the Cheyenne's turn to hide the bone. When Daveko guessed, he reached over with his opposite hand as if he were pulling on someone's nose and produced the bone, showing Daveko to be wrong. So when it was Daveko's turn to hide the bone again, he did the same thing.

The third time, the Cheyenne pulled his hand down from up in the air and produced the bone, making Daveko wrong again. So when Daveko hid the bone again, he reached with the opposite hand as if to draw the bone out of the fire, and showed it to the Cheyenne.

The people were beginning to get tired of singing all this time. When the Cheyenne hid the bone again and Daveko guessed, he made a motion with his other hand toward the Apaches across from him, and showed them the bone.

On Daveko's fourth turn at hiding the bone, instead of putting his hands behind him, he showed the Cheyenne the bone in his right hand, then closed his fists. When the Cheyenne guessed, the bone wasn't there. Daveko reached over toward the rib that the Cheyenne had put on the ground, and picked up the bone. It was the Cheyenne's turn to hide the bone once more, but he suspected what Daveko was going to do next. He said everybody was tired and the game should stop. Daveko told him, "Go ahead and hide it again. Whenever your power or my power runs out, one side will win. We are going to sit here until we use up our powers."

The Cheyenne began talking among themselves. They said, "We have already lost. Our man has refused to hide the bone again. He knows the other man has more power." So the Apaches got all the stuff that the Cheyenne had bet.

100   CHAPTER 2

Alfred Chalepah reported that Sam Klinekole, Daveko's stepson, was given a handgame hiding bone that may have been associated with power. During a game against the Comanche, Klinekole was apparently hiding very well, and they began to suspect him of having two bones or being able to change them from hand to hand without them seeing it. A Comanche man named Dah-nah-koe tried to guess him and missed. Chalepah recalled, "[After several misses], they were afraid of him, Sam Klinkole."[86]

In 1935 William Bascom recorded a Kiowa account of a handgame in the 1880s involving the use of "power" between Comanche and Kiowa who were camped near one another north of present-day Lawton, Oklahoma. One day the Comanche challenged the Kiowa: "You Kiowa don't know much. We'll show you we can beat you." It was to be a "medicine hand game" including demonstrations of power. Reputed to be the most powerful Kiowa medicine man in the 1880s, Tónàuqàut (Rough Tailed or Snapping Turtle) accepted the challenge, and a large tipi was put up that evening. When Snapping Turtle arrived, the Comanche were already inside. Snapping Turtle stopped to prepare for the power contest, painting his face and head red all over and tying black and white beads to his hair and black handkerchiefs around his wrists.

Snapping Turtle suggested that they "practice a little" before they started. He took a stick and then had them guess in which hand he had it. When he opened his hands it was in neither. He rubbed his hand on the ground and shook his head and the stick came out of his ear. He said he was ready for the Comanche, so all entered the tipi. The Comanche were on the south side, the Kiowa on the north. Opposing Snapping Turtle was a Comanche man known among the Kiowa as Câidàuhà (Comanche Medicine), who was famous for his powers. Bets of horses, saddles, guns, and money were made. Using elk teeth to hide, they began to sing. The Comanche missed the first guess, so the Kiowa began on offense.[87] Snapping Turtle hid the elk teeth, showed the others that he did not have them, and then drew them out of the eagle feather worn by his partner.

When the Comanche got the teeth, he said, "We'll throw the teeth in the fire and if you take it out, you win the game." But Snapping Turtle didn't want to. Then the Comanche said, "We'll take it outside and hide it, and if you find it, you win." Snapping Turtle agreed, so the Comanche went out with it. Snapping Turtle meanwhile asked everyone to be very quiet. He touched the ground with his fingers and cleaned out his ear with dirt and listened intently. When the Comanche returned, Snapping Turtle announced that he hadn't heard the tooth drop and that the Comanche still had it. This the Comanche denied,

The Traditional Handgame 101

but Snapping Turtle told him to stand up. When the Comanche stood up, the tooth fell out of his clothes, and the Kiowa won.[88] For the most part, competition between medicine men from different tribes was friendly, but rivalries sometimes led to sorcery. Snapping Turtle is attributed with dispatching at least one Wichita who insulted him during a game of monte, and one Caddo medicine man through sorcery (Nye 1962, 257–66).

Accusations of power in handgames continued into the 1930s. During a handgame between the Kiowa and Apache against the Comanche in the summer of 1934, McAllister (1949, 10; 1970, 54–55) witnessed a game in which Alonzo Chalepah (1875–1943), an Apache, although blind at the time, was accused of possessing and using medicine or power in a game.[89] As McAllister described, Chalepah "was liked and respected by many, and by some feared, for he had medicine powers. Even the Comanche knew of him." McAllister's work on Daveko also states that the Comanches were afraid of his father, who was known to have handgame medicine. The following is a well-known story in the Apache community. Late that summer the Kiowa and Apache were engaged in a handgame against the Comanche just west of Apache, Oklahoma, in which the betting was heavy, and the Kiowa and Apache had lost every game. The Apache sent for Chalepah, who was taken to the game by Dr. McAllister and asked to play. McAllister reports that a murmur arose among the Comanche, from which the word "medicine man" could be heard, and the Comanche objected to Chalepah's playing. The Comanche had been winning, but the Kiowa and Apache demanded that Chalepah be allowed to play or they would cease playing. In order to continue, the Comanche acquiesced and agreed to his entrance. To show that there was to be no deception, Chalepah ensured that everyone could plainly see him by taking off his coat, rolling his sleeves up far above his elbows, and holding his hands far out in front of his body as he hid during the game. With Chalepah hiding, the Apache immediately began to win until the Comanche objected, accusing Chalepah of using medicine and insisting he cease playing. Afterward the Apache continued to lose.[90] Accusations of using medicine commonly accompany too much success in the handgame.

Alonzo's son Alfred Chalepah did not attend the game but stated that his sisters did, and he was well informed about the proceedings. His father was blind by this time and was taken to the camp where he hid for the Apache and won three straight games. After the third game, the Comanche reportedly became suspicious of him and stated that he was a "medicine man." Alfred Chalepah stated that he did not believe his father had power, just luck, and was just like any other man.[91]

Alonzo Chalepah (Plains Apache). Photo courtesy of Alonzo Chalepah.

Alfred Chalepah may have been modest about his father's success in the handgame. Alonzo Chalepah, son of Alfred Chalepah and grandson of the earlier Alonzo Chalepah, related an account his father Alfred told him about a form of handgame medicine. In this medicine you were to kill a bison and take a large handful of hair from it. You would put some of the hair in both hands and rub it over all of your joints (ankles, knees, hips, shoulders, elbows, wrists) to keep you flexible and able to stand and sit. The hair was then rolled into a ball and placed in a small buckskin bag. The medicine bag could be worn around your neck while playing or could be hung on the north side of a tipi or from a house window and was said to increase your chances of winning in the game.[92]

Many Plains tribes used protective medicines for various reasons, most often as protection from witchcraft (from a fellow tribal member or that of another tribe) and ghosts. Both men and women wore forms of personal protective medicine, including that for handgames. Handgames are often intertribal events involving travel and play in the community of another tribe. The KCA each maintain a lively fear of ghosts of the dead that could return to haunt the living and cause sickness and disaster, particularly while outside at night. Brant (1969, 55) lists several Apache precautions for preventing ghost-sickness, one associated with preparing to travel to a handgame. As a consultant described, "Before I would leave home at night to go around to the hand games, she [the consultant's mother] would take ashes and put a cross of ashes on my forehead and on my chest to protect me."

THE RESERVATION ERA

While the handgame continued to be played throughout the reservation era (1875–1901) and post-reservation and pre–World War II era (1900–1941) of the Kiowa, Comanche, and Apache, little mention of the game appears in ethnographic accounts. This paucity of material is most likely because the majority of ethnography conducted from 1900 to 1940 focused on capturing the last of the alleged "pristine" or "golden days" of pre-reservation Plains Indian life. Often, little or no attention was given to the current developments regarding change and continuity occurring in this period. Marriott (1945, 140) mentioned the Kiowa playing the handgame during the winter of 1874–1875, when they were imprisoned in the open-air stone corral at Fort Sill: "Some of the other men had managed to get some bones and carved and polished them, and made a hand game set. They sat around most of the time, gambling for what little meat they had."

Another pattern that was common among many tribes involves who continued to play handgame. Because the game is associated with more-traditional culture, it was primarily played by those maintaining men's societies, powwows, giveaways, the Sun Dance, and the Native American Church, rather than Christian converts. From the 1890s to World War II, many Christian sects heavily discouraged and sometimes excommunicated individuals who participated in traditional activities. For several decades a considerable divide regarding participation in social and cultural events was created between Christians and the traditionalists who most regularly played handgame. As Alfred Chalepah explained, "They always do what's on the agenda, they do it together. . . . Mostly the same people, handgame, peyote meetings, and powwow. They are the same people."[93] The divide may have been weaker among the smaller Apache tribe. According to Chalepah, some Apache Christians also camped at midwinter encampments spanning Christmas and New Years and participated in handgames, in part because Apache Christians were small in number and sometimes had no regular preacher, and because the Apache tribe was such a small population.[94]

Agency Suppression

Between 1870 and 1934, the year the Indian Reorganization Act was signed by Franklin Roosevelt, dramatic efforts were made by the Bureau of Indian Affairs to suppress most traditional Indian political, linguistic, religious, and sociocultural forms. Kracht (1989, 820–75) and Meadows (1999, 113–26) discuss the effects of these policies on Kiowa, Comanche, and Apache dancing, giveaways, military societies, and Peyotism during this time. The Kiowa and neighboring tribes frequently participated in a wide variety of gambling. Guy Quoetone (Kiowa) reported that the Kiowa commonly engaged in horse racing, monte, stickgames, shinny, and arrow games, all of which were commonly bet on with money, horses, saddles, moccasins, quivers of arrows, blankets, cooking utensils, or any other item an individual might have—as Quoetone described, "anything of value . . . whatever is valuable and pretty."[95] Likewise, Cecil and Jenny Horse reported the betting of arrows, blankets, shawls, horses, saddles, guns, rings, and later money, and they noted that essentially anything could be bet, possibly including items such as tables, chairs, clocks, and quantities of gasoline.[96]

While the suppression of handgames in Oklahoma was not of major importance to some agency officials compared to other larger sociocultural and religious forms, gambling in general was, and this was affected by the collapse of the pre-reservation economy and widespread reciprocity, governmental policies, and Christian missionaries that affected social institutions and structures.

For tribes associating the handgame with the Ghost Dance, the game was sometimes targeted for suppression by local Indian agents. In the first mention of the ceremonial handgame among the Pawnee, their agent reported in 1902, "They have frequent and protracted dances and hand games. . . . A large number of the tribe remains in camp from one to two months—in fact, as long as someone can be found with the necessary funds to furnish refreshments for recurring dances. The demoralization and loss of time is great."[97]

In 1894 the Otoe tribal agent similarly wrote, "The greatest evil we have had to contend with at Otoe is the insatiable desire of nearly every member of the tribe for dancing. It would not be so bad if they would indulge in harmless dances, but they have what they term the 'Hand Game,' and claim it to be their worship of the 'Great Spirit,' which is really a form of the 'ghost dance.' We have worked hard to suppress this evil and have had partial success."[98]

In other areas, agency efforts were even directed against groups who did not associate the handgame with the Ghost Dance. In 1865 the agent at the Yakama Reservation stated that he had at times imprisoned individuals for gambling.[99] From the late 1800s through the 1920s Crow continued to hold handgames at winter gatherings and horse races at summer gatherings. In both cases betting was frequently involved and frowned on unless the organizers could show that the handgame teams and horse racers were playing solely for honor, prestige, and the spirit of competition (Hoxie 1995, 213). As reported in November 1922, Crow handgames were also held at Beaver Dances. "Gambling games have been going on night after night up at this camp, and when asked in regard to the games they all deny that any such games have been carried on. But it is a known fact that last week for five nights steady this game of 'Hand Game' was played" (Hoxie 1995, 216).[100]

Economic shifts in the reservation period also affected traditional forms of gambling. Flannery and Cooper (1946, 418–19) report that Gros Ventre gambling, especially with the wheel and handgames, rapidly decreased with the end of the pre-reservation bison-based economy in 1884. With an economy of abundance shifting to an economy of scarcity, gambling seems to have decreased. The last big handgame is reported to have occurred in 1891, although some play continued as late as 1922 in a match against the Flathead. The introduction of non-gambling handgames around 1887 grew in popularity and continued. By the 1940s little gambling occurred on the reservation, and neither the wheel game nor the two-button handgame were being played. Most gambling was held in off-reservation non-Indian towns where Gros Ventre gambled in poker and other card games with whites.

Several accounts report Indian Agency attempts to suppress Kiowa cultural forms.[101] Kracht's (1989, 820–75) discussion of agency efforts to suppress

106   CHAPTER 2

Kiowa culture between 1880 and 1934 indicate that efforts were primarily focused toward ending the Sun Dance, Forty-nine Dances and other dances, powwows, giveaways, and Peyotism. While betting and gambling occasionally occurred with most traditional KCA sporting forms—including handgames, awl- or stickgames (also known as "sticks," different from the form of handgame known as "the stickgame" among western Montana tribes), horse racing, shinny, and arrow throwing—gaming traditions began to change more rapidly among the KCA as the reservation era began in 1874–1875.

With increased non-Indian contact, new forms of gambling, primarily forms of card games, were introduced by Anglos, Hispanics, and African Americans and grew in popularity in some circles. Josiah Gregg mentions Cherokee and Choctaw playing card and dice games in the 1830s (Thwaites 1966, 20:307), while John K. Townsend mentions Sauk (Sáque) Indians "playing a Spanish game with cards" in 1833 (Thwaites 1966, 21:124). Flannery and Cooper (1946, 391, 418–19) also report the rapid decline of traditional Gros Ventre games, including the handgame, following the disruption of their traditional economy and lifestyle and the introduction of Anglo card games. Likewise Desmond (1952, 9–10) reports the introduction and eventual predomination of card games and associated gambling among the Yakama from the late 1800s through the 1940s. Helm, Lurie, and Kurath (1966, 81, 93–94, 97) cite several sources mentioning the role of card games in undermining and sometimes replacing the handgame as an informal pastime, and they note ensuing problems such as addiction and gambling losses among the Dogrib, Great Bear Lake, Kaska, Slave Lake, and Snow Lake Chipewyan that were not associated with the more occasional and communal handgame. However, Elmendorf (1960, 240) states that the handgame surpassed the disc game in popularity among the Twana in the late 1800s, and that the "surge of popularity was a phenomenon of the reservation period."

The introduction of new Anglo gaming forms such as card games quickly became part of Indian relations with non-Indians, often preceding the establishment of reservations by decades in their respective geographical areas. Several accounts note the decline of traditional gambling games following the introduction of Anglo card games. In 1848 George Ruxton (1951, 11) noted that "Euker" (euchre), poker, and "seven-up" were the fashionable card games among trappers and traders on the Arkansas and Platte Rivers.

These forms increased with intercultural contact in the pre-reservation period and intensified in the reservation period for tribal populations. In discussing the handgame, Dodge (1882, 327) describes these processes and the introduction of Anglo and Indigenous card games:

The Traditional Handgame   107

This and other old games, though holding a strong place in the affections of the Indians, because they permit an unlimited number of players, are generally discarded by the more ardent gamblers, who like the whist-playing lady, regret the loss of time "taken in dealing," or getting ready. All the tribes are sufficiently civilized to possess and understand cards. Those who come in contact with Mexicans are well versed in all the mysteries of "monte," while the reservation Indians acquire a knowledge of "poker," and "seven up," sufficient for all purposes of gambling, in a quarter the time it would take to learn the alphabet. The wilder tribes invent games for themselves.

In the late 1800s and early 1900s, the KCA began leasing portions of their reservation to Texas cattlemen to graze their herds—the Comanche in the summer of 1885 and the Kiowa in 1886 (Mooney 1898, 354). Creating a source of income, tribes gathered in large encampments twice a year to receive their grass lease and federal government annuity payments, which were often paid at the same time. Such gatherings were typically referred to as "payment camps" and often involved payments of $50 to $100 per individual, typically in silver coin. With long periods between payments, many Kiowa engaged in rapid and intensified periods of spending at local stores, alcohol consumption, and gambling.[102]

Lease payments, known as "grass money," and annuity payments shifted gambling toward the use of money. As Cecil Horse explained, "Sometimes, here about 1891 they began to get their money and they gamble with money. But way before that they always put up their blankets and moccasins and maybe a gun or something—just so it be worth something, you know."[103] These encampments attracted Anglo gamblers eager to relieve the Indians of their money. Ironically, present-day tribal casinos are likely recouping these funds and more. Guy Quoetone described the activities at grass payments camps:

> See the government paid the Indian every six months. "Grass money" we call it. Cattlemen had leased the entire Indian reservation for a hundred thousand dollars a year. And the government paid in two payments. Semi-annual payments. Fifty dollars to everyone—babies, children, and all. Even if he is one day old. He got fifty dollars. And they . . . pay it off in silver coins. And I love to make them sound pretty, you know. And play with them dollars. The government tell the Indians to come in and camp, that it was time for payment and the Indians all camped west of Anadarko around the river in them villages, waiting for the day of payment. . . . The money comes to Ft. Sill and the Army escorted it to Anadarko to make the payment.

108   CHAPTER 2

> They don't know the value of it. The Army cavalry men taught the Indian how to gamble. And they played cards. They gamble. The soldiers win all our money and take it back with them. And the Indians gamble among themselves. I got pictures of them gambling. They gamble in different spots. Just all over gambling. And when the soldiers, early traders, cattlemen, trade with the Indians, they'd sneak off and get all the Indians' money and the government found a law. No more non-Indians gamble with the Indians. So they sent the United States Indian Police and the United States Marshals to see if the white man is gambling with the Indians and to arrest them. And the gambling went on as late as 1920. The gambling went on around the Agency and the river. After the towns opened, those townsmen sneak away to creeks and gamble with those Indians. And 1907, 08, 09, and 10, I was on the Indian Police. I arrested some of them.[104]

With the marked decrease in traditional activities, including subsistence and warfare, people had more time on their hands, particularly men. Combined with payment camps and the traditional wintertime gaming season, the quantity of time gambling appears to have increased. As Dodge (1989, 281) described in 1876, "Having but little to lose and work to do, their sittings are protracted. The bucks [men] play from morning to night, and from night to morning again. In the winter camps, scarce anything else is done." As with traditional handgames, men and women both played, but they played separately. Non-Indian accounts in the Oklahoma Indian-Pioneer Papers, a WPA oral history project, indicate that, through the 1880s and 1890s, monte and poker were common forms of gambling at grass payment camps among the Kiowa and neighboring tribes.[105] In addition, some traditional dance, games, and "medicine meetings" were held at Christmas encampments, while other Indians attended Christian church services (La Verre 1998, 97, 114, 167, 207, 211, 223).

Born in 1893, Louise Saddleblanket (Plains Apache) recalled large encampments of Apache just west of Anadarko, Oklahoma, who gathered to receive annuities and lease payments. Tribes regularly gathered at designated locations to receive these redistributions. She reported encampments of several days duration, before and after the payments, by the Apache and sometimes the Kiowa and Comanche, with considerable gambling, playing of cards, drinking, and visitation by Anglo traders.[106]

As part of the "Jesus Road," missionaries strongly opposed any form of gambling, equating it with sin. Isabel Crawford, a Baptist missionary among the Elk Creek (November 23, 1893, to April 1896) and Saddle Mountain Kiowa (April 1896 to December 1906), reports numerous instances of gambling by both sexes at payment camps, card playing, and Fourth of July horse races (Crawford 1998, 24, 121, 127, 140, 145, 149–50, 204, 227, 229, 278). The Kiowa name for the Fourth of July is XángàkꞮ̀dà (Race Day) from the widespread horse races that were heavily bet on.[107]

To reduce Native lands in Indian Territory in preparation for land runs, Boomers and Sooners (non-Indian speculators and settlers) took any opportunity to point out negative characteristics they perceived of Native peoples. These included vices such as gambling, including the very game forms that non-Indians had introduced to the Indians. As an excerpt from an April 1897 edition of the *Chickasha Express* (Crawford 1998, 65) stated, "These full-bloods should be given the opportunity to go to some other country if they want to. Almost any country would welcome them with open arms. They are first class citizens at a shooting-match or at a game of monte or make a full hand at loafing, but as a benefactor in making two spears of grass grow where one grew before they are a failure."

Cecil Horse described how card games grew in popularity between 1871 and allotment of KCA lands in 1901. Referencing grass payment camps, Horse noted, "Well they played a little bit before that [1901] because I remember when they used to have . . . big payments, you know, in the big camp at Rainy Mountain and Anadarko. The white people, that's when it started. Big gamblers, white cowboys. They go in there and they play cards." Jenny Horse, who described her father Haumpy as a great gambler in his youth, recalled, "I remember when I was a little girl, north of Anadarko, right below Riverside [Indian] School was Indians with white people and coloreds playing cards. All tribes gambles a lot—Chickasaws, Caddos, Comanche, Apaches and Kiowas."[108]

Horse also described four-day encampments at Hobart, Anadarko, Lawton, and a meadow near the end of the Wichita Mountains focused on horse racing. Men commonly practiced with their horses in the morning hours, raced them during the mid- to late afternoon, and then participated in evening dances. Accusations of using medicine and witchcraft to fix the races were common. Such witchcraft was said sometimes to give one's horse increased speed (through the feathers of a swift hawk) and to detrimentally affect the performance of another's horse (through the application of chewed cocklebur seeds). Cecil and Jenny Horse remembered Bob Koomsa (Kiowa) as having a racehorse named Grey Dick that was especially successful around 1900 to 1912.[109] Iseeo (Meadows 2015, 440–41) described a root he used as medicine to make horses long-winded and thus to win races.

Many accounts of Kiowa gambling in the late 1800s and early 1900s and agency efforts to suppress gambling among the KCA were recorded from Guy Quoetone (Kiowa), who served as an agency policeman. He reported that Kiowa and neighboring tribes regularly acquired whiskey from soldiers and travelers, and he noted the regularity of gambling: "Indian do nothing but gambling in those early days. The colored soldiers learned them how to gamble, and the cattlemen and everything. I have a lot of those pictures where they are gambling. . . . Early day gambling."[110]

While Native peoples acquired many new gambling forms from non-Indians, in some cases the opposite occurred. As Ritzenthaler and Ritzenthaler (1991, 113) describe for southern Great Lakes populations, "When the government annuities were given out at Madeline Island, much of the money was redistributed by gambling on the moccasin game. Early white settlers took over the game so zealously that in Indiana a statute expressly forbade gambling at the moccasin game (among other gambling games), and stiff fines were set."[111]

By circa 1900, gambling associated with Anglo card games was of greater concern to agency officials than traditional forms, some of which were declining in frequency and intensity. Guy Quoetone reported that whites, Blacks, and Mexicans, including traders, commonly entered the reservation to gamble at cards with the Kiowa. Raids occurred at Rainy Mountain, Anadarko, and other locales. Often communication was limited between the participants, with some Kiowa understanding a little English, but all were able to play, being familiar with the games. Efforts were usually aimed at arresting the Anglos more than the Indian participants, and fines of $25 were typical of the period.[112]

Military service as cavalry also helped spread new gaming forms. Kiowa, Comanche, and Fort Sill Apache men served in Troop L of the Seventh Cavalry at Fort Sill from June 30, 1891, to May 31, 1897. Members of L-Troop, as it was known, and their families resided on the post during the tenure of their service. They primarily policed the reservation for non-Indian trespassers and criminals and hunted supplementary wild game for military staff, and they participated in no combat-related activities (Meadows 2015, 57–65). As Mooney (1898, 223) and Nye (1962, 261–62) describe, scouting duties were light, and much of their time was spent playing the card game monte.[113] According to Guy Quoetone, card games were learned from soldiers at Fort Sill and from traders. Quoetone reported gambling among Kiowa on horses, cards games such as monte and poker, the traditional stickgame (played mainly by women), the women's game of shinny, and arrow games.[114] Grinnell (1908, 28) and Van de Logt (2010) report several instances of Cheyenne and Pawnee scouts gambling among themselves, with other tribes, and with non-Indians during their enlistment. Although these tribes all had traditional forms of gambling, military service provided other opportunities for gambling with other Indians and non-Indians.

The Traditional Handgame

Efforts to end gambling, dances, and other activities deemed detrimental continued under Agent John P. Blackmon and, following his untimely death, under Special Agent Charles H. Dixon and then Agent Ernest Stecker. Guy Quoetone, Oscar Ahpeahtone, and Enoch Smokey were appointed as US marshals under Stecker to help in stopping "gambling" and "clan dances" and to stop "Indians gambling with whites and Blacks." Quoetone described several instances of participating in raids on card games with Stecker and fellow policemen Smokey and Ahpeahtone and on payment camps in efforts focused on stopping Indian gambling.[115]

While many Kiowa resented the respective efforts of agents Ernest Stecker (1908–1915) and C. V. Stinchecum (1915–1922) to suppress cultural forms, Quoetone described Stecker in a positive manner, possibly reflecting his own background in Christianity and law enforcement: "He knew most of the Co-manches and Kiowas. They just love him. And he made a wonderful Agent. He was their friend. But—the government told him to stop the pow-wows. This clan dancing. So he went—and stop gambling with white people and colored people. [They] could gamble among themselves, but not with any other kind of citizen. It was under his power."[116]

As Indian agents and missionaries attempted to teach Native Americans that gambling, one of their favorite pastimes, was a crime, this also included the Indian members of the police force. In 1886 Kiowa-Comanche agent J. Lee Hall lamented that some of the "most expert" gamblers on the reservation were found in the Indian police force. Efforts to outlaw other forms of Native American games and gambling occurred in several states.[117]

When asked if individuals ever lost everything they had, Quoetone responded, "They do lots of times. Lots of times they lose everything they had. And relatives have to start them off again."[118] Quoetone also noted that if a man bet and lost all of a couple's possessions, the wife might get mad and or leave: "Well, naturally she would, but it seems that the man is the boss. They never did have any trouble over it. They just lost everything. Once in a while the wife would get mad and go to her parents."[119]

Cecil Horse described how his mother Po-e-to-mah (Fíjómà) once lost all her possessions gambling and was subsequently taught a lesson by others:

> Yeah, women gambled too. They'd gamble all their—everything—even their ponies—and horses. Well, my mother would bet bedding, tipi, plates, dishes—my mother was a great gambler. [And she lost] everything she had, her tipi, her bedding—sometimes they bet their [relatives'] things too. . . . Bracelets, earrings, buckskin, everything. She lost everything. Dishes. One time when she lost everything—her father was still living. So

he told her, "This gambling is not a good thing. Sometimes you get lucky. Sometimes you don't." So she got everything beat [lost everything]. So one time visitors come to eat dinner with them. She didn't have no dishes. She lost everything gambling. Then she went to another place to borrow some plates—dishes. And when she went in there, this man said, "We not going to loan you nothing." See they got mad. . . . Well, they all don't like it, as far as that's concerned. And she said, "Get out of here. We not going to loan you a cup!" And my, she [my mother] said, "My, how did I get hurt!" She said, "I cried. Didn't have no dishes. No spoons. No nothing to set the table." That's the time she learned. She quit that time."[120]

Quoetone also reported that non-Indians to whom Indians owed money commonly came to payment camps to collect their money. In instances when Indians had not yet cashed their checks and did not want to pay their debts, they resorted to tricking the collectors in various ways. One method was to have a fellow Kiowa run into one's tent and announce that the law was coming, resulting in the Indians hiding the money and sending him out the back of the camp to "protect" him. Sometimes lights were extinguished, and non-Indians left in such a hurry that they left the bets of the ongoing game where they lay. Another ploy involved feigning illness. As Quoetone described,

> Well, one collector was hunting another Indian and he wanted to know where his camp was. And my uncle, he's always joking, so he said, "He's camped over there. I'll see whether he's home or not." So he walked over there and says, "Hey, your collector is coming over here to see you. You get in bed and pretend you're sick with small pox or some other disease that's contagious." "All right, tell him to come in. Tell him I'm sick with smallpox." It was in the daytime. Late evening. Well, he says, "He's home but he told you to come in there but he's got an awful case of smallpox. He says for you to come in there. He's got smallpox but he wants to talk to you.' "No, tell him I'll see him some other time." That was just a trick, see. And he got by. So he just try all kinds of tricks and the white people too—both sides.[121]

Handgames declined in the early 1900s, depending on whether one was raised in a more-traditional or a church-oriented community. Christian missionaries taught the Kiowa and other tribes to view the handgame as a form of gambling, and thus a sin and something that should not be practiced. The following account from Cecil Horse about his mother, Po-e-to-mah (Fíjómā̀), reflects both the fact that some Kiowa bet and lost goods to an excessive level and the impact of missionaries on those who converted to Christianity: "My mother, she played with a Shoshone, why, she lost. When she came to her sense, and know that it's not good to play that, she lost everything she had. The beds, sheets, blankets, dishes, the tipi, everything. And when she lost all

The Traditional Handgame 113

of that, they took it away from her. She didn't have no place to live. Weren't no quilts to sleep on for the babies—nothing."

This event occurred before he was born in 1891:

> I just heard that story because my mother used to tell it when she became a Baptist. She become a Christian. She talk about gambling. She talk about her own sin—that's the time I heard her. . . . She always say that her husband told her to quit: "Quit, don't do that." She gets mad at my father. Of course, he don't really get mad and fight. He gets mad because she lost everything and he's got to provide. Jenny's father used to gamble a whole lot here in 1914. But it was card game—gamble with money. He was a great gambler.[122]

Noting that Kiowa did not play handgame in the summer, Jenny Horse also revealed, "The Missionaries came and they call it gambling. So they ask them not to—Christian people not to play on Sunday. So they don't play on Sunday and summertime, they don't play."[123] Parker McKenzie, born in 1897 and raised in a church-oriented family, stated that he heard very little of handgames in his youth. They were held only in the winter, when large aggregations of Kiowa camped together, usually for the two annual grass payments. Allotments split people up even more than pre-allotment camp areas, segregating Natives into smaller units most of the time.[124] McKenzie also noted, "Church-oriented Kiowa did not play hand game. It was played mostly by Ghost Dance people, and it was they who knew the songs."[125]

In contrast, Alfred Chalepah Sr. (Naishan Apache), born in 1910, remembered many handgames and much gambling during his youth. Once, while camped with his parents and members of several tribes at the Caddo County Fairgrounds, his parents and others were gambling in an adjacent field of thick sunflowers and bloodweed. They were all arrested by police from Anadarko. As Chalepah recalled, "The fine was two bucks a person, which was a lot of money back then."[126]

Ernestine Kauahquo Kauley described the impact of the missionaries on the Kiowa community around Hobart, Oklahoma:

> Kiowa are great gamblers. They love to gamble. And she'd go walking among them, and just cry, Miss Reeside, and just cry because they thought they were so sinful, gambling and not observing, you know the Christian rules. But that's how it was really for a lot. It was probably—let's see, I was born in 1934. So probably from 1934 to about the seventies, Christian religion was absolutely strong here. . . . All of that, that missionary concept. Sin was deeply instilled, so they didn't do any powwows or they didn't do any handgames, gambling. It was shut down.[127]

114   CHAPTER 2

An elder Kiowa man also noted that churches were against handgames, viewing all traditional ways as wrong and the handgame as "gambling."

Following the World War I armistice in 1918, a large contingent of Kiowa began camping on the allotment of White Fox, two miles northwest of Carnegie, Oklahoma. These encampments continued into the late 1930s and possibly until the start of World War II. Prior to Scalp and Victory Dances held every November 11, Kiowa often arrived and camped several days in advance to socialize. White Fox's niece Delores Toyebo Harragarra, who grew up on the adjacent allotment, recalled that her aunt put up two large tents for a series of handgames that were played on the evenings of November 8–10. No dancing occurred on these days.[128]

Photos of gambling on the reservation exist, but because they were usually taken from behind the players, identification of the game being played is often inhibited. Southwell and Lovett (2010, 14, 109, 204) provide three photos of gambling on Kiowa Agency lands. The first one is Wichita, the other two of Kiowa and Plains Apache. In two and possibly all three photos, two separate groups of people can be seen gambling at the same time. Tree foliage indicates that two of the images are winter scenes (2010, 14, 109), while one of the Kiowa and Apache depictions (2010, 204) under a recently constructed willow arbor suggest a summer event. The seating positions and body language in the latter photo suggest that the activity is a card game.

By the 1930s, most handgames seem to have been held in conjunction with larger dance gatherings. In 1935 Mrs. Horse noted, "Nowadays what dances they have are given on the Fourth of July and on Armistice Day."[129] These two holidays became the largest Kiowa aggregations, and by the 1930s at least some handgames began to be held in the summer months at these or other special gatherings. Alice Marriott attended and documented a large Jáifègàu Society Gourd Dance held on George Tsoodle's allotment near Carnegie on July 14–18, 1937. Contingents of Otoe, Pawnee, Ponca, and Osage attended. While focusing primarily on fancy war dancing, social dances, and some military society dances, intertribal handgames were also held. The event was held to reciprocate a similar exchange a number of years before between the Kiowa and Otoe.[130]

While most play continued during the winter months, the Craterville Park Indian Fair (1924–1933), the American Indian Exposition (1934–present), and summer and Armistice Day aggregations became the largest annual gatherings and opportunities for holding handgames. Bill Koomsa Jr. and Parker McKenzie both stated that handgames practically died out in the 1940s but began to be held again in the 1950s, as people went to houses in different communities to play in canvas arbors and shelters. The decline in the 1940s was

The Traditional Handgame 115

likely due to the priority of supporting World War II. As a child Koomsa Jr. recalls his family having a building at their house in which games were held.[131]

Elder Kiowa remember handgames at the allotments of Mrs. Hummingbird or Maunkaugul, Dupoint, and William "Cornbread" Tanedooah (east of Carnegie), Haumpy (northeast of Carnegie), and Domebo (near Stecker, Oklahoma). Later games were held at Adrian Satepauhoodle's (east of Carnegie), Marshall Beck's (Beck was an Anglo married to a Kiowa), and Steve Mopope's (east of Fort Cobb). An old shed boarded up with boxes was used at Bruce Haumpy's home west of Carnegie. A fire was kept inside the barn for heat, and the shed was used until catching fire and burning down. Sadie Nestell, a Kiowa married to a Plains Apache who had a dance ground with a cement floor, also hosted handgames at her home between Fort Cobb and Carnegie.[132] Jackie Yellowhair stated that Rogers Tofpi related how older people sometimes sat around and played handgame inside the tipi after Native American Church meetings.[133]

Born in 1915, Ina Paddlety Chalepah (Kiowa) first saw the handgame as a child at the Domebo home near Stecker. The players sat on a canvas and played beneath a shade. Bets were matched and tied together, then placed in a bag that was tied to the ridge pole of the arbor, in clear sight of everyone during play. Two elk teeth, one marked and one plain, were used. Teams had one medicine man who did the guessing. At that time players played until dark, then quit to return home since few people had lanterns and according to Ina Chalepah, many Indians feared being robbed on the roads. Later, when electric lights became available, they sometimes played all night. Games were confined to the fall through early spring.[134]

Marie Yokesuite Haumpy (Comanche), born in 1929, remembered regular Sunday afternoon handgames at Mah-kah-nas-sy's place one mile northwest of Apache. People came by horseback and wagon, as few had cars then, and played in a large arbor behind the house. At this time only men served as guessers in the game. Many Comanche and Apache came to these games, sometimes camping there at Christmas. Women commonly bet their bracelets, rings, and earrings, and men bet their rings with one another. At this time bets were matched up in pairs and laid on the ground.[135]

Gregory Haumpy Sr, who was born in 1918 and lived two miles east of Carnegie, remembered playing handgames at Cornbread Tanedooah's. Individual bets were typically a penny, nickel, or dime and did not exceed a dollar. Some games lasted all night, after which Mr. Tanedooah's wife cooked breakfast for everyone. He attended games there frequently, often attempting to make enough money to buy Bull Durham for rolling cigarettes (Bull Durham tobacco was then five or six cents a bag). Haumpy recalled walking

116   CHAPTER 2

down the railroad tracks to games, then going home the following day to sleep. He would then wash up, go to town to buy tobacco, and return the following night to play again. He and his friends raised money by picking up and selling pop bottles for their deposit, sometimes making as much as twenty-five to fifty cents, and chopping firewood to buy kerosene in order to have lights at night.[136]

A Bag of Bull Durham

There are many humorous stories associated with the handgame, and, typical of southern Plains Indian humor, often feature self-deprecation. Gregory Haumpy related one such account from the 1930s that features the back-and-forth nature of the old style of play with four sticks in the middle. One time, Gregory Haumpy and Edgar Satepauhoodle wanted a bag of Bull Durham tobacco, then costing six cents. Having only three cents, and unable to find any work at this time during the Depression, they decided to double their money by betting it at a handgame. They walked down the railroad track from Carnegie to the home of Major Baldwin Pewenofkit (a Plains Apache) several miles east of Carnegie where a handgame was being held that evening. Upon arriving they placed their bet and awaited the outcome of the first game. Being played in the old style, the first game seesawed throughout the night with no winner. At dawn the game was declared a draw, and all bets were canceled and returned. The two men then had to walk back to Carnegie with their three cents—still short half of the money needed to purchase the tobacco they desired.[137] Haumpy commented on the style of play and their long walk back to town, "That's the way it [was] run, see. In that old game, old way of four, four, four; when them four sticks they go back and forth, back and forth. And nobody gets all of them sticks, you just quit and take your bets back or leave your bets and come back and play again. That's what happened. Yeah, we walked about five miles, you know."[138] Although accounts are lacking regarding how individuals living at distances from one another were notified of upcoming games, news likely came through individuals traveling by horse and wagons, or it was known ahead of time through visits at towns and other Native gatherings.

The Cheyenne and Arapaho

Having described KCA handgames, a brief discussion of the game among the neighboring Southern Cheyenne and Arapaho is essential since they are two of the six Plains tribes in western Oklahoma who regularly play the KCA. Grinnell (1923, 1:326–28) describes the Cheyenne style of handgame, known as No'o ïts ïn ïs' ta (They Are Hiding), that included two sets of marked and

The Traditional Handgame

unmarked bones. A hider on each side took turns hiding their set of bones until one lost to the other; the winner then took both sets of bones and began the offense with two hiders. Grinnell reports variations in hand signals for guessing and reverse (split finger or V) guesses and the practice of guessers holding an item in their signaling hand that, when shown, reversed the guess signaled.

The Southern Cheyenne traditionally used the same four guessing patterns as the KCA but used a decorated wooden "pointing stick" of twenty to thirty inches in length with paint and feathers at one end to guess with. Guesses were made by holding the stick horizontally (outside), or pointing vertically downward (inside), to the right, or to the left toward one's opponents. As Mary Beaver described, "It was just a stick, and at the end of the stick there was feathers. . . . The feathers would indicate, like an arrow, which way [you were guessing]." For left or right, the stick was held by the end, and the other end, with the feather attached, was pointed to the desired direction. For an inside guess the stick was pointed straight forward, with the feather hanging down toward the opposing side. For an outside guess, the stick was held in the middle and held up horizontally toward the opposing side.[139]

Pointing sticks in the Cheyenne handgame appear to date back to the use of decorated handgame counters being distributed through Cheyenne camps to women to solicit donations of food for an upcoming feast for guests. As Grinnell (1923, 1:215) reports, "The custom of sending about these sticks at such a time and for such a purpose is very old. Such sticks are merely counters for the handgame, but in their ornamented form are modern, having been trimmed in this way by the ghost dancers since about 1890. This association gave the sticks a sacred character, hence they were handled reverently."

Some Cheyenne handgames were associated with religious aspects, in particular fasting, prayer, and blessings. Sam Dicke (Cheyenne), born in 1902, described how during his youth the sponsor of a Cheyenne handgame was required to fast three days and nights. The games were held in a tipi in which those who vowed to fast had to remain. A meal was served each evening to the visitors. The visitors took part because eating the meal was related to the persons who vowed to fast, who were considered to be sacrificing for their people so that they might receive a blessing from God. Dicke also described how an individual vowing to fast and hold a handgame took the counter sticks and placed one in front of a Cheyenne camp. Each stick in front of a camp seemed to represent an invitation and the requirement that they bring food such as a covered dish to the event. Dicke described these events as social gatherings without gambling, and they correlate with Grinnell's account.[140]

Gregory Haumpy described one form of play in which the Cheyenne singers sat around a large bass drum, with only the guesser in the middle. When the music intensified, women and sometimes men arose to dance during the game. In one form, the guesser of the winning guess wins all of the bets.[141] Myrtle Lincoln, an Arapaho born in 1888, reported one version of play among the Cheyenne in which three hiders hid a single bead and then had to be guessed by the opposition.[142] The Cheyenne use of pointing sticks is continued by some Cheyenne near Seiling, Oklahoma.[143]

Mary Beaver remembered that the use of a pointing stick was fading out by the early 1980s. "We'd go to Hammond . . . and they have a lot of people probably in their seventies and eighties who remember that style. And when we go up there to play our regular style, those ladies always say, 'You don't have no stick?' I said, 'No, not now, we use our fingers.'" She laughed.[144]

At the first Cheyenne handgame I witnessed at the 1993 Colony Powwow, near Colony, Oklahoma, players were playing the current western Oklahoma style, with no pointing sticks.[145] Cheyenne consultants report that handgames in the second half of the twentieth century in the Cheyenne area were common around Canton, Clinton, Geary, Hammond, and Weatherford, Oklahoma. Mary Beaver remembers playing at the home of her father's cousin Alfrich HeapoBirds on Deer Creek west of Weatherford, and at the community halls at Canton and east of Clinton (the latter now a smoke shop). Pete Bearshield sang several older Cheyenne handgame songs that he learned from his uncle Alfrich.[146]

Although the handgame was originally a wintertime game, the Oklahoma Cheyenne and Arapaho now play handgame most of the year. As Mary Beaver described, "For us it started out as a winter [activity], and then eventually it evolved to anytime. . . . We go through the summer now, except for the time when we have our Sun Dances. . . . We Cheyenne-Arapahos actually close off all of our community halls, out of respect for our Sun Dances, so we won't open our community halls to be able to be used for benefit dances or handgames until after the Arapaho Sun Dance."[147]

Arapaho

While little ethnographic data has been recorded on the Arapaho handgame, Myrtle Lincoln, an Arapaho born in 1888, provided an extensive account of the Southern Arapaho style of play in 1969. Her account resembles that of the KCA style of play in most aspects, including the use of one or two decorated beans. The Arapaho style of play was generally similar to that of the Cheyenne, including the later use of hair pipes (in which a marked one was sought), use of a decorated wooden guessing stick, four forms of pointing or "guessing" (inside, outside, right, left), "making medicine" against one's opponent,

The Traditional Handgame 119

the use of matching decorated beans and fourteen score sticks, starting play with seven sticks on each side, and obtaining all fourteen sticks to win the game. The Arapaho style also involved competition between two individuals for the first point, the passing of a bean to the winner of the first point, and then the use and guessing of two beans or sets of hair pipes thereafter, requiring the successful guessing of both hiders in one or two consecutive guesses to win the offense. Another version using four hiders, and the ability of the first two hiders to come back in upon missing the last two hiders, was also reported. Arapaho play originally involved men who drummed and sang and women who sang and kept time with wooden sticks. Later on, it involved players of any age. Myrtle Lincoln also reported that the Arapaho did not bet on handgames but elsewhere stated that they regularly bet against the Cheyenne and noted the use of prayers for blessing prior to playing.[148]

Kroeber (1907, 368), who visited the Arapaho in 1899, reports the use of pointing sticks with feathers in the Arapaho handgame associated with the Ghost Dance of 1899. One Arapaho player stated that during games at Canton, Oklahoma, in the 1960s, a single bead was used as the hiding object.[149]

CHAPTER

3

The Modern Kiowa, Comanche, and Apache Handgame

HANDGAMES REMAINED A traditional part of the Kiowa, Comanche, and Apache social calendar throughout the nineteenth and into the twentieth century. After World War I the Kiowa began having handgames a few evenings before each Armistice Day celebration at White Fox's allotment west of Carnegie, Oklahoma. This annual November gathering appears to have set a standard that continues today. Following World War II, Kiowa began holding similar celebrations hosted by the Victory Club in Carnegie Park. Kiowa, Comanche, and Apache continued to play handgames through the 1950s. Several elders spoke of a "revival" of the handgame in the late 1950s and early 1960s when, as one described, a "number of people became interested in getting it going again."[1] Handgames seem to have never completely died out and then to have gained a renewed emphasis at this time, which coincides with the revival of the Kiowa Gourd Clan (1957), the Kiowa Black Legs Society (1958), and the larger growth of pan-Indian powwows and ethnic identity in the mid-1950s.

In the 1950s, the Kiowa, Apache, Comanche, and others frequently held winter handgames in tents at Carnegie Park, west of the present-day 4-H fair building. Bill Koomsa Jr. recalls that elongated structures of wooden pole frames covered with canvas, resembling miniature Quonset huts, and called "bungalows" by the Kiowa, were used up through the 1950s.[2] At this time most games were still played sitting cross-legged on pallets on the ground.

Men sat in the front row, women behind them. Koomsa Jr. described a gradual shift in the architecture associated with handgames. During his grandfather Bob Koomsa's time, the Kiowa played in tipis against the Apache and other local tribes. During the time of his father, Bill Koomsa Sr., games were held in canvas tents. During his lifetime play shifted to buildings and barns, then to modern community buildings and gymnasiums in tribal complexes.[3] The KCA began holding handgames, once confined to the winter months, throughout more of the year. In 1969 Jenny Horse reported that the game was then being played in the summer: "They do now. They play it anytime."[4]

During the late 1950s and 1960s, several modern innovations occurred. Games began to be held in community fairgrounds or park buildings that were warmer than tents. Wooden benches, like those used at powwows, began to replace sitting on the ground. Eventually lawn chairs began replacing benches. Whereas only one or a very few drums were used during the game, more singers began bringing their own hand drums to play in unison. During this period Stephen and Jeanette Mopope hosted handgames at their home east of Fort Cobb. Vanessa Jennings showed me her grandfather Stephen's handgame set from this period that consists of a wooden rack that holds four sticks in a horizontal fashion on each end, four in a vertical fashion in the center, and two sets of bones (one marked and one unmarked in each set). The family of

Handgame set of Stephen Mopope (Kiowa), circa 1950s. Author's photo.

Jack Yellowhair has a similar set from this era. The traditional style of play continued. As Gregory Haumpy described the old style of play, "They played a long time. Boy it was a long game. The sticks they go back and forth. That's how come the games last so long, they go back and forth."[5]

THE "SOUTHERN" OR "OKLAHOMA" STYLE HANDGAME

Around 1960 a new style of play was created that became variously known as the "southern," "Oklahoma," "southern style fast handgame," or "tournament style" of play. This style involved a new form of wooden rack with a larger center stick and an even number of sticks (usually from fourteen to eighteen) on each side. An uneven number of points was played for, and when a point was scored a stick was taken off the rack and could not be regained. This style was created to speed up the game from the traditional style of play that could last all night.[6]

Most elders state that Bill Koomsa Sr. was instrumental in developing this style of play along with contributions by his uncles Bruce Haumpy and Gregory Haumpy Sr., and Jasper Sankadota. The shift from the older 4–4–4 style to the use of a rack, a center stick, and an even number of points on each side of the center stick became the common form of handgame in western Oklahoma.[7] As Bill Koomsa Jr. described:

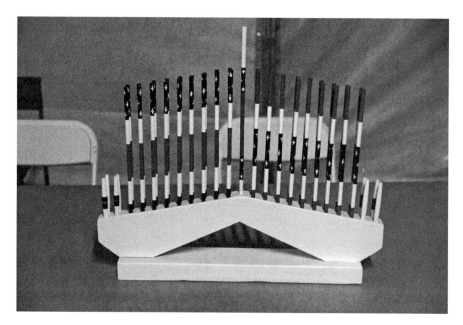

Contemporary handgame scoring rack and bones. Author's photo, 2017.

The Modern Handgame 123

> The old rules, the old type of game, one game could last all night, and I've seen games that went pretty well all night, and when they finally come back to even, when they get back to even like the game started, sometimes they would quit right there and divide up the bets and call it a night. But then it came to these more modern times. My dad was one of them guys that was kinda instrumental in changing the rules a little. That's when they went to the scoreboard and playing for odd number. . . . These guys came along and wanted to try and make it a winner, a game somebody can win within so long a time. So, Dad and them, they timed a lot of games, and a long game at this time is about forty-five minutes. It may be longer, and it may be shorter sometimes. . . . With the points, when they go down, they stay down. They don't come back up like the old-time game. So that's the way we play anymore, and . . . we call it "the KCA style," more or less. Kiowa, Comanches, and Apaches, we play that rule [style].[8]

With games averaging forty-five minutes or less, several games could be played in a single gathering.[9] This style also eliminated draws. As Bill Koomsa Jr. explained, "It made it a game where one side must win; there is no tie. One game lasts about forty-five minutes, and we play seven to eight games a night."[10] Elders report that the fast version started out with fifteen sticks but was eventually lengthened to nineteen.

Exactly when this style of play started is difficult to determine. Several elders state that it was introduced in the late 1950s. Jack Yellowhair recalled that the new style of play was already in existence when he began attending handgames around 1963: "They call it a fast tournament, southern fast tournament."[11] In 1984 Nell Pappio reported that this style had been in use for over fifteen years, placing its origins nowhere later than the mid- to late 1960s.[12]

However, the new style of play did not completely end the traditional form. In the games Tony Isaacs (1969) recorded in November 1968, KCA were still using the old style of play with four sticks in the middle (placed upright in a wooden rack) and four sticks to each team. The four counter sticks between the two teams were being kept on a table between the two teams, and a stand was often used so that the counter sticks could easily be seen by all. Mary Beaver, who started playing in the early 1980s, remembers that the new style occurred shortly before, although the older style of play still occurred as well.[13]

Other changes accompanying the shift to the new style of play included a scorekeeper who sits at a table between and at one end of the two teams and moves the counter sticks as points are scored, a referee who checks and signals each guess and the points scored to the scorekeeper, and a judge from each team—these sit on each side of the scorekeeper. Today a single scorekeeper is often used, and two referees have largely replaced the judges. KCA all play

Carnegie Roadrunners versus Billy Goat Hill, Carnegie, Oklahoma, November 1968. Photo by Tony Isaacs.

the same style of handgame. Although adopted by the neighboring Wichita, Caddo, Cheyenne, Arapaho, and other local tribes, some of these groups still occasionally play their own style among themselves.

The increased speed of play and set number of points needed to win quickly became popular. Jack Yellowhair described the difference between the older and newer styles of handgame: "Well I didn't care too much about that [old style] really. It's too slow. It took a long time, you know, it took forever and a day, you know, to win a game.... But now it just takes a few minutes... to play a game. So everybody liked it. The first time they couldn't get used to it, you know. But then they got used to it, and it's here today now. There's no other way. I don't think they'll ever change the way."[14]

Adam Kaulaity (Kiowa) described the difference between the two styles of play, "The new way's all right, yeah. You take those sticks down until you get to the last stick, yeah. Those old ones [games] they had, boy, they go back and forth sometimes all night. . . . I don't know when we quit playing that old style. It was at Bruce's out west of town here, Bruce Haumpy's place out there, we used to play that old style. But they brought that new style on, and they don't play that old style now, Kiowa style."[15]

Carl Atauvich (Comanche) also commented on the popularity of the new style of play, "Today's style is tournament style. The game goes a lot faster, and the game don't last as long. Back then they played the old way, the original way. Sometimes they last as long as three, four hours or longer, one game. That's the reason why today they've turned to the tournament style."[16] Carla Atauvich (Comanche) succinctly added, "The southern style is the tournament style."[17]

Seating Arrangements

Most seating today consists of two sets of opposing wooden benches (one or two rows per side), like the benches used at powwows. Additional seating for more players and the crowd, usually consist of folding lawn chairs brought by individuals and/or folding metal chairs kept at the facility being used. Most teams contain intertribal membership due to the overall small size of the handgame crowd, intermarriage, and friendship. Players tend to sit in team- and family-oriented clusters around the arena, moving to the benches when their team is called to play, then returning to their chairs after each round. Men continue to sit on the front row and women on the second row behind them. Women do not sit on the front but commonly come forward to guess.

Drums

One- or two-sided rawhide-covered hand drums are used. Today the cost of single-headed hand drums average around $75 to $100, while double-headed hand drums may cost around $150. In the late 1990s Jack Yellowhair was a major producer of hand drums, and his sons continue to make them. He bought cowhides at the local slaughterhouse, then stretched, dried, and scraped the hides before cutting a circular portion and tying the drum. While handmade rims can be made from wood, many prefer rims from commercial snare drums, which are sometimes difficult to find.

Once, while watching a wildlife program on television featuring zebras, Jack Yellowhair thought their hides would look good on a hand drum. On the next drum he tied, he used black and white shoe polish to paint the head in the design of a zebra hide. The drum was an instant hit on the circuit, and, informing everyone that it was made from a "zebra skin," Yellowhair got a good laugh from everyone out of it. In the fall of 1998, Yellowhair raffled the drum off during a fund-raiser, and it was won by a Crow. The next winter when the Crow came down to play the Oklahoma teams, one of the Crow had it. Years later, when *SpongeBob SquarePants* was popular with his children, Ace Yellowhair made a bright yellow hand drum with a vivid image of SpongeBob on both sides. When he used it at a public school program on handgames, the children began crying because he was "hitting Sponge Bob." He later disassembled the drum and replaced the cover.

Most individuals carry their drums by an attached strap or have loose cloth bags in which they put their drum and drumstick. One individual had an octagonal wooden case with a metal latch in which he carried his drum. Because drums can lose their tightness from humidity and cold during the winter season, many individuals set their drum near a heat source, such as a space heater brought by one of the players, to tighten it to the right pitch. Heating the drum surface tightens it, producing a more resonant sound when played. Some individuals use hand-held hair dryers for this purpose.

Rattles

Rattles are an important part of handgame music. Most rattles are made from thick milk cans fastened to wooden dowels and decorated with one or more colors of paint and tape. Ribbons or bright iridescent streamers attached to the top act like pompons when shaken in time to the music. Most are not made from thinner salt and pepper shakers as in the Gourd Dance or wild gourds as used in the Native American Church and are shaken much harder, in a more frontward-and-backward manner. Handgame rattles also usually have little or no beadwork, compared to other rattles. Small gravel or BBs are placed inside to produce a sound when shaken. Several are normally carried in a single cloth bag, unlike Gourd Dance Rattles and Native American Church rattles that are more delicate, contain beadwork, feather work, and horsehair, and are more gingerly kept in cedar boxes with other ritual paraphernalia. Rattles add a pleasing quality to the men and women's voices and the men's drumming.

Women shake the rattles in time to the drumming and singing of their team and in cheering their side on and taunting the opposition. Although rattles are primarily used by women, a few men sometimes shake them, but in all of the games I attended men shook rattles only if sitting in the second row of players

The Modern Handgame   127

or farther back. Rattles are never used on the front row with the male singers. Of the heavy use of rattles in the western Oklahoma handgame teams, Bill Koomsa Jr. commented, "That goes along with your cheering and jeering, more or less. Each team, when you're on the offense and wanting to score, that's when . . . the better the rhythm is, seems like the harder people want to play. That's where the rattles and bells, or just anything that they can get, they use to make rhythm with."[18] Bill Koomsa Jr. and Ina Paddlety Chalepah both reported that the use of rattles in western Oklahoma handgames is largely a Crow influence.[19]

HANDGAME MUSIC

Music is intimately linked with many Plains Indian cultural forms, including the handgame. This section provides a summary of the general characteristics of southern plains handgame music. Music is one of the most emotionally engaging aspects of the game. The rapid tempo, undulating nature, and repetitive, rhythmic pulsations gives handgame music an entrancing, almost hypnotic, and in some instances medicinal quality for player and spectator alike. One psychological anthropologist reported that it is physiologically possible to achieve a trance-like state during percussion with three to seven beats per second. Stuart reports an average of 252 pulses per minute, or 4.2 pulses per second in Coast Salish Slahal songs (Stuart 1972, 11). A most noticeable feature of the handgame is the fast, hard-soft drumbeat, the cadence of which resonates with the heart's rhythm. As Garcia (1996, 230) describes, "This counterpalpitation creates psychological excitement, confusing the guesser and adding to the general emotion of the game."

In the early 1900s Frances Densmore (1918) and other ethnomusicologists transcribed several handgame songs. Although not identified, Herzog's (1935) early description of Plains Indian handgame music appears to be based on his observations from the Plains, Southwest, and perhaps other areas. Herzog mentions several characteristics associated with handgame music that are present to a large degree among both the Blackfoot and Kiowa. Herzog notes that although gambling songs have distinct tribal styles, they also have much in common throughout a group of otherwise distinct Indian music repertories. According to Herzog (1935, 6–7) most handgame songs are

> comparatively short (but repeated any number of times) and consist of brief phrases. Each phrase contains a small number of tones; the range of the song is very often limited to a fifth or thereabout. The melodic movement of the song, as well as of the single phrase, is meager. Each phrase may be cut up into still smaller sections by staccatos or rests and intakes of breath which are more frequent than is physiologically necessary.

128 CHAPTER 3

> Another mark of the style is a comparatively simple balance; in most of the songs of this group the single phrases are of approximately equal length. The initial rhythmic figure may be carried throughout the song. The tempo is frequently quite fast. All this makes Indian gambling songs, on the whole, more tense with rhythmic pulsations than any other Indian songs. The accompaniment is always with the drum, or with whatever percussion instrument substitutes in the music of the tribe for the skin-covered drum.

Nettl and Blum (1968, 15–16) found that although Herzog excluded Blackfoot music in his study, he still discovered several features of handgame music that applied to their later study of Blackfoot songs. Songs are comparatively short, and their range is more limited than many other types of songs. Handgame songs have a "choppy effect" due to frequent staccatos and rests and commonly contain a repeated rhythmic figure. Phrases are relatively equal in length, "and in other ways also, structural balance is achieved."

Blackfoot handgame songs are generally brief but contain varied forms and composition techniques. Nettl and Blum (1968, 19) regard them as "most sophisticated musical products of the Blackfoot in 1966." Nettl and Blum (1968, 15) list the following as major characteristics of Blackfoot handgame music, which occur in some other forms of Blackfoot songs: a relatively tense vocal technique, a generally descending pattern, the use of transposition as a composition devise, and tetratonic and pentatonic scales. Nettl and Blum (1968, 19) also list several other prominent characteristics of Blackfoot handgame music, including songs that may be exceedingly simple or contain great intricacy, repeated rhythmic patterns, transposition (both tonal and approximate but rarely precise), incomplete repetitious form, and a general tendency of a beginning followed by a decreasing melodic contour. Nettle and Blum (1968, 16–19) maintain that despite a range of variety in Blackfoot handgame songs in terms of melodic contour, range, and rhythm, they constitute a clear genre of music and culture. Another important aspect is improvisation. As Nettl and Blum (1968, 15) describe, "The social situation surrounding the singing is perhaps closest to improvisation among the various public singing activities of the Blackfoot, since the leader or singing leader of a team must, on the spur of the moment, when his team suddenly receives the sticks to be hidden, begin a song. Thus it seems that the song closest to his musical consciousness will be the one chosen by him."

Southern Plains Handgame Music

Many of the features that Nettl and Blum (1968, 15–19) describe for Blackfoot handgame or stickgame music also apply to Kiowa and southern plains handgame music, including short songs, repetitious rhythmic patterns, a metric structure, short rhythmic units with staccatos and stops, a descending melodic contour, and a small number of note values per song. Notable exceptions among southern plains tribes include using rawhide hand drums (rather than drumming on wooden planks or logs with wooden sticks) and the shaking of metal rattles by women in accompaniment to the drumming. Songs usually do not have names associated with them, and improvisation appears rare.

Like other types of southern plains singing, handgame songs begin with the lead singer singing the first line. Other men join in on the second line, and the women join in on the third line singing an octave higher than the men. Most songs are fairly short in duration but can be repeated as long as needed because a round of hiding can last for several minutes. The same song may be sung several different times over an evening of play. Elder Kiowa singers state that older handgame songs have a straighter and faster beat than the 1-2, 1-2, or hard-soft, hard-soft beat that is common today.

Most KCA songs begin with a slower tempo that gradually increases and then stabilizes. A significant rise in the pitch of the singing also increases as the momentum builds. Pitch seems to increase when a song is sung through many repetitions. A team must score points to maintain the offense and thus continue singing. Prolonged rises in pitch appear to correlate with the quick tempo of the game, the excitement emanating from the play, and the increased energy associated with scoring successive points, not from song variation. Most songs have an undulating contour and are descending in shape. Bill Koomsa Jr. related that all Kiowa songs should be sung with an up and down or rising and falling quality and not in a flat or monotone style. Older Kiowa signers often have a quavering quality to the pitch of their singing. This was stressed to him by his father and other elders and was easily audible in his singing style.[20]

Originally play began with the singing of the Starting Song by both sides as two individuals competed to win the first point and the right to hide first as a team. The team that won the first point continued singing the Starting Song as they began to hide in preparation for their first offensive exchange. Later a coin toss was adopted to decide who would hide first, the winner gaining the offense but no points. The Starting Song is still used today, usually after the coin toss at the start of the first game of a tournament, but this is not done consistently.

Following the coin toss the winning team often starts with any song they choose. The choice of which song is used to begin play is largely at the discretion of whoever is starting a song. Some teams have an informal "theme" song, a song that they have a particular fondness for and begin with. Today it is largely up to what the lead singer chooses to sing, often a song that the singer thinks will stimulate his team and gain them momentum by getting them in the mood. As Jack Yellowhair explained, "Some people can sing a song, you can get a person into the song. He'll get lucky. Then [sometimes] you can sing a song, and the person won't get into it, you know, he gets beat, he gets caught. It takes the rhythm of the drum, the sound. . . . You can sing anything you want, or some song that comes to your mind, or whatever you want to sing. You like a song or [you are] trying to get your group in the mood, in the groove or in the mood, you know. That's what we try to do. . . . We're trying to get the people into the groove, to start moving around."[21]

Some nights one or two individuals may start most of a team's songs. In other instances, five or six different people may start songs for a team throughout a single game. Often the medicine man will take some time before handing out the bones, allowing him time to make his choices but also allowing the team to sing a song two or more times to build up momentum for hiding.

Singers are sometimes chosen to hide. When someone singing and drumming is asked to hide, they may put their drum down and hide or pause long enough to hide the bones behind the drum or in closed hands before continuing to drum and sing. When guessed, they simply open their hands to show how they hid. Many teams with only one or two singers often have someone else sit in to help them sing. Those players seated with a team but singing to help another team who lack singers are not supposed to hide as they are registered as players on their own team.

As with songs in other cultural events such as the War Dance or Gourd Dance (Meadows 1999, 2010), songs can be sung with or without lyrics. Brief lyrics can be inserted into handgame songs, and elders report that in the past more handgame songs contained lyrics. According to Bill Koomsa Jr., some Kiowa songs have words, but most do not pertain to the game. Of the samples I collected, the lyrics appear to focus on two main themes: 1) daring or taunting the opponent to find the marked bones, or 2) humorous references that from a musical standpoint easily fit into the rhythm of the song.

One Kiowa handgame song recorded by the Santa Fe Laboratory of Anthropology in 1935 contained the following lyrics.

> 1. Hè-gáu náu táun, ém-chò è chél
> (and then / you to me / found; / within over here / it is / contained within)
> And then you found it, but it is on this side (in this hand).[22]

This may be an abbreviated form of a longer Kiowa song recorded by Elsie Clews Parsons (1929, 121):

1. À sái dḛ́–gá yà ó̱-dè
   In winter I like going to sleep

2. Há-òi, há-òi
   where it is, where it is

3. À sái dḛ́–gá yà ó̱-dè
   In winter I like going to sleep

4. Hè-gáu náu táun, ém-chò è chél
   And then you found it, but it is on this side (in this hand).

Most southern plains handgame songs that I have heard since 1997 lack lyrics. When lyrics appear, they are typically one or two brief sentences or phrases inserted into the song. Flannery and Cooper (1946, 403) describe the same structure in two Gros Ventre handgame songs they recorded.

Bill Koomsa Jr. explained that handgame songs are designed to tease and confuse the other team.[23] Woody Kipp (Blackfeet) similarly stated (Roberts 1992, 45), "The songs are songs of power which are meant to confuse the opposing side, preventing them from guessing correctly."[24] Songs with lyrics often taunt or challenge the opposition, as in the following Gros Ventre handgame song (Flannery and Cooper 1946, 403): "It's no use you trying to guess me; I'm holy." Like Trobriand cricket songs or chants sung during American basketball games, handgame songs with lyrics incorporate taunting lyrics toward the opposing team.

The following translations of two Kiowa handgame songs reflect these competitive themes:

1. You think you guessed / found it.
2. But you didn't get anything.

Bill Koomsa Jr. composed a song that translates to state:

1. So, you think you're lucky.
2. Why don't you bet a lot of money?
3. Let's see who wins.[25]

Ina Paddlety Chalepah described the lyrics in some Kiowa handgame songs, including the occasional inclusion of an individual's name to more directly challenge and taunt them. "Kiowa [songs] got words, you know, 'Well, you can't find it on me.' 'Let's see you find it,' like that. 'I'm hiding it on this side, you can't find it.' That's what they say in Kiowa. 'You cannot find it.' And

132   CHAPTER 3

they call [out] this certain Indian name. 'You can' find it, look at me. Look at me in the eye. You can't find my bone.' Just like that."[26]

Gregory Haumpy translated a Kiowa handgame song that blends both genres of songs described earlier.

1. Háun-àn nàu ta̱u-mâu
   You cannot find it.

2. Èm áu-fa̱u, yà jép-jè-da̱u, yà jép-jè-da̱u
   Wait awhile, you are my relatives, you are my relatives.

3. Jò-hâu-ta̱u nàu chél
   I've got it hid over the cliff (and you can't find it).

4. Èm qa̱u-náu-tâu èm chó-chòl.
   You are a spider, don't forget it.

5. Bél-tó̱ a têm-da̱u, gàu há-yá-kó-ba̱
   He's got a broken knee, and he went somewhere.[27]

One handgame song ended up with two versions of English lyrics, like Round Dance songs with English lyrics. The Carnegie Eagles composed the following song about the Wild Bunch which they sang as played them.

We are the Eagles
We'll dust the Wild Bunch
We are the Eagles
Hey yah hai yah, Hai hey yah hai yah.

The Wild Bunch soon reciprocated their own lyrics for the same song.

We are the Wild Bunch
We'll dust the Eagles
Hey yah hey yah yo, hay yah hai yah.[28]

In 1998 Jack Yellowhair reflected on the handgame songs he had composed. "Songs come to me like this, and I put words in it. Now I composed about four songs so far. Two they sing a lot now. One they don't hardly sing. Now I compose another song. Haven't brought that [one] out yet. . . . I haven't sung it out in the handgame world yet. But I am planning on singing it if I get that building Sunday."[29] Some singers of many genres record new songs on tape, and now digitally, until their composition is finalized and in order not to lose them. As one singer described of a song he composed only two weeks before, "[I] just put it on tape where I won't forget it." Players also commonly

The Modern Handgame 133

tape-record songs from other tribes, learn them, then later sing them in their home area in Oklahoma.

William Bittle recorded four Apache handgame songs with lyrics from Rose Chalepah in 1961. The translations to the Apache lyrics include:

Song 1: "I'm going to get my sticks back."
Song 2: "Get out, I'm going to beat them."
Song 3: "Smiling at me, he can't see it, can't guess it."
Song 4: "Look at me good. I'm the one that's hiding it."[30]

Comanche consultants stated that about five Comanche songs have lyrics in them. As Carla Atauvich commented, "They don't really refer to anything in particular, just words that they put in there that they say."[31] The brief lyrics are usually humorous or phonetically catchy, as demonstrated in the following translations collected from consultants:

Song 1: You've got a stinky skunk for your friend.
Song 2: You have grey flat feet.
Song 3: The red donkey is loping.
Song 4: The red donkey doesn't have a forehead.
Song 5: The red donkey has no neck.

Sometimes referred to as "Eka-muura" (Red Donkey), one consultant explained, this song was originally sung "A red donkey with no neck" but today is simply sung as Red Donkey with vocables:

Eka-muura, Eka-muura?
hey yah hai, Eka-muura?
hey yah hai, Eka-muura?"[32]

Variations of another Comanche song I regularly heard in the 1990s refer to a cedar tree. One version states, "He's standing on a hillside looking like a cedar tree." Vernon Atauvich told me of a Comanche song with words that state, "A cedar tree is standing on a hill; when the wind blows, it looks white" (referring to the shaded, light gray, dead branches in the lower part of the tree).[33]

Some old songs have been recomposed or innovated on, often with a different rhythm or the addition or deletion of words to make new compositions. Elders state that the older songs typically had a slower beat than those sung today. Comanche consultants commented that other tribes pick up their songs and slightly modify them. As one individual described, "Today they've got a little more liveliness to them, the beat and the singing. . . . They've got a little bit more rhythm to it, you know. They're a little bit faster. They've got little additions to most of them."

Jackie Ray and Ace Yellowhair shared a Plains Apache handgame song that their grandfather Ace Chalepah composed. The song references the disappearance [inability to correctly guess the location] of the hiding object and the cawing of a crow.

> Say-ah-wah coo-coo
> The rock [i.e. hiding object] disappears.
> Say-ah-wah coo-coo
> "The rock [hiding object] disappears.
> Cah-cah, Say-nay-way coo-coo.
> [Crow cawing] The rock [hiding object] disappears.

Reflecting the spirited competition in play, Alonzo Chalepah composed one Apache handgame song with the words "*Chee dah kah*" (We are the winners [or champions]).[34] His son Alfred Chalepah Sr. described how the song leader tries to choose a song that serves to motivate their team to win: "He's got a choice. They sing songs you know, he tries to pick out [one] that's got good morale [spirit] in it, that's got a lot of like he wants to win you know. He gets that, that maybe that song, that song will help him win you know."[35]

An elder Kiowa stated that in the Kiowa handgame you traditionally sang the same song over and over during one set of offense (hiding), however long it lasted, until you had scored four points. Upon scoring four points in a row, you could then switch to another song. However, this individual stated that he was afraid to do so from fear of breaking their luck, so he sang the same song no matter how long they continued to hide in a single run. Some singers maintained it is best to keep on the same song if making a run of several points.

According to Gregory Haumpy Sr., a team should sing a single song as long as the other side is missing your hiders until scoring four sticks. After scoring four sticks, or after being guessed and later starting your next round of offense, you can start a new song. He stated that it sounds better if you periodically change songs and get as many songs in as possible rather than singing a single song throughout.[36] Usually when a team is guessed correctly and the opposing side begins their offense, they will begin a different song from what the other side was singing. However, a few times I have noticed that the other side will begin singing the same song that the last team was singing. Whether this was coincidence or unconsciously chosen is unclear. Singers also noted that is it important in how you start a song at the beginning of a new round of hiding to maintain momentum from the previous round.

The tradition of the winner singing a victory song immediately after winning a game continues. This is an old custom dating back to at least the reservation period (1875–1901), and possibly earlier. This song begins with a distinct ruffling of the drum that distinguishes it from other regular handgame songs. In one instance when the Kiowa beat the Crow in a game, all but two of the Kiowa team were so excited that they jumped up and forgot to sing the song. As the two remaining members began the song, the others quickly retook their seats and joined in.[37]

Victory songs sung at handgames can come from several genres of songs. Kiowa elders in 1935 reported the use of Jáifègàu Society songs. Reflecting change, my elder consultants stated that while one could sing a song of this society as a victory song in a handgame, they had not heard of one being used. A victory song is usually sung at the end of a round-robin tournament by the winner, and at the end of a free-for-all after a tournament (free-for-alls are described below in this chapter). Victory songs are sometimes begun near the end of a game as a team is gaining momentum and about to win. In this situation it implies that the side singing is going to win and thus serves to harass or intimidate the other side, adding to the intensity of the competition. Consultants reported the use of Forty-nine, Horse Stealing, Wind or Traveling, War Dance, and Round Dance songs as victory songs at handgames.[38] Bill Koomsa Jr. described the use of victory songs at handgames, sometimes referred to as "winning songs," and how they add to the excitement of a close game.

> There's also songs we call winning songs. When your side, your team, is about to win the game, they usually change the beat of the drum and harass the losers, you know. They know they are going to win . . . so they kinda harass them a little while they are singing these slower type songs. It's just different, you know. The hurrahing I guess you'd say, is when your team has got some people that like to [do that]. But that makes the game, you know. It really gets exciting sometimes, especially when it's a tight game. Sometimes the games will go back and forth, and that's when the crowd gets into it. It really becomes a hard-fought game. So sometimes the game goes down to the last point . . . and that gets pretty exciting. Especially if you have a pretty good bet, you know. You want your side to win.[39]

Mary Beaver acknowledged that the singing is important to gaining momentum during play and that teams often have noticeably different singing styles. "I always think of it this way, it's like A, B, and C, you know . . . they're good singers . . . powwow singers. They got the voices, and I like to hear them because their team really gets into it. And then take D and E, you know, they pound their drums a little bit more, harder. They sing just a little bit, harder,

136   CHAPTER 3

you know. And then you come to F—F has that . . . soft drumbeat . . . F is
slower. He likes this slow tempo so that everyone can listen to the songs. He's
not the fastest. I think it's just his style. He's always been like that, it's just a
real even tempo. . . . So, it's just kind of, you know, up to each singer.[40]

Changes in Singing

A noticeable change since the 1960s has been a decline in singing older handgame songs and songs with lyrics in them. Elder players frequently mentioned
the reluctance of younger people in singing old songs, especially those with
words, versus newer songs. As Gregory Haumpy described,

> You know it's funny, them old songs that I'm singing, that's got words in
> it. You get in the handgame, and you happen to sing one of them songs,
> they won't help you sing it. I don't know why. But when you start a new,
> kind of up-to-date song, boy, they'll drown you out. You know, but you
> sing these old songs, they won't hardly sing them. It looks to me like they
> should, they should try to keep them up, you know, learn them and then,
> even if you don't sing them, well, learn them, and just like now, sing them
> every so often. It's a lot of fun. Some of them have funny words in there.[41]

Aside from generational tastes and the decline of fluent speakers, confidence in using the language is a likely factor. Singers state that some individuals are not taught the language and song texts. However, many songs with
words are still sung at powwows, society dances, and especially in Indian
Christian church services in which hymns in most sects, all with lyrics, are
sung a cappella. Several older handgame singers also sing songs with lyrics
at other venues including Flag, War Mothers, Gourd Dance, and Black Legs
Society songs. Singing does not require fluency in a language, and many
singers, Native and non-Native, sing songs in a language they do not speak.
There seem to be many factors in the reluctance to sing songs with lyrics in
handgames.

Sometimes an individual attempts to introduce a new song with lyrics,
only to find others reluctant to embrace it. Ace Chalepah (Plains Apache)
led the team called KCA. His son-in-law Jack Yellowhair Sr., who succeeded
Chalepah as the head of the team, took a Crow song and put Kiowa words to
it to make a team song.

> When I first made that, I told my wife, "Listen, I'm gonna sing you a song,
> put words in it." Keep going [singing it] over and over for her. It kind of
> got to her. She said, "Hey, that sounds all right." Said, "That's going to
> be our song, KCA song." Boy, one night we're at Carnegie. I started out
> on that song. When I put them words in it, boy, everybody was laughing.

The Modern Handgame 137

They thought it was funny, then yet it was good. They were hollering. Our bunch was just hollering. . . . But nobody ever did use them words in that song, no other team. They just sang that song, wouldn't even put the words in it.

Brief but poignant, the lyrics to this song state:

1. KCA è zél-bé
   Kiowas, Comanche, and Apache are bad [i.e., fierce].

2. KCA-chó è dàu
   Kiowas, Comanches, and Apaches, that's how they are.

3. KCA ó-báui-dàu
   They are really Kiowas, Comanches, and Apaches.[42]

Another shift involves a decrease in singing older, faster-paced KCA songs. Ace Yellowhair commented on this trend:

When I first started, I always used to hear them old people sing. Boy, they'd be getting it. What I mean is . . . that they'll be having that, make you want to tap [your foot], dance around kind of music and feeling. And that's what's changed about now days . . . [the] drum beat and all that has changed too. They used to have that [taps a faster, steady beat], now it's a slow kind of casual drum beat, you know, boom-boom, boom-boom, boom-boom. But way back there, you know, ninety miles an hour, you might say, boom-boom-boom-boom-boom, then they take off. . . . The old style of music is gone. Just a very few people still sing that style, I mean really get up and go fast. But I think that's what has changed a lot, the singing.[43]

Singers also report fewer people singing during handgames in western Oklahoma. In the games recorded by Tony Isaacs in 1968 (Indian House Records 1969, 1974) or Crow games with large teams, many individuals, male and female, are singing, producing a broader, fuller sound. While men on the front row, and some women in the second and third rows sing, the percentage of singers per team has decreased. Some teams have many singers, while others have only one, two, or a few singers on a team of six to twenty players. As one Kiowa singer described, "Once . . . everybody would sing, and then it's just very seldom now. You know very few people will sing."

In most tournaments, if a team has no singers, they are allowed to pick up two singers to enable them to play. The singers can sit on their side and drum and sing for them but cannot hide, guess, coach, or contribute in any other fashion.[44] Sometimes when the only singer on a team is asked to hide, one or

138 CHAPTER 3

more women will sometimes pick up drums and start drumming as he hides, while all continue to sing. In the 1990s Flora Weryackwe, whose team The Gang was all-female, sometimes picked up a hand drum and led the singing. In other instances, one or more men would sing for them.

Although some singers periodically switch back to older songs for those who enjoy and can sing them, most singers stated that the more contemporary songs dominate the repertoire at handgames today. Elder players report having sung some of the same songs since they first started playing, as well as learning new songs from other tribes such as the Crow and Ute. Handgame songs used to be faster, with a steadier, more regular beat. Now the tempo has been changed or altered to fit the modern rhythm, which is described as more "jumpy."[45] This description reflects the 1-2, 1-2, or hard-soft, hard-soft rhythm of most contemporary handgame songs.

Another major change in southern plains handgame singing has been the introduction of Crow songs. In 1993 Bill Koomsa Jr. stated that Kiowa were beginning to sing more Crow-style songs. Many southern plains handgame songs are still known, but most southern plains players now sing Crow songs. The KCA all sing one another's songs and sing together against the Crow every November, but they sing an even greater number of Crow songs. Whereas Kiowa songs are repetitious, some Crow songs have verses. Koomsa stated that he tried to sing Kiowa songs at least one or two games per match to keep them active. He used to receive a tape every year containing new Crow handgame songs and learn all of them each year, but he eventually could not keep up with the quantity. Singer Phil "Joe Fish" Dupoint also noted that Crow and Kiowa commonly "trade songs."[46]

The exchange of songs has a long history. According to Alfred Chalepah Sr. (Apache) the KCA had many of the same handgame songs for a long time. In his youth he remembered that KCA songs were sung at handgames. He reports that in the 1930s several Tonkawa songs were learned and mixed with Apache songs. Later the Apache began to use Cheyenne songs. When the Crow began coming down in the late 1960s, he recalled that some did not like the KCA style of play as it was slower, with the four sticks on each side and in the middle.[47] The intertribal exchange of songs and singing styles continues. At a handgame at Clinton, Oklahoma, in 1998, an elder Kiowa singer identified Northern Cheyenne, Comanche, Kiowa, and numerous Crow songs sung that evening. This singer noted that everyone likes and sings one another's songs. In 2017 a singer identified Kiowa, Comanche, Plains Apache, Cheyenne, Crow, and Ute songs in a single evening of play in Oklahoma.[48]

The Modern Handgame   139

There appears to be less concern for the ownership of handgame songs than Gourd Dance and other dance society songs. In the Kiowa Gourd Dance there are "open" songs that may be sung by any Kiowa. There are also "family" or "society" songs that are associated with ownership and use by a specific organization or when requested by the members of a specific family. Ownership of handgame songs depends on the composer of the song, some of whom want individuals to ask and perhaps give a small gift before being given permission to sing the song, and others who put no restrictions on it. While certain handgame songs are known as Kiowa, Comanche, or Crow songs and were composed and introduced by particular individuals, most appear to be "put on the drum" or "open" songs that are public domain in the handgame community and can be sung by anyone. While a team may have a favorite, elders I interviewed stated that everyone is essentially free to sing any song when they desire to. When singing another's song, some singers will make slight changes in how they sing the song, eliminating exact duplication.[49]

SPONSORSHIP, FACILITIES, AND COST

An individual, family, organization, or team may sponsor a handgame for many reasons, including birthdays, memorials, to honor someone, or simply to have a tournament. The winner of larger tournaments, such as the Oklahoma State Handgame Tournament or the Crow tournament, must host the next year's tournament. Putting on a handgame generally involves three things: 1) rental of a building, 2) providing a meal and running a concession stand, and 3) trying to recoup the money required to fund the first two items.

Facilities

Foremost, a facility large enough to host the event is needed. Because participants exceed what an individual house can usually accommodate, some form of public building is needed. In the summer, games may be held outside in a shaded area, such as under a large arbor or tent. A public building is commonly used. In the 1980s the handgame began to be affected by the growth of high-stakes bingo, as it became an important source of gaming and income for many tribes. Regularly scheduled bingo began to limit the availability of building space for handgames. Adam Kaulaity said in 1984, "Bingo has knocked us out of places to play. At the Kiowa Complex, on Tuesday, Friday, and Sunday we cannot get the building for handgames."[50] However, organizers are resourceful and usually are able to come up with a location for a tournament.

Over the last few decades most handgames have been held in county fair or community buildings or in gymnasiums at tribal complexes. In March 1998 an elder consultant sponsoring a tournament called around to check the rental prices on several public buildings in Southwest Oklahoma, which were as follows: Red Buffalo Hall (Carnegie) $200, no refund; Wichita Tribal Building (Anadarko) $250, no refund; Apache Fair Building (Apache) $175 ($100 returned if cleaned after event); Carnegie Bingo Building (Carnegie) $75, no deposit, cleanup required; Clinton Community Hall (Clinton) $35, later $50; Geary Fair Building (Geary) $50; Anadarko Fair Building (Anadarko) $70, $30 deposit return.

After the mid-1990s, many buildings in the KCA area became so expensive that many handgames began to be held in the Cheyenne and Arapaho community building at Geary, Oklahoma, regardless of the sponsor. As Jack Yellowhair reflected in 2003, "Around here now we don't hardly have no handgames. The simple thing is the buildings which I have to rent cost too much. They charge too much. Up there [Geary], well, they don't charge them people like that. My granddaughter's going to have one up there. She has to have it up there because the building's cheaper. . . . [at Geary it's] $65, I believe, for one day, from that day clear to midnight or maybe later. See, that's cheap. Round here they're almost $200. So that's why I say it's cheaper up that way." At that time, Mr. Yellowhair reported that $300 was more than enough to sponsor a basic one-day handgame tournament, which for some families was a significant amount to raise for an event.[51] Recently several tribes have frequently used the new Cheyenne tribal multipurpose building in Geary for handgames.

Although larger buildings typically cost more to rent than smaller ones, a host often chooses a site based primarily on cost. To reduce overhead costs or receive a partial refund, the sponsors and other players remain to help clean up the facility after the event. Team leaders recalled renting several of these locations for $25 to $35 prior to the mid-1990s. The increasing growth of bingo at these locales has led some facility managers to raise prices. At one popular city park building, city officials threatened to cease renting the facility for powwows and handgames in 1998 on the complaint of drinking in the parking lot and beer cans left on the grounds. However, as many people, Indian and non-Indian, use the same facility and recycle the cans for cash, there is little long-time concern and, from my observations, no difference from non-Indian events I have seen.

The Modern Handgame

Meals, Concessions and Fund-raising

Because handgames usually run from 2:00 to 11:00 p.m. or later, concessions are needed. The long day requires providing an evening meal for all in attendance and supplies for a concession stand. To offset the costs of the building rental, evening meal, and concessions, fund-raising activities are undertaken. As with powwows, the host typically runs a concession stand to recoup their overhead for holding the event by selling soft drinks, water, coffee, potato chips, popcorn, pickles, candy, hamburgers, hot dogs, frybread, Indian tacos, and chili.

Donated raffle items provide another way to make money. Usually grocery baskets, serapes or blankets, hand drums, and 50-50 raffle tickets (for which the winner of the drawing gets half of the money and the host retains the other half) are raffled by the host. Individuals or other teams may also contribute to another's event by donating a grocery basket, blanket, trophy, prize money, or other raffle items.

Jackie Ray Yellowhair described the generosity of handgame people to buy raffle tickets to help the host offset the cost of the event and to contribute during blanket dances where money is collected for an individual or a cause. "People like to buy raffles. They know you're trying to raise money, you know, and handgame people are generous in that regards to help one another. Someone's having hard times, you know, maybe in their health, and they'll spread a blanket out, and they'll sing a song, you know, and everybody will put in whatever they got, you know. A dollar, two dollars, fifty cents, whatever, you know, and handgame people have been generous like that."[52]

Similar to passing a hat to collect money, a Blanket Dance can be used to raise funds for a cause. Between games a blanket is spread out on the floor. Singers come forward with hand drums and sing a song for the recipient. Although most songs are War Dance songs, handgame, family, or Gourd Dance songs can be sung. The recipient usually stands beside the blanket and individuals come forward during the song to place money on the blanket and shake hands with them. Unlike Blanket Dances at powwows, individuals may choose not to dance at handgames. At the song's conclusion, the money is collected and given to the individual being honored or the event host.

Five factors determine the success of an event: 1) the date, 2) the type of handgame held, 3) the starting time, 4) how many people attend, and 5) support from other teams. The sponsor tries to pick a date that does not coincide with other handgames and cultural events. Sponsors must sometimes reschedule a tournament to prevent doubling up with another event and thus splitting a fairly limited crowd.

142 CHAPTER 3

With numerous teams, more people, larger prizes, and lasting all day, round-robin tournaments are usually the most productive type of handgame. Free-for-alls and match games tend to involve limited betting, offer smaller prizes, and draw fewer people and less money. The earlier a sponsor opens their concession stand and begins a tournament, the better chance they have to recoup their expenditures. The more people and teams that attend, the more money that is circulated in terms of team entry fees, prize money, individual bets, concessions, and fund-raising. Participation of teams at one another's events is key to a successful tournament. Most individuals report they can make their money back and sometimes profit.

The host may attempt to raise money for a specific purpose such as sponsoring an upcoming tournament, like the next state tournament, or simply to pay travel, medical, or other bills. Although some people question fund-raising efforts, others do not and simply support another team any time they have a tournament by attending and participating. As Jack Yellowhair explained, "We all go to help one another, [help] the club out, you know. Maybe they might be having a benefit or just a round-robin, you know. Maybe some people need money to pay certain bills or whatever they want to do, you know. We don't question that. . . . We're just there, we're gonna help them out, you know. That way . . . at the same time, we're enjoying ourselves, you know, playing, meet people, talk, tell stories you know, different things like that."[53]

TYPES OF HANDGAMES

In western Oklahoma three main types of handgames are played: match games, free-for-alls, and round-robin tournaments.

Match Games

Match games are based on play between set teams that seem to have begun in pre-reservation times with intertribal play. Born in 1918, Gregory Haumpy recalled that in his youth there were no set teams; everyone played by tribe, such as the Kiowa, Apache, or Comanche. Intertribal exchanges of games were essentially a series of match games.[54] Adam Kaulaity told of meeting at the homes of Bruce Haumpy and Bill Koomsa Sr. west of Carnegie, Oklahoma, where four or five match games might be played in an evening.[55] In the late 1990s Jack Yellowhair and Carl Atauvich both described having previously held occasional match games against other teams at their homes.[56]

In match games, one team invites another team for a series of games. The host provides the structure in which to play and all needed equipment, although the guests bring their own hand drums. After feeding the guest team lunch or dinner, depending on the starting time, play begins. Originally teams could play as many games as they wanted, with games often lasting all day. Today the two teams will usually play a couple of games and then shift to playing free-for-all style. In some match games, teams allow anyone to sit and sing for a team, but only the actual members of the two teams can hide and guess. The same applies when men are asked to sing for an all-female team.

Table bets are placed prior to each game, matched to equal amounts on each side, and collected by the winner immediately after each game. In match games the losing side of the previous game sets the amount of betting prior to the start of the next game to ensure their monetary resources are not depleted and to ensure that another game is possible. There is no pot or purse as in a round-robin tournament.

Both match games and round-robins were common in the early 1980s and used the modern set of sticks on a rack. Sometimes the two were combined. As Mary Beaver explained, "It was a little bit of both when I started, but it was the match games that really got people coming because we would invite. I remember my dad inviting a team to come early, and he would feed them, and then they would play like . . . two out of three with the same team, and then other teams would come for the round-robin tournament later. . . . And then in return this team would later invite my dad's team down to a handgame in their vicinity, and the same thing would take place. And then everybody was inviting everybody, you know, and that's how people got to know each other, become acquainted."[57]

Today match games are rare among the Oklahoma teams but continue in the Crow community and when the Crow visit each November and are hosted for several evenings by Kiowa, Comanche, Apache, Cheyenne and Arapaho teams. While the Oklahoma teams in these games are always mixed and vary each night, and some Oklahoma players will sit and play on the Crow side, the games are played as a series of games against a single opponent, the Crow, and are thus considered match games. Occasionally a team will still invite another team over to one of their homes for a set of games.

Free-for-Alls

"Free-for-all" refers to a handgame in which membership is not based on formal teams and anyone can play on the side they choose. Betting is not required, and, as one player described, "it is free for all." This form is also sometimes called an "open handgame." Once a game begins, you must remain on the side you have chosen until it ends, then you are free to remain on that side, switch sides, or not play at all in the next game. Membership often changes from game to game as people switch sides or sit out a game.

144 CHAPTER 3

In free-for-alls, the same basic rules apply as in other handgames, except that they are much looser. As the name implies, almost anything goes. Hiders can include members of the audience, scorekeepers, the master of ceremonies, and even people working in the concession stand. Those asked to hide for a team are generally on the same side of the building. Guessing and hiding motions may be comical and more spontaneous, such as guessing with one's hands, feet, or lips. The guesser can cross the line down the middle of the floor between the two teams, even walking behind the bench of the other side to examine hiders in the crowd against the far wall and sometimes getting nearly right up in their face.[58]

Humor and pantomime add to the lighthearted nature of play. At one game the guesser walked around behind a girl hiding on the other side and feigned looking to see how she had hidden the bones. Everyone laughed as he walked back to his side, where he sat down, allowing her to re-hide the bones before arising and proceeding to guess. One night at the start of the fourth game of a free-for-all at Apache, Eddie Longhat sat down on the east side to begin play. He quickly got up and switched to the west side, where he stayed for the rest of the night. The MC and everyone immediately razzed him about switching sides.[59]

While an evening of handgames used to consist of several free-for-alls, they are now typically held before and after round-robin tournaments. Prior to a tournament beginning, individuals may start a free-for-all as a means of warming up and a way of filling the time as teams gradually arrive. Those held after a tournament usually occur when the tournament has ended early, the evening is still young, and individuals desire to play more before going home. Someone will call for a free-for-all, and any combination of players will gather to form two teams. With this format, teammates on named teams may become opponents, and former opponents may end up playing with one another. Typically, two or three free-for-alls may be held after a tournament ends, depending on time and interest.[60] Games held after the end of a tournament allow individuals additional opportunities to place individual bets and socialize. The annual American Indian Exposition usually includes one evening of "open handgames" or free-for-alls the day before the round-robin tournament.

In free-for-alls, individuals regularly place bets at the score table, and the sides are evened up before play starts. Individuals may also at any time make individual bets with someone sitting on the opposite side. However, because the betting in free-for-alls is generally very small, often only $90–$125 per side today, this form of handgame is less attractive to those interested in winning the larger pots associated with tournaments. Practically any form of

The Modern Handgame   145

guessing is permissible, including hand gestures, double-finger or fork guessing, and tongue pointing. While guessers are not supposed to make excessive hand motions in tournaments, which are considered harassment of the hider, they are allowed in free-for-alls.[61]

Free-for-alls have declined in frequency. As Jack Yellowhair described in 1998, "We don't hardly have that anymore you know, free-for-all. We don't hardly have any match games either, mostly just round-robins."[62] One elder player remarked, "I get tired of round-robins, you know. I like the money all right in a way, but then I like to sit down and just enjoy myself with a free-for-all, you know, and just do [my] thing. But now they don't have that. They want to play round-robin all the time, . . . there's money in it."[63] Jack Yellowhair and Gregory Haumpy both recalled that match games and free-for-alls were the norm until the late 1980s, when round-robin tournaments slowly began to be held.[64]

Round-Robin Tournaments

Today round-robin tournaments are the most frequently appearing form of southern plains handgame. Inspired by round-robin softball tournaments, this format was adopted in the mid-1980s. Gregory Haumpy, who recalled playing "straight handgames" or match games at Cache, Chandler Creek, Anadarko, and Carnegie, Oklahoma, also believed that round-robin handgame tournaments started in the 1980s. Believing the idea came from the Cheyenne at Clinton, Oklahoma, Bruce Haumpy, Bill Koomsa Sr., and Carl Atauvich started this style of play in the KCA area. Gregory Haumpy also believed that someone saw it played and brought it in, possibly from the Cheyenne.[65] Adam Kaulaity stated that the idea to hold tournaments and to change from the old to the new style of play came from Montana.[66] One elder felt these tournaments should not be called round-robins because all teams do not play one another as in a true round-robin tournament but simply play against one another until losing two games (double elimination).

In round-robin handgame tournaments each team registers under a team name and pays an entry fee. When all teams have entered, they draw numbered tickets to determine who will play one another. In one tournament I attended, the MC placed eight numbered slips of paper into a hat. Each team captain drew a slip. Number 1 played 2, 3 played 4, 5 played 6, and 7 played 8.[67]

Teams remain in the tournament until their second loss. After the first round of play, teams who won their first game are placed into a winner's bracket, and teams who lost their first game enter the losers' bracket. Beginning with the

146 CHAPTER 3

second round, play continues until one team remains in the winner's bracket (having no losses) and one team remains in the loser's bracket (having only one loss). These two teams then play for the tournament championship. If the team from the winner's bracket (A) defeats the team from the loser's bracket (B), A wins the tournament, as B has acquired two losses and is out. If the team from the loser's bracket defeats the team from the winner's bracket, both teams now have one loss and must play a second and final game. The team that wins this game wins the tournament, as the opposing team now has two losses. Although any form of bracket can be used, most sponsors use a softball tournament bracket.

RULES

With the shift from match games to round-robin tournaments, more rules developed. These include a time limit for hiding and guessing (often thirty seconds each), usually kept by a judge or timekeeper at the score table. Hiders must hold their hands chest-high while being guessed, and no fancy guessing (two-finger or tongue pointing) is allowed, only the standard inside, outside, left, and right signs. A center line of black electrician's tape is usually placed down the middle of the playing area that guessers cannot step over. Guessers cannot try to fake the hiders into giving themselves away, are limited in the range of "medicine" or "power" motions they can make in guessing, and cannot consult with anyone while guessing.

Any breach of these rules typically results in the loss of a stick (the opponent removes a stick from their side of the scoring rack). Some individuals stated that they do not really like all the rules, saying these have "taken some of the fun out of it" and "commercialized" the game to a degree. However, the rules help to standardize the play and keep the games moving in a timely fashion. How strictly tournament rules are enforced varies. As one team captain explained, "Some of them are pretty strict on that. But I don't see any danger in them, you know, making motions. That's making medicine man, trying to voodoo them, like trying to throw them off by doing that to them. But a guesser cannot get up there and go like [one player] always does. That's trying to make him give himself away. . . . He always does that. He always goes [makes a fist and shakes and moves it from side to side]. You can't do that."[68]

Tournaments often require a team roster with the names of every player on it prior to the start of play. At the Red Earth Tournament one year, a player with a large family recalled how a woman demanded a roll call on his team, making each member on the list stand as their name was called. Some of their children and grandchildren who were not on the list were made to leave. Not understanding why he had to leave, one younger grandson who drums and

The Modern Handgame 147

Bill Koomsa Jr. (Kiowa), *in white hat, center*, and Virgil Williamson (Crow), *in white hat, right*, scoring two points, Caddo County Fairgrounds, Anadarko, Oklahoma, Author's photo, 1997.

sings no longer wanted to go to handgames anymore. As his grandmother noted, "How can you get your children to learn your traditions with rules like this?" Exact rules, which vary from tournament to tournament, are usually announced prior to starting, often handed out in printed form. It is best to get a copy of the tournament rules and become familiar with them prior to play.

Individuals and organizations frequently ask Mary Beaver (Cheyenne) to run tournaments, and she tries to do so when asked. She has run handgame tournaments for the Red Earth Festival, the Jacobson House and American Indian Student Association at the University of Oklahoma, the Oklahoma City Pow Wow Club, individual tribes, tribal casinos, and others for many years. Indian students at the University of Oklahoma used to have both a fall and a spring handgame, with the spring event as a fund-raiser selling raffle tickets and running a concession stand to make money for the Indian student association. Mary keeps a set of materials with her to run a tournament or hold an educational demonstration anytime. Included are a set of score sticks and bones, rattles, copies of tournament rules, blank team rosters, and round-robin brackets for four to twenty-four teams that were drawn by Myron Beaver (Kiowa/Caddo). Mary laughed after adding, "I have another set of sticks at home

148   CHAPTER 3

that I carry because they're always saying, 'Can you come run this tournament for us?,' you know. I'm ready."[69] For drawing team numbers prior to play, she uses a small plastic bottle with miniature billiard balls inside designed to draw positions for billiard tournaments. Teams draw by shaking the bottle and rolling one of the numbered balls out. The matching of opponents, winner's and loser's brackets, and double elimination rules are the same. As she explained, "The loser has to defeat the winner twice to win it, and if the winner beats them in the final game once, then it's over. So, double elimination."[70]

PRIZES

Originally round-robin handgame tournaments contained only one prize, later changing to two or three prizes depending on the sponsors and the number of teams playing. As Jack Yellowhair explained, "In a round-robin you're supposed to play for the whole. Winner takes all is the way it's supposed to be. But we got to thinking the way some of them play so hard all day long, you know. Why don't we just have two prizes? So that's the way they made it, now to this day that's the way it is. Because then, if you win second, you don't win anything. Well, you played hard for nothing, you know."[71]

Prizes are set and advertised by the sponsors. Much of the prize money comes from the entry fees of the teams playing. If six teams enter with a $50 entry fee, the $300 of prize money will usually be divided into a $200 first prize and $100 second prize. Eight teams produce a $300 first prize and a $100 second prize, and so on. If not enough teams enter to match the advertised prize money, the sponsors must make up the difference. If enough teams enter a tournament, three or more prizes may be awarded. Over the last twenty-five years, the entry fee and prizes in round-robin tournaments has continued to increase. Gregory Haumpy recalled how the entry fee for round-robin tournaments with seven to ten teams had risen from $25 to $50 to $100 and even up to $300 and $400 at some larger tournaments, such as at the Red Earth Festival in Oklahoma City in the early 1990s.[72]

In addition to team entry fees, the tournament sponsor may add to the prize money. Most often this is done through raffle and concession income or donations. Team leaders are sometimes called together to decide how many prizes will be given. Individual and team bets can still be made between the sides but are not as common when playing for the larger tournament pots.

SPONSORED TOURNAMENTS

Sponsored tournaments started in the 1970s and differ from round-robin tournaments in that the sponsors usually offer three to five prizes, larger prizes, provide all prize money and any trophies or other awards, and provide a meal for the event. These tournaments cost more to hold than a round-robin since the sponsors must fund the entire event. The annual Jacobsen House tournament in Norman, Oklahoma, and the Oklahoma State Handgame Tournament are examples of this. Except for a few large events, sponsored tournaments have largely been replaced by round-robins. Jack Yellowhair said, "And then they stopped the [sponsored] tournaments. Now hardly anyone has a tournament. It's always a round-robin." When I asked Mr. Yellowhair what caused this change, he replied, "People like to gamble. They'd rather play for money, and then, see, if you go for a free-for-all you don't hardly get too many people there. They don't go for that no more, you know. Just certain ones that like to play—that really, really likes to play handgame—go for free-for-all."[73] The style of betting is a major factor behind the change, reflecting an increased emphasis placed on rules, betting money rather than goods, and winning prize money.

The Oklahoma State Handgame Tournament

Each year Oklahoma has a state tournament in May. Several Kiowa reported that it was started by Bill Koomsa Sr. His son Bill Koomsa Jr. recalled, "We have what we call a state tournament. That's usually one of our last handgames of the season. My dad kinda started that also. . . . We sponsored it, just himself a few years, and then he finally went to making it a rotating [event]. . . . Usually the tournament is held after we get back from Montana. We go up there the end of April, first of May, and when we get back, maybe the second week in May, then we'll have our state tournament."[74]

Most players I interviewed stated that the Oklahoma State Handgame Tournament began in the late 1970s. Ace Yellowhair, born in 1967, recalled, "When I was a kid there was hardly ever . . . a tournament. . . . They didn't have too many of those until the state tournament start coming out, and then that's when they changed and put those, made those sticks, nineteen and then that one in the middle." Most games were free-for-alls, in which people simply showed up and formed two sides, or match games. Yellowhair also recalled handgames during his youth at places named Shady Front, the Astrodome, and Billy Goat Hill that still practiced the old style of play with four sticks in the middle. "That's the way they played back up here at my old home place there, Shady Front . . . even back down at the Astrodome, and down there, like I mentioned Billy Goat Hill, there's that style, you know, four. . . . Back then that was the only way they played."[75] This suggests the older style of play continued into the 1970s. Some individuals state that the new style of play, with sticks on a wooden rack, came in or at least increased with the start of the Oklahoma State Tournament in the late 1970s or early 1980s. This correlates with Koomsa Sr. running the state tournament for several years prior to passing in 1990.

Although a few teams from northeastern Oklahoma have occasionally played in the Oklahoma State Tournament, most are from southern Plains tribes. One individual recalled going to the state tournament several years when it was first held at Oklahoma City. Later the Carnegie Eagles hosted the annual state tournament for several years at Carnegie and surrounding locales in Oklahoma. Later, each year's winner became responsible for hosting the next year's tournament. The winner will usually hold one or more benefit handgames through the fall and winter to raise funds to sponsor next year's tournament in May. The winner can hold the next state tournament wherever they like, but it is usually held somewhere in their tribe's home community. Prizes often include trophies and cash for the best-dressed team, best guesser, best hider, and a king and queen.

In western Oklahoma handgames the major differences between the state and weekly tournaments are the number of teams playing, the amount of prize money, and special awards. A larger pot is played for, and there are more prizes, such as team trophies, individual prizes (for best hider, best guesser, and best singer), best-dressed team, and best banner. The best hider is usually awarded to the player who scores the most consecutive sticks in the final game, male or female. Best guesser is given to the individual who makes the most consecutive guesses in a row without missing any hiders. The best medicine award is rarely included unless the sponsor has special funds to sponsor it. This involves noting who is most effective in handing out the hiding implements as reflected in points scored. In Oklahoma handgames, a team can change a medicine man in a game if he or she is not performing well—if one's team is not scoring points. In some past tournaments an award for "best medicine" was given for the most unique and decorated item created by a team and brought to the tournament, an item that they referred to as their medicine. The best-dressed award is usually only given during the state tournament or occasionally by a team that sponsors the award. In such cases, the dress code, either T-shirts or colored dress shirts, is announced beforehand, and the award is chosen for the team with the most artistic or striking shirt.[76] One year that I played with the Red Thunder team in the Oklahoma State Tournament we had matching iridescent-blue dress shirts made to wear in the tournament.

State tournament rules fluctuate, depending on who is sponsoring the event and what rules they choose. To eliminate confusion and conflict, some individuals formally write up their set of rules when they run a tournament and hand out copies beforehand. People add and delete rules from year to year as desired. The following are the 2018 Oklahoma State Handgame Tournament rules sponsored by Dozen Excuses.

2018 OKLAHOMA STATE HANDGAME
TOURNAMENT RULES

SCHEDULE
9:30 a.m. RESIGTRATION
11:45 a.m. DRAWING TIME
12:00 (noon) LUNCH

ROSTER
1. Sponsors will check rosters.
2. Rosters must be handed in prior to first game.
3. Player is only allowed to be on one roster.
4. There will be no add-ons once roster is turned in.
5. Any team allowing a non-roster player to play will forfeit the game.

AGE LIMIT
18 years and above.

SCORING
All initial games will be played with 18 sticks with a winning center stick. All loser bracket games will be played with 14 sticks and a winning center stick.

PLAYER RULES
1. Each team is required to submit a roster. (Individuals can only be on one roster and no add-ons).
2. Any players thought to be under the influence of alcohol or drugs will not be allowed to participate and will be escorted from the premises.
3. If teams do not have singers, they are eligible to recruit two singers to sing only.
4. Teams are responsible for selecting proper judges. Judges must stay involved and pay attention to all games. Team selected judges should be knowledgeable in all phase of tournament play.
5. Both team selected judges will be responsible for making fair play decisions.
6. Tournament sponsors will make and have final decisions if needed.
7. No disorderly conduct, no foul language is acceptable and can result in disqualification.

GUESSING RULES

1. Guesser will have one minute to make guesses.
2. Guesser must notify judges if selecting a new guesser.
3. Must say "HO" loud enough for judges to hear.
4. Must stand in front to make a guess.
5. Must hold guess for judges to see.
6. NO FORK < NO FINGER < TRICK GUESSING OR COIN GUESSING [flipping a coin to guess].
7. Hand gestures are allowed as long as guesser says "HO" to true guess.
8. Judges have the final say, with the sponsors breaking a split decision if needed.

GUESSES

A. Center Guess—Palm vertical [in] direction of players with thumb down.
B. Outside Guess—Palm horizontal [in] direction of players with thumb outward and fingers outward.
C. Left Guess—Thumb extended to left of players with palm closed.
D. Right Guess—Thumb extended to right of players with palm closed.

HIDING RULES

1. Hiders will have thirty seconds to hide bones.
2. Once hider comes up they cannot go back down.
3. Judges must notify of new guesser, and then hider can go back down and re-hide.
4. Hiders must open both hands for judges to see.
5. No one handed hiding. Unless physically handicapped.
6. Hands must be visible, chest high so judges can see. Judges will determine if hider is incapable of doing so.

MEDICINE MAN/WOMAN

Have one minute to pass out bones.

JUDGES

1. Must know Oklahoma Handgame Rules.
2. Captain of each team is the only person who can make a protest to the judges for a ruling.
3. Judges are responsible for keeping time (time will be enforced).

BONES TO BE PROVIDED BY SPONSORS ONLY

TEAM

The use of alcohol or any other disorderly conduct will not be tolerated. Team captains will be responsible for the conduct of their team members. No foul language (including trash talk) will be tolerated. Parents must keep children out of the playing area, this is a distraction to players and may impair players from proper decision making.

Decisions of any protest will be directed to the judges with coordinator having final ruling. Failure to abide by any rules can cost your team the tournament. Event coordinator has final say to ALL decisions pertaining to the tournament.

The Dozen Excuses Handgame Team, 2017 Champions, would like to thank all teams who came to participate in the 2018 Handgame Tournament. *Good luck to all teams!!!!*[77]

BENEFIT HANDGAMES

Funds raised at benefit handgames are usually raised to help defray the costs of a later handgame tournament. A benefit handgame resembles a regular game except for more raffles held throughout the event to raise funds for a particular event or cause. For example, the Comanche Nation Fair Board held a Free-For-All Benefit handgame to raise money for the Comanche Nation Fair that coming Labor Day weekend. As with raffles noted earlier, raffle items include blankets, grocery baskets, donated amounts of money, donated items, 50-50 raffle tickets, and tickets for other fund-raising events. I once saw two teddy bears raffled at a handgame near Valentine's Day.

The costs of putting on the Oklahoma State Hand Game Tournament require the host to sponsor one or more benefit handgames. Travel to a distant handgame, like the annual trip to Montana to play in the Crow Senior Tournament, will usually require a benefit to defray a team's costs and entry fee. Typically the entry fees are discussed by the team leaders prior to starting. The same procedures found at benefit Gourd Dances or powwows are used.

One year I attended a benefit powwow at the Apache Fair Building to raise money for the Kiowa team to travel to the annual Crow tournament in Crow Agency, Montana. The program included an afternoon Gourd Dance and an evening War Dance, with a Straight Dance competition. Grocery baskets, serapes, shawls, beaded bracelets, pillows, and a small painted model tipi were raffled. Several of the better guessers, including Carl Atauvich, Willie Bearshield, Eddie Longhat, Ken Chasenah, and Del Wermy, were brought forward at different times and honored with a song. Two blanket dances were also held to draw donations. The money donated in front of them went toward the trip. That evening a dance contest for small boys and a Straight Dance contest for adult men was held. While a goal of $2,000 was set, $874 was raised. Bill Koomsa Jr., who served as head singer of the event and would lead the team to Montana, remarked that this was all right, because the team entry fee was $500 and the Crow always took up funds to help the southern players with their travel costs, just as the Kiowa and other tribes do when the Crow visit each November.[78]

Several regular teams did not attend, choosing to participate in a handgame in nearby Anadarko. One of the benefit sponsors shook his head and remarked, "Well, you know how we are, we can't get along on anything." The sponsor noted that even though all could not pull together to support the benefit, it turned out pretty well.[79] After arriving at Crow Agency few days later, our team of twenty-two Oklahoma players and eight Crow from Black Lodge District, including Ed Little Light, were seated and preparing to play our first game, when the Crow judges announced that our entry fee had not been paid. Everyone looked at the individual entrusted with the entry fee who had arrived earlier than the rest of us. We had noticed his truck parked at the Crow casino the evening before when we entered town. He maintained that he had paid the entry fee to the Crow; they solemnly maintained that he had not. After several awkward exchanges and silence, the team had to pool another $500 before the game could begin. It definitely affected us—we were flat and quickly lost the first game.[80]

Other forms of fund-raising may also be used to raise money toward playing in a handgame tournament. One elder couple raised around $700 by holding four bingo games, enabling them to participate in the Red Earth Tournament one year. The money was used toward the $400 entry fee and their family's hotel rooms.[81]

TEAM SIZE

Although large team size can be beneficial in terms of changing hiders and guessers and gaining spirit, momentum, and crowd support, teams do not have to be large. Technically, as long as there are two players to hide, one or both may hide while they drum and sing or others may drum for them. Usually, a team will have four or more members, and some tournaments may require a minimum number. I have heard players comment that they "need support,"

The Modern Handgame   155

especially in singing. Carl Atauvich described the importance of having many singers: "Yeah, that's got a lot to do with how you feel in hiding your bones, is the singing. If you got some good singers, man, they can liven you up pretty good where you could do some pretty good hiding. I know there's certain songs that certain hiders like to have sung when they're hiding, and it really puts them in a pretty good mood to really be able to hide the bones pretty good."[82]

Team size does not always determine the outcome of a game or tournament. Over the years I have seen teams of four to six and teams with many times that number win and lose. However, a bigger team is commonly perceived as having advantage in providing more choices in hiding and guessing, being harder to memorize, and being harder to predict. As Carl Atauvich described,

> You have more to choose from in your hiding, and a lot of times some hiders are flat, they can't get out. So you have to, if you're a medicine man, the medicine man's the one that the team captain chooses to give out the bones. That's called the medicine man, he looks for the hiders that can really win some of those sticks. If you get more players, then you got more choices, and there are some of them that are flat and some of them that can hide pretty good. And then the next time it's just the opposite. The players that were flat will be getting down, and the others are, you know, cold. That's the way we were this weekend. We were all flat. One or two of us were getting out, and that was it. But, boy, sometimes my bunch can . . . every one of them get out, every one of them.[83]

TYPES OF BETTING

Whereas a wide array of items were traditionally bet in handgames, Jack Yellowhair Sr. noted the change: "Now days it's different, nothing but money."[84] While the earlier betting of goods involved items that were highly varied and usually distinct (for example a pair of earrings bet against a bracelet), money is more homogenous and anonymous. Individuals also report that people are not able to remember who bet what today. To prevent disputes and keep the names and wagers straight, they are written down. Today there are three kinds of bets in Oklahoma handgames; regular bets (often called table bets), individual bets, and tournament entry fees.

Regular Betting or Table Bets

Table bets are bets taken before a match or free-for-all game begins. Prior to the first game an announcement is made that betting is now open, with someone "taking up" on each side, usually north and south. Individuals, each with a sheet of paper, sit on each side of the scorer's table or at tables on each side of the room and record the name of each bettor and their bet.

Handgame score rack with bets, Carnegie, Oklahoma. Author's photo, ca. 2019.

Anyone can place a bet on either side, whether they are playing or not and regardless of age. The money is then counted, recorded, and kept by this individual. After bets have been taken for a while, the two sides will compare the amounts placed. Usually, the higher side stops taking bets, and as soon as the other side matches their amount the game begins. To facilitate the start of the game, someone may place money on the lower side to equal the two sides, or one or more players may withdraw their bets from the high side to bring the two sides to equal amounts. When both sides are closed, the lists and money are brought together and kept at the head table. The bets for the first game of a match can be set by the sponsor or may be cut off to match at any given point. This practice speeds up the play by eliminating the seesawing in betting before one side sets a limit and waits for the other side to match it.

When the game ends the winners report to the head table to collect their winnings. With no odds in betting, one either doubles one's bet or loses it. Winners double the amount they wagered; losers win nothing. The losing side of the previous game is allowed to set the amount bet on the following game as a sort of courtesy, to not deplete their remaining funds, and to ensure the next game can continue. This process continues for each game. Table bets can

The Modern Handgame 157

vary tremendously, ranging from one dollar to one hundred dollars per person. Most individual table bets I have seen, however, fall into the two-dollar to twenty-dollar range. Collectively, table bets vary tremendously depending on the type of handgame being played, the size of the crowd, how many games have been played, and the remaining cash participants have. Collective bets may range from as low as twenty dollars per side in a small free-for-all game to over three hundred dollars per side during the annual Crow visit, to two thousand to three thousand dollars during games such as I witnessed at the Senior Handgame Tournament in Crow Agency, Montana. In Oklahoma free-for-alls, more than three hundred dollars bet collectively is considered a lot of money.

Individual or Floor Bets

Bets between two individuals are sometimes made, especially after a game begins. Individual bets can occur at any time during a game if someone matches it before the end of the game. This provides individuals who come in after the table bets have closed and a game has started to place a bet. Usually these are between men on the front benches but can be from anyone. An individual will take the amount they wish to bet, walk to the front of the playing bench on their side, and either hold the money up or simply throw it out in the middle to be matched by someone. These bets are almost always matched, placed together on the center line on the floor of the playing area, and remain there until the end of the game when the winners claim their winnings.

Most individual bets I have seen have been relatively small, ranging from one to twenty dollars. Where some games may have three or four floor bets, other games have none. Because most betting occurs prior to each game's beginning, floor bets are usually fewer and smaller than table bets. Although most of these bets are small amounts of money, virtually any items can be bet and sometimes include cigarette lighters, pocketknives, and even hand drums.

Sometimes, as the score sways during a game, an individual will reach out with his foot and pull the money slightly towards his side, taunting and jeering his opponent as they regain the offense and vice versa. The reciprocal shifts in these acts are one of the most entertaining parts of the game as players tease one another. Alfred Chalepah Sr., who played handgame a lot from the 1920s into the 1950s, described the spirit associated with intense play and the need to not let the taunting of the other side distract you

> Well, it's according to the rhythm. You know, just like anything. You've got something going, you speed up, and you just put in more pep and some morale and more aggression. You put a lot of spirit in that, you know. It's just like a big game . . . morale [is involved]—and you have to like it. These people enjoy it. You know, that's kind of a spirit. That's the way I

158 CHAPTER 3

look at it, you know . . . Morale. You get that feeling, you know, and it's kind of you're winning something, you know. It makes you try that much harder, you know, just like a ballgame. And you get that, sometimes it goes with it. Sometimes you hide those bones, and that's built up here [points inside his head]; sometimes it goes with it. Because your opponent has the same chance. But both of them has the same kind of feeling, that music, you know, and it goes. You've got to have a good sense of humor that goes along with it. They koo-hoo-raugh you [ridicule you]. They try to disturb you. . . . Well, it was like that way back there, you know. When a lot of that good and fun comes out, the spirit. They make all kinds of monkeyshine to the guesser, you know. Some of that magic, magic signs [makes hand motions]. As long as it is respectable, then you've got to have a good sense of humor in spirited competition.[85]

Although smaller cash bets are almost always matched, some bets are not. During one game between the Oklahoma tribes and the Crow in 1997, Carl Atauvich (Comanche) who was guessing for the Oklahoma side, took off his watch and laid it on the floor as a bet in front of Ed Little Light on the Crow side. Mr. Little Light did not accept the bet, but the Crow went on a sixteen-point run in the second round of hiding, won the game, and would have won the watch.[86]

The antics and humor accompanying play add to the fun and spirit associated with handgames. During one game Jack Yellowhair tossed a folded pocketknife onto the floor as a challenge and a bet to someone on the other side. A man on the other side matched his bet. When the other side won, he claimed Jack's pocketknife from the floor—only to discover that all of the blades in it were broken. As Yellowhair recalled, "They didn't know it was broken up or damaged like that . . . he won, and he got my knife [begins laughing], and he couldn't find any blades [more laughter]. . . . We try to have a little fun in between, you know and it's just joking like to make everything just fine."[87]

Ideally, individuals are told not to bet more than they can afford to lose and heed this caution. Some people bet large amounts and, after losing, blame the guesser of their side. An elder Kiowa man stated that this was not appropriate since the game is a team sport and depends on both the hiders and guessers. During round-robin tournaments table bets are not taken, although two individuals may bet privately during any game.

Tournament Entry Fees

In tournaments a team entry fee is collected prior to the start of play and serves as a team wager. This can range from fifty dollars to several hundred per team depending on the size of the tournament. Ideally, the entry fee is pooled equally from the number of individuals on a team; the amount decreases, the larger the team. If a team places high enough to win a prize,

The Modern Handgame   159

usually first and second in a small tournament, the prize money is distributed equally between the team members. Of course, the larger the team, the smaller the winnings per person when divided (and the smaller the team, the larger the individual winnings).

OFFICIALS

In the old style of play, teams were smaller and played in a tipi. With everyone sitting on the floor and with hiding limited to certain individuals, all could see and follow the game. Some forms had a referee who sat by the four neutral sticks on the west side. Today, with larger teams and venues, you cannot always see both hiders, and even the hiders cannot always see one another. Hiders may be chosen from different rows or sides of a team, or from the crowd in a free-for-all, and cannot always be seen from a seated or standing position. Thus, referees became necessary to check the hiders. Today there are three game officials, two referees and a scorekeeper.

The two referees stand in the middle of the floor and provide hand signals, which direct and communicate the progress of the game. The two referees are responsible for signaling when hiders are ready, when guessers may guess, checking both hands of each hider after they are guessed, reporting the results of each guess, and announcing the status of the remaining hiders and from time to time the score of the game. When a hider is hiding, the referees will hold an arm out with the hand toward the defense in a "wait" gesture. When the hiders are ready, the referees make a sweeping motion of one or both extended hands toward the offense, inferring "go ahead" to the guesser. Following a guess, the referees signal the guess with one hand (inside, outside, right, or left), check the hider's hands, then signal the number of points scored with the other hand held high: one with an index finger, two with an index and middle fingers. Some referees call out the guess and points scored verbally while simultaneously signaling them. A correct guess is usually signaled with a closed fist made in a downward motion from around chest high to the waist (guessers also commonly use this motion after studying a hider and before signaling their guess to indicate they have figured out where the hider has the marked bone, thus signaling their confidence prior to guessing). If one hider is guessed correctly and one missed, an index finger will be extended to indicate the point, followed by a fist to signal that the other hider was guessed. If the remaining hider is missed on the second guess, making the first hide active again, the single point is signaled, followed by a two-armed upward sweeping motion with open hands toward the offense, to signal that two hiders are now active.

Referees are usually experienced players who have been playing for at least a few years. In tournaments, the two teams playing are each allowed to ask

Edward Nevaquaya (Comanche) guessing Camp 7, Handgame tournament, Comanche Nation Fair. Author's photo, ca. 1993.

an individual who is not a member of their team to serve as a referee for their game. Some individuals are frequently asked to serve as a referee, and some have stated that they enjoy serving in this capacity. Many people serve as judges, which, depending on who is available, changes from one game to the next. Referees can place bets on games they are officiating but must function in a neutral manner in their position.

One or more scorekeepers sit at the head table behind the scoring rack and are responsible for watching the referee's hand signals and removing the appropriate number of counters as points are scored. Scorekeepers may be from the tournament sponsors or experienced players asked to serve in this position. Some rotation of scorekeepers may occur if they are playing on a team in the tournament.

MASTER OF CEREMONIES

Most handgames today have an announcer or master of ceremonies sitting beside the scorekeeper. Using a public address system, they welcome everyone and keep everyone informed on the progress of the game. According to one Kiowa elder, in the past this was not necessary as everyone understood the game and could follow along. The use of announcers is reported to have begun in the early 1980s. In some instances, a single individual serves as scorekeeper and master of ceremonies. The noise is often so loud that you cannot hear the announcers, and thus the easiest way to follow the play is to watch the referees' signals or the response of the teams, as the cheering, taunting, shaking of rattles, and drumming of the hider's side will briefly accelerate if they score a point, while the cheering and taunting of the guesser's side will accelerate if they have just correctly guessed their opponent. A good MC is much like a sports announcer, being familiar with the players' names and calling the action of hiding, guessing, and scoring in play-by-play fashion.

DISPUTES

As in any sport, errors by players, referees, or the scorekeeper occasionally occur, and in almost every instance these provide a moment of drama and tension until resolved. One of the most common errors, though occurring only occasionally, is the dropping of one or more bones during play. In the past this commonly resulted in the guessing team quickly calling the error to attention and demanding a stick. By the time I started playing, this rule no longer seemed to be enforced. Collier Oyebi (Kiowa) often jumped to his feet when this occurred and declared, "Stick! Stick!," but I never saw the point awarded, and play simply continued.

Because so many people are watching, any error by the referees or the scorekeeper is usually quickly noted, whether accidental or intentional. As one elder explained, "Scorekeepers can also cheat. You may score two sticks, but they only take one off. You have to watch them closely every score. When two points are scored and only one is taken out, it causes a big argument."

A referee may miss a call or assume that the other referee made the call. In one game the referees missed the second part of a double hide (two hiders). The first guesser was declared out, but the opposing team protested when the second hider began to hide again. The game quickly stopped, and the scorekeeper was asked which way the second hider had been called. Unsure himself, he asked the two referees, who also seemed unsure. Finally, a stick was awarded to the team on offense, and they were permitted to continue hiding. This scenario was the most common dispute that I have witnessed. Occasionally the scorekeeper may start to take sticks off the wrong side of the scoring rack, resulting in an immediate correction by the players and referees and often a good deal of teasing.

HIDING IMPLEMENTS

Today southern plains tribes generally use two four-inch or four-and-a-half-inch hair pipes (real bone or plastic) that are commonly used on breastplates, necklaces, and other items of dance regalia. According to Gregory Haumpy,

162 CHAPTER 3

large bones came in with the new style of play in the late 1950s and early 1960s. "You can't switch those things. Now they make you open both hands out."[88] While individuals with large hands can hide the bones in their closed hands, the ends of the bones can usually be seen in the closed fists of individuals with smaller hands. In each set of bones, one is painted with black paint or marked with electrician's tape in the middle, while the other is unmarked. In southern plains handgames the marked bone is still the one sought in guessing. Both bones must be shown after each hide to ensure no cheating is occurring, such as using two unmarked bones. Referees must check to make sure hiders open both hands.

ALTERNATE FORMS OF GUESSING

As the handgame has evolved, several changes have emerged. One area in which changes have developed involves variations to the four guessing signs. For a right side guess, the guesser may point with his index finger to the right of the two hiders. For a left side guess, a guesser may point with his index finger to the left of the two hiders or may point both the right index and middle finger toward the hider's right. For an outside guess, a guesser may use both hands and point outward with his two thumbs (Isaacs 1969).

Tongue Pointing

One style that developed is known as tongue pointing, where the guesser points with his tongue at different angles out of his mouth to signal their guess. This style of guessing can be used in free-for-alls or open games but not in tournaments. Before doing so, the guesser is required to tell the people that they are going to use this form. This form of guessing is reported by some to override hand guesses. The signals include pointing out of the left side of your mouth (to your left), out of the right side of your mouth (to your right), straight out in a forward motion with tongue narrowed to the center for an inside guess, and straight out and flat to signal an outside guess. While some people are fond of this style of guessing, many are not and try to prevent its use. Some players report that some guessers, on missing a guess with a hand signal, have tried to stick their tongue out at the last moment to override the hand motion. Those reporting this interpreted it as an attempt to cheat. This form of guessing was popular among men for a number of years.[89]

According to Alfred Chalepah Sr., this style dates to the early 1920s. He also reported that it originated among the Apache, however I have not been able to verify this. Chalepah recalled seeing this style of guessing used at handgames between the Cache Creek and Washita Apache communities at the Red Bone Dance Ground southwest of Fort Cobb, Oklahoma. According to him, only a couple of the older handgame leaders used this style.[90] Marie Yokesuite Haumpy stated that Edgar Monetatchi (Comanche) often used this. When he missed, Comanche women would tell him, "We're gonna cut your tongue off."[91] This style was sometimes still used by Eddie Longhat (Delaware) in the 1990s.

Two-Finger Guess

Another style of guessing is the two-finger guess or "Lazy V" guess. This style originated in Montana and was reportedly introduced in the KCA area by Jasper Sankadota (Kiowa). In this style, the guessing sign, made with the index and middle fingers of one or both hands, indicates the opposite of what is signaled. Two fingers pointed to the right signals a left guess, and two fingers pointed to the left a right guess. Two fingers pointing forward or inward (vertically) signals an outside guess, while both hands with two fingers pointing to the outside (horizontally) signals an inside guess.[92] For those unfamiliar with this form it can be confusing, and one night I saw a controversy arise over its use. This form was often used by Eddie Longhat (Delaware) in the late 1990s. This style of guessing is allowed in free-for-alls but not in round-robin tournaments. One night during a round-robin a member on our team made this style of guess and was penalized a point.

Coin Guessing

Eddie Longhat had another unique guessing style for a single hider that he often used. When guessing two hiders and getting one of them correctly, he would take an item out of his pocket and rotate it in his hands as if he were hiding the bones. When he was ready to guess the remaining hider, he opened his hands with the object in the hand on the side he wished to guess. He most often used a dollar coin while making this type of guess. This style enhanced the antics of the play, and people seemed to enjoy it.[93]

Score Keeping and Scoring Racks

In the modern Oklahoma form of play, scoring is kept by removing sticks from a wooden scoring rack at a head table. A table in the center of one end of the playing area where the two teams are seated is used, allowing the counter sticks to be easily seen by all. A scorekeeper and an announcer or master of ceremonies usually sit at the score table. They watch the two referees in the middle of the floor who signal the guesses and when points are scored, then remove the number of sticks signaled from the rack, hold them up for all to see, and put them onto the side of the table. Like sports announcers, some MCs provide play-by-play commentary, announcing the names of the hiders, guesser, and medicine men for each team, as well as the number of hiders being guessed, guesses and their results, and the current score (number of remaining sticks needed to win for both sides). While these positions were earlier held by men, today men and women serve in this position. In free-for-alls, even the MC or the scorekeeper can be asked to hide by either team.

These positions are usually staffed by the host group, but in a tournament they may just as commonly be rotated to various individuals whose teams are not currently playing. Each team has a wooden scoring rack with holes drilled to insert the scoring sticks usually made from wooden dowels. The scoring rack and sticks are painted, often in a two-tone design with half of each stick one color and the other half another color. The sticks are then placed in the rack with one color upright on one side and the opposite color upright on the other. The center stick extends higher than the other sticks in the rack and may be made from a larger-diameter dowel. These may be more elaborately decorated and usually contain colored plumes, horsehair, or beadwork at the top. At the end of each rack are four holes to hold the four hiding bones for each side.

Because the hiding sticks are in a two parallel lines, and due to the elongated linear seating arrangement of the game and the depth of the seating on each side, one often cannot determine the score. Some tournament hosts use a large spiral-bound score pad with bold black numbers that hangs over the front of the scorer's table to show the score. The wooden sticks are generally removed from the rack before the numbers are adjusted. The score is frequently read aloud over the public-address system by the announcer—such as, "The south side needs two sticks, the north side needs seven," and so on. The current score is also frequently signaled by the judges and members of the teams with the appropriate number of fingers.

The only concern for scoring is during a game. Unlike some cultures who keep statistics on many sports, Indian people are not concerned with keeping detailed tabulations of play, scoring, wins and losses, and averages. To do so would be extremely taxing and would defeat the entire purpose of the game—to have fun. Everyone knows who the good hiders and guessers are, and who is currently hot (effective) and who is not. The primary concern is in choosing who will best benefit the team effort. All efforts are ideally team-oriented because when the team wins, everyone on it wins. The only exception to this occurs in tournaments with awards for high-point man, high-point woman, and best guesser, usually only for the final game when brief tallies are

The Modern Handgame   165

kept to determine the winners in these categories. In these instances, only the individual's name and number of points is kept. Once a game is over, the winning side is announced: "The south wins game three." There is no reading of a final score as in baseball (noting how many sticks the losers had remaining). To do so would be rude, poor sportsmanship, and not conducive with Native concepts of hospitality and modesty. Everyone already knows who won and approximately what the score was. The score is not recorded in any fashion, and the sticks are immediately returned to the stick holder for the start of the next game.

However, there are advantages that keeping score holds in terms of explaining the progress of games, especially for someone unfamiliar with the handgame. During my fieldwork I devised a method to record the scoring in handgames for ethnographic analysis. Table 3 illustrates an evening of five games between the Oklahoma players (South) and the Crows (North) on Friday, November 14, 1997. The South won four of five games. Each game was nineteen points. Because play begins with two hiders and both hiders must be guessed within two consecutive guesses to shift the offense, scoring may occur as 0; as 1, 1, 1, or 2; as 2, 2; 2, 2, 1, 1, 2; as 2, 1, 1, 1 or 2; and so on. Scoring cannot occur as simply 1 or 2 because there would only be a single hider left on the second guess.

That evening's play was typical in several aspects of handgames in general, in that there were both close games with multiple ties and several lead changes (games 2 and 4), complete blowouts (game 3), and games with wins of medium margins (games 1, 2, and 5). As with other sports, large scoring drives may occur more than once in a single game (game 2), followed by periods of little scoring (games 4, 5). The unpredictable nature of the game adds to its constant, exciting qualities.

Medicine Men

Traditionally one or sometimes two male leaders served as guessers and handed out the hiding objects to players. Today in larger games a designated person is chosen to hand out the hiding objects to whomever they wish to hide. Both men and women serve in this role, a position known as "medicine man," a term said to have come from the Crow. After handing out the hiding objects, the medicine man may hold up a hand until the hider is ready and then signal with a wave for the opposing guesser to guess. If the hider is successful, they continue hiding. When one hider is guessed correctly, the medicine man may take the bones away, or the hider may voluntarily give them back. In some instances, a missed hider is allowed to keep the bones and, if the second hider is missed, hide again. During actual play the medicine man picks only the

166 CHAPTER 3

Table 3: Scoring Notation of Sample Games

Game 1		
	South	North
1.	1, 1, 1	1, 1, 1, 1
2.	0	2, 1
3.	2, 2, 1	2
4.	1, 1, 2	1, 1, 1 (tie)
5.	1, 1	1, 1, 1
6.	2, 1, 1, 1	
Game 2		
	South	North
1.	2, 2, 2, 1	1, 1, 2
2.	0	1, 1, 1 (tie)
3.	0	1
4.	1, 1	1 (tie)
5.	1, 1, 1	1, 1, 2
6.	2, 1, 1, 2, 1	
Game 3		
	South	North
1.	0	0
2.	2, 2, 1	1
3.	1, 1, 2, 1, 1, 1, 1	0
4.	1, 1, 1, 1, 1, 1	

The Modern Handgame

Table 3: Scoring Notation of Sample Games continued

	Game 4	
	South	North
1.	1, 1, 1	0
2.	2, 1	1, 1, 1, 1, 2, 1, 1
3.	1, 1, 1, 1, 2, 1, 1	2, 1, 1
4.	1	2, 1 (tie)
5.	1	
6.	0	1 (tie)
7.	1, 1	0
8.	0	2 (tie), 1
	Game 5	
	South	North
1.	1	0
2.	1	1, 1 (tie)
3.	1, 1, 2, 1, 1	1, 1, 2
4.	1, 1, 1	0
5.	1	2, 2
6.	0	1
7.	1	2
8.	0	1, 1, 2
9.	1	1, 1

CHAPTER 3

hiders; guessers are chosen by the captain or the team by consensus and can pass the position on to another guesser whenever desired.

Guessers

Teams or their captains may choose a set number of guessers for a game, from which the position of guessing is rotated when one individual passes the role of guesser to another. Some teams may have most of their guessing done by one or a few individuals who are noted as good guessers. As with hiding, a guesser performing successfully is allowed to continue. In other situations, a team may allow the guesser to pass it to anyone they desire. When a team is not having any success guessing, they sometimes pass the position to someone else that may not normally be a guesser, to bring in a fresh guesser.

Today both men and women frequently serve as guessers. Among the Kiowa, traditional gender roles are still strongly held in some areas, especially positions of leadership. One elder Kiowa man felt that it was all right for women to hide but that only men should hand out the bones and serve as guessers, citing the more conservative role of women in the northern plains, sitting in the back rows at games, eating after the men, et cetera.

In free-for-alls and many round-robin tournaments there is no age restriction, allowing entire families to play. Many elder handgame players have children and grandchildren on their team. I have seen players as young as four and five years old and elders into their early nineties chosen to hide and guess. The only games I have seen with age restrictions for playing are those on the grounds of tribal casinos, for individuals eighteen or older.

Some people are known as being a good hider or good guesser and will be chosen more frequently than others. Several Kiowa elders reported Bertha Domebo (Sànémà or Snake [Woman]) as an especially good hider, and she was reported to have had a form of snake medicine.[94] Mary Beaver (Cheyenne) remembered a Kiowa man who intimidated some by his prowess in guessing.

> Way back I remember we had a person like that. We would go down to, it was called the Astrodome at that time. I was young and . . . I would go with my dad and my mom, and every time this certain guy would come through that door, I just knew, because it just seemed like he just would find everybody. He was just like, 'I got you. I don't even have to look at you,' you know, 'I know where you're at.' So it was just like, 'Oh God, you know, so and so is here' [laughs]. There are stories like that because there are some people like that that are actually really sharp at handgame.[95]

Often when a team gets in trouble, getting behind several points, near the end of the game, or have repeatedly missed guessing the opposing side several times, they turn to their older, more experienced players. Sometimes they can

The Modern Handgame

169

stop the other side; sometimes they cannot. The efficacy of individual players, and sometimes entire teams, can ebb and flow from one game or tournament to the next.

Hiding Strategy and Variations

From my experience playing in handgames, hiding is a largely individual strategy—trying to outthink the guesser. As hiders are not supposed to consult with one another, there is rarely an opportunity to consult with other hiders, and one hider may not know who the other hider is until after the bones are handed out. Hiders may end up beside one another, on opposite ends of the same row, on different rows, or include members of the crowd or scorekeepers during free-for-alls.

An almost unlimited number of styles of hiding exist in the contemporary KCA handgame. Individuals may hide the bones behind their back, underneath one of their legs, under a blanket, coat, or hat, behind the back of a player in front of or beside them, or behind a drum held up by another individual. Adult male hiders often hold their hands together to mix the bones in full view of the opposition before separating them, a style said to have come from the Crow. Women often hide the bones behind an object, another player, or under an item of clothing or blanket.

Once an individual comes forward with a hide, there is no end to the range of hand, wrist, arm, and body motions employed. The variety and artistry to the kinesics used during play are part of the spectacle and a highlight of handgames. Usually each person has a certain style or number of styles used in hiding. Individuals may raise and hold their arms outward at about shoulder level and then hold them in place as they sway and rock their body. Some extend their index fingers in this style, resembling a large bird with its wings spread wide. Others retain this relatively still posture or periodically contract and extend their arms toward their chest and then back out again. Alternating one closed hand in front of the other is the sign language sign for handgame. Many produce rapid gyrations, crossing their arms back and forth in front of their chest, in figure eight directions, at angles or simply in-and-out motions from their chest. Some men simply place their closed fists on their thighs, not moving them, or may hold them just above their thighs and make a slight back and forth motion that resembles running. Most players keep their closed fists at chest-to-shoulder level. Some women simply hold up the back of their hands toward the guesser with the bones exposed toward themselves.

Hiding movements follow the rhythm of the song and add an especially theatrical quality to the game. While the hiders are hiding and making their hand motions, teammates often make shaking hand motions or "medicine"

170   CHAPTER 3

motions, shake their rattles, raise their drums, wave their hands, or raise coats and hats in front of their own hiders to inhibit the guesser's concentration. Some singers will stop drumming and rub their drum beater across their drum at the opposing guesser before they make their guess. Because hiders rarely have the same hiding motion, this adds to the spectacle of hiding and to the variation and confusion for the guesser.

In western Oklahoma, hiders are not required to look at the guesser, producing highly varied responses. Some individuals, from small children to adult men and women, look the guesser directly in their eyes, unflinching, flaunting their hiding and body motions, and taunting and daring the guesser to guess them correctly. Others lower their head, often closing their eyes to not give anything away. Some players have stated that when they first began hiding, they were very intimidated by the hider's medicine motions and direct stares and that it took time before they could look at them and stare them down without giving themselves away. Some individuals who hide this way and with vigorous hand motions become so focused that they do not hear or see the guesser's or the referee's calls and keep hiding until a teammate taps them and tells them to open their hands. Everyone gets a good laugh out of this.

Sometimes a hider will intentionally dare a guesser. During a game between the Oklahoma tribes and the Crow, a female scorekeeper was given the bones to hide. She scored one point, then hid for the final point of the game. She swayed back and forth and extended her arms forward, then pulled her left hand back against her body, leaving the right hand extended toward the guesser. The Crow guesser guessed the left hand but missed, and the south won the game.[96]

Once a hider has made their hide and come out with their hands, they may not "go back down" or re-hide unless the other side changes guessers and they receive permission from the referee. Emphasizing that hiders also have patterns, one team captain explained, "If they change guessers, then you can go back down and re-hide because you got to prepare for this guesser. He guesses a certain way and this one here guesses a certain way. You gotta go down and prepare for him."

Guessing Styles

As with hiding, there are myriad styles made by guessers. In open handgames great variation in guessing is permitted, such as hand motions, the nod of a head, tongue pointing, and so on. In Kiowa games the standard rule is one of the four guessing motions with the thumb of that hand extended. According to Bill Koomsa Jr. there were originally only limited hand motions in the

Kiowa handgame, but these increased after the Crow began coming down to play the Oklahoma tribes.[97]

One elder Kiowa stated that there are three primary forms of deciding a guess: 1) following a feeling; 2) seeing in their hands; and 3) body language. About the first form, intuition, he explained, "Sometimes you just get a crazy feeling and go with it, and you are right." The second form is where a hider gets up, closes their fist, and puts their head down, sometimes on their clenched fist. Closing their eyes and concentrating, some guessers say they can literally see the bones in the hider's hands. When they have decided, they look up and signal their guess. Some guessers will lower their head and look at the ground in concentration, whether still seated or after standing up between the two teams, then raise their head and signal their guess. The third form focuses on reading an individual's body language to determine which hand the marked object is in. Many people have a "tell" or do something to give themselves away—nervous eye or hand movements, favoring the side they are hiding the object on (such as moving a foot or leaning their body that direction), or hiding the marked bone differently in their hand, often lower or closer to their body. Many guessers study hiders to see if and how they give themselves away.[98]

Ace Yellowhair described two of the styles of guessing, basically intuitive or a combination of seeing and reading: "There's some people that won't even look at you either and just guess. . . . He'll kind of close his eyes and think, think, think. . . . And then there's that type that'll just keep watching you, you now, throughout the whole game. They'll know what you're going to do."[99] One long-time player described their guessing strategy: "I've probably tried it all, you know. I just close my eyes, like when I get up to guess. But mainly to me I'd rather watch them, you know. Maybe if I get up, I'll close my eyes when I am getting up, and maybe I can see it there, or something like that. Overall, you know, I'd rather keep my eyes open and watch them."[100]

Some of the most animated action occurs on scoring a point. Many whoop and holler. Men may beat their hand drums with increased tempo. Female hiders will ululate or trill before hiding again. After scoring a point one woman kissed the bones before hiding them again. Many players reach down to touch or rub one or both hands on the ground before hiding again. Some women will rub their rattles on the backs and shoulders of male hiders in front of them before they bring their hands forward to be guessed. The more flamboyant hiders make creative and sometimes ridiculing gestures at the guesser and the opposing side such as waggling their open hands with the plain bone after being missed.

172 CHAPTER 3

LUCK, SKILL, OR MEDICINE?

Is successful hiding and guessing in the handgame based on luck, skill, or a combination of these? While most recorded accounts classify the handgame as a game of chance attributed to luck and contemporary opinions vary, there are clear elements of both luck and skill in the modern form of the game. Among the Kiowa the basic rule is that as long as a hider or guesser is doing well you let them continue.

Observations associated with luck are common. One elder Kiowa man stated, "I've never seen a good handgame player. It's mostly luck. It's all luck. Some night you may be lucky, some night you're not." Another Kiowa elder also attributed success solely to luck:

> It's not how good you are. It's luck. Sometimes, like I was saying, concentrate, you know, [but it's] mostly luck, you get lucky . . . like that one girl got lucky on us you know, when we was playing . . . so lucky we couldn't guess her, none of us. We just couldn't get her, you know, and that's luck. It's not how good you are. Everybody's good, but there's not what you would say [is] extra or professional. No, there ain't nobody that good; it's just luck, you know. A lot of times you're lucky, you get lucky. You know, people will say "Boy, he's a good hider" or "He's a good guesser." He's just lucky, that's all it is. People often say someone is good, but really all it is, is luck."[101]

During one night in 1993 against the Crow in Carnegie, a Kiowa player related, "There's not much skill in this. Some guys can put on a pretty good act, but as far as I know I've never seen anybody that was extra good. It's just luck. Some nights you're lucky, some nights you're not. That's what it all comes down to."[102] After several games at a round-robin, one evening an elder player observed, "The east side was lucky. Whoever is sitting on the east side was winning each game." That day the teams sitting on the east side won eight of twelve games.[103]

Observational Skill

While many players associate success in the handgame to luck, several consultants make a conscious effort to study and remember people's hiding and guessing patterns as an important part of their strategy. To be a good in the handgame one must be able to observe and remember people's habits for both hiding and guessing. Similar to the skills needed to play chess, where one must be able to look ahead several potential moves, in the handgame one must be able to remember what an individual hider or guesser has been doing.

The Modern Handgame   173

Although luck always exists, skill in studying players and remembering their habits is clearly present in today's handgame.

During handgames many people are watching. Except for the larger tournaments, where multiple games may occur simultaneously, smaller tournaments play one game at a time. Many players have related how they watch the other teams, guessers and hiders, and try to learn their frequencies and habits. As one Kiowa explained, "Just like any sport, you know, you have scouts. You do scouting, you watch them. You watch them from the previous games they played . . . and we try to remember what they did." With a relatively small number of teams and players in the western Oklahoma handgame circuit, many of the teams and individuals have been playing one another frequently for many years. According to this individual, everyone has patterns in hiding and guessing, sometimes using one pattern in tournaments and another in free-for-alls.

Some guessers believe that hiders have "tells" or give themselves away. Most commonly, actions such as bringing one hand forward before the other, squeezing the marked bone harder than the unmarked one, tapping one foot while hiding, looking away from the guesser, eye movement in one direction, or chewing gum on one side of the mouth were cited as a sure sign of the side an individual was hiding the marked bone. While some individuals give themselves away, these actions are not always accurate, as some hiders always look to the same side or have a regular hiding style. Behaviors can also be done unconsciously or consciously, sometimes intentionally to encourage a guesser to guess a certain way. One time a guesser was studying me closely and had me focusing on the hand I had the marked bone in. As an experiment, I intentionally moved my opposite foot an inch forward as they were about to guess. It drew their attention to that side, and they guessed incorrectly.

One long-time Kiowa player described their approach to the game, classifying hiding and guessing in relation to observations focused on chance, science, and superstition, which correlate with luck, observed behavior, and psychology:

> To me . . . there's three parts of a handgame that I look at. One, it's a game of chance. It's either on your right or your left, and then the other part is a scientific part of it. It's like a person, they have a pattern that they follow all the time. They stay home twice, and then they jump, or they're gonna guess in the middle first, or they're gonna guess on the outside. Patterns, you know, numbers, math, those kind of things. And then the other part is superstition, which is like the hand motions or like maybe a person's

getting ready to hide or you're getting ready to hide and you kind of twitch to your right, and then you're trying to trick them, you know, to think you're gonna put it on your right and come out hard, and you've got it on your left. I'm gonna make medicine, shake my hand on the right side, but I'm gonna put it on the other side to make them think I got it over here, you know, superstition. . . . Those three things there. Game of chance, superstition, and scientific.[104]

Soon after I began playing, skill in watching hiders became apparent when a young Comanche man who was a good guesser sat down by me after a free-for-all one day, correctly recounted the order of my last several sets of hiding that day, and told me that I needed to change my hiding pattern. Realizing he was memorizing the habits of players to more effectively guess them, he explained how he watches individuals to learn their habits and patterns. He related that he studies every hider and their habits as much as possible for five to six hides, then, having learned their tendencies, uses that information to guess them.[105] Similarly, a Comanche elder stated, "The thing to handgame is the guessers. You have to know what they are gonna do. They have habits that you have to get to know. Then you know how to hide."[106]

An elder Comanche described the value of learning other players' hiding habits:

> Oh yeah, you got to look for that. There's quite a few guys that's got a habit of giving themselves away. And I'm not gonna name any names [laughs]. There's a lot of things that I know of, you know, that I keep it to myself. I don't even tell my own guessers. I don't even tell them. They might give it away and hurt us. That's like hiding habits and things like that, that you have to watch for, and if you know something don't give it away because it'll be used against you. So I don't give nothing away.[107]

Two elders described how one woman with small hands gives herself away in her hiding habits by clenching the hand with the marked bone hand too tightly. One explained they were afraid to tell her for fear she might become offended by telling her how to hide, quit, and play for another team. "She was a good hider for a while there. Finally they got wise to her ways of hiding, you know. You learn everybody's habit. They all got habits, and you learn it."[108]

An elder Kiowa player also described studying the opposition by watching and remembering the order of their previous several guesses and hides to try to figure out what a player is most likely to do. He also related particular patterns that he observed in studying hiders and guessers in general, which I will not repeat here. In preparing your next hide or guess it takes considerable concentration and memory to remember the past several hides and guesses for numerous players. Although a player will sometimes lean over and inform you

The Modern Handgame   175

that so and so has been hiding or guessed a certain way, once a guesser has gotten up, there is not supposed to be any consultation or coaching. The trick, of course, is to outguess the hider or guesser as to what they are likely to do. In several instances elder players have sat by me during games and informally coached me while we watched the play.[109]

Eddie Longhat told me that hiders often hide twice in one hand then "jump" to the other hand, and that guessers also sometimes fall into patterns of guessing one way then switching to the other. The trick he said was to outguess the other, whether hiding or guessing.[110] Jack Yellowhair told me that guessers catch on to everybody after a while. Hiders must mix up your hiding patterns to confuse the guesser and psyche them out.[111]

Often an offensive player who is not guessing will watch the play of the opposing side and predict what the hider is going to do—sometimes to themselves and other times to the player sitting next to them. In several instances, players sitting beside me have related several sets of correct guesses before the guesser signaled his guess. Some players practice guessing from the sidelines. Studying and memorizing other player's habits has likely increased over time as handgames have increased in frequency since the 1950s and involve regular players.

With increasing prize money in tournaments, some individuals state that the level of competition has also increased. As Gregory Haumpy noted,

> They're better players. They learn how to play, how the other people play, and it's pretty hard to win. When we first started, well, it was easy. Nobody paid any attention; all they did was want to get out there and play, you know, and whoop and holler, but now everybody, well, the leaders are the ones that watch that, how they hide and how they guess and all of that. Yeah, that's what it is, that prize money. . . . If the prize money is up high, well, that's the way you see them play. And they won't guess as quickly as they do with not much money in there. But they study your motion[s].[112]

Haumpy asserted that one's playing ability was "more skill than luck." As he explained,

> In guessing and hiding, yeah. Yeah, you have to watch the hiders and every time each team plays you gotta watch the guessers. They watch them, who hides them and how they hide. And when you're playing well you guess them, you know pretty near how they hide when they come out, see. But if you ain't got it in here [points to his head], then you just blowed up, they'll beat you. That's the way I look at it. When you're sitting outside, when you're sitting and not playing, sitting on the side, well, you watch them, how them guessers guess, you know. And also how they hide, each one, each side. And that way, that's how come a lot of times I always come

176 CHAPTER 3

out on my left side. I have the marked stick, and sometimes I change.
I change on my right. And then when they miss me, that's when I'll go
to town on them. Once they miss me, well, the next time I know where
they're gonna guess, see?[113]

Haumpy recalled one game when a woman hider had stayed home (hidden
in the same hand) five times. Noticing this, he told the other guesser, but she
would not listen to him. Finally she did, and she got her. "That's what it takes,
memory. If you can remember what's going on, you're all right."[114] The key to
this is practice and analysis. One man stated that he had his wife watch him
hiding and guessing to establish his patterns.

Mary Beaver described her approach to guessing and her love of the game:

It's a mind game. When they're hiding and you're guessing, you know.
You look at them, you look at their face, you look at their expression, you
look at their movement, and you're trying to figure out, well, what's going
on in their head. Is he going to stay in the same hand? Is he going to try to
trick them? Is he going to jump to the other hand, you know, do the quote
"switcheroo?" And it's just whatever comes to my mind, and, you know,
I'll say "Okay, I got it." It looks like he didn't even move, so I'm going for
him to stay. So there's just a lot of things that are involved. It's really fun.
It's really a fun game, and I just really enjoy it tremendously.[115]

Some individuals still carry medicine bags or wear paint, yet players vary
in their beliefs of its efficacy. One long-time player stated that he believed
more in luck and observation than the ability to use medicine or power to
determine the play:

Well, I'm thinking more on luck. Maybe they've got a better outlook at it,
or maybe . . . they're using something to help them out to guess. That's
all up to them, you know. Like, say, "Well, go ahead," you know, and they
use whatever they think. Maybe they got a medicine bag around them or
something like that, and they'll go with that, you know. Basically, I think
it's luck and observing. Studying. . . . It has to go back to luck again, you
know. Everybody has their day in that handgame. Some days you're gonna
be able to run them sticks.[116]

This player did acknowledge that sometimes individuals carrying medicine
are effective:

Well, they get into them predicaments like getting down to two, maybe
three sticks, about ready to win. Then they might give it to somebody
that's packing, we call it packing, you know, because they got something
[carrying medicine]. And maybe they'll get up and do their thing, and
they'll get 'em, they'll get 'em. . . . Basically if they keep going to that
certain person, like for hiding or guessing, each game, each time they

The Modern Handgame   177

play, yeah, something's up. You can just tell, I guess, observing, you know. If they keep playing that one person, then that's the one that's got it, or they've got a little extra. They might have their [medicine] bag or something on them. Or even women too. I've seen the women . . . carry it in their purse, you know, set their purse real close to them, and they hide and they go behind that purse."[117]

One woman in 2018 stated, "I don't think there's any medicine. I think it's all luck." This individual attributed the game to odds and studying the behavior of other players. "I like to sit and watch people, and I tell my team members, I said, 'If you ever watch so and so, he has a pattern. His first guess will always be this way.' You know, then: 'If you miss her, she's gonna go this way.' And they go, 'Ahh [gasp of surprise], you're right.'"[118] To be successful, both hiders and guessers must not become predictable.

Some players maintain that if someone uses medicine to win, they will suffer repercussions in the future, such as illness or bad luck of some kind. Some individuals also stated that those who use medicine to win also act differently toward those they played. As one player described, "I know if they do something to you they won't look you in the eye, you know. Maybe they'll glance at you or look off you know, but they won't look you in the eye and tell you hello, or greet you, you know."[119]

Cheating

In the past, skilled players and people believed to have medicine often switched the hiding object after being guessed to avoid being guessed correctly. Although cheating was officially not allowed in the old form of play, it occurred. While not really sanctioned, cheating seems to have been permissible—as long as you were not caught doing it—and seems to have been an accepted part of the game to which opponents tried to remain vigilant. The dim lighting in tipis and later in canvas-wall tents undoubtedly aided in the success of sleight of hand practices.

Cecil Horse reported the presence of disputes between teams centering on accusations of cheating that resulted in starting games over. "Both sides, sometimes they have a squabble. They say, 'That man's cheating.' And this man says, 'No.' So on, and they get to squabbling. Sometimes they just gather up their stuff because they're cheating over there, and they play over again."[120]

Ina Paddlety Chalepah described combining sleight of hand and the use of medicine in past play:

And if they see you throwing, a lot of them knows how to throw them elk teeth. Some of them got big hands, you know, big calloused hands, and when they going this way [swings hands back and forth in front of her],

CHAPTER 3

every which way, they got ways. They throw it some way where you can't see them, and then they guess them, and you can't guess them because they're throwing them. One of them, how do you say it? They using voodoo [medicine] things. Yes, in them days that was going on. . . . Yes, they cheat. You know they throw it, and then they open their hand and it's on the other side.[121]

Gregory Haumpy noted that during his youth, when teams played with a single elk tooth per hider, the older, experienced players used to switch the object, especially when guessed. "You ain't supposed to do that. But they're crooks. Sometimes they miss them, and it falls on the floor." Cheating could result in immediate accusations that usually produced hard feelings and, if proven, immediate forfeiture of the game and all bets from the cheater's side. If a player dropped the item being hid while attempting to switch hands, the game was automatically forfeited for the entire team. As Gregory Haumpy explained, "You could throw it if you want to. If you don't catch it . . . you lose, you automatically lose. The whole game. And then they beat that guy out. The women will get up and beat on him and make him go out [laughs]."[122]

Haumpy spoke with firsthand knowledge, describing an instance in which he tried to cheat in a handgame, but was caught.

I tried it one time, over there east of Carnegie at Julia Daingkau's. They had just one bone, an elk tooth, and they had another one, and they had given it to my buddy over here, and they started out. Boy, we went to town [laughs]. They guess, you know, and by golly they guessed me right quick, you know. Boy, I was going to throw it, you know, and, doggone, it hit right here [the area between the bottom of his thumb and index finger] and it popped, bounced out, you know [laughs]. Boy, them women got up and . . . just beat on me [with their purses], you know. They told me to get out of there. "You're a cheater." They won't let me back in [laughs].[123]

Getting caught automatically disqualifies one's team during match games, free-for-alls, and tournaments.

Bill Koomsa Jr. explained, "A long time ago [there were] some hiders who move their hands so fast they could switch the elk teeth between their hands with no one seeing. Some said magic was used. But if you were caught cheating it would cause your team to lose the whole game."[124] When the Kiowa played with a single hiding item, Koomsa reported, if you suspected someone of cheating you could take something out of your pocket and hand it to them to force them to open their hands to ensure that both hands weren't empty. If they refused the item, it meant that they were cheating by having both hands empty.[125]

The Modern Handgame

To help eliminate the possibility of switching the game piece after being guessed, two game pieces were introduced for each hider. However, some individuals responded by hiding two unmarked game pieces or by showing only one hand when guessed. This resulted in requiring hiders to open and show both hands and game pieces on each guess. As Gregory Haumpy explained, "That's how we got them bones, two of them to hold. She's got a pair, and I've got a pair, and we hide together. And the other side has got two [sets] of them too. Then there's no way that you could throw them. But sometimes I heard that they had two white [unmarked] ones that they can hide, them two white ones. They play, and somebody they guess on that side, and they guess, and they show the white one [showing only one hand], and they don't show this one . . . [but now] you got to show both of them."[126] Marie Yokesuite Haumpy agreed, "Now they make them open both hands."[127]

The new form of play, requiring hiders to open both hands after each guess, makes it virtually impossible to cheat unless a hider can bring his hands back down quickly after being guessed and switch the bones without being seen. One elder described how an opponent did this at a game at Geary, Oklahoma. "One guy came down like that [makes hand motions], and he came back up, and he had that bone, it was on the other side. We saw it. But we didn't say anything, we just, you know, let it ride at that time. . . . Anyway, we beat them [laughs]."[128] This is where referees must be diligent.

In the 1990s and the decade following, allegations of cheating were common and usually consisted of accusations of 1) switching the bones after being guessed, 2) changing the marking on a set of bones, or 3) using two unmarked bones. However, when I interviewed senior handgame players and began to investigate this aspect, I found it to be more a matter of speculation than cases where there had been solid evidence.

SWITCHING THE BONES

Today the use of long bone or plastic hair pipes inhibit switching one's hide. Accusations commonly occur when someone makes an unusual form of hiding, such as using only one hand to hide, or continues to make hiding motions after the guesser has signaled his guess, such as a hider in a second row swinging their hands down low behind the chairs in front of them to obscure the opponents' view of their hands. Any unusual type of behavior may draw suspicion of cheating. One woman who claimed a physical inability to hide with both hands frequently hid with only one hand, reaching down into her purse to hide. She was often very hard to guess correctly and frequently

180   CHAPTER 3

suspected of having another set of bones in the purse and switching the bones or taking the tape off of the marked one. As one elder described,

> She hides one hand, you know, she's always sticking her hand in that purse, and a lot of times they miss her, you know. But it's like I say, she might have took the tape off of the other one and just held it there or had another white bone. Now I always thought to myself, now she's got another set of bones in her purse. She'll bring out the two white ones. Every time you guess which way it is, you'll miss; it's always the white one, you know. I don't really know, to tell you the truth, but . . . why she hides with one hand I could never understand. . . . I don't really know if they are cheating or not. It's kind of hard to do. But she is hard to guess a lot of times.[129]

Switching can be nullified by the judges making the hiders keep both hands in view, separated after coming out with their hide, and having them immediately open both hands after each guess. Why she was not made to keep both hands visible is unclear.

CHANGING THE MARKINGS ON BONES

One day I was interviewing an individual about another elder who had made accusations to him about people changing the markings on the hiding bones and whose team had lost the previous weekend. Changing the marking on bones that are painted or have inlaid markings while hiding is virtually impossible. If someone removed markings of electrical tape, it would leave a sticky residue on the bone it had been on and likely a stained area around the middle. When I asked him if that really happened in games, he replied, "No. Not really. He was just sort of angry because he got beat. . . . No, I've never seen it done before, and I don't know why or how they can do it." The only advantage in switching the markings on the bones would be if your hider was relying on being able to see the ends of the bones well enough to detect some difference in color, diameter, or shape.

Differences in the thickness, color, or other features of the hiding items could allow a guesser to differentiate them if a hider holds his hands still and permits a prolonged look. Some players cover the entire game piece when hiding to prevent this. Illustrating how players study their opponents and make adjustments in play, Adam Kaulaity discussed a strategy he used one time in a game against the Crow:

> I got to hide against the Crows down here one time, and I come out, and I covered the bones up. They couldn't guess me [laughs]. Yeah, I covered everything up. They look at you, they look at your hands and try to figure

out which bone to guess. I think I caught on to them the way they kind of watch the bones. You might say they might know where they're at. I don't know what they can do about them bones. You know if they see them bones, they can kind of guess which way to go. Yeah, I covered all the bones up, and I got away. They couldn't guess me. [130]

Scratching the bones to gain an unfair advantage is another allegation that appears to have little substance. Some bones exhibit evidence of scratches on them that have been put on them by players. Often this is alleged to be efforts to remove the paint or tape marking the bone. Such scratches are usually attributed to women who have longer fingernails. While this may be done to allow a hider to identify the bones better by feel, or simply from a nervous habit, it does not represent a change in the items that would alter the game. When asked, some individuals did not know why people did this other than possibly being "nervous." Some sets of bones are so smooth that it is sometimes hard to distinguish those with painted markings unless the marking extends above the surface of the bone (as with black tape) where one can feel it. Some intentional alterations to bones such as scratching may be to make the objects easier for some individuals to identify by feel or to make people think that they were being manipulated. But because each team uses a separate set of hiding implements for an entire game—provided by the tournament sponsor for the event—the effect may be more psychological than an actual advantage during play.

TWO UNMARKED BONES

Allegations of using two unmarked bones are also common, often when a guessed player is alleged to open one hand with an unmarked bone but not the other, then quickly lowers their hands out of sight to hide again. The use of two unmarked bones will only work if the hider does not open both hands to show both hiding items and is easily prevented by making the hider clearly open both hands after each guess. When an accusation occurs, the hider can be asked to open both hands to quickly settle the matter. During my fieldwork I occasionally heard some people claim that sometimes when a tournament had ended there would be additional unmarked bones turned in, meaning that someone had brought extra unmarked bones to the game. Whether this was done for psychological reasons, such as to make the hosts believe there had been cheating during the tournament, it would have no real advantage as long as the hiders are required to keep both hands visible and open them after each guess. To alleviate these problems, hosts supply their own set of bones.

Alcohol

While the handgame is for enjoyment, it is not without some problems. Drinking is the most visibly observed and verbally cited problem described by players. In the early 1990s and in the first decade of the new millennium, elders stated that drinking was not present at earlier handgames but had become common, especially among the younger crowd. Gregory Haumpy recalled that during his youth people commonly smoked Bull Durham, Country Gentleman, and Prince Albert tobacco but that there was no drinking at handgames. According to Haumpy, drinking began to be a problem in the 1940s, sometimes resulting in fights in the periphery of the camps. He recalled that many older people attending handgames at this time, including some of his own close family, quit attending because of the drinking. Intoxicated individuals were problematic because the position of security workers associated with today's powwows had not yet been developed, and attempts to remove drinkers during this period often resulted in fights.[131]

While some handgame tournaments include security today, drinking continues, primarily in vehicles parked nearby. As with powwows, drinking is not condoned or permitted in the arena or primary area of activity but is somewhat tolerated as long as it remains on the perimeter of the event and does not directly affect it. However, drinking is always noticed and impacts the game, even if indirectly. As one elder Kiowa man commented,

> I hate to say this, but a lot of people go down there just to drink nowadays, you know. It didn't used to be that way, but now it's getting that way. People just like to go to drink. Them kind we try to keep them out several years back, but they just kept coming in. And now, I guess they're all right as long as they can control themselves. We had several fights in the handgame. Some drunks, you know, they got straightened out, and, well, after that they realize what they done, and they apologize to one another, and then back at it, handgame again.[132]

An elder Comanche woman offered a similar view. "It's a lot of fun. It's more fun if those drunks don't come around. Them drunks just mess it up. Now that's what it is today, that's why we don't go that much [anymore]."[133]

Several times I have heard elders say to one another in Kiowa or Comanche: "They are drunk." One elder reported, "Some people come to handgames just to get drunk anymore." Many handgame players do not drink, at least while at handgames. Some do but not to the degree of resulting in any problems or inappropriate actions. Officially, alcohol is not allowed at handgames or in a building where the handgames are played. Some host teams have even posted signs stating that drinking is forbidden on the premises, including the parking

The Modern Handgame 183

lot. One such sign read simply: "No drinking in the parking lot." Many people drink out of coolers in their cars and trucks. Some drink but not amounts that inhibit their playing or singing, and the effects are hardly visible unless one is looking for the signs. However, a few individuals who enter and exit repeatedly during a day or evening become more and more visibly intoxicated. Although these are a small minority, sometimes their actions impact the game. As Marie Yokesuite Haumpy explained, "There's been a lot of arguments, especially right now. Just like I say, in them earlier days there was no body drunk or drinking [and] playing, but now they do that. In our round-robin games we play, there's certain guys, they drink a lot. They go out and come in [and their actions are sometimes noticed]."[134]

One evening, a Crow elder took the microphone and arose to announce that there were police outside and that one man had already been arrested. He continued: "Those of you that are drinking outside, be careful. There's police around here. They've taken one man in already, and they'll take you in too if they see you drinking." Later that evening one of the Oklahoma players with a bad drinking problem had played very well in the first two games but then left. He returned visibly inebriated and fell asleep sitting upright in a chair. In the middle of the fifth game, the music suddenly stopped. The individual had fallen to the floor, hitting it quite hard. As the man was helped out of the building, the MC eased the tension, making light of the situation: "He's been drinking for seven nights, and it's finally caught up to him. It's hard on him. He's okay." People laughed, and the game resumed as if nothing had happened.[135]

At one round-robin, I was visiting with several individuals in the parking lot. One man who had sat his beer down couldn't find it and decided to drive to town, only about a mile away, and get more. As he pulled out, in broad daylight, everyone noticed it was on the back bumper of his truck and began to laugh. In a few minutes he returned with more beer; the can was still sitting on his bumper. After it was brought to his attention, he resumed drinking it, and everyone laughed. No harm occurred.

At another tournament a man going through a separation continued to drink as the day went on, with obvious impairment to his ability to stand and retain his balance. Several times he dropped his drum while singing and the bones while hiding. Although people talked much about his actions, nothing was said to the individual. Nevertheless, these incidents serve as a reminder of the substance abuse problems that individuals struggle with.[136] Since the mid-1990s I have seen a decline in drinking by those playing the handgame.

By the twentieth century, the handgame remained the primary traditional game played by the KCA. By the 1950s the Kiowa, Comanche, and Apache were again playing one another with increased frequency across Southwest

Oklahoma and with the neighboring Cheyenne and Arapaho, which continues to the present. Major changes involved the use of community buildings, shifts from goods to cash in betting, more family-based teams, a shift to the modern "Oklahoma" or "fast" style of play, and a decrease in match and free-for-all games with the emergence of round-robin and state tournaments. This regional focus expanded further as the Kiowa and Crow renewed their friendship and began annual reciprocal handgames in the 1950s and 1960s.

CHAPTER

4

The Kiowa-Crow Association and the Handgame

THE KIOWA HAVE a long history of friendship with the Crow (Apsáalooke, the Children of the Long Beaked Bird) dating to at least circa 1700, when the Kiowa lived near them in the Yellowstone area of Wyoming and Montana. Kiowa elders interviewed in 1935 stated that some Kiowa continued to travel to Montana to visit the Crow as late as the 1850s. The Kiowa likely played handgame with or against the Crow during these periods. The Crow are a northern plains tribe now with a reservation in south-central Montana.

Contemporary handgames between the Kiowa and Crow derive from a relationship between these two tribes in the Native American Church (NAC). In the 1930s, small contingents of Crow began coming through western Oklahoma on their way to gather peyote in Texas for their meetings and to attend Kiowa peyote meetings. Many of these visits included staying with Kiowa around Hobart, Oklahoma, especially at the home of Moses Botone, an active NAC leader. These visits continued into the mid-1950s, when the Crow began attending the annual Kiowa Armistice Day celebrations around November 11, sponsored by the Carnegie Victory Club. The Crow, who have their own style of the handgame, saw the Kiowa playing their version of the game at these encampments at the city park in Carnegie, Oklahoma. By the 1960s the Kiowa and Crow had established several friendships and were beginning to travel to play one another in handgames. In the late 1960s the Kiowa began hosting the Crow each November for a series of nightly handgames. An announcer at one Kiowa-Crow handgame in 1997 stated that this was the twenty-eighth year of such reciprocal visits, inferring that they began in 1970. However, elder Kiowa who were active players then have stated that the reciprocal relationship started a few years earlier, by at least 1964. The Crow began to come down annually each November to play the Kiowa in handgames.[1]

When the Crow come to Oklahoma to play, attendance is usually much larger than regular handgames. These games are an attraction, and many individuals consider the annual visit to be the highlight or event of the year in the western Oklahoma handgame. According to Bill Koomsa Jr., Bruce Haumpy was the first Kiowa to take a team to Montana to play the Crow.[2] Since that time, contingents of Crow have traveled south to play the Kiowa, and later other southern plains tribes, in Oklahoma, while a Kiowa team and increasing numbers of other Oklahoma tribes have traveled north to play the Crow at Crow Agency, Montana, in late April or early May. Especially large contingents of Crow began coming to Oklahoma annually after 1968, when they began their annual handgame tournament at Crow Agency, Montana. The size of the Crow contingent varies. Over the years it has varied from forty or fifty members to around fifteen. In 1999 a sizeable contingent came to play, but a mining accident in Montana that killed four Crow and injured several others forced many to return early with only five nights of play held. When the Crow travel to Oklahoma they are obliged to play the southern or Oklahoma style of handgame. When the Kiowa and other Southern Plains tribes travel to play in Montana, they play the Crow style.[3]

Among western Oklahoma tribes the Crow are known for loving the handgame and being willing to bet much larger sums than their southern hosts. Some winters, heavy snowstorms between Denver and Montana make it difficult for the Crow to travel to Oklahoma. One Kiowa woman remarked, "It's gotta be pretty bad when a Crow can't make it down." Since the Crow began coming to Oklahoma to play handgame, they have generally come for at least a week, playing at the site of a different host every night, usually five to seven nights. Although a specific tribe (Kiowa, Apache, Comanche, Cheyenne, Arapaho, Wichita) or family serves as host each night, with more members of their respective tribe normally turning out for games in their home area, participation is essentially open and intertribal. Many families have sought to host the Crow but have had to wait many years to get the honor. Members of southern plains teams will sit on the south side of the building, while the north side is reserved for the Crow. Adam Kaulaity described one such game in which a Kiowa playing with the Comanche helped to beat the Crow: "We went down there to Comanche Country one time when they [the Crow] came

The Kiowa-Crow Association   187

down. We went down there to the Comanche, and they bet about three thousand [laughs]. Three thousand, yeah. Boy, they was lucky, they had a Kiowa guy guessing for them. Boy, he saved the day for them. Yeah, he won that three-thousand-dollar game. Yeah, those Comanches, they like to bet too."[4]

In Oklahoma the Crow do not play by districts as they do in Montana but as a collective tribal team of whomever can make the trip. They also do not wear their distinct matching dress, identifying their district, just regular clothing. The Crow also typically exhibit less hand motions than when they play in Montana. Crow medicine men playing in Oklahoma do not take nearly as long to prepare and hand out the bones as in Montana. Some will feign hiding, open the missed hand, and then shake their hand and arm briefly at the opposition before handing out the bones. Crow hiders also use less gyrations in their motions, mostly just extending their arms and occasionally moving them back and forth or in and out. In accordance with playing the style of the host, in Oklahoma hiders do not have to follow the Crow guesser's hands while they study them.[5]

With lengthy friendships between the two groups, a good-natured rivalry in the play is obvious and may involve actions that are not normally allowed during a tournament. During one game the Crow medicine man stepped out and rubbed his hand down the arm of the Oklahoma side's guesser. He then wiped his arms off with his hands and made a motion of throwing it away, producing smiles and laughter. The motions implied taking his ability to correctly guess their side and throwing it away.[6]

Although the Oklahoma team sits on the south and the Crow on the north, some members may choose to play on the opposing side. It is not uncommon to see a few southern plains members playing on the Crow side and a few Crow playing on the Oklahoma side, especially if one side has a small number of players or needs additional singers. Regardless of who is hosting, most players travel night after night to attend the matches. Games are usually held by the following tribes and at the following locations: Kiowa (Carnegie, Anadarko), Cheyenne and Arapaho (Clinton, Geary), Apache (Apache), Comanche (Cache, Lawton), and sometimes by Wichita (Anadarko). Some locations may be used more than once during the Crow visit, and thus visits can involve six to eight consecutive nights of handgames against the southern plains tribes. In 1993 the Crow played at Clinton (Cheyenne), Cache (Comanche), Apache (Apache), twice at Carnegie (Kiowa), and again at Apache (Apache).[7] The 1997 schedule included eight consecutive nights of play at Clinton, Apache, Clinton, Cache, Lawton, Carnegie, Anadarko, and Carnegie, with the Comanche requesting an extra night to play the Crow. More recently

188   CHAPTER 4

Handgame flyer, Crow 2012 Oklahoma schedule. Author's collection.

Kiowa, Cheyenne, and Comanche have been the main hosts, using sites at Carnegie, Geary, and Lawton, Oklahoma. The last night's game is typically sponsored by the Kiowa at Carnegie.

Traveling night after night around Southwest Oklahoma to play against the Crow is physically demanding. Marie Yokesuite Haumpy described it:

The Kiowa-Crow Association

When they first came down, [my husband Gregory] and I, we were much younger, and we used to go, and we followed them every night. Like ten nights, every night straight, every night. They were playing different places—Oklahoma City, Clinton, and Watonga, and Geary, and Carnegie, and Apache, and Cache, and Lawton, and just different places, you know. And in Anadarko they played a couple of times over there in a building, and I tell you what, when they left, I was sick. I had handgame hangover. We played, way into the night, say when we come home maybe two, three o'clock in the mornings and then kind of rest up like this during the day and then leave early again to get good seats, you know. But we enjoy it. It's a lot of fun.[8]

Over the years, numerous friendships, marriages, and adoptions have resulted from these intertribal visits. I have recorded intermarriages between members of Kiowa and Crow, Kiowa and Comanche, Cheyenne and Comanche, and Cheyenne and Crow handgame families. Ed Little Light cited several intermarriages, kinship adoptions, and deep, long-term relationships between the Kiowa and Crow. These relationships involve individuals and families reciprocating in housing and feeding one another, extensive gift exchanges, donations of money for travel costs, and a shared love for traditional ways that include the handgame. As Little Light told me of the reciprocal Kiowa-Crow handgames, "Its a lot more than just a game."[9]

Crow hospitality is highly regarded by the Kiowa and other Oklahoma tribes, as is the Kiowa's hospitality in November. I can attest to the reciprocal hospitality. When playing with the Kiowa team in the 1998 Crow tournament, I was taken to dinner on several occasions, invited and fed at people's homes, and taken to participate in a Crow sweat lodge. In Oklahoma similar hosting occurs, including housing, meals, gifts, and nightly gifts of money to each carload of Crow to help offset their travel costs.

Typical of Indian kinship and the making of relatives through adoption, several Crow and Kiowa have adopted one another as relatives. Ed Little Light adopted Bill Koomsa Jr. as his son. Koomsa was also adopted by several other individuals in various kinship roles. Mary Bearshield Beaver and Pete Bearshield (Cheyenne) were adopted by Crow. As Mary described, "Pete and I are real close to the Crows cause we started going up to Crow Agency. I started going up in 1985 with my folks. Pete started coming up in 1986 with my folks, and with the exception of the years that my folks died . . . we've went just about every year since. And through that, you know, a lot of people have taken us. I'm talking about Pete and I, as their kids. Those people . . . they've passed since, but a lot of people know what clan we belong to." Pete and Mary were adopted into the Greasy Mouth Clan. As Mary explained, "We belong to the Greasy Mouth children. So, when they have their clan games up there on Sundays, we play with the Greasy Mouth Clan."[10]

Before each night of play the host group typically welcomes the Crow over a public address system, then, following a prayer, invites the Crow to go through the dinner line first. Meanwhile bets begin to be taken at a table on one side of the arena. Like the tournament forms described, any number of individuals may bet, and bets may vary in amount but must total an equal amount on each side before play starts. Although bets are evened up prior to each game starting, southern plains tribes regularly comment that the Crow bet more than they do. One elder Kiowa remembered that the first time he played against the Crow, the fifteen or twenty visiting Crow had compiled $250 in bets, while all of the Kiowa, Comanche, and Apache had amassed $50. This elder told me of how he felt embarrassed one time when he was in line at Crow Agency, Montana, to place a $5 bet and discovered a Crow man behind him was ready to place a $100 bet. As this individual perceived, "The Crow are not that much more financially well off. They just like to gamble." While many Kiowa and other southern plains individuals often place $5 or slightly larger bets, individuals recording bets in the 1990s stated that Crow individuals regularly bet larger amounts of $25 to $40.

As one elder described, "The Crow people that we invite down here every year, they are great gamblers, them people, it's nothing for them to bet $50, you know, or even more. But they'll gamble. . . . Today, $10 is a big bet for a Kiowa." Another Kiowa elder stated that the Crow are "true gamblers" and will continue to play even after losing several games in a row. This individual stated that, in contrast, the KCA teams often quit after they lose three games in a row. As one Kiowa elder remarked, "The Kiowas want to quit while they are ahead." He then told of how the Crow lost the first four games at Apache one night that year but were ready to continue playing. After the Kiowa lost the fifth and sixth game, they all left and "it was a short night." An early exit after losing a few games makes it difficult for the remaining players to collect enough money to hold another game and can result in a short evening.[11] Marie Yokesuite Haumpy noted, "When the Crows come down, now that's when the big betting starts."[12] In games I witnessed, the combined Oklahoma-Crow bets ranged from $160 to $832 per game. One long-time player remembered a game in which each side once put up $1,500.

Betting is the same as in match games in the south. Additional individual or side bets of any equal amount can occur between two individuals after a game starts. A coin toss decides the start of the offense. At each offensive exchange some individuals will share their hand drums with players on the other side. Often two men sharing a drum or sitting across from one another will engage in a great deal of good-natured taunting, with extensive hand motions, shaking hands, rubbing the floor, pointing fingers at one another, and periodically breaking out into big smiles and laughter. The winner of the first game starts on offense for the next game. However, the loser of each game sets the amount bet for the following game so that the previous winners do not bet so much that the other side cannot continue to play. The number of score sticks can be adjusted to partially determine how long a game will last, most commonly involving eighteen points per side and the center stick.[13]

During one game when the Crow began to get far ahead, they broke into an especially peppy song that contained the lyrics "eeny, meeny, miny, mo, heh yah, hey yah." Many of the Crow pointed at the south side and danced in their seats as they sang these lyrics. Some of the women stood up and pointed with their fingers or rattles, while some of men did likewise with their drumbeaters. After the south side caught on to the lyrics, many of them broke into smiles and began laughing. The Crow won that game by twelve points.[14]

It is the element of unpredictability that creates a constant atmosphere of uncertainty, surprise, and excitement in handgame. In one game between the Kiowa and Crow, the head of one of the southern singer's drumbeaters flew off its stick as he was drumming. As it flew through the air toward the Crow side, one of the Crow men reached up and caught it. His then tossing it back to its owner produced great laughter.[15]

The Crow medicine men sometimes place the bones on the ground in front of them, kneel behind them, and engage in extensive motions over them known as "making medicine." The following example from a 1997 game between the Crow and Kiowa illustrates this. The Crow medicine man placed both sets of bones on the floor in front of him at the east end of his side's bench. He knelt behind the bones and began swaying back and forth over them with his hands raised and arms extended forward. Periodically he would rub his hands on the floor, rub them together, and then shake one hand, with arm and fingers extended and quivering, while pointing with his other at the opposing side, then back and forth across all the players and spectators on the KCA side of the building. He then feigned picking up the bones three times, gathering them up on the fourth motion. Standing up, he chose his hiders, gave them the bones, and then shook and pointed his quivering hand at the opposing side.[16]

At first the Kiowa were not used to the more animated hand motions of the Crow style of play, and the accelerated hand motions and faking or feigning of guessing motions led many Kiowa to show their hands and give themselves

Crow (left) versus Kiowa (right), C. C. Whitewolf (Comanche) in plaid shirt guessing. Red Buffalo Hall, Carnegie, Oklahoma. Author's photo, 2018.

away before the Crow had committed to a guess. As Gregory Haumpy described, the Crow will clap their hands, hit their stomachs, and shake their hands. "They're trying to jew you out, you know, trick you. They'll find out just about where you've got it, you know."[17]

During the Crow visit, many players may change seats between games on the nights when the Kiowa are the hosts. Some Kiowa will play on the south side one game, then shift and be on the north or Crow side the next game. Likewise, some Crow may play on the south of Kiowa side. In other instances, an individual may play the entire night on the opposing side's team. This is most prevalent among those Kiowa who have personal relationships (friendship, adoption, or intermarriage) with the Crow. Some nights the Crow may ask a particular person to sit and sing or play with them.

RECIPROCITY AND SOCIAL ASPECTS

A great deal of reciprocity occurs between the Oklahoma group and Crow. The Crow are typically housed with Kiowa or other families when visiting Oklahoma, and Crow families provide housing when the Kiowa go to Montana. When the Crow visit Oklahoma each November, the southern plains tribes collect money to give to the Crow to help with their travel or whatever they might need. As one Kiowa adopted by a Crow explained, "You try to do all you can when they come down." Fund-raisers are often held prior to their arrival. Families and relatives take up donations of food, and raffles are conducted to raise money. After a host's expenses are covered, the rest of the proceeds are given to the Crow to offset their travel expenses. Some years I have seen a blanket dance held during an evening to raise money to help the Crow return home. Often as much as $600 is raised through blanket dances, raffles, and donations and given to the Crow. As Jack Yellowhair described, "We entertain them now, you know, different groups feed them, give them money. We collect money for them at handgames, give it to their leader, which is Ed Little Light."[18] These efforts are reciprocated every spring when the Oklahoma team travels to Montana to participate in the Crow tournament.

Giveaways at handgames are similar to those at powwows, although sometimes without dancing. When Bruce Haumpy took the first Kiowa team to play at Crow, they held a giveaway for the Kiowa. When the Crow came south, the Kiowa reciprocated, and the tradition began. Today whoever sponsors a particular event is expected to have a giveaway. A song is sung, and gifts are presented to the Crow. When Bill Koomsa Jr. hosted the Crow during their annual November visit, he sponsored a meal before and after the evening's set of games and a giveaway, usually held during a break in the play, especially if the visitors had lost two or three consecutive games. In this situation the giveaway provides a break in the play while lifting the spirits of the others before play resumes.[19] One giveaway for Bill Koomsa Jr. that I witnessed involved the southern side singing a song with hand drums while he danced in front of the score table. His family placed four folded blankets over his shoulders and money on the floor in front of him. After the song he addressed the crowd, then the family called people to come and receive the gifts.

The Crow visit is an important social event. One of the most observable trends associated with their annual visit pertains to participation. Many southern plains people in Oklahoma come out to watch or play with or against the Crow when they visit but are rarely ever seen at handgames the rest of the year. Several individuals stated that there is an unspoken "need to be seen" when the Crow visit. One Comanche elder commented: "Some of them people that play, they don't come, and we always call them 'Oklahoma Crows' [laughs], because they only come out when they come down and they play with the Crows, and they try to act professional, you know, big time, and they get up, and they strut, and they go through all this fancy thing that they do, and they try to get up there, and, boy, you'd think that they were king roosters or something the way they do [laughs]. But they don't come out and play week after week like we do."[20] Another individual described, "In fact, we see sometimes

194   CHAPTER 4

people you don't see until these people [the Crow] come down this way. They like to come out and, you know, hear the music and watch it."[21]

When the Crow are in Oklahoma to play, you will often see some of the regular players sit back and watch the other less-frequent players who assume a more prominent role in the play. One long-time player described this pattern: "Once a year you'll see them guys up there, different ones will be up there singing and guessing and, you know, doing everything, but the ones that really go every week, they kind of sit back. They'll sit back and watch them other people." This individual described one night at Carnegie when the Oklahoma team kept getting beaten by the Crow until they convinced the others to put their team into play. When their team's hiders took over, they won the next two games. Regarding the people who only play once a year, one individual stated it is often easy to tell how they are hiding, although acknowledging that sometimes they get lucky and get away.[22]

Members of several tribes commented independently of one such individual who rarely plays handgame but always comes out when the Crows are down. In particular, they commented at length on what they described as the overconfidence of this individual during the games with the Crow. As one woman described, "I just love to get out on him. Boy, he always thinks he's really something. He hardly ever plays. But when he comes out . . . the way he struts. He thinks, boy, he's just it in the handgame."[23]

A Kiowa man described those who turn out only to play the handgame when the Crow visit in November:

> There's a lot of those. One-timer, one time a year, you know, once a year.
> Yeah, there sure are, boy. [Dressed] to the T, you know, the best they can.
> It's kind of like when you're up there playing, everybody's watching you,
> everybody's looking at you, you know, and I guess the people that crave
> attention, that want to be up there, that want to be seen, you know. Some
> people's personalities are that way. They crave the spotlight, you know.
> Those are the ones that you see, that come out just once a year, you know,
> and they'll come and show off and be seen in there."[24]

Others may come out for the Crow matches for varied reasons, including the presence of another tribe, match games that rarely occur the rest of the year, larger games and betting than normal, and the uniqueness of the Crow style of play and music. One Kiowa elder attributed the increased participation to the popularity of the Crow musical style, as well as a chance to show off.

> I don't know why it's like that. They like the way they play, the Crows . . .
> [they] give us these songs and all that, you know, and then their songs.
> They got good songs. They got good singers, good drum beat. Everything

The Kiowa-Crow Association 195

about the Crows is good. . . . We started learning the Crow songs. We all started learning them. I like the beat. Everybody likes those songs. That why the people come around, just to hear them sing and play, things like that. That's why they all come out. When they're gone you don't ever see them people no more. Just the diehards we call ourselves. . . . Yeah, mostly big showoffs.[25]

Levels of dissatisfaction in this regard are most readily apparent in the annual November and May matches against the Crow. In the November matches when the Crow visit Oklahoma there is a social importance attached to "seeing and being seen" at the handgames. The opportunity to play during these games is a socially valued activity in addition to the ongoing rivalry associated with the annual matches. Beyond social prestige associated with winning, considerable amounts of money are bet, adding to the pressure to play well. When the Kiowa and members of other southern plains tribes travel to Crow in May, the overall group size is smaller, but there is a great desire to play—especially after traveling so far. However, as one elder noted, some people complain after traveling so far: "I never got to hide," or "I never got to guess." In these instances, this individual maintained that some people are much luckier in hiding and guessing than others and that they should be the ones who do most of these functions. In addition, this elder stated that individual interests should be put aside for the benefit of the team.[26]

The Crow have greatly influenced the western Oklahoma handgame. According to Ina Paddlety Chalepah, the Kiowa and southern tribes continued playing the old style and did not use hair pipes and rattles in the handgame until the Crow began to come around.[27] Over the last fifty years the largest influence on the western Oklahoma handgame has been the Crow style of handgame and singing. When the Crow come to play in Oklahoma, the southern plains teams will sing a wide variety of KCA and Cheyenne songs, but more Crow songs are sung as well. In the 1990s, singers reported that fewer new Kiowa or other southern plains handgame songs were being composed. Those composing songs were mostly elders over the age of sixty, and, while a few of the eldest players provided a few songs they had composed, they stated that they are rarely sung. Elders also pointed out that the singing of southern plains handgame songs in general is declining. So, what songs are being sung? Although several Kiowa and Comanche handgame songs are still known and sung, many of the songs now sung at KCA handgames are of Crow origin. Alfred Chalepah described the more recent shift to singing more Crow songs: "Northern tribe [songs], that's what they use here now. Like a match game or a tournament. Even here, Kiowas and Comanche and Apaches, they use

196   CHAPTER 4

the northern style now because it's fast. They don't sing the [southern] songs. They use northern songs and some songs that was just maybe newly made."[28]

Jack Yellowhair described the popularity and increasing adoption of Crow songs among the Southern Plains tribes:

> We like their singers real good. They're real good singers . . . and we really enjoy their singing. People like to go when they come. . . . We learned. All we sing now is their songs. We don't have our own songs, the old-timer songs—we done away with them. Now we sing nothing but their songs. That's all we sing pretty near every handgame we go to now. All them songs you hear are Crow songs . . . because they got more rhythm in it. . . . In my days we call it jive. . . . Their rhythm has got a jumpy beat, . . . you know, it makes you get in, it's just a medium, it makes you . . . kind of shake with your body. You know, you get into it . . . and get with the beat, the drumbeat. And that makes it a lot better for hearing.[29]

The Crow style of singing has also influenced the singing of southern plains handgame songs. As Mr. Yellowhair continued, "When I first got in there [started playing], there was that fast beat. Man, I mean it was fast. Okies, when they sing [taps slower rhythm on leg]. . . . But then yet we kept slowing our beat down as the years kept coming. Now they get into that rhythm. The old-timers, if you see an old-timer at the handgame now, that's all they want to do is a fast beat. Sing one of them old songs, fast beat, you know."[30]

Ace Yellowhair offered a similar view regarding the popularity of the Crow songs. "I think they have more beat and more rhythm to them. More jive, I guess, bouncing, as in, you know, fast, straight songs. You just wanna get that adrenaline going, but the other kind of songs, you know, you can sway with them . . . their drumbeat is a little slower than our beat down here."[31] Another singer noted that while the Kiowa have adopted many songs from the Crow, the Oklahoma tribes have increased the tempo a bit and "put that swing to it."

Southern plains tribal members exchange tapes of recorded songs with Crow individuals. For several years Gordon Plain Bull of Pryor District sent tapes of new Crow handgame songs to Bill Koomsa Jr. and Phil "Joe Fish" Dupoint in Oklahoma. Most of the songs did not contain words. Many of the Crow songs sung by Oklahoma players in the 1990s were reportedly composed by Mr. Plainbull.[32] Koomsa stated that when the Crow come to Oklahoma, he tried to sing only Kiowa songs.[33] These patterns shed insights into an intertribal-tribal dialectic model of song maintenance and change.

With the adoption of Crow songs in the Oklahoma handgame, southern plains songs have also been learned and are sung by the Crow. As Carl Atauvich explained, "They still sing quite a few of them around here, Crow songs.

Pat Alden (Crow) guessing, Carnegie, Oklahoma. Author's photo, ca. 2017.

And then too they sing a lot of our songs up there. They've taken them up there, and they sing quite a few, and they've taped them and learned them, and they've revised them, you know, and there's quite a bit of songs. That one song goes all over the United States, wherever they play handgame."[34]

For many, the annual Crow visit is the highlight of the handgame season. As one elder team leader described, "We enjoy ourselves when the Crows come. Boy, there's a whole bunch. Everybody, each club . . . entertains the Crows, you know: Carnegie, Clinton, Apache, Cache." The Crow have long been hosted by Bill Koomsa Jr. and now Phil "Joe Fish" Dupoint at Carnegie, Jack Yellowhair at Shady Front east of Fort Cobb, Carl Atauvich at the Cahoma Building in Cache, Oklahoma, and the Bearshield family at Clinton and Geary.

The Crow visit culminates with the November 11 Kiowa Armistice Day [Veteran's Day] Observation, hosted by the Carnegie Victory Club at Red Buffalo Hall in the Kiowa Tribal Complex at Carnegie, Oklahoma, followed by the last evening of handgames with the Kiowa before heading home. At

198 CHAPTER 4

evening's end, prayers for the visitors' safe return home are offered. Many Crow begin traveling back to Montana that night or the following morning.

The next spring, the exchange begins again as a contingent of players from the western Oklahoma tribes travel north to play in the annual Crow tournament. Attending the Crow tournament is important for some individuals. One year an Oklahoma couple put in for a leave from their jobs two months in advance to go to the Crow tournament. Just before they were prepared to leave their request was denied. The couple quit their jobs and journeyed to Crow. While this is not typical, and they indicated that they likely would have eventually left those jobs, it reflects the importance that the handgame and the tradition of the annual visits holds for some individuals.[35]

THE CROW HANDGAME

An understanding of the Crow style of handgame is integral to this work for three reasons. First, the Kiowa and Crow continue annual, reciprocal visits to one another's communities to play handgame. Second, in each visit the host's style of play is used. Third, over the past three decades, Crow handgame songs, more than those of any other tribe, have been incorporated into the southern plains handgame. This section provides a brief sketch of the Crow handgame based on interviews with Crow and Kiowa players, fieldwork and participation in the 1998 Crow Senior Handgame Tournament as a member of the Kiowa team, and observing Crow players in Oklahoma.[36]

The Original Crow Handgame

The handgame is one of five traditional games mentioned in Crow mythology (Lowie 1922, 234). Among the Crow, the gambling game par excellence was the handgame. Published data on the Crow handgame is limited (Lowie 1922, 234–36; 1983, 98–99). This section describes the content and organization of the Crow handgame, comparing it with the KCA or western Oklahoma version. Lowie (1983:98) recorded the Crow name for the handgame as *báxuə-(h) irùə* or "hiding making," which is also interpreted as "soul-making" (Lowie 1922, 235), suggesting a supernatural component associated with the game. Medicine Horse (1987, 58) gives the similar name of *baa aa xua hi lúua* as "hide something intentionally."

There are both mythological and historic accounts of the game's origin. Old Man Coyote once assembled all the winged and un-winged creatures and instructed them to play the handgame. Throughout the game he helped each team alternately. The game lasted all night. In the morning, the birds finally won. Magpie flew up, raised his wing and got the first light on it; hence his wing is white (Lowie 1922, 236).

Related to Lowie's (1922, 235) translation of the Crow name of the handgame as "soul-making," the Apsáalooke Place Names Database at Little Big Horn College contains another origin story of the game.

> The handgame originated when some young Crow men were scouting in the hills within the Black Lodge District. They came upon two hills, [and] on the sides of these two hills facing each other were ghosts chanting back and forth across the gully between them. They were playing the handgame, but instead of losing sticks they lost a ghost player, until there was no one left on one of the sides. At this point the winners would call out a name and collect a soul. The young men witnessing this game took it home with them and soon imitated the motions and songs. Over time this became the handgame we know today.

The database lists this site as Aashkaatbaaaaxuahiluua (Hand Game Creek), modern-day Ash Creek in the Black Lodge District of the reservation.[37]

Another account from the Old Horn family, tells a variation of the former account, when the Crow were camped near Fort Union, North Dakota. Two brothers, out as scouts, heard singing and a lively crowd. Coming over a ridge they saw several ghosts playing the handgame in a ravine. Every stick the ghosts took involved the taking of a soul of a departed person from the earth to their camp. Because of this, the Crow say never to get mad over the handgame. After watching their play, the two brothers returned, bringing the game back and teaching it to the people. The spirts shared it with the people.[38] This version closely resembles the prior one except for the location, but a unique set of ravines follow the bluff just downstream from Fort Union. The game is also reported to have been used to settle disputes between groups without bloodshed.[39]

This account was explained as representing ghosts playing for souls, with each stick representing a soul taken to the other side when won. Today when a stick is won from the middle of the floor, where they are laid at the beginning of play, the head guesser picks up a stick and holds it up toward the mountains or shakes it at the other medicine man or head guesser. One consultant believes this represents when the soul makes the journey at this time. According to one consultant, the Crow are not really afraid of ghosts, because they know they were alive once and that they are around but are cedared (ritually incensed with cedar smoke accompanied by prayer) or cleansed for protection against the spirits.

200   CHAPTER 4

Related to this origin for the game, there is a concern for playing hand-game too much. Lewis Walks Over Ice (Johnson 2001) explained, "There is a contention that if there is too much handgame being played on the Crow Reservation, to an excess, there's a saying that the people that are sicker, that are about to die, will be called home. Because you find that if there's too much handgame played on the reservation, people start dying. So we don't play to excess. We don't abuse it."

For the Crow, the traditional handgame season occurred after it began getting cold, some say after the first frost through April. Both men and women played the game, but they played separately. Originally games were small, with only four of five players per side. The marked increase in the size of Crow handgame teams may have been an indirect influence of earlier competitions between rival military societies such as the Lumpwoods and Foxes, who competed to outdo one another in warfare, hunting, feasts, romance, and the stealing of one another's wives (Lowie 1983; McGinnis 1990, 166). Lowie (1983, 98) reports that later games held between the Lumpwoods and Foxes involved large numbers of players sitting in several rows on opposite sides of a large tipi. Each society first met in its own lodge, then in a large lodge prepared for playing handgame. Robes, beadwork, feathered bonnets, and other items were wagered and placed on each side of the lodge. When the wagers were equal, a man on each side took a seat in the rear of his side. These individuals kept a pipe lit and worked magic on behalf of their respective team throughout the duration of the game. Henry and Barney Old Coyote (Bauerle 2003, 83–84) told of a great handgame between the Greasy Mouth and Whistling Waters clans, with the great warriors Spotted Horse and Red Bear seated on each side to guard each clan's bets. Both smoked pipes during the game, blowing smoke toward the other side that "invoked powers to turn the game in their own favor."

Lowie (1983, 98) states that one player represented each side. "Each appealed to his familiar spirit, pawing like a horse, snorting like a bear, hissing like a snake, or flapping his arms bird-fashion, according to the nature of his protector." Today these forms of imitative magic, usually called "making medicine," are very much alive in Crow handgames, and the individual who enacts them is commonly referred to as the "medicine man."

Each side alternated using two hiders on offense and one guesser on defense. Hiding implements included individual elk teeth, sets of differently marked bones, and later sets of bones with strings. Bones or elk teeth used for hiding in the Crow handgame are known as *ba le waa aa xuá*, "something that is hidden" (Medicine Horse 1987, 58). In one case the use of a shell hidden

The Kiowa-Crow Association 201

beneath a bison robe is recorded. Lowie purchased a set of two spindle-shaped bones, one marked around the center with a string, and ten counters. Each missed guess resulted in the loss of one counter. and the game ended when one side had all the counters.

Each guesser or *ak·chi·weé* "one who tells" (Medicine Horse 1987, 58; cf. Lowie 1922, 236) struck his chest hard with one hand, extending the other arm to signal his guess. According to Lowie (1922, 236), the guesser had to indicate his guess at the other player's "second movement." Lowie (1922, 235; 1935, 98–99) reports the four standard types of hand signals used in guessing two guessers: "outside two" (*asa'ka rū'pdak'*), "the middle" (*ku'onak*), left or "he went to the door" (*biri'ac-dēky*), and right or "he went to the lodge" (*acu'c-dēky*). Each incorrect guess was jeered and meant the loss of a tally stick. Sticks used in the Crow handgame are known as *ba·la·kí·sshe*, "imitation wood" (Medicine Horse 1987, 58). In this form of play, which appears to have been specific to the form of play between the Lumpwoods and Foxes, each side had only three counters (Lowie 1922, 236) and the game was over with the loss of only three sticks. At this point, two customs associated with warfare came into play. With the game's conclusion, the winners sang victory songs to mock their opponents and gave the tally sticks to a noted chief who held them up and recited a war honor for each counter (Lowie 1983, 98). Bauerle (2003, 84–85) recounts the recitation of several coups by Water Edge after the Greasy Mouths defeated the Whistling Waters Clan in a famous handgame.

The Modern Crow Handgame

Following establishment of the Crow Reservation and the formation of Crow Agency in 1883–1884 and at the lead of band and clan leaders, five (later six) districts were created: Lodge Grass, Reno, Black Lodge, Big Horn, Pryor, and later Wyola (Voget 2001, 698). Among the Crow, handgame teams and play are usually determined by residence in a district. According to one individual I visited with, if you move to a new district you must play with that district's team.

Variations occur in an adoption-like process that involves making the uniform for an individual transferring to your district to play. An individual, usually a relative or close friend, may bring an individual or even a whole family from another district to play for their own district by "outfitting them" (making them clothes) and dressing them. The adopter does not have to give anything to the other individual's district. When Jeremy Shield of Reno District was younger, his cousin and best friend's mother made his clothes, and he played with their district, Wyola. As he described, "Later, when I started

202 CHAPTER 4

to know songs, started to guess, and started to be medicine man, then my mom started making my stuff to play in our district." His mom told his aunt, "I'm gonna outfit him; I'm going to take him back, and I'm going to have him play with us." Shield said, "There is a kind of adopting going on wherever you play." In another period he was dressed by an uncle and played in the Big Horn District.[40]

Other variations can occur. One Crow played with Reno for many years. After getting married, his brother-in-law began outfitting him and continued to do so every year so he could continue to play in the brother-in-law's district. In still another instance, a noted Cree singer was dressed and brought to play on a Crow district by one of the Old Horn family because he sang so well.

Dressing an individual from another district can also be used when bringing someone out of mourning. As with powwows, many individuals sit out from public events following the death of a close relative. One individual related how his mother, whose cousin had lost a son, made a new outfit for her. After bringing her and seating her at the handgame, she brought her forward, announced that she was bringing her out of mourning, and gave a present to a clan uncle who prayed for her.

District teams may contain fifty to eighty members during tournament time. Each district has a community building or district hall for holding basketball games, handgames, and other activities. One Crow man reported that there is no rental fee to use the hall, but whoever uses the hall must pay for the electricity.

As one individual explained, Crow "still live by the seasons." There are certain activities for certain seasons. For the Crow, the handgame, along with Round Dances and Push Dances, is an indoor, winter activity. Today the Crow handgame season begins with the annual visit to Oklahoma in November. After returning home, Crow districts play against one another all winter in invited matches. The handgame season concludes with the annual senior and junior tournaments in late April and early May at Crow Agency. After the first thunder and lightning in the spring, they begin to switch to summer activities such as arrow throwing. Although more recently participation in some handgame tournaments occurs over the summer months, arrow-throwing tournaments and rodeos take priority. Crow handgames are found in three primary forms: 1) invited matches between two districts held throughout the winter, 2) the annual Crow Junior and Senior Handgame Tournaments in April and May, and 3) other handgame and stickgame tournaments sponsored by Crow and other tribes throughout the year.[41]

MATCH GAMES

In district match games, one district invites another district to their district hall for an evening of games. District matches occur most weekends throughout the winter. Matches may occur after local basketball games or comprise the entire event of an evening. Attendance averages thirty to fifty members per side, depending on people's schedules. Everyday dress is worn. Teams may play anywhere from one to four games, then eat around midnight. If people feel like it, additional games may continue. Matches on weeknights typically conclude with the meal, while those on Friday and Saturday evenings may continue far into the night. Some games are short in duration, and several are played; in other instances a single game may sway back and forth and last nearly all night. Games are known to last from ten minutes to over six hours. In match games the winner of the last game retains the offense at the start of the next game. A district may invite one district one night and another the following night.

Crow districts are said to be very competitive against one another. Table bets are matched before each game begins. Players report that table bets during district matches may start out as small as $200 to $300 per side on the first game and became as large as $3,000 per side in later games. Late players may hold up money as a challenge to someone on the other side.

District matches may be held as fund-raisers, with a concession stand and "box socials." In a box social, members of the host group prepare two boxed meals that they donate for the event. As a gesture to the visitors, the donors buy back their box from the district at midnight, seek out a clan relative from the visiting district, often a clan aunt or uncle, and go sit, eat, and visit with them. This tradition dates to a time when people traveled less and did not see clan relatives as often. Some districts may opt to provide a regular meal for all in attendance. District members may also donate drinks and sides for the meal. Other fund-raising activities include 50-50 drawings and raffles of hand drums and auctions of blankets that are carried around the arena as people bid on them. Match games can serve as both fund-raisers and social events. With increasing Crow–Northern Cheyenne intermarriage, the Crow and Northern Cheyenne sometimes invite one another for an evening of match games.[42]

THE CROW JUNIOR AND SENIOR TOURNAMENTS

For decades the annual Crow Senior and Junior Handgame Tournaments were held every spring in the wooden "Round House" (Ivan Hoops Memorial Hall), now no longer standing, at Crow Agency, Montana. The junior tournament, open to those aged thirty and under, is held around the third weekend in April. The senior tournament, for those thirty and over, is normally held one or two weekends afterward. The two tournaments have the same rules. Both tournaments run from Wednesday night through the championship game on Sunday. The senior tournament will be discussed in greater length later.

OTHER TOURNAMENTS

The Crow traditionally did not hold round-robin tournaments, and thus, unless playing in a match against another district, the annual junior and senior tournaments were the only ones held on the Crow Reservation.[43] More recently Crow have developed some round-robin tournaments and travel to play in those of other tribes. Black Lodge District usually sponsors a Thanksgiving tournament, and other districts may hold tournaments as fundraisers to prepare for the costs of the annual Crow tournament in May. The winner of the annual Crow tournament usually holds a couple of tournaments to raise funds for next year's tournament, which they must sponsor. Other tournaments may be held to celebrate a birthday or be sponsored by a district to raise funds for individuals with medical and travel costs to reach distant locales such as Denver.[44]

The Crow have a relationship with the Cree at Rocky Boy Reservation, including significant intermarriage. Many Crow in the Black Lodge District are part Cree, and Crow once sent a delegate to help the Cree obtain a reservation. Groups of Crow form independent teams and play in the stickgame tournament at the Rocky Boy Powwow in August. Crow teams also participate in the stickgame tournament at the Arlee Powwow hosted by the Salish and Kootenai.[45]

As in Oklahoma, where many people play handgame only when the Crow come in November, some Crow do not play throughout the entire handgame season, only coming out to play or watch the annual Crow tournaments in the spring. Likewise, some Crow do not play handgame at all, especially those who associate the game with ghosts and spirits, and others, especially some Christian and Pentecostal Crow, who associate it as a "ghost game" or as gambling and a sinful activity associated with the devil. The tournaments are also associated with erratic spring weather. Erratic or extreme weather in the form of rainstorms, late snow, and tornadoes often occurs during the junior and senior tournaments of April and May. Some Crow attribute this to the handgame players "pulling their medicine out."

THE CROW STYLE OF PLAY

Crow handgame teams are characterized by several organizational principles. First, teams are formed by reservation districts. Second, a man traditionally plays on the team his wife plays with. Third, most Crow teams are based around extended families. Reflecting a matrilineal basis, this rule is reportedly still followed by most. At Crow, each team must have a medicine man, five guessers, and others to sing.

The Crow handgame differs significantly from the Oklahoma version. According to some Crow, originally only men played handgame. Gender roles at Crow handgames dictate that men sit on the front row, women in the rows behind. Women may hide, sing, and shake rattles but not serve as guessers or medicine men. In addition, the traditional belief in menstrual blood breaking medicine required women to avoid Sun Dances, powwows, handgames, and other rituals during their monthly cycle, a custom that is still supposed to be followed. One individual cited this practice as the reason why women are not allowed to be guessers.

In the Crow style of play there are no referees in the middle of the floor, as the teams simply watch one another. There are four hiders instead of two, and woman may hide but not guess or serve as medicine men. Compared with handgames in western Oklahoma, the Crow style of play is more intense in several aspects. The Crow teams are larger, contain more singers, and wear elaborate matching uniforms. Brand-new uniforms are made for each district each year. Parts of the old ones are worn at powwows, for nice dress, or sometimes not at all. In addition to an award for best-dressed team, there is an award for best designer, and Crow women in each district eagerly seek to win this status. The medicine men make elaborate, sometimes lengthy preparations over the hiding objects; hiding and guessing motions are more elaborate; and at times the visual and auditory intensity of the singing, gestures, and play is greater.

Crow pride themselves on their fierce competitiveness in the handgame. Willie Stewart described, "Our game is very aggressive. It gets very complicated, and you got to have a lot of patience and a lot of endurance." One Kiowa man remarked, "Up at Crow, I mean, they do take it serious . . . they have sweats and different things like that." One Crow man remarked, "Some Crow women are just as vicious and ruthless handgame players as the men." The junior tournament is especially noted for its competitiveness. Some individuals have stated that they feel the younger players in the junior tournament are even more competitive and intense than the senior players.[46] Crow women and

206   CHAPTER 4

children participate in handgames, frequently as hiders. However, one of their primary contributions is in singing and shaking rattles while on the offense to distract the opposing team's guesser, and when the other guessing side misses their side and they score a point.

Guessing Signs

The four basic guessing signs have continued and are generally similar to those used in Oklahoma. Inside is the same as in Oklahoma. The outside guess is the same, except the Crow hold the back of their hand toward the opponent rather than the palm side. Left and right can be signaled by pointing with the thumb or an index finger. While signs are not as set as in Oklahoma, the Crow do not use two-finger (V) guessing and tongue pointing.[47]

Singing

Crow singing is higher in pitch than the southern plains style and is characterized by a double beat that many groups like. When playing intertribally, some tribes ask Crow singers to sing older Crow handgame songs. While southern plains hand drums are normally two-sided, Crow hand drums are one-sided and thus also often higher in pitch. In the past, Crow handgame songs were slower than those of the KCA. At one time the Big Horn District was especially noted for its slow-paced songs. The Crow are known for producing many handgame songs, and they place a great deal of emphasis on the rhythm of singing. One Crow man remarked that the pace of the music is what is most important. "Anyone can sing, but it's all in the rhythm." Perhaps reflecting a decline in language fluency, Crow players have recently stated that, as in Oklahoma, they are not singing as many songs with lyrics.

Large teams and elongated seating arrangements make it difficult for some players and spectators to see all that occurs during a game. The five guessers sit close to the floor on small upholstered stools. Behind them, two rows of men sit on long wooden benches. The women sit then behind the men in several rows on bleachers. Only a few feet separate the two sides. One end of the rectangular formation is blocked by three seated judges, while the other end contains a table with an announcer. However, the audience easily follows the flow of a game by the reaction of the teams—in particular the drumming, rattles, cheering, gestures, and general body language of offense and defense.

Medicine (Magic and Power)

The use of *baaxpée* (spiritual power, medicine, power transcending the ordinary, something mysterious or spiritual, good luck) and *xapáaliia* (a medicine bundle, the tangible image of baaxpée) permeate the Crow belief system. Baaxpée and xapáaliia are used in several situations, including healing, preventive medicine, divination, and competitive and gambling-related activities such as horse races, basketball games, and the handgame (Frey 1997, 59, 144–48, 183–84). Reflecting the vibrant motions made during play, Frey (1987, 144) describes the successful use of baaxpée in a handgame against the visiting Kiowa:

> The Kiowa hand-game team is up from Oklahoma, challenging the six district teams on the reservation. They're undefeated, and about to play the weakest of the Apsáalooke teams. In the school gym the stage is set. The Apsáalooke team sit in their bleachers and anticipate the worst—that is, all but one. On the floor the two teams face one another. Among the Kiowa, one stands and begins to sing his medicine song, "making medicine for his team." He's the key to their success. Just as he's about to finish, a man on the top row of the bleachers reaches out with his hand and grabs at the air in the direction of the Kiowa team. The singer immediately stops his song and looks around in wonder. All he can do now is sit down; his power is gone. The Apsáalooke team, the poorest on the reservation, beats the Kiowas.

Frey (1987, 146) reports, "The guesser on each team often has xapáaliia that is clearly designated for hand games." According to Crow dictates, an individual should have such handgame medicine in order to have the "right to guess" in a handgame. To guess without having the medicine, and thus the right, may result in ultimate failure as recorded in one case (Frey 1987, 146, 148). At handgames, arrow-throwing tournaments, and parades, a clan uncle (*áassahke*; the men and women of one's father's clan) will sing praise songs as he dances before all in attendance to publicly honor and recognize his *baakáate* (clan niece or nephew) for a deed (Frey 1987, 45, 49).

In Crow handgames there are four primary kinds of medicine: medicine for hiding, guessing, protection, and good luck. In contrast with the southern plains handgame, stronger concepts of supernatural power or medicine clearly remain in the Crow handgame. As one Crow man explained, "It's not just a game here like it is in Oklahoma. There's medicine involved here." The medicine is used by the medicine man to protect his teammates and to help his side win. Many Kiowa believe that the Crow possess and use medicine in playing the handgame. Following a record-setting six-hour, thirty-eight-minute game in which the Northern Cheyenne team finally beat Lodge Grass in 1998, one Crow man commented that it was an example of "too much medicine" being used between the two medicine men on the teams.[48]

To be a guesser or medicine man in the Crow handgame, a man must have medicine. In accordance with their matrilineal descent, most Crow obtain

208   CHAPTER 4

their handgame medicine from a maternal clan uncle, who teaches them specific procedures or "rituals" for preparing the hiding implements before handing them out to play. As Ed Little Light described (Johnson 2001):

> You take those people who guess, who make those motions. They imitate an elk, maybe a buffalo or a bear or a coyote or a bird of some kind. They buy those ways. You know, a guesser cannot guess unless he buys one from somebody, one of his uncles. Okay, a young man who wants to be a guesser or a medicine man, he has to go and ask one of his uncles. They probably have a sweat, and they'll have a big feast for that man. Then they'll give him four things, four good things. Then the man would accept that. Once you accept that, you give them your way, how to motion. That man would tell that boy, 'You do this. You do this.' It's been handed down for years and years and years. We don't just get in there and play.

Medicines and their related practices and taboos can vary highly depending in part on associated rites. In Crow handgames the medicine men often wear a physical form related to their medicine, such as red paint on their face, wrists, or hands, elk teeth, an eagle claw, bentonite clay, colored plumes on their hats, or a strip of fur as a bracelet. As one consultant described, "A lot of people use sage and then bear root. A lot of them have paint, you know, they paint themselves. Some people have it [paint] on their face; some have it around their wrist or on their hands. It just depends on how their medicine was given to them. It's kind of like a protection, and then at the same time it's a right to do things that are like ritual to that medicine itself."[49]

Some forms of medicine are visible, others are not. Formal handgame medicines are often physical objects contained in a small bundle or a pouch. Some medicine men wear their medicine in the form of bracelets, in pouches attached to the bottom of a bandoleer worn over their shoulder (much like a Gourd Dance bandoleer), or under their vest, and these are often touched when making medicine over the bones. Some bandoliers contain items such as bison horns or elk teeth and have eagle plumes and other items hanging from them. The head guesser of one team I observed wore a bracelet around his left wrist that contained a bear claw extending down the back of his hand. The head guesser of another team wears a mescal bean bandolier over his left shoulder (like those worn in the Gourd Dance). Another Crow wears a bandolier with items suspended from it. Included in his medicine are certain things he must adhere to, including food taboos. One individual explained how he paid $500 for his handgame medicine and how his brother-in-law paid $1,000 for his. An elder Kiowa described a Crow guesser who wore a small strip of beaver fur around his wrist as medicine but noted that this man's team sometimes lost. One Kiowa player who attributes success only to luck told me of a Crow medicine bundle that he was given, but he wears it under his shirt only as a gift and not as a source of medicine.

One time a group was forming a team to play in a tournament sponsored by Black Lodge, but no one wanted to be the medicine man. A clan uncle took his nephew outside to teach him the motions and ritual associated with his medicine. The team entered the upcoming tournament and won under the new medicine man. Afterward the nephew and his family prepared a sweat and a meal and took cigarettes to the clan uncle's house, where they thanked him for teaching the nephew and letting him use his medicine and formally asked permission for him to continue using it. The uncle accepted and came to the sweat and meal. He told his nephew of the stories behind the medicine and said he would share it with him.

Several individuals state that medicine is sometimes shared with others, in which cases the original owner keeps the objects associated with the medicine while the new recipient makes a replica for himself. From the individuals I visited with, the transfer of handgame medicine is associated more with knowledge and its teaching than physical objects. Although many Crow try to keep their medicine in the same family when sharing it or passing it on, there are also instances of individuals giving it to younger men from other families. Some forms of handgame medicine go back several generations. Henry "Sargie" Old Horn's medicine went back to his great-grandfather Two Leggings, who obtained it from his father Sits in the Land.[50]

Derived from animals, the various types of medicine used in handgames are often reflected in the movements made by the medicine man and what they do with their hands while preparing the bones prior to each round of hiding. Each medicine man has his own style with their medicine and rituals. During the 1998 tournament I was able to watch one medicine man with Bear Medicine, who got down on the floor on his hands and knees and performed a series of scratching and pawing motions. A medicine man with Elk Medicine made motions with his arms extended outward like the broad horns of an elk. Another, with Eagle Medicine, made a series of motions with his arms extended outward and then moved in a flapping motion. Each medicine man has his own medicine and his own style of making medicine over the hiding objects before passing them out to the hiders on his team. According to one consultant, some men do not use their medicine during the district match games but only bring it out for the final tournament each year.

One elder Crow medicine man explained how he had Magpie Medicine. He said he had seen magpies attack and peck out a bull's eyes until it was blind. Soon the bull died, and the magpies ate on the bull for a long time. This individual compared magpies to sharks in that they can smell the blood of a bleeding animal and quickly swarm together to attack it.[51]

When preparing the hiding implements, known as "making medicine," the medicine man usually rolls or presses the bones on the floor while kneeling. He may make several motions, then individually (for each elk tooth or set of bones) pick up one hiding object, hide it in his hands, make motions toward the opposing side, then open the empty hand (symbolizing the hand soon to be missed) and shake it at the other side. Most medicine men will do this for all four of the hiding objects, then pick the objects up, stand up, proceed to select hiders, and hand the hiding objects out by throwing them to the individual or by walking behind them and handing them to the person. The medicine man will do everything in his power to choose the best hiders and help their side. As Lewis Walks Over Ice explained (Johnson 2001), "The medicine man, he is the captain. He is the one, when he makes medicine, he makes medicine, and he tries to fool the guessers. So, he looks over at his charges and he'll say, 'I wonder. I think I'll give it to this guy. I'll give it to that women. They seem like they got the best luck."

In contrast to formal handgame medicine, often handed down through family lines, some individuals also carry other simpler forms for protection during handgames. Crow consultants report that sage, cedar, bear root, plumes, and paint on their faces, wrists, and hands act as protection from malevolent medicine. Similar medicines may be used in other events such as powwows. As one Crow player explained, "[My uncle used to say], 'Make sure you cedar yourself or, you know, use protection in there because sometimes people want to win so bad that they forget they use medicine that don't belong in there.' . . . He said, 'Make sure you're using the right medicine in there.' . . . I was always taught to wear protection in there because my uncle always said, 'People are starting to bring medicine in there that doesn't belong in there. . . . You always want to protect yourself.'" It seems that an individual may use both types of medicine, formal (often inherited) and informal (personal items), and the only way to determine the nature of a form of medicine is to ask the individual involved.

Crow refer to many aspects associated with playing handgame as "medicine." Medicine can involve physical items, ritual routines, or both. In the Crow handgame both men and women can have medicine. In anthropological terms, these kinds of beliefs and actions comprise much of the kinesics (body language) associated with the Crow handgame, especially that of the medicine men, hiders, and guessers. They represent imitative or sympathetic

The Kiowa-Crow Association   211

magic—the acting out of a desired effect or activity prior to undertaking it to ensure the desired result. This is primarily conducted through the motions to prepare the hiding implements prior to passing them out, hand motions made toward the opposing team that imitate the missing of guesses, the deflection of the other team's efforts toward one's own team in play, the pantomimed pulling of the hiding object or objects and thus the offense to one's side, and ridicule of one's play—missing a guess as a guesser or being guessed correctly as a hider.

Other forms involve contagious magic or magic that is associated with physical contact with the source of power or onto which the power has been transferred. Some medicine men carry objects related to their source of power, such as a bear claw, magpie feather, fur from a particular animal, or red paint. In many cases, both forms appear to be combined, as in the case of a handgame medicine man pantomiming his source of power (often an animal) while bearing a physical item from that power (such as a feather or claw) on his person.

The elaborate motions associated with the handgame make it a visual spectacle. For example, a medicine man or a hider often feigns hiding the objects, then opens his or her hands to show an empty hand (in the use of the elk tooth) or a hand with the non-desired bone (the marked bone in the north, and thus a missed guess) to imply the guesser is going to guess them incorrectly. Even players who are not hiding often make a motion of brushing off one hand with the other toward the opposing team, imitating the reversal of the other team's power being used against them. Similarly, some players make motions of catching and then throwing or brushing off the others side's medicine. The intense and spirited nature of these actions add greatly to the atmosphere of the game by adding kinetic forms of taunting, ridicule, and competition to the play. Probably the most common form seen is the shaking of one's hand or quivering fingers motion—either in an upright vertical fashion or in a horizontal form—toward the opposing team.

The extensive use of hand and body motions and their association with power and medicine adds a significant aura and element of performance to the play in terms of entertainment. As Ed Little Light explained, "You play the way you feel. If you feel good, cut up. People like to see a little action. Give them something to talk about."[52] The elaborate hand gestures in the Crow style of play make the game visually intriguing and dramatic. As news reporter Ed Kemmick described of a Crow handgame he attended in 2017, "What mattered was the spectacle—the teams in their elaborate, mostly handmade outfits, the constant yelling and chanting, the gesticulations of the players themselves."[53]

212   CHAPTER 4

The particular actions and taboos associated with handgame medicine can vary greatly from one individual to another. As one individual explained in relation to the handgame played between the ghosts, "The medicine that I was given, every time I pick up one of those sticks [counters], I have to motion with my hands toward that area, wipe the sticks off with my hand, and then wave in that direction . . . Everyone has different things, different ways."[54]

A range of activities are undertaken by some Crow for obtaining protection prior to handgames. Some attend sweat lodges, pray, and seek power before playing. In 1998 several of the visiting Kiowa and I were taken to a sweat lodge ceremony hosted by the Little Light family prior to playing in the senior tournament. Some Crow may also wear a strip of otter skin around their wrist or attach some other amulets or form of charm for luck and success in the game. One Kiowa elder told me how he was given such a charm long ago to wear but usually doesn't use it. This individual stated that he sometimes likes wearing it but that, when he does, it is solely for luck. However, this individual also carried a small bundle containing red paint in his left pants pocket, a bundle his grandfather gave him long ago when he was a dancer. Because some tribes "have a feeling about others sometimes," meaning they wish to harm someone by putting magic on them, this individual stated that he carries this bundle not for "luck in any way" but "for protection."[55]

Crow that I spoke with stated that all men have handgame medicine, especially for hiding, and that some women have it as well. One Crow man reported going on vision quests to obtain power for playing the handgame and that this form of power was needed to be a medicine man in the game. As he explained, "You must dream the dream in order to be a medicine man in the handgame. You must have power. Otherwise, what right do you have to get up and shake your fist in another man's face!"[56] While players exhibit their individual styles, their play and degree of success also reflect on their family's, clan's, and community's social standing.

Medicine Men

In the Crow handgame each team has a medicine man whose principal job is preparing the hiding implements (two elk teeth and two pairs of bones), selecting the four individuals who will hide them, and "making medicine" for his team during play. In the past these items were real teeth and bones, but today imitation elk teeth and plastic hair pipes are commonly used. The medicine man has medicine that he uses in the game. In Crow handgames a team cannot change their medicine man during a game as allowed in Oklahoma. Medicine men can take as long as they want to make medicine in preparing the hiding objects. You will often see a medicine man making hand motions toward the other team, often slapping the side of their waist, touching their medicine pouch, their source of power, and then extending their other arm and shaking their fingers at the other team. This is commonly done while their own side is hiding and the other team is trying to guess them.

Making medicine over the hiding implements is important, both from a theatrical and entertainment perspective for all in attendance and from its relationship to building spirit and confidence in play for the offense (hiding team) while simultaneously serving as a form of intimidation or psychological distraction for the defense (guessing team). One year when the Kiowa team lost one night, two Crow playing with the team remarked that the team was flat that night and that the medicine man "didn't have anything to him" ("he wasn't dressed up nice and didn't do anything to make any medicine"). We were easily beaten. Oklahoma handgame players rarely use uniforms and do far less preparation in handing out the hiding objects, but from the Crow observations, inferably, medicine associated with handgames can be anything that helps one, whether in winning, protection, or something else.[57]

When the medicine man has finished making his medicine, he will choose who he wants to hide for the round. In the Crow game, individuals are not permitted to walk up and down the center playing area as in the Oklahoma style. For individuals sitting on the front or guesser's row, the medicine man generally gains the attention of the individual he desires to hide, then throws the hiding objects to them. Because mobility is limited and the music is extremely loud, conversation between the medicine man and an individual sitting down the row is often not possible. A team's medicine men may signal an individual to ask what type of hiding object he or she wants to hide by holding up one finger to designate a single elk tooth or two fingers representing a set of bones (two). The hider will respond by holding up one or two fingers, and then the medicine man will give the corresponding type of hiding object to the hider. The hiding objects are generally tossed to men and handed to women. There is little or no concern as to whether the thrown objects are caught, and players are not taunted nor do they lose a point if they drop an elk tooth or the bones as in older Oklahoma games. The player simply picks them up and begins to hide. Sometimes the objects are simply thrown on the carpet on the floor in front of male hiders, near their feet, to pick up and begin to hide. For hiders closer to the medicine men and for men and especially women in the back rows, the medicine man walks to them and opens his two hands together containing the hiding objects. In this instance, the hider is allowed to reach and take whichever they prefer. Often after each hider receives a hiding object, the medicine man pauses to motion at the other team by extending his arm and vigorously shaking his hand at them. The process is generally repeated as each of the four objects is distributed to a hider.

Some medicine men may hold both types of objects in their two open and cupped hands and allow a hider to choose the type they desire. Most often medicine men will throw the objects to the men in the first two rows and hand them to players in the remaining back rows, including the women hiders. Older players reported that the throwing of hiding objects was common among the men in the first two rows, in part because the medicine man cannot walk down the center of the floor in front of the other men and because it is often difficult to walk between the first two rows of men. One Crow explained that when he received his style, he was told to hand the objects to hiders and not to throw them: "Because you want your medicine to rub off on their medicine and get stronger together." One medicine man reported that to pass the hiding items down the line would allow portions of its medicine to rub off onto non-hiders and that one should not walk back and forth in front of the others since all are wearing medicine and might be throwing medicine during the game. If any hiding objects are thrown and accidentally knocked across the center line of play, that object or set of bones is forfeited for that round.

On defense, medicine men, guessers, and other players can often be seen making medicine (making body and hand motions) against the other side. Often the medicine man of the guessing side will be making motions against the other side as they are preparing and hiding their objects. The first time I saw this it reminded me of the role of conjurers in Cherokee stickball, where opposing conjurors continually worked medicine against one another's teams and, according to Cherokee belief, the side with the stronger conjuror won the game.

First Point

Match games and tournaments begin with competition for the first point, known as *ba chii chi le* (Medicine Horse 1987, 58), which involves the award of two sticks and the offense. Crow handgames begins with fourteen score sticks lying on the floor between the two teams. Each side uses a single guesser, typically their main guesser, and their medicine man. Each side guesses the other side's hider. When one side wins this exchange, they are awarded two sticks and the offense, and regular play begins. For purposes of illustration, I will refer to the two teams as Teams A and B. To determine the first point, and out of courtesy, one side is told to hide (Team A), while the other (Team B) will guess. If the first guess is missed, the team hiding (A) is one point ahead (although no sticks are used). The other team (B) then hides. If a correct guess is made by team A, they win the first point. However, if Team B is incorrectly guessed by Team A, then the teams are tied, and Team B then hides again. If they are incorrectly guessed, they are now up to two points to one. Team A then hides. If they are missed by Team B, the score is tied again, and the process begins again. If they are guessed correctly, Team B wins the offense, takes two sticks from the pile of fourteen in the middle of the floor, and continues to sing and drum as their medicine man begins making medicine over the bones and elk teeth before passing them out to four hiders to begin regular play. Play continues until one side has all fourteen sticks. Teams must put up $250 as "first point money" for every game in the tournament. If one wins that game, that money can be divided among the team or kept to use as the first point money in future rounds.[58]

Hiding

In the Crow handgame, following the first point, there are four hiding objects and four hiders at the start of every offensive exchange. At the beginning of each offensive exchange the medicine man takes the bones and elk teeth and makes medicine over them before handing them out to players on his side to hide. When the medicine man has finished making medicine on the hiding pieces, he begins to choose the four individuals to hide for his team. If he can reach the individuals, he usually walks behind them and hands them the hiding object or objects. If he cannot easily walk to where they are seated, which is often difficult in the cramped area, he simply tosses them to the hider. Two of the hiders each hide a single elk tooth in the hand of their choice, the other hand being empty. The other two hiders each hide a pair of hair pipe bones, one bone in each hand, with one bone being plain and the other one marked with black tape around the middle. In guessing, the guesser tries for the hand containing each elk tooth and, opposite the Oklahoma style, the unmarked bone of each of the other two hiders.

Men must hide with both hands in front of them or under a leg but not behind their own back. They can hide the objects behind the back of one of the guessers if they are sitting on the second row. Women are allowed to hide under a shawl or blanket or behind other players. In Crow-style play, you can hide both bones in one hand, which then become the one to guess for. If the guesser chooses the hand with both, you are "hit" and must give up the bones. If the guesser chooses the empty hand, it is a miss and your side scores a stick. Men with large hands can hide in this manner (they must be able to completely hide both bones without giving themselves away).

Crow guessers are known for making elaborate hand motions, moving their guessing hand from side to side while watching the hider's eyes and feigning guesses until an actual guess is made. Both Kiowa and Crow have told me that the guessers do this for two reasons: to get the hider to give themselves away by faking them out to think the guess has been made and thus opening their hands and exposing the hiding objects before a guess is made, and to induce an individual to give themselves away through a tell or mental or physical fatigue. When playing with the Kiowa team against the Crow, I was warned not to be fooled by their attempts to fake me out and not to open my hands until members of our own team told me to.

Most hiders follow the guesser's extended hand as he moves it back and forth in making his motions, making sure to maintain their stare exactly in the middle of the guesser's hand so as not to favor one side and potentially give away which side they are hiding the object on. Some hiders have stated that they sometimes attempt to fake the guesser out by looking slightly more at the incorrect side than the correct side after the guesser has made several motions. Some individuals stated that the guesser will often fall for this strategy. Then many hiders will do the same thing again by looking to the side where it was the first time but having switched the hiding item or items in their hands.

Bill Koomsa Jr. described the Crow style of hiding and guessing and some of the differences between the Kiowa and Crow style of play:

> Up there in the north . . . they like to look for you to flinch at a certain time when they make a certain gesture, and that's where they go. Up there, once you come out with your hiding object, when you break your arms away from your head, they like to check your eyes. . . . They say you gotta look right at the guesser. Maybe there's something to it, but we don't play it—we play for luck, just on luck. And we like to play for fun too. Some persons . . . play that way, [but] we don't really like to play that way. In fact, some people up there, up north, they really take it serious. Some guys that are going to guess, they'll go into a sweathouse and whatever and prepare.[59]

Louis Walks Over Ice explained that a great deal of psychology is involved in the play. In particular the guesser tries to detect a number of "tells," as if playing poker. A hider may unconsciously squeeze the hand holding the elk tooth extra hard or hold that hand lower than the other. The hider may also do these things intentionally to fake the guesser out.[60] As one Crow told me, "It's a lot of psychological warfare, and the Crows are the masters of it."[61]

In the Crow handgame, if a hider wishes to re-hide the object prior to being guessed, they signal this by holding up an index finger from one of two closed hands. The guesser will acknowledge this by throwing one or both hands in an upward motion toward the hider to signal "go ahead." The hider will then

The Kiowa-Crow Association 217

re-hide the object or objects and then bring their closed hands forward and outward again. The guesser then resumes studying the hider and prepares to make his guess.

The guesser may also instruct the hider to re-hide by bringing his two extended index fingers together then separating them to the side. As Lewis Walks Over Ice explained (Johnson 2001), "When you take an elk tooth, you go like this this [hides it in two closed fists, one on top of the other, moving them together up and down], and you go like this [separates hands]. See, you make the motion [to] try to confuse the guesser. And you, he's watching your hands. . . . Sometimes he'll go like that [puts two index fingers extended out together, then separates them to the sides], which means put it together again [hide again]. So, you're in effect trying to fool him again."

When a hider is guessed they must open their hands to show their hiding positions. If guessed correctly, they are out for that round and must give up the hiding objects. Once a hider is correctly guessed they are down for the remainder of the offensive exchange and cannot come back in, as in the Oklahoma style of play. When correctly guessed, the men tend to simply toss the elk tooth or bones to members of the other side to catch or onto the floor across the center area toward players on the other team who pick them up and give them to their medicine man. Women tend to hand them back to their medicine man, who passes them to the other side at the exchange. On one team I noticed that the Crow medicine man gathered each of the hiding items from the hiders as they were guessed correctly and held them together in his hands. After the last hider was guessed correctly, he gave all four items to the other side to begin their next offense. At Crow there is no penalty for dropping a bone or elk tooth. The only penalty consultants recalled was when during the first point a hider was guessed correctly and tossed his bones before the other side hid and got guessed, resulting in two sticks and the offense. For each point scored, a player from the offensive team will take a stick from the center to their side, or if all fourteen have already been won from the center, from the other side's sticks to their side. When all four hiders have been guessed correctly and their hiding pieces collected, the medicine man on that side will begin a similar ritual in making medicine over the hiding pieces, choosing hiders, and passing the hiding pieces out to begin their offense.

In the past the Crows allowed an individual to wager more than one point on a single guess, including hiding or guessing all four hiding implements. For example, a hider might lay three of the four hiding implements on the floor in front of him and then hide the fourth as a challenge to the other side to guess a single hider for all four points. This is a very high-stakes and daring form since the guess is then worth four points instead of one. If the hider is correctly guessed, the hiding implements and offense pass to the other side. If the guess is missed, the offense scores four immediate points and can hide again. Ed Little Light, who was commonly known among the Crow as "Mr. Handgame" for his playing ability, successfully did this several times, including hiding all four twice in a row and being missed both times.[62]

One Crow man stated in 1998 that cheating can and does occur, both by male and female players. Most commonly this occurs with a player hiding a single elk tooth. The key to successful cheating is to either 1) move one's hands side to side and throw the tooth from the open area between the thumb and slightly extended and curled forefinger in an almost closed fist, or 2) move one's hands up and down, and then, if correctly guessed, raise the hand with the tooth in it, with the other hand below it, next to the elbow, and let the tooth drop down the inside of one's raised arm, and catching it in the opened area between the thumb and forefinger of the lower hand. If the guesser misses, there is no need for this maneuver, of course. If the tooth is dropped, which this individual said he had seen occur, it is considered an automatic hit (correct guess), the tooth is given up as if correctly guessed, and the other side takes a score stick for the point. According to this individual the tooth is considered dropped, and no accusations of cheating are made.

Guessers and Guessing

In most match games and in their annual tournaments, each team has five designated guessers who sit together in the front row on small wooden benches in the middle of the floor. The guessers are ranked. The head guesser in the center of the five directs all the guessing. The second guesser sits to his right, the third on his left, the fourth farther on the right, and the fifth farther on the left—or in order from left to right: 5, 3, 1, 2, 4. The head guesser does most of the guessing, but if he misses a few times, he may turn the position over to one of the other guessers. If they are unable to guess the opposition correctly, the position of guesser can be passed down the ranks of the other guessers. If a guesser misses several times, the head guesser can take the position back or appoint another guesser. Although the main guesser will usually pass the position to his second guesser when needed, they can choose another, including the medicine man, to guess. Often a new guesser will be put in if a guesser misses two consecutive guesses. On regaining the offense from an opponent, the last active guesser can resume guessing or return it to the head guesser. At one time a single hider could hide all four points (hiding one and laying the other hiding objects in front of them) and be guessed, or two hiders could hide for two points each.

In the Crow tournaments there is no middle line marked between the teams as in Oklahoma. Guessers can stand up and walk back and forth in the center area studying the opposition, but they must remain on their side of the center area. Although there are four hiders, a guesser can choose how many he will guess at a time and will signal to the judges: one, two, three, or all four. Most guessers single out one or two hiders at a time and then, after getting them, go on to the others. Once you begin guessing a set number of hiders (one to four), you must continue until all have been guessed correctly before you are allowed to guess the remaining individuals. Although it is rare, individuals are known to have guessed all four individuals correctly in a single guess.

Phil "Joe Fish" Dupoint described one time when they were at Crow, the Kiowa were losing, and Tom Kaulaity got up to guess. After conferring with others, he turned to face the Crow. "So he went like this [indicating all four guesses], he went 'four,' and the crowd went wild." After rubbing his hands together to make his medicine, he slapped his side with one hand, motioned with his other, and went "Ho!" "So he went that way, he went to their right, and they all open up, and dang if he didn't get them all. He guessed all four of them, and that crowd went crazy man. . . . So, anyway, he got best guesser. They gave him $100." Guessers can still guess up to four hiders at a time if they choose.[63]

A key element in the Crow handgame is the guesser's motions. The Crow employ a rule for hiders that provides a certain amount of consistency in how one can hide and thus, in theory, a degree of control for the guesser. In the Crow handgame, a male hider must follow the hand motions of the guesser with his eyes. Most often this involves the hider extending one arm and hand, with his index finger and thumb extended, with the other fingers folded inward. If he does not follow the guesser's hand motions, the guesser can request the judges to make the hider do so. This is done so that the guesser can study you. In having your eyes fixed constantly upon his moving hand, a guesser can study your eyes for the slightest change in motion and dilation. The guesser may also ask a hider to remove their sunglasses, which has to be complied with. The Crow also study various elements of the hider's body posture: their movement of arms, legs, and feet; the position they are sitting in; their degree of tenseness; the favoring of one side, arm, hand, or leg over the other; greater tightness in one fist than the other; the veins on one's hands. Any of these might give the hider away. The Crow players I spoke with stated that while all of these factors are taken into consideration, the movement of the eyes is given priority, and Crow are experts at detecting the slightest, subtlest change. Ed Little Light (Johnson 2001) characterized the game as "a scientific game."

220   CHAPTER 4

Most guessers go through a series of side-to-side and up-and-down motions at various angles, with their arms extending back and forth, while shaking their hand at the hider with thumb and index finger extended open as if in an L or pistol shape. According to one Crow consultant, this hand motion is similar to the sign language sign for "do you understand?" or "do you get it?" Many guessers have a set style, the motions associated with their guessing medicine. As one Crow man explained, "The people that have an actual guessing way, like there are certain hand motions that you have to do, you know, like a routine. . . . It's not just throwing your hand up and down and sideways, you know. You're given a rite, and you have to do it that way."

As Kiowa and Crow elders explained to me, the guesser is trying to get you to give yourself away with your eye motions by looking too far one way or the other to one side of his hand. They told me the key is to concentrate exactly between the center of his outstretched thumb and forefinger. If you look too far to one side, the guesser may detect which side you are hiding the object on and guess you. After several such motions, some hiders will intentionally look to one side attempting to mislead the guesser, but if the attempt is too obvious the guesser may pick up on it and realize the hider's efforts to mislead him.

Crow guessers are noted for vigorously faking their guesses to get hiders to prematurely open their hands and give themselves away. At one time the guesser's motions did not count in the Crow style of play unless their pinky was extended or curled away from their fist, but I have seen some players use their thumb as the principal indicator. While one consultant knew of an older player who guessed with his pinky, this style seems to have faded. Guessers may make several fake motions to make the hider think he has signaled his guess and make them open their hands. This worked many times in the past on Oklahoma players unfamiliar with the style who opened their hands and showed the hiding objects before an actual guess was signaled, resulting in being immediately guessed and caught. The guesser may also make prolonged motions to attempt to wear the hider down until they give themselves away. While a team is on defense and guessing, the women players on that side can often be seen reaching toward the offense and pulling toward their side with cupped hands. Some players stated this is in imitation of bringing the bones over to their side, thus gaining the offense.

The Crow are noted for making highly energetic and prolonged hand motions that are much more extensive and intense than those used in southern plains handgames. Crow players often change their motions, trying to make you give yourself away through their combinations or by tricking you into showing the bones before they signal their actual guess. Often they walk back and forth in front of a hider, studying them. There used to be no time limit for guessing, often resulting in each guess taking several minutes, but around the mid-1990s a one-minute limit was implemented. This has not always been enforced in games I have witnessed and played in.

Out of respect, in the Crow style of play male guessers do not make excessive hand motions toward women, motions associated with power such as shaking the hand, pointing a finger, or faking motions. Men may raise a straight hand, a closed or laid down fist, shake their hands, and make the regular four signs of inside, outside, right, and left. As one man explained, "There's no trying to fake them out, right or left. That's kind of out of respect for the women folks." Women are not required to follow the hand motions of the male guessers or to even look at the male guessers. As Jeremy Shield explained, "I remember my grandma telling my mother and my sisters and all that not to look at the guesser. To close their eyes and put their head down. Don't even look at them."[64] Many women close their eyes or lower their head and look at the floor while hiding. The only rule applying to women is that they must hold their hands high enough to be seen while hiding. More recently some Crow women will look at the guesser.

Matrilineal clan association also affects the guessing in the Crow handgame. In general, many men do not guess their female clan relatives. Prohibitions on who one can guess can vary from individual to individual. Some men will not guess their sisters. A guesser's individual medicine may also impact who he can guess. One male reported that when he was given his medicine it was explained to him that he cannot guess his mother-in law, his mother's sisters, or the wives of his wife's brothers. In cases when a man cannot guess a particular clan relative, they will pass the guess to the next-ranked guesser of their team's five guessers. In theory, an opposing team can take a particular guesser out of the game by choosing hiders an opposing guesser is not allowed to guess.

Handgame players study one another's habits, sometimes concentrating so long and hard that it can become exhausting. According to one Kiowa, one year at Crow an individual studied the hiders so long that he was catching on to how they were hiding and was doing well guessing them. But finally he studied them so long that he got physically sick and couldn't do it anymore. One Kiowa who has played against the Crow for many years stated that the key to success was to have a good medicine man that watches the guesser's actions (faking and otherwise) and tells you when to open your hands to show your hide. According to this individual, the Crow may ask you to watch their pointing hand, but you really do not have to.[65]

A lot of good-natured competition, taunting, and jeering often accompany the game, just as in Oklahoma, and the teasing and ridicule can have a kinship basis. The Crow have what are known as "joking" or "teasing" clans in which members of a man's father's clan undertake public censorship and mentoring through mockery, ridicule, and rebuke for inappropriate or inept behavior (Lowie 1983, 22–23). Among the Crow, members of one's "joking" or "teasing clan" are on the opposing side during handgames, and thus a lot of joking and teasing between the two groups of relatives occurs during play. There have also been years when the competition resulted in fistfights. Before one game in 1998, one of the judges asked over the microphone that "there be no fighting after the games." Stating that the previous year there had been fights, the speaker said that this set a bad example for children and asked for good sportsmanship to be demonstrated.

An individual who has just been guessed may act as if the guess was correct and begin to hand over the hiding object or objects only to suddenly open the guessed hand to show that it is empty (if hiding an elk tooth) or contains the marked bone (if hiding two bones) and then make a series of hand motions at the opposing side. Having just scored a point, the hider's side will holler, beat their drums, shake rattles, and verbally celebrate as the player begins to hide again.

Often when a side gets more than five of the fourteen score sticks, they begin to hand them out down both sides of the front line of guessers who each begins keeping time with them by tapping them on their knee or in their empty hand. Other people make similar motions with an empty fist. This is a form of psychological intimidation and taunting that correlates with the increased momentum of the game as a side continues to successfully hide. One Crow described this as "keeping time in their face." As a team begins to acquire many points or makes a run, its players continue to more actively display the sticks as they sing and drum.

THE ANNUAL CROW HANDGAME TOURNAMENTS

The Crow junior and senior tournaments are the highlight and the formal end of Crow handgame season. Prior to the formation of the Crow tournament, handgames among the Crow were largely match games between two districts, in which one district would invite or challenge another for an evening of play.[66] For many years among the Crow there were only two handgame tournaments a year, the junior and senior tournaments held in late April and early May. The annual senior tournament held at Crow Agency, Montana, is reported to have begun in 1966. Players thirty years old or younger play in the junior

The Kiowa-Crow Association 223

tournament, while players thirty and older play in the senior tournament. An individual who is thirty can play in both tournaments that year.[67]

More than just a recreation, the annual handgame tournament has several levels of social importance for the Crow. As Willie Stewart described (Johnson 2001), "During the handgame season in April we prepare ourselves as men, as women, and as clan members to represent our district to the fullest that we can. And we represent our families. We represent our clans. We represent our mothers, and fathers, and grandfathers." Like other cultural traditions, handgame can serve as a source of pride and focus for individuals and, like other cultural forms, an avenue away from alcohol. Lewis Walks Over Ice (Johnson 2001) explained, "Before I got involved in handgame, for my own personal experience, you know, I was quite lost. I was aimless. . . . I was doing a lot of alcohol, you know. I got involved in handgame. So I forgot about drinking and alcohol, and I got into taking pride in handgame and arrows [arrow-throwing contests]. And I want to win it for my district, and I haven't touched alcohol or drugs in . . . a good ten years."

The creation of the senior tournament is credited to Ed "Buck Day" Little Light, who was inspired with the idea to create a handgame tournament for the Crow while attending a six-team basketball tournament. His idea was to invite each of the six districts of the Crow Nation to form a team and send it to the tournament, and to have everyone dress in elaborate clothing as a way of showing respect for the tradition and pride in their districts.[68] As Little Light described (Johnson 2001) of the formation of the tournament, "The six districts on the reservation, they invite one another. And when the sun goes down they go into those little halls and they start playing handgame. That went on for years and years and years. And we had a little meeting one evening, and, by god, I been watching these basketball tournaments and all that stuff, and it got into my mind. 'Hey,' I said, 'I got an idea. Why don't we start a little tournament." According to some Oklahoma players, the Crow had been coming to Oklahoma for a number of years and had observed their style of play, which influenced their formation of a Crow tournament. Both events may have been influences. For the Crow, the senior tournament became the second-largest event of the year, second only to the Crow Fair in August.

Ed Little Light, Jim Big Shoulder Blade, and Ira Lefthand are reported to have been the original founders of the Crow Senior Handgame Tournament. For many years Lefthand placed the counters between the teams before each game. Several years later Lefthand sponsored a junior tournament that has continued to the present. As noted, the junior tournament is usually held in mid to late-April, one to two weeks prior to the senior tournament. In the

224 CHAPTER 4

original Crow tournament only the six Crow district teams were allowed: Lodge Grass, Wyola, Reno, Black Lodge, Big Horn, and Pryor. Several years ago, a number of the Lodge Grass District players splintered off to form a seventh team called No Water. As the Crow were already making annual visits to the Kiowa when the Crow tournament began, they invited a Kiowa team to participate. Little Light also had children attending Riverside Indian School in Anadarko, Oklahoma, and thus the trips to Oklahoma also allowed him to visit them and visit the adjacent Kiowa community. As the popularity of playing in the Crow tournament grew in Oklahoma, members of other western Oklahoma tribes (Comanche, Apache, Cheyenne, Delaware, and others) asked to join the Kiowa contingents, resulting in what is now a mixed Oklahoma team. The Crow neighbors to the east, the Northern Cheyenne, were also invited to participate in the annual tournament, bringing the total number of teams in the senior tournament to nine.

When the tournament began with just six Crow teams, it was a two-day event, typically held on a Friday and Saturday. With the addition of a seventh team, No Water, which split from Lodge Grass, the tournament was shifted to a program of Thursday evening, Friday, and Saturday. With the addition of the eighth and ninth teams of Oklahoma and the Northern Cheyenne, the schedule was against shifted to begin with two games on Wednesday night followed by play on Thursday, Friday, Saturday, and sometimes into Sunday. The 2021 tournament ran from June 9 to June 13. The event is played as a double elimination tournament, winner take all. Whichever team wins the tournament has to sponsor and host it the following year. The Kiowa have won twice at Crow, in 1988 with Pete Bearshield as head guesser, and in 2005 with Ace Yellowhair as head guesser.[69] The winning team also wins the sticks used in the tournament. These are usually made by the previous year's winner as part of hosting the tournament. Because the tournament involves all Crow districts, it brings people together, allowing Crow to visit with dispersed relatives and friends.

From its origin the tournament was long held in the octagonal log "Round House," a large octagonal wooden community building at the park in Crow Agency, Montana. This is the site where the well-known Crow Fair is held each August. Inside, nine sets of bleachers were arranged in a circular fashion around the central area where the games are played. Above each set of bleachers was a banner with the name, in both English and Crow, of each of the nine teams in the tournament, the seven Crow districts, the Kiowa-Oklahoma team, and the Northern Cheyenne. Seating was fairly limited, and the bleachers filled to capacity every time a game started, with some people standing on the ledge behind the bleachers or squeezing into the areas between them. Once a game started, then as now, people focused intently on the play.[70] In the center of the bleachers was a small open area between the two opposing sides where the counter sticks were laid at the start of each game. One player likened this space to the gully separating the two groups of ghosts playing for souls in the origin myth.

A small concession stand selling drinks and food was located on one side of the building. The only difference between the Crow and southern plains concession stands was that at Crow you bought tickets at an adjacent table for twenty-five cents apiece, then exchanged them for your food and beverage choices at the stand, whereas at southern plains games you simply paid cash directly at the food stand. Between games the bleachers and area around the playing area was swept and all trash picked up, keeping the area clean and reducing the final cleanup at the end of an evening's play. Around 2006, the Round House, by then considered unsafe, was taken down, and the tournament was shifted to the Multipurpose Building, containing a gym, a short distance south and beside the rodeo arena (Nabokov 2007). The same basic arrangement continues in the new facility.

Entry Fee and Rules

The Crow tournament is a winner-take-all event, with the entry fees used to pay the prize. Over the years the team entry fee has grown. In 1998 a $500 entry fee for nine teams produced a pot of $4,500. Later entry fees rose to $1,000 per team, resulting in a pot of $9,000. In 2017 it was $1,200 per team. One year when the Kiowa won the tournament they received $5,600, with the remainder of the entry fees covering other prizes.[71] Today team entry fees average around $1,000 for the junior tournament and $1,500 for the senior tournament.

Reflecting nine teams in the tournament, one consultant explained that for his district, if he put in $10 toward their team's entry fee and his team won the tournament, he would get $90 back. Games are typically scheduled to start at 7:00 p.m. but often begin later, accompanied by jokes about "Indian time." The games often go late into the night.

The winner of each tournament, junior and senior, must sponsor the next year's tournament. In 2016 Wyola won both the senior and junior tournament, which was a very rare feat. There are also pots of prize money and awards for high-point man and high-point woman (most consecutive points in a single hide) throughout the tournament, best medicine man, and best guesser (the five best guessers of the winning team in ranked order). In the 1998 Crow senior

226   CHAPTER 4

tournament each team put up $500 as entry fee, $100 for the first point bet for each game, $100 for the best male hider pot, and $100 for the best female hider pot. Winners in the "high-point" and "best" categories sponsor their respective award for the next year's tournament, usually through family members pooling things such as money, hats, boots, benches, jackets, and hand drums. Each individual and their family decides what the prize will be. Another tradition occurs when the head guessers of the last four remaining teams in the tournament are auctioned and "bought" by individuals who sponsor them. These funds are put in a pot, and the sponsor of the head guesser whose teams wins the tournament wins that money, sometimes as much as $5,000. The practice is comparable to the "Calcutta auctions" in rodeos.[72]

There is also a table on one end of the arena where side bets on the two teams playing are taken before the start of each game of the tournament. Unlike southern plains handgames, there is no effort to make sure the amount bet on each side is equal before play begins in Crow handgames. If Team A has $240 bet on its side, and Team B has only $210, the people bidding the last $30 on Team A's side will neither win nor lose their money; it will simply be repaid to them at the end of the game. A large chalkboard is used to post the amounts bet and can be viewed by all. The amounts are also announced by the master of ceremonies. The Crow also often have prizes for the best-dressed team, and best singing group at their annual tournament. Overall, the betting between the Crow and Kiowa is much smaller during the games in Oklahoma than those in Montana. At the annual Kiowa-Crow handgames in Oklahoma, bets average around $300 per side per game. One time a game's bets totaled $3,000, which the Crow won.[73] The Crow are known as great gamblers. Ed Little Light said (Johnson 2001), "Crow Indian like to gamble. You'll see those ladies up there. They bet $50, $100. They like that. You might lose today; maybe tomorrow you night get real hot. We believe if you don't have anything, you're gonna be in bad luck."

The rules for the two tournaments are the same. Both are double elimination and run similar to the round-robin tournaments in Oklahoma, with the exception that the Crow have a different set of rules and the speed of play is much slower. Often the Crow do not begin their first game of the evening until after 9:00 p.m. or 10:00 p.m. and play until near dawn. In speaking of this, one Kiowa individual jokingly stated, "[There is] white man time, Indian time, and Crow time!"

Three or four judges sit at a table between and at the end of both teams and watch the game closely to ensure that all rules are followed. The judges are not from either of the teams currently playing that round. In the Crow style of play there are no judges on the floor between the teams as in the southern plains. Other rules and specifications may be dictated by the host district. The following senior handgame rules and regulations as posted by the Lodge Grass District for the 1998 tournament, which follow on the next page.[74]

Each Crow district team has a standard uniform they wear for the tournament. For the men these usually consist of matching-colored long-sleeve ribbon shirts, vests of another color with appliqué or beaded designs, jeans or trousers, cowboy hats or baseball caps, and cowboy boots. The women of each team typically wear full-length dresses and elaborately embroidered or beaded and fringed shawls that match the color of the men's shirts, beaded buckskin leggings, beaded or tack belts, bone chokers, feather pendants, scarves, and associated necklaces and jewelry. The colorful uniforms are very attractive and are one of the most visible aspects of each team. With teams averaging fifty to seventy members, the matching attire of such large groups can have an intimidating affect. In 1998 the Northern Cheyenne men wore matching long-sleeve white shirts, and the women wore white and light-purple dresses and shawls. The Kiowa team wore long-sleeve red shirts and jeans or slacks. The visitors' dress is typically not as extensive or matching. Jeremy Shield suggested that colorful dress for the spring tournament correlates with the colors of the season and said: "That tournament that we dress up and go all out for, we give it our best because that's the last time we're supposed to play handgame for the year."[75]

Many Crow players also wear red paint on their foreheads and cheeks, some with lines extending back from the corners of their eyes. During the 1998 tournament many of the guessers on the Crow teams wore this form of paint. Some of the Oklahoma players wore similar red paint. Many of the Crow change back into their regular clothes after each game, as some teams will only play one game on certain nights.

At Crow handgames, men and women typically sit separately. A man is commonly teased, especially by members of specific clans, if he sits with his wife or spends too much time around her at a handgame.[76] At the start of each game, a seating order is followed. The women on each side are seated behind the men on two or more rows of benches on both sides. The five male guessers, with their small individual benches, are seated on the center of the front row. These are small three-legged stools or small rectangular benches on which the guessers sit in a semi-squatting fashion, lower to the ground then the other rows of players behind them. Next, the remaining male players and medicine man are seated on the first full row of wooden benches, followed by the male singers with hand drums on the second row. Spectators sit in lawn chairs on

1998 SR. HANDGAME RULES AND REGULATIONS

BETS

Each team participating in this year's tournament shall have $500.00 for the main game bet, $100.00 for the first point bet, $100.00 for high point woman and $100.00 for high point man, teams shall have all bet money ready when the scorekeeper calls for it.

1. Each team will be ready within fifteen (15) minutes when called to the playing arena, immediately after the conclusion of the proceeding game. When unusual circumstances warrant, a team may be allowed an extra (15) minutes to report to the playing arena. After fair notice and warning, the team that is not ready as scheduled to play will forfeit to the team that is ready and on the playing arena. The first game will begin at 7:00 P.M.

2. Judges will be selected by the Lodge Grass District and will be responsible for decisions rendered to common playing rules. Judges may stop the game for any infraction of any of the rules at any time. All decisions made by the judges will be final.

3. Playing area will be designated before each game and will be occupied by judges, announcers, players, singers, and coaches only. The coin toss for the seating arrangement will be done by the coaches.

4. Each singer shall have his own drum and not pass drums across to the other team during the game.

5. Number of guessers: Guessers shall be the front row lineup.

6. First point: during the first point contest, the hider and guesser shall be male participants.

7. Guessing: There shall be no guesses from the sidelines or singers after the games have started.

   A. All guessing shall be done by male participants.
   B. Extra motions used to guess men shall not be practiced on the women. Opened one handed motion is allowed, but any waving motion of any type will not be allowed. The closed fist motion is a pattern used to guess men. The closed fist motion will not be allowed to guess the women.
   C. When a guesser chooses to guess two (2) hiders and is unsuccessful, the next guesser is required to guess the same two (2) hiders until a successful guess is made.

D. A guesser will not stop a hider who is making a run and jump to another; but will continue until a correct guess is made on this person.

E. No Lazy V signal and/or forked finger signal will be allowed during the tournament.

F. The guesser shall indicate whether he wants to guess one (1) player or two (2) together and so forth, and shall notify the opposing team medicine man of his intentions.

G. A guesser will be allowed up to one (1) minute to make his final motion and guess. The one (1) minute time limit will begin when the hider is ready. On the one (1) minute lapse, the team hiding the bones will be awarded a point stick. This rule will be mandatory.

H. If the line of view of the guesser to the hider is obstructed and judges deem it necessary, judges will ask the obstruction—shakers/bodies/hands—be moved.

I. If the obstruction continues[,] the guesser has the option not to guess until he is in clear view of the hider.

8. Hiding

A. A player hiding the bones shall have both hands in view of the guesser at all times. When a guess is made, the hider shall expose the bones without first taking the bones out of sight with both hands.

B. Bones will not be thrown to the center, but will be handed to the medicine man, or nearest player after a player has guessed correctly.

C. A person given the bones has the option to pass off to someone else after successfully scoring a point, but points will not count for the award of high point man/woman.

D. A man hiding the bones will be awarded up to two (2) additional re-hiding motions after the initial move. On the third re-hiding motion by the hider before a guess is made, the medicine man may collect and re-issue the bones to someone else. This infraction will be strictly enforced by the selected judges.

E. If a guesser has already indicated his decision and the player hiding the bones brings both hands together, he/she shall forfeit the bones. If the bones are tossed in by mistake, it will be a forfeit.

F. The medicine man may exercise the option of one hider, going for four (4) [points]. He can also have two (2) hiders going for (2) points [each].

G. If a male hider is asked to take his dark glasses off by the guesser, he must do so.

9. Each team will be dressed in their traditional Indian attire before they can be seated to play with their team. This rule will be strictly enforced.

10. Qualifications: a person wishing to play, shall be thirty (30) years of age on the dates of the tournament or older.

Note: guessing of two (2) after one (1) hour will not be exercised. It's up to the guesser, throughout the whole game on how many he wants to guess.

Good Luck And May The Best Team Win!!

The Lodge Grass District Committee Is Not Responsible For Any Accidents, Theft or Stolen Articles.

additional benches around the arena. Accommodations are made for some older or physically disabled players by allowing them to sit on small chairs. The judges are seated, and the first point money is brought to the committee table. A coin toss is made to determine the choice and assignment of seating. A prayer is offered (either by a Crow or a visiting tribal elder). The fourteen wooden score sticks are then placed in the center of the floor between the two teams by one of the three original founders of the tournament (Ed Little Light, Jim Big Shoulder Blade, and Ira Lefthand), who have always been given this honor. The sticks used in the 1998 tournament were all painted solid red and were about twelve inches long.[77]

The time is marked by the announcer, and then both teams begin to drum and sing simultaneously in what can only be described as a burst or explosion of music. The medicine man on each side makes medicine over the hiding objects and then passes one out to an individual to hide. Play begins with competition for the first point When the first point is won, that team is given two of the score sticks from the center, takes the offense, and continues to sing and drum as their medicine man begins to make medicine over the bones and elk teeth before passing them out to four hiders to begin regular play. The other side has ceased singing, and one of their guessers prepares to begin guessing the other side. In the Crow tournament there is a $100 bet required by each team and awarded for winning the first point of each game. At the beginning of each game a bucketful of candy and throat lozenges is usually passed around for the two competing teams to partake of to ease their throats while singing.

The Oklahoma Team

The Oklahoma team that first began traveling annually to Crow Agency in the 1960s was originally composed almost exclusively of Kiowa. In time the group has become a more intertribal, comprising individuals from nearly all of the western Oklahoma tribes. As the Crow continued to visit every fall and play handgames with the Kiowa, they began to receive invitations from other nearby groups who wanted to host them for an evening of matches. In time, as several tribes each began to host the Crows for an evening, members of the various western Oklahoma tribes began to travel to each other's sites and play collectively against the Crow. Likewise, when the Kiowa began reciprocating with a visit to the Crow every spring, members of various Oklahoma tribes began to join the group in playing against the Crow. Today at Crow Agency, the team from Oklahoma is still referred to as the "Kiowa Team" although most players in some years are not Kiowa, and the banner above their section of the bleachers reads "Oklahoma."[78] The size of the Oklahoma contingent varies and has declined over the past twenty years from around forty to twenty. Some years the contingent has been as small as nine members. In 2005 the Oklahoma team had only around twelve members but managed to win the senior tournament.

One elder Kiowa explained that it was easier to make everyone happier when the entire team was Kiowa because with a mixed team someone always complains about something. For example, if the Oklahoma team wins and there are Crow playing on their team, other Crow complain that the Crow players won the game for Oklahoma. Conversely, if they lose, some of the Oklahoma players may complain that the Crow lost the game for them.

Before the annual Crow and Oklahoma exchanges, a great deal of excitement occurs in anticipation not only of the upcoming play but also of the other side's singing. When the Crow go to Oklahoma, older Oklahoma people want to hear the old Crow handgame songs, and then when the Kiowa come to Crow Agency the older Crow want to hear the old Kiowa handgame songs. One Crow singer described,

232   CHAPTER 4

> Everybody gets excited when . . . we come down there. Like, when we go
> south, you know, a lot of people want to know who's coming and . . . what
> style they're gonna be singing. Because, like, in Crow . . . if a lot of Black
> Lodge people are coming, it's going to be some pretty good music, you
> know. It's kind of like that, and I remember when Bill Koomsa [Jr.], he used
> to go [to] Crow. They used to get real excited because . . . [of] the way he
> used to sing. Like, in my mind, if I said I want to hear an Oklahoma style
> song, the way Bill Koomsa used to sing is . . . what Oklahoma style would
> sound like. . . . Because it used to be him, a couple of other gentlemen,
> and all his sisters behind him, and, man, they used to really belt it out.
> At Crow, older people really liked that. Oh, man, the Oklahomans are
> coming, you know, they used to say. That old style, you don't hear
> anymore.

Prior to the tournament, the host (the past year's winner) gives a set of the official rules to each district. Our team met at the home of a Crow family in Crow Agency to go over the rules, choose guessers and medicine men for specific nights, and discuss strategy for play. Members of one Crow district having political differences joined our meeting and discussed how some of the members in their district wanted to play in the tournament while others did not; some even wanted to split into two teams. This family decided to join our team that year and play on the Oklahoma team. Crow who have kin (marriage or adoption) connections sometimes join the Kiowa to help supplement the size of the Oklahoma team, which is typically much smaller than those of the Crow districts due to the time and cost involved in traveling to Montana. One Crow member encouraged our team's guessers to take their time in guessing and not get in a hurry since each bone was worth $400.[79]

Medicine men make medicine on the hiding objects every time they gain the offense. Thus, a medicine man might perform this series of ritual behavior several times in a single game. The following two descriptions of medicine men, filmed during the 1998 tournament, illustrate these actions and give the reader a sense of the elaborate body language accompanying the game.

At the start of one game between the Lodge Grass District and the Northern Cheyenne, the medicine man for Lodge Grass got down on his knees and began making medicine on the hiding objects contained in his two closed hands. He extended and retracted his arms in a hiding motion four times and then opened an empty hand and shook it at the opposition. He then got up, signaled to a hider on the front row, pitched a set of bones to him, and then shook his empty hand again at the opposition. Standing, he continued making medicine on the hiding objects, handed one out to a second hider in the second row, then again shook his empty hand at the opposing team. He repeated this process, handing the hiding objects to be passed down to another hider in the second row, and then again to a woman in the back of the team's seating section. He then took a seat but continued, along with some of the other members of the team, making hiding and empty hand motions toward the opposition as they began to guess. The men in the front row who were not drumming began keeping time on their legs with a closed fist. The medicine man continued to make motions against the guesser as he prepared to guess each hider. As the guesser missed, the women called out, ululated, and pointed their rattles at the guesser and shook them. Following a correct guess, the medicine man made an underhanded pitching motion toward the guesser with an open and empty hand, as if to infer a return of his power or that he would next choose an empty hand. When the fourth hider was missed twice, the intensity of singing, cheering, and drumming increased markedly. When she was missed a third time, the intensity of the offense increased to the point that the men were literally coming off their benches to lean toward the opposition, all the while shaking their hands at them. She was missed a fourth time before finally being caught on the fifth guess to end that round of offense. This game went on to set a tournament record: the longest game on record, six hours and thirty-eight minutes, finishing after 5:00 a.m.[80]

In one game between the Black Lodge and Big Horn Districts, the medicine man for Black Lodge knelt before the hiding objects on the floor. He raised his arms upward and swayed back and forth and side to side several times, and then he shook both open empty hands at the opposition, picked up the objects, made a series of hiding motions, and again showed his open, empty, shaking hands to the opposition. He repeated his actions and then motioned his hand toward the opposition as if catching their medicine and then turning and throwing it away. He then arose, handed a hiding object to a hider, and shook his hand at the opposition. This process was repeated for all four hiders in handing the hiding object or objects to them. Each of the first three hiders was guessed correctly on the first guess. The fourth was missed on the first three guesses, during which the medicine man repeated the motions he used in handing the hiding objects out and catching, turning, and throwing away the power of the opposition. As Big Horn prepared to hide, their medicine man rubbed his hands together, reached his left hand under his vest on his right side (possibly to touch his medicine), and then pulled his hand out and rubbed his hands together again. He then put his hands out, rubbed the inner top portion of his right hand on the floor, extended his arms, lowered his head, and swung his extended arms and swayed back and forth on his knees around eighteen

Crow Senior Handgame Tournament, Crow Agency, Montana, May 1998. Author's photo.

times, rubbed the back of his right hand on the floor, and then shook his left hand at the opposing team. Repeating this with the bones on the floor in front of him, he picked up the bones and repeated the swaying motions. Rubbing his left hand on the floor, he shook his left hand at the opposing side, hid the bones in his hands, swayed back and forth, rubbed his left hand on the floor again, and shook his left hand at the other team. The medicine man then got up, handed out one of the hiding objects, and shook his empty hand at the opponents. He repeated this with all four of the hiders. As the hiders hid the objects, he continued to sway from side to side but with less emphasis. The first hider was guessed; the second hider scored a point and then was guessed on the second guess. The third hider was guessed, and then the fourth hider scored a point before being guessed on the second hide. At the end of this first exchange the score was Black Lodge 3, Big Horn 2.[81]

Guessing

There used to be no time limit on guessing, and Crow guessers are renowned for sometimes taking five or six minutes to make a guess. More recently a one-minute time limit was implemented, but this is rarely enforced. The guesser may also make prolonged motions in an attempt to wear the hider down until

The Kiowa-Crow Association   235

they give themselves away. One Kiowa hider sitting beside me in the 1998 tournament was worked on by the guesser until he was profusely sweating across his forehead, and his arms became so tired that he began to lower the one with the unmarked bone in it. He later told me that, as the guesser went on and on, the bone began to feel heavier and heavier until his arm began to sag, and he was correctly guessed. He was later told to start working his arms in some motions to relieve the tension from extending them so long, but he said he was concentrating on the guesser's hand so much that he forgot about moving his arms. Although this guesser took almost five minutes to guess, the time limit was not enforced. This part of the game involves a true battle of wits. One Crow man stated that guessing was much harder in Crow games in Montana than in the southern plains games where sometimes he does not even look at the hiders when he is guessing.

Around 2003 the Crow implemented a new tournament rule that during the first hour of a game a guesser could guess any number of hiders they desired, from one up to four, but at the start of the second hour and thereafter you had to guess at least two hiders at a time. In doing so, if you get one correct and miss the other, another hider comes in on the following guess. Occasionally, if the games of the first two nights are running long, after all fourteen sticks are off the floor the host may shift all guessing to at least two hiders at a time to speed up the play in order to finish by Sunday evening.[82]

Throughout the play one of the judges serving as master of ceremonies serves as an announcer, regularly calling out "*ikche*" ("got him," or "guessed correctly") or "*k'ahikche*" ("did not get him," or "guessed wrong"). During play the names of those serving as medicine men, the hiders (as they receive the hiding object or objects), and the guessers (as they begin guessing) are announced by the master of ceremonies. The score of the current game is also read aloud at each exchange.

On the final day of the 1998 tournament (a Sunday), the Crow fed all in attendance. Several Crow men sang and drummed as all passed through the serving line. The final two games of the tournament were then played. In 1998 the Northern Cheyenne defeated No Water in the championship game. Following the final game, the winning team sang a victory song on their side of the floor. Afterward the awards were presented, and these included a large trophy and the cash prize ($4,500 that year) for first place, a smaller trophy for the runner-up, and Pendleton blankets, a hand drum, and other gifts for the best medicine man, high-point man, high-point woman, and the best-dressed team. Similar to Oklahoma handgame tournaments, the high-point man and woman are not awarded to whomever scores the most consecutive sticks in a hide but rather applies to the entire tournament. A judge keeps track of scoring runs during the tournament. "Best guesser" is awarded to the man who makes the most consecutive guesses without a miss. "Best-dressed team" goes to the most-stylish team, usually wearing matching shirts, vests, and hats.

After the tournament ends there is usually a break when people will eat, followed by some free-for-all games. In 1998 the first free-for-all game was between the winner and loser of the final tournament game. A second game was between three Crow clans and the Kiowa team on the south against the remaining three Crow clans on the north. The south won the second game, with Bill Koomsa Jr. of the Kiowa scoring the final four points.

Following the free-for-all games, the Northern Cheyenne invited the Kiowa to come to Busby, Montana, the next day (Monday) at noon to play a series of handgames on their reservation east of Crow reservation. Three games were played, all were won by the Kiowa. That morning the Crow Nation fed the Kiowa breakfast at the Little Big Horn Casino (since closed), hosted by Crow tribal chair Clara Nomee. After playing the Northern Cheyenne, the Kiowa were invited to return to the fairgrounds at Crow Agency later that evening for more free-for-all games with the Crow. Just as the Kiowa do when the Crow come to visit every November in Oklahoma, the Crow gave the Kiowa contingent money to help with their travel home. The following morning most of the Kiowa contingent departed to return to Oklahoma.

Clan Games

If the tournament ends early on Sunday or, if it does not, on Monday afternoon, a number of games called "Clan Children's Games" or a "clan tournament" is normally held." The Crow are matrilineal, with their mother's clan their principal clan and each person being "a child of" their father's clan. The Crow refer to clans as *ashammaléiaxia*, or "driftwood lodges," a metaphor comparing the unity of a clan to how driftwood intertwines and piles up in a stream. As a Crow clan stands together against turbulence in life, so does conjoined driftwood against the turbulence of water in a stream course (Frey 1987, 3). Oral tradition states that the clans were named by Old Man Coyote. The ten clans organized into five phratries include 1) Greasy Mouths; Sore Lips; 2) Whistling Waters; Bad War Deeds; 3) Ties in a Bundle; Brings Home Game Without Shooting; 4) Big Lodge; Newly Made Lodge; and 5) Blood Indian Lodge; Dung Eaters.[83] While thirteen matrilineal clans were reported in the pre-reservation era (Lowie 1983, 9), Frey (1987, 40) reports eight surviving clans (Ties in a Bundle, Whistling Water, Bad War Deeds, Sore Lips, Greasy Mouths, Piegan, Big Lodge, and Newly Made Lodge).

The Crow clan tournament games usually consist of the members from three or four clans playing a series of match games against the other clans, the Oklahoma team, and the Northern Cheyenne. Each Crow clan has several leaders, and the remaining members, regardless of age, are considered the children of that clan. The members of each clan are also considered the children of another of the clans.[84] Those who have taken individuals as relatives through kinship adoption typically stay with their relatives when visiting to play handgames and play with their host district and clan.[85]

In this tournament all ages can play together, but individuals must play on the team of their maternal clan. As Jeremy Shield explained, "When they do that, they're making you understand who your clan sisters and brothers are and all that. It's kind of an educational time for people."[86] A bracket is made for single-elimination play. Prize money is usually pooled by the sponsors and by each clan putting in some money. In the clan games there are no rules regarding guessing members of other clans. In some occasions, mixed teams hold a series of match games in which three or four of the Crow clans play against the remaining Crow clans and any visitors.

Highlighting several of the major aspects of the Crow style, family, medicine, and singing, Jeremy Shield reflected on what he likes about the handgame:

> The thing I like about it is I get to sit with my family. My mom goes all out, and she pretty much buys all the material for our outfits, you know, and she . . . outfits all my brothers, my sisters. And then, secondly, I get to use my family's medicine, you know, at the time. So it's kind of like an honor. Honor, and then a lot of those old people that see those old medicines, they like it. It makes them feel good to see that people are still using those ways. So those are the two main things I like about it. And the third would probably be the singing. Like I said, our family has made a lot of the handgame songs, and . . . now it's kind of like up to me and my nephews, you know, making a lot of the songs today.[87]

Recent Play and Changes

The 2021 Crow Senior Handgame Tournament rules demonstrate that the senior tournament has remained largely the same over the years.

In recent years a number of changes have developed in the Crow handgame. Although many individuals state that the multipurpose building does not have the ambiance of the wooden Round House, it has become the setting for the annual junior and senior tournaments. As in Oklahoma, Crow singers report that old Crow handgame songs are sung less often as new compositions from the younger generation become popular.

2021 SR. HANDGAME TOURNAMENT RULES

Multi-Purpose Building
Crow Agency, MT
June 9–13, 2021

1. All pots ($1,200-MG, $100-FP, $100-HPM, $100-HPW) must be submitted together before the start of the team's first game in the tournament or the team will forfeit.
2. Judges' decisions are final.
3. There will be 5 guessers and 1 medicine man for each team. Once players are seated, coaches are required to fill out roster sheets before each game.
4. The ladies can stand during games, but cannot obstruct the guesser's view, after one warning the hiding piece(s) will be forfeited.
5. All female players must wear complete outfits, women must wear belts, moccasins or leggings. No tennis shoes or boots. If the female does not follow this rule, she will be asked to leave the playing floor.
6. All male players must be matching in appropriate attire.
7. After the end of each game, teams will have 15 minutes to be seated and ready to play.
8. Absolutely no drugs or alcohol will be tolerated during the handgame event. Law enforcement services will be notified immediately or anyone suspected to be under the influence of drugs or alcohol will be asked to leave.
9. Each game will have 3 judges randomly selected by the Committee.
10. All sticks must be in plain view on the playing floor.
11. During the loser out games, guessers must guess two after all the sticks are off the floor.
12. Please be respectful and have good sportsmanship.
13. CDC guidelines will be adhered to: sanitize, wear masks, practice social distancing.

HIDERS

1. All hiding pieces cannot be placed on one hider.
2. Hider has 1 minute to hide, judges have the right to ask the hider to forfeit the hiding piece(s) if the hider is taking too much time.

3. All hiders must show both hands in plain view of the judges when hiding or hiding pieces will be forfeited.
4. Hiders cannot put their hands together when hiding or hiding pieces will be forfeited.

GUESSERS

1. Guessers have 1 minute to guess.
2. No fake guessing on women.
3. No buying of guessing ways on the floor.
4. Guesser must clearly indicate to the judges which way he is guessing.
5. A guesser must indicate to the judges how many hiders they are guessing.
6. A guesser cannot stop a hider from making a run.

For many years the annual junior and senior tournaments were the only handgame tournaments at Crow. Although far less than in Oklahoma, other tournaments are beginning to appear on the Crow Reservation. From January 8 to January 12, 2020, the Honoring the Memory of Edmund Old Crow, Crow Style Handgame Invitational was held at Crow Agency, Montana. Held in honor of Old Crow, who passed the previous April, the events included several daily singing and Push Dance contests in addition to the handgame tournament.[88] A Father's Day handgame tournament selling $10 plate lunches was held at Pryor, Montana, June 17–20, 2001, as a fund-raiser for a group traveling to Las Vegas. Fees included $175 for the main game and $15 for first point. From June 20 to June 22, 2021, the Crow Native Days Handgame Tournament was held at Reno Hall at Crow Agency, with a ten-team limit, a $100 main game, and $25 first point fees.[89]

The Crow have started occasionally playing the Oklahoma style of handgame in their home area and have ordered several sets of score sticks. As Mary Beaver described, "When we go up there, they like to play Oklahoma style, so they actually have their own sticks. Yeah, they actually have their own sticks, and my daughter was telling me sometimes they will play Oklahoma style. . . . They ordered sticks and paid for them, they take them up there, so they have them whenever they feel like, you know—that's the way they want to play." The Oklahoma style is not used in the Crow tournaments, though.[90]

240 CHAPTER 4

Despite changes, the Crow continue to emphasize the importance of maintaining Crow ethnic identity and recognition of respect, family, and good sportsmanship. Living in two worlds, the handgame offers a release from the dominant non-Indian society. As Lewis Walks Over Ice (Johnson 2001) described, "During the week I'm shirt and tie, nine to five. You know, I live in the white man's world, so you say. And so on the weekends I can [do] something like this. I can shed my suit and tie, and I can once again be what I am, a Native American." While maintaining good sportsmanship is widely associated with the Native American handgame, for the Crow the spiritual aspect from its origins adds another element. As Jeremy Shield explained, "A lot of the competition comes out in people. But then at the same time, you know, when you get beat you're not supposed to get mad, you know. Because of the spirit thing [association]. Playing over those souls, you're not supposed to get mad. You're supposed to show good sportsmanship. But, yeah, you know how people are—they get competitive, and they really want to win, you know. That always comes out."[91] Respect and remembering ancestors is another important component in the Crow handgame. Discussing what the Crow emphasize about playing handgame, Jeremy Shield explained, "The respect. You know, learning that respect for each other, for your own relatives. You know, especially if you're playing against them. And they, like at the end, always say, 'Shake hands. Shake hands.' You know, because those spirits are there, and then . . . being that spirit game, you know ghosts [are] playing for those souls, you know. They say when you're sitting down to play, the relatives that have passed on, they're sitting there with you, you know . . . you get to sit down with those that are gone."[92]

CHAPTER

5

The Kiowa, Comanche, and Apache Handgame Today

TODAY THE WESTERN Oklahoma handgame is primarily a southern Plains Indian tradition. Although a few members of other neighboring tribes (Wichita, Delaware, Caddo, Fort Sill Apache) sometimes play, most teams consist of Kiowa, Comanche, Plains Apache, Cheyenne, and Arapaho. Their style of handgame earlier was generally similar and was easily blended together into what became the "southern style" of play. Consequently, many Cheyenne, Wichita, and Caddo, who all have their own and slightly different styles of play, have increasingly begun to play the KCA style. The annual reciprocal visits with the Crow, and occasional play in Great Basin and Plateau tournaments represent other influences. Elder players have reported that Pawnee and Ponca teams came a few times to play in the past but no longer do. Northeastern Oklahoma tribes such as the Ponca, Pawnee, and Osage play handgame while seated around a large center drum and use pointing sticks to denote the four basic guessing signs. Some groups also hold sets of dances between games. In the late 1990s several Prairie and Southeastern tribes in eastern Oklahoma were known for playing older, traditional styles of handgame rather than the newer western Oklahoma tournament style.

Some individuals from handgame families are born into the game. Newborns and infants of all ages are commonly taken to Native cultural events before they can walk or fully participate, and just as some individuals grow up around the drum at powwows, others do so at handgames. Jackie Yellowhair

241

242   CHAPTER 5

was taken to handgames while in the womb and only five days after being born in 1974, which he calls "handgame immersion." Yellowhair began to drum and sing around the age of five and has played handgame his entire life. As he recounted,

> I heard the stories from my dad, my grandma, my elderly people that I was no more than a week old when I went to my first handgame, and I've been going ever since. The stories I heard was that I used to cry when the drumming would stop, when the noise would stop maybe—[they were] taking their bets and going on with different things. And my grandpa had to sit there and hit the drum, you know, like "Stop crying," and then when the game would start again . . . I'd go on, you know, carry on. So, I wouldn't be crying then. . . . People know me as the handgame baby.[1]

Yellowhair's mother, Lela "Doll" Yellowhair, also grew up with the game. Taken as a little girl, she often slept in a blanket at her mother's feet while her parents, Ace Yellowhair and Ina Paddlety Chalepah, played. She was called a "handgame kid."[2] One individual noticed that when his two-year old niece got bored, she went to pick up handgame sticks rather than toys. This girl began singing the songs before she could speak and is now a regular player.[3]

Others may start playing by coming to watch and sitting far in the back. Later they begin to participate as hiders and singers, and eventually they work their way up to guessing and serving as medicine men. Reluctant at first, Jack Yellowhair Sr. was introduced to the game by his wife around 1963. At first he wasn't interested and didn't participate, he just took his wife and waited in the car. Later his cousin got him to come inside and watch a game. Later he sat closer. Eventually his relatives had him sitting in the second row when he got the bones to hide. Although he was quickly guessed, he soon learned more about the game and the songs and became a regular player for the rest of his life. Mr. Yellowhair described how he became involved:

> It took a while before I got into the handgame. My wife was into it—since she was a little girl she'd been playing handgame. I'd take her a lot of times, her and her grandmother, take them to the handgame wherever they're having them. They'd go, I'd wait on them. I'd sit in the car, or I'd just wait on them till they got through playing handgame. Then they'd come out, and we'd come home. I didn't know nothing about it. That's the way it went for a while. She begged me to go in. I said, "No, I don't want to. I don't know what's what." . . . It took me a long time to go. Finally I got a little courage to go into one, down in the Astrodome they call it, down in Boone. And there was just a little shack, round, covered with paper boxes and they just nailed them on, all the way around. But we played

Jack Yellowhair Family (Kiowa–Plains Apache). *Standing, left to right*: Leland Yellowhair, Jackie Ray Yellowhair, William Meadows, Ace Yellowhair. *Seated*: Jack Yellowhair. Author's photo, 1998.

handgame in it. We didn't care what it looked like or what. It's altogether different between . . . then and where we play now. So I went in one time, and I sat way in the back, just listening. Pretty soon they started hollering and everything like that. So next weekend we came back. Sat in the back row for several times, you know. Pretty soon I was in this, moved down. Kept coming my way down every time. Before you knew it I was sitting in the front row.[4]

Yellowhair learned many handgame songs from his wife. Several KCA players have told me that they were "nervous" or "scared" the first time they were given the bones to hide and that it took some time to build up their confidence until they were comfortable hiding.

Mary Beaver (Cheyenne) related that she began playing handgame in the early 1980s with her parents Willie and Bertha Thunder Bull Bearshield. After Bruce Haumpy (Kiowa) invited her father down to play at his home just west of Carnegie, Oklahoma, they began going regularly to play at Haumpy's, Bill Koomsa Sr.'s, and elsewhere. At this time the modern Oklahoma style was

244 CHAPTER 5

already in use. Willie Bearshield was very active in powwows, but after being introduced to the handgame he stopped participating in powwows and started focusing on the handgame. As Mary Beaver explained,

> They got into it later in life. They were probably in their fifties. They were more of a powwow group. [My brother] Pete and my dad were well-known MCs and were head man dancers at many powwows. And then eventually someone invited them to a handgame, and my dad really did like it. He really, really . . . took a big interest in it and started going everywhere. You know, taking . . . the older kids . . . with him and my mom, and that's how we got involved. Not right off. We kind of stand in the background and, you know, watch—watch the adults have their fun, you know. And then we started . . . to see what it was that was so exciting, and you kind of have to understand the concept of the game. And it was interesting, and I thought, Well, I can do that. You know, I can play, . . . and then "I can guess." . . . And that's how we came about getting involved in that.[5]

Jack Yellowhair and Gregory Haumpy (Kiowa), also shifted from participating in powwows and Gourd Dances to playing handgames.[6] One individual described how their family was heavily involved in the powwow world but, after being invited to attend a handgame, switched to the latter, in part due to financial aspects:

> It was like they quit going to powwows and started going to handgames. That was something new for them. Because, when you actually think about it, if you're on head staff, weekend after weekend after weekend, it takes a lot of money, because you have to have . . . giveaways and grocery baskets, and . . . financially I think it was kind of draining them. So this handgame was easier. All you had to do was get gas and go and, you know, put in [money toward the] entry fee with other people, which wasn't probably much at that time, and then, you know, [you were] able to just have fun. And they like meeting other people.[7]

SPONSORING

Games used to be played in tents on private allotments, such as that of Julia Daingkau, who set up a tent outside her house and placed a wood-burning stove in it to heat it. Some games were held in a room inside a house. Bruce Haumpy had a barn on his land near Carnegie that he modified to facilitate handgames, and many were held until the barn caught fire and burned. The Apache built a large, permanent, tarpaper-covered structure resembling a hybrid between a bungalow and a Quonset hut, on Julia Mulkahey's land at Boone, Oklahoma, that was dubbed the Astrodome.[8] Mary Beaver, who went to many handgames at the Astrodome with her parents, described it:

The Handgame Today 245

As I remember, there was . . . wooden benches that were already set, and there was . . . maybe four benches like this, and maybe a couple of benches on this side because they had a stove, like an old cast-iron stove, . . . wood-burning. That was there, and . . . everything was just, like, put together. It was, like, wood, and then inside the wood there was, like, paper and tin, you know, just to . . . keep the wind out. But it was like, like, real ancient, I mean. But they call it the Astrodome, and you could go there any Sunday and they would be playing, just to be playing, and a lot of people do that.[9]

Since the 1980s most games have been held in public buildings that are rented for the day, such as county fairs or community buildings or tribal multipurpose buildings or gymnasiums. These typically rent for anywhere from $50 to $250 daily. With some, a significant portion is returned if the renter cleans up after their event. For example, one building that rents for $150 comes with the stipulation that $85 will be returned if the renter cleans it, so it really costs only $65 per day. Concessions continue to help offset the cost of holding the event. As one individual described, "Its run like a powwow. At a handgame you've got to make things up to raffle off, like baskets of groceries, serapes, Pendleton blankets, anything that . . . will bring in money. Even towels and . . . and shawls and jewelry—rings, bracelets, necklaces, or whatever you want to raffle off."[10] Hand drums are another popular and practical raffle item at handgames. The event host typically serves supper and runs a concession stand throughout the event. Singers and players often have coffee, water, or soft drinks at hand, while children may be snacking on a pickle or frybread.

Team entry fees continue to provide prize money for many round-robin tournaments. For larger pots, trophies, and any special prizes such as best guesser or hider or best singer, the sponsor typically contributes additional money beyond that raised through team entry fees. This may require the collection of individual or family pledges, or it may entail fund-raisers, including benefit handgame tournaments, prior to the event at hand. The winners of larger tournaments such as the Oklahoma State Handgame Tournament, often hold a benefit handgame to raise money prior to hosting next year's event.

Participation at handgames is directly linked to the prize money being offered. As one player stated, "The bigger the money, the more teams you're gonna have." Simply put, the more prize money that is offered, the more players and teams will come to participate, which also suggests the importance placed on the opportunity to win these funds, even when divided between team members. While teams undertake varied fund-raising activities such as benefit handgames, raffles, and Indian taco sales, large prize money is often directly linked to the amount of funding one's tribe will provide, which increasingly comes from tribal budgets and casinos.

246   CHAPTER 5

In recent years the increasing number of tribal casinos are often asked to help sponsor handgame tournaments, the success of which is strongly linked to the current tribal chair. While some tribal chairs support handgames as a traditional cultural event, others do not. As one individual explained, "The [tribe], when they were really going and had the support of their chairman, . . . gave out good money. It just depends. It's political too. If you try to go . . . for them and they don't know anything about handgames, [you won't likely] get any support, you know, from their chair or political groups. . . . [But another] chairman even came to the handgames, and he even played. That's what I call supportive, you know, rather than, 'Here, here's a check, here,' you know."[11]

TYPES OF PLAY

A major change has been the near demise of match games, except for the annual Crow visit in November. Occasionally a team may invite another over to their home for an afternoon of match games, such as Southern Thunder (the Yellowhair Family) and North Spur Heights (Robert Old Bear). Although individual bets occur, these events are more for enjoying the game, fellowship, and eating together than for financial gain. Some individuals state that they do not attend such smaller gatherings when invited, attending only "real tournaments."

Free-for-alls have also declined in frequency. As one elder explained, "They don't hardly have no free-for-alls, just once in a while . . . they usually have about one or two or three free-for-alls before the tournament starts at these handgames now. Then they'll start the tournament. That's all they want to do [now]."[12] Free-for-alls are still held before or after tournaments, such as a special night of games during the American Indian Exposition.

Today most southern plains handgames are round-robin tournaments. Tournaments are frequently held to honor someone, such as for a birthday, a baby shower, a memorial after a player's passing, or a homecoming for a soldier or another individual who has been away for a long time. They are also held at holidays such as Valentine's Day, Easter, and Veteran's Day, and they are sometimes benefits to raise funds for a cause, such as to sponsor the upcoming Oklahoma State Handgame Tournament or support a tribal Head Start program.[13] In one instance a couple got married and then sponsored a wedding handgame that afternoon.[14]

The host team typically determines the style and rules to be played and typically announces these verbally or provides paper copies of rules before play begins. During round-robin tournaments, this usually occurs just before teams draw numbers to begin play. Most games today are nineteen points,

The composition of the handgame crowd overlaps to some degree with that
of other cultural events. Some of the more well-known singers also sing at
powwows and society dances. Several players relate that the handgame is
their primary cultural and social activity and that they rarely attend other
events. Jack Yellowhair Sr. told me that he used to be a powwow person and
frequently sang and drummed before he got interested in handgames. In explaining that he gave up participating in powwows, he said: "I have more fun
at handgames."[15] Greg and Marie Haumpy likewise stated that they preferred
handgames to powwows.[16] Another player stated, "Yes, that's the best to me.
Handgame is the only one. I don't go powwows anymore or anything else."[17]

The Handgame Today

with eighteen sticks on each side of the larger central stick; a few may be
seventeen or fifteen points. If a tournament ends early, most sponsors will ask
if anybody wants to play free-for-all, which people usually do, and will start
collecting bets. If it has been a long day, some people will start to leave, but
others, the "hardcore players" who were knocked out early on in the tournament and have just been watching, will want to play. Occasionally a match
game between two designated teams or a Crow-style game will be held prior
to starting a round-robin tournament.

CROWD COMPOSITION

The composition of the handgame crowd overlaps to some degree with that
of other cultural events. Some of the more well-known singers also sing at
powwows and society dances. Several players relate that the handgame is
their primary cultural and social activity and that they rarely attend other
events. Jack Yellowhair Sr. told me that he used to be a powwow person and
frequently sang and drummed before he got interested in handgames. In explaining that he gave up participating in powwows, he said: "I have more fun
at handgames."[15] Greg and Marie Haumpy likewise stated that they preferred
handgames to powwows.[16] Another player stated, "Yes, that's the best to me.
Handgame is the only one. I don't go powwows anymore or anything else."[17]

Of the smaller weekend tournaments I attended between 1997 and 2021,
which usually drew from four to ten teams, the size of the crowd varied from
around 60 to 125 people. These events are typically smaller than most Gourd
Dances and powwows. Annual tournaments, usually held as special events or
in conjunction with other tribal celebrations, are typically larger. The annual
Oklahoma State Tournament, the Crow visit in November, and tournaments
with large prize money such as the Kiowa casino tournaments at Devol and
Verden, Oklahoma, and those held at Red Earth, the American Indian Exposition, the Comanche Nation Fair, or the Labor Day powwow in Colony,
Oklahoma, are typically larger, with twelve to over twenty teams and crowds
easily in excess of two hundred people. At the 2017 Oklahoma State Tournament, twelve teams competed, nine being Cheyenne and Arapaho teams. Two
other teams showed up after registration closed and could not play.[18]

Although people still express the beliefs that the handgame should only be
played in winter and that the primary handgame season is between October
and May, tournaments throughout the summer now make play year-round.
These developments increased with post-reservation intertribal proximity,
increased adaptation to the twelve-month calendar, and the post–World War II
growth of community buildings, such as tribal gymnasiums and county 4-H

fair buildings. Howard (1965, 50) reports similar developments among the Ponca in north-central Oklahoma: "Peyote ceremonies, handgames, and church services are held at any time throughout the year. Usually special Peyote meetings, handgames, and other festivities mark Easter, Memorial Day, Thanksgiving, and New Year's Day."

Many recognize the older, more traditional style of play. However, everyone indicates that they like the new style of play. As Adam Kaulaity noted, "[Playing the old style] could turn into a long game. So they just say 'Use that northern style—you take those sticks out now.'"[19] Gregory Haumpy also preferred the new way of play: "I'd rather have these sticks that goes down and doesn't come back. The other way [the old way] is too long, too long. Man, it takes you all night for one game."[20]

The positions of hider, guesser, and medicine man have tended to remain held by adults but now include more women and occasionally youths. Like the adults, how long a youth maintains one's position in a game largely depends on the efficacy of the hiders they choose. Likewise, in the modern style of play, younger individuals are commonly included as hiders and sometimes include small children. In 1998 Jed Querdibitty, who had played handgame since around World War II, told me that he was trying to let some of the younger players get more experience, especially in guessing. Although some team members complained because they were not winning very often, he said, "The old ones did the same with us. You have to learn sometime. So I'm just doing what they did with us."[21]

While teams usually have preferred hiders, virtually everyone gets to occasionally hide. However, several senior players stated that it is important not to give the bones to a bad hider if a game is close and near the end. Far fewer people usually serve as guessers than as hiders. Teams use a relatively few guessers most of the time, with others used occasionally. On some teams one individual may perform most of the guessing during a tournament. The use of youth as guessers and medicine men is usually less frequent in tournaments than in free-for-alls or games with smaller stakes.

NEW RULES

One of the most frequently cited changes entails the rules of play. Because the host sets the rules, whether intra- or intertribal, it is easy for a group to implement changes in play. Some of the most common changes include requiring a roster listing all members of a team before a tournament starts. Afterward no other players can be added. However, some team captains have stated that they have seen the lists turned in and then seen players added on later. Another issue is starting time. While "Indian Time" is regularly joked about in Indian communities, many older players report that round-robin tournaments used to start on time. If too few teams arrive on time, then there are not enough to start the tournament or to have sufficient entry fees for prize money. On the other hand, a late start allows teams to play that otherwise would be disqualified for arriving late. Usually when a late start is imminent, free-for-alls are held to fill the time and allow people to warm up.

One rule involves a set number of seconds to hide and bring one's hand out to play. A guesser cannot cross the midline between the teams, upon penalty of a point for the opposition. If a player drops a bone, it costs the player's side a stick, although this rule is rarely enforced. Each team selects one judge before the start of their next game, and judges are responsible for checking the guessers and hiders and conveying the scoring to the scorekeeper or scorekeepers.[22]

Some individuals do not like any hand motions by guessers beyond the four basic signals (left, right, inside, and outside), considering other motions to be power play, Crow-style play, or "trick guessing," attempts to trick the hider into giving themselves away. But the creative hand motions used by guessers adds to the excitement of the game. The most common way to deal with such hand motions is to either prohibit them in the rules prior to play or require that hiders call out the traditional "Ho!" to indicate their final and real guess. As one individual described, "Now, in your rules, some will state that hand gestures are allowed as long as you say, like, Ho! to the true [guess]. 'Cause the worst people about this . . . I cannot stand it when they get up there and go like this [makes different hand motions with their fists and open hands]—like, try to trick you . . . But when you say Ho!, that's your true and final guess, and a lot of the rules will state that . . . When you say Ho!, that's your final guess."[23] The hider should maintain their hiding until they hear the call and the referees tell them to open their hands.

There used to be a tournament rule that if a team was late, even if they had their entry fee, they could not play. Some tournament organizers maintain this rule, which others dislike. Today if a team is late they are sometimes allowed to pay their fee, are given one loss and placed in the loser's bracket in a tournament, and are allowed to play. Other recent changes are the addition of judges located between the two competing teams, a center line that players cannot cross during play, and time limits to hide and guess. In round-robin tournaments I have occasionally seen individuals make a double guess (inside or outside) when the opposing side had only one hider. That mistake results in the offense being awarded a point (one stick taken off their side). The hider then hides again, and the game continues.[24]

250   CHAPTER 5

The most widely reported problem, it seems, entails not so much the rules designated at a particular place as much as the level of consistency in enforcing the rules to ensure fair play, such as time-limit rules in hiding and guessing. As one player described, "They don't have a hold of their rules. There's a lot of them say what they're gonna do or what they want, but they won't enforce the rules."

One complaint I periodically heard involved the choice of hiders by the medicine man during free-for-alls. Some individuals stated that while each side on a free-for-all may be made up of members of many regular teams, the medicine men tend to choose the players from their own regular teams more often to hide and guess. As one individual described,

> We got money on that. Let us guess, or let us hide, or something, I tell you. If they don't hide, they get mad too. You know, but you can't cover everybody, just certain ones, and they would say, "That woman there hid about five times," which is the truth. I've seen it done. Or, "That guy over there, you keep giving him the bones, but he's missing and getting caught all the time." But they still turn around and give it back to him. It's things like that, you know. People get mad. . . . The medicine man belongs to one certain team, [and] he's going to give it to his team's [members] before anything else. That's the way it works, and that's what people get mad about."

One elder Kiowa man stated that he felt you should not hide for a team unless you have a bet placed on that team.[25] While the contrary occurs, and people notice, it is hard to say how often, and several factors can lead to this. A game may end before everyone gets to hide or guess. Some players may make a successful run, which means they are not going to be changed as long as they are hot. On some teams, relatively few members do most of the hiding and guessing, which may carry over to free-for-alls, when one's own medicine man is in that role. However, some medicine men make a concerted effort to rotate the hiding and guessing and to include as many people as possible.

ETHNICITY

While the overwhelming majority of players in western Oklahoma handgames remain Native American, there is a small number of non-Indians since around 2004. A few whites and African Americans have married into Indian families or are close friends with members of a particular team. The African American players I have seen are just as enthusiastic and competitive as everyone else. One older Kiowa woman commented that African American singers have "powerful voices." Characteristic of Native American kinship patterns, members of other tribes and non-Indians are readily incorporated into the kin networks of Native families and communities as relatives or friends. Although an occasional tournament only allows play by Indians with a CDIB (Certified Degree of Indian Blood, or popularly called an "Indian Card"), which lists one's tribal affiliation and percentage of Native blood and is used to identify federally enrolled tribal members, I have witnessed no overt discrimination toward non-Indians at handgames.

In one instance, however, blood quantum became an issue. In 2008 the Kiowa casino at Devol, Oklahoma, began sponsoring a tournament with $10,000 in prize money that required a federally recognized CDIB to play. Some people were angered since it excluded non-Indian relatives and friends and Indians possessing too low a blood quantum to be tribally enrolled and thus federally recognized. As one individual pointed out, "[This is] just something we don't do at handgames. Everyone is welcome." Nevertheless, the rule was enforced, possibly because the casino, an enterprise of the tribal government, wanted to ensure that the money it put up went to Natives. This is an interesting example of how sovereign tribes may practice discrimination based on race that would be illegal outside of their sovereign territory.

BETTING AND SUPPLEMENTAL INCOME

Betting on handgames has changed over time. Nearly any kind of item used to be bet in the past. Adam Kaulaity said, "Yeah, they used to bet . . . horses, cattle, [and] stuff way back there. There used to be big betting."[26] Today bets are almost strictly cash. Elders also report that bets have increased in size. While some people had money during the early 1980s oil boom, fewer games were held, with match games and free-for-alls, occasional tournaments, the annual state tournament, and the annual Crow visit. As Jack Yellowhair Sr. described, "They bet more now. Way back, before I started, they were telling me they used to bet material and maybe a horse or whatever, something like that. And it got to where they started betting money. Bet a quarter, nickel, but they were playing the old way. . . . When they changed . . . to play . . . quick games, [people] started betting more money and just kept going like that."[27]

Comanche elders have reported that during the Oklahoma oil boom of 1978–1983 and shortly thereafter, the number of Comanche handgame teams, the frequency of games and tournaments, and the amounts wagered reached all-time highs. One Comanche noted in 1998 that matches against the Crow as Eagle Park had formerly drawn bets from $3,700 to $4,500 per game but had decreased to around $400–500. "Times are changed. Money is—living is getting high, and money is kind of hard to get now." Extra money during the oil boom also allowed some individuals to sponsor tournaments. Gregory and Marie Haumpy sponsored a handgame tournament in 1984 after receiving a large payment from an oil lease. Requiring only a $100 team entry fee,

252   CHAPTER 5

sixteen teams entered. The Haumpys provided supper for all in attendance and made up the remainder of the purse to offer five prizes ranging from $1,500, for first place to $1,000 for second, $800 for third, $500 for fourth, and $100 for fifth. To provide food and beverages and to help offset the cost, the family ran a concession stand.[28]

Several factors draw people to tournaments. They are now held almost all year long in western Oklahoma. Players frequently mention money, seeing friends, socializing, catching up on news, and the music. However, despite the social aspects, many emphasized that they are drawn by the chance to win money. As one elder player described, "Money. That's all it is, money. . . . But a lot of times we'll go just to meet people. Socialize and all that, gather and talk with your friends. . . . It's a friendly deal, that's why they go. And then there's the drumbeats and the singing. One of them, they got a lot of good handgame singers. They can [really] sing, some of them boys."[29]

With the increasing prizes from a few hundred to a few thousand dollars, economic opportunity is a draw for some individuals, and different forms of play offer different opportunities. As one individual explained, you cannot make much money in a round-robin tournament because you sit much of the day waiting to play the next round, side bets are not allowed, only first- and second-place prizes are normally given, and winnings, if any, must be divided between one's teammates. In free-for-alls, each game is usually over quickly, and you can bet as much per game as you want. Therefore, you can make money quickly and repeatedly in multiple games.[30]

As one individual described, "It's a lot about money today. It's a big money game now." One woman concurred about the biggest change in the handgame since the 1980s: "It's been the money. The money part." While the money is a major draw, it is not typically enough to constitute any major form of income. When Greg Haumpy's team of around fifteen took second at the 1997 Red Earth Festival tournament, each member took home around $80. As one elder described, "[It's] not enough, really. You know, because it's divided. You don't get much out of it, really. Just to pay your way over there and back and that's it. In the free-for-all you can win more than you do in a round-robin. You might win a big pot, but look at how many people will be on your side. It has to be split up. You don't get much, you know. . . . But if you lose, it hurts. [You think] *I could've had this money* and stuff like that."[31]

Flannery and Cooper (1946, 407) note that while those possessing supernatural gambling power were spoken of by contemporary English-speaking Gros Ventre as "professional gamblers," no professional gamblers actually existed since no one, even in the old days, made a living or most of their living at gambling. However, Stuart (1972, 6) describes some players in the Northwest known as "professionals" who travel the handgame circuit all year round and earn a living by playing. Like some of the best dancers in the contemporary contest powwow circuit, very few earn enough for those earnings to constitute a sole source of income.

While the larger number of tournaments and prize money in the Northwest United States make this a possibility for a few, it is not possible with the smaller prize money in Oklahoma. Even with increased prize money over time, individual payments are small. A pot of $2,000 at a larger tournament, divided between ten players, provides only $200 apiece without taking into consideration the entry fee, travel, and other expenses.

Larger tournaments and prize money draw more teams to play. Teams that do not play frequently often enter these tournaments. Because they have had less opportunities to observe them, the other teams are less familiar with the players' hiding and guessing habits. Ace Yellowhair described this type of team: "The kind that get lucky where, you know, [they] don't play for a long time, and then you haven't watched them, and then they'll run the sticks on you. . . . The last one that gave us a good challenge was at Norman. . . . They haven't played in six, seven years or more, and then they come out and they win the tournament up there."[32]

Beginner's luck and being unknown can be advantageous. One year at the Schemitzun Powwow in Connecticut, a small handgame tournament was scheduled between a Kiowa team, two Crow teams, and a Blackfeet team that did not show. Phil "Joe Fish" Dupoint (Kiowa) showed some Pawnee who were there and wanted to learn how to play, and they ended up winning the tournament.[33]

In 2021 Jackie Yellowhair, Lydia Meat, Jeremy Yellowhair, and four of my field school students and I entered a tournament as a team. Three of the students had never played except for a few informal games a couple of weeks before. Our unfamiliarity was an advantage that day, helping us to make several extended scoring runs. As the tournament went on and we continued to win games, individuals began to cheer us on and came over to tell us they hoped we would win it. The only game we lost was when our main singer had to leave temporarily. The only team that beat us (in round three) was the same one that helped hold the informal games for the students earlier. We later played them twice in the finals and beat them both times to win the tournament. I teased them about teaching my students too well.

Smaller weekend tournaments, offering only a few hundred dollars for first place, offer occasional supplementary income at best. I am aware of no one who is able to win enough to live on, and those teams that do win significant amounts must divide the winnings between ten to twenty members. But for some individuals the money won at handgames, although small, is important. As some teams are family-based, the winning of a sizable pot in a tournament can represent considerable income when pooled in a family.

In 2004 a Comanche man told me that, although he especially enjoys singing, the chance to make money was a major reason why he played. With an income of around $250 per week from his regular job, additional money from handgames, especially at tournaments with larger prize money, helped him through the week. He stated that he especially liked tournaments due to the larger prize money.[34]

Jackie Yellowhair described the shift in the importance of money in the handgame and how he sometime looks to the game for supplementary income. "A lot of younger ones play it for the money; a lot of older ones play it for fun. Probably a few years ago it was all for fun, but . . . it's a source of revenue now. Indian gaming, I guess. . . . I'm living proof of that, you know [laughs]. Little handgame, you know, go get me some money, going to handgame. But, yeah, it's possible to . . . supplement, yeah, big supplement."[35]

Ace Yellowhair also described how some individuals earn supplemental income from playing handgame. "I guess it goes back to where you know you're an addict [laughs], handgame addict. Sometimes you can make money, sometimes you can lose money. But, yeah, it gets to that. Well, I'm gonna bet ten, I can maybe win ten." One chance to win larger sums is when the Crow come from Montana to play match games, with bets placed before each game. There is no limit to how much an individual can bet, though the two sides must be even before play can begin. Ace Yellowhair said, "A lot of that comes to when the Crows come down, the big money. . . . A fellow could make some money if he gets on the right side and bets good. There's no limit too during that time, you know. Moneywise you can bet a hundred dollars, two hundred dollars if you want."[36]

Mary Beaver said, "Only when the Crows come down do people actually bet that big. . . . When the Crows come down you know you can bet—it's unlimited, and they are the ones that will usually bet really high. 'Cause that's what they come down here for is to play, you know, . . . Oklahoma style and make some money. You won't find that going on in Oklahoma [otherwise] 'cause, if you do, you'll be sitting there all night waiting for the other team to match you."[37]

Despite the chance of winning some money, most players cite the social aspects of the game as the most important feature. Consequently, many individuals try to ensure they have a few dollars to play in weekend tournaments. My consultants pointed out that most of the handgame community are not wealthy but will sometimes go to considerable lengths to come up with money to play on the weekend. One memorable account involved the late George "Woogie" Watchetaker, a well-known Comanche man. "Yeah, Woogie, boy, he would do that, come to the handgame with black fingers. You'd know he'd been shelling pecans all week, you know, and everybody does their own thing, you know, to get handgame money. You know, all the handgame people, they're not rich. . . . Maybe a few of them they have a job, you know, that they go to, and they have money . . . every weekend."[38]

The most common criticism of round-robin play involves the amount of actual play time and the lack of table bets. Unlike free-for-alls, in round-robin play you only play when your team is up. As most Oklahoma tournaments have only one game being played at a time, you might sit out three out of four games in the early part of a tournament, waiting for the others teams to play. However, this gives people time to socialize and get a snack, and it allows the singers time to rest their voices and time for all players to study other hiders and guessers. Another criticism is that with all prize money coming from team entry fees and additional amounts from the tournament sponsor, the total prize money is limited. With usually only two prizes and no table bets, only individual side bets are left. As one player explained, "I'd rather play a free-for-all. In round-robin you don't play too much, only when your turn comes up. . . . Then you sit, all day long. You don't bet any money. It's tiresome, real tiresome, you know, to me. But this other one, you get a seat there, anywhere. You bet your money, whatever you want to bet."[39] While some past tournaments allowed tables for side bets, most round-robin tournaments do not.

One Comanche player described:

> That's what it is nowadays: number one is round-robin, and free-for-alls are second, when it used to be the main attraction. . . . If you play that money and you keep winning, then there's more money in it. A lot more. It depends on what you want to bet. It's not like the old way. Shoot, them old folks used to bet a quarter, you know, just to be playing. Some of them didn't even bet, they just loved to play. But nowadays it's how much you can gain. Boy, if you can gain forty or fifty dollars, you're doing good.[40]

While these amounts would seem like little money to most non-Indians, it represents important supplements in communities with high unemployment. From 2016 to 2018, American Indian and Alaskan Natives (AIAN) in Native communities had a jobless rate of 11.4 percent, while those outside of Native communities had a 6.6 percent unemployment. Both are significantly higher than the national average. Among full-time wage and salary workers in

256 CHAPTER 5

2016–18, AIANs tended to have lower earnings than the population as a whole. Twenty-six percent of AIANs earned less than $500 per week, compared with 17 percent for the total US population. For those with higher weekly earnings, 19 percent of AIANs earned $1,200 or more per week, compared to 32 percent for the national average, due in part to differences in education levels, occupation, industry, and geographic region (Monthly Labor Review 2019). In April 2020, during the COVID-19 pandemic, over 26 percent of the Native American workforce was unemployed, compared to a 14.5 percent national average. On some Indian reservations in the United States, the unemployment rate among residents has ranged from 20 to 80 percent (R. Miller 2021).

In this light, the handgame is best viewed as an extremely enjoyable social activity with the potential to win small amounts of supplemental income in an economy with significantly high unemployment levels. However, many of the regular players that I know have regular jobs or regularly pursue other avenues of income and thus do not rely on the game for its income potential. This suggests that on the southern plains, income from handgame is typically irregular supplementary income associated with a pleasurable activity and that the enjoyment of the game draws participants more than anything else.

As with any event, individuals who enjoy a particular activity often miss or crave it when it is unavailable. I have heard individuals joke about returning to Oklahoma to get their "handgame fix" after a prolonged absence. Similarly, one consultant reported that when he was gone from the community for approximately two years, he missed handgame and had "cravings" for it.

TEAM COMPOSITION AND NAMES

In the past, teams were not named. A group (team or tribe) challenged another for a set of match games, or people simply gathered for free-for-alls, with everyone choosing which side they wanted to sit on. Up through the early 1980s, when most games were free-for-alls or match games, teams were fewer, larger, and composed of members of several families and individuals. However, with the shift toward round-robin tournaments in the 1980s, the nature of team formation changed. Elders have reported that families began to pull out and that teams became more numerous but smaller. The increase in round-robin tournaments in the 1980s led to an increased number of set teams that began to be named. The increase in smaller, named handgame teams with more intertribal and non-kin membership mirrors the increase in singing or "drum" groups in the development of the powwow circuit in the latter twentieth century. Most teams today are extended family-based lineages or structured as clubs and are rarely larger than twenty-five members. When a free-for-all is

The Handgame Today 257

held before or after a tournament, the number of players often exceeds that of two regular teams during a round-robin.

Because handgame play is between groups who share tribal ethnicity (as Kiowa or Comanche) and are often related through kinship, there is a different structural basis than that found in forms of non-Indian gambling pursued by individuals or couples. While formal teams did not exist in earlier times, family members tended not to play or bet against their close relatives. Today most relatives do not play against one another, but sometimes a large family team may split to create two teams (and thus lead to intra-family competition).[41]

Determining precisely when named teams began to form on the southern plains is difficult. Older individuals report that they began to form in the 1950s, most likely toward the end of that decade. A Kiowa team named Jack Rabbits formed in the 1950s and was followed by the Carnegie Roadrunners (Bruce Haumpy), the Eagles (Bill Koomsa Sr.), the Wild Bunch (Bill Koomsa Jr.), Billy Goat Hill (Thurman Kadayso), and others. Bill Koomsa Jr. explained that teams initially formed not from political divisions but to facilitate tournaments, as opposed to match games where two teams would play a set of games in one evening.[42] Tony Isaacs (1969) reported that while players were not normally organized into teams, definite memberships and team names had recently developed, as with the Carnegie Roadrunners and Billy Goat Hill, which he recorded in November 1968 (Indian House Records 1969, 1974).

Some teams grow so large that they fission, and in time may fission again. The Challengers, a Cheyenne team, is one example. As Mary Beaver described,

> I've always played on my dad's [Willie Bearshield's] team, and then Pete [Bearshield] was with us and then my uncle Moses. . . . It was really Moses Starr and my dad's team, and then it got to be so huge that my dad wanted to branch off from Moses. And, yeah, they talked about it, so my dad eventually broke off, and . . . all of the kids went with my dad, and then Moses and his kids, you know, his big family went with Moses. And they remained the Challengers, and they still go by that name, and then my dad, the name of our team was the Oklahoma Indians. . . . When my dad died in 2001, I guess I took over as the team captain. At that time Pete branched off to his own team, which is called Magic.[43]

Today most teams' core consist of members from one family and in some instances a smaller number of individuals from other families. During my fieldwork in the late 1990s, this was easily observable with teams focused around elders including Jack Yellowhair, Bill Koomsa Jr., Carl Atauvich, Willie Bearshield, Jed Querdibitty, Alonzo Sankey, Gregory Haumpy, and Flora Weryackwe. While most teams are based around extended families, members

Pete Bearshield (Cheyenne), in pale blue shirt, and Magic. Watchetaker Hall. Author's photo, ca. 2018.

of the same family may occasionally play against one another. However, kinship is not always the determining factor of what team an individual plays with. I have seen examples in which Cheyenne teams led by a brother and sister and predominantly Comanche teams involving a father and son played against one another and at other times together. I have not seen any detrimental effects to these arrangements.

While many matches prior to the 1950s involved games between members of the same tribe or between two tribes, elder players have pointed out that most teams are now made up of members of several tribes through intermarriage and friendships. Team size tends to increase during the winter months, then decrease in the warmer months as powwows and other activities begin. Some handgame teams have set colors, like in other sports, wear matching shirts or jackets, use matching rattles or other accoutrements, and may have team songs.

Traditional respect-avoidance relations between mother-in-law and son-in-law, and between father-in-law and daughter-in-law, continue in some families but not in others. Consultants have occasionally pointed this out or commented on this, which most often involves individuals not moving the other's chair

The Handgame Today

or speaking directly to them. As is common among Oklahoma Indians in general, most players have nicknames and are introduced by their nicknames. Often, unless asking someone, I found myself not learning some people's real names for weeks or months.

By the late 1950s, some teams began adopting colorful names, some chosen by them and some given to them by others. A 1969 interview on a tournament held at the Hub City Powwow in Clinton, Oklahoma, names the Boone Raiders (Gregory Haumpy), Carnegie Eagles (Bill Koomsa Sr.), Carnegie Roadrunners (Bruce Haumpy), and the Clinton Challengers (Roger Reynolds), the latter of which formed in 1968. Kiowa, Apache, Comanche, Cheyenne, and possibly other tribes were represented.[44]

Team names are often based on nearby geographic characteristics, town names, or tribal membership. Dip City is named for the prominent dip in the street in downtown Geary, Oklahoma; Buzzard Creek and South B C. are named for nearby Buzzard Creek east of Fort Cobb, Oklahoma. Thurman Kadayso (Apache) kept several goats and lived on a hill south of Boone, Oklahoma. Players began calling his group Billy Goat Hill, which became the team's name. The Canton Indians, Carnegie Eagles, and Elgin Indians are all named for nearby towns. Carl Atauvich's family team Camp 7 is named for an area just west of Cache, Oklahoma. Located on the northwest corner of present-day Cache Road and Quanah Parker Road Northwest, Camp 7 was the name of an Indian Agency building where local Comanche drew rations and conducted other business.[45] Teams such as Arapaho Nation, C and A [Cheyenne and Apache] Renegades, and KCA are named for the tribal affiliations of their members. Some teams retain the same name for many years, while others periodically change, as with KCA, Buzzard Creek, South B.C., Red Thunder, and Southern Thunder, all variants of a single-family team. Others have interesting names such as A Dozen Excuses, No Shame, Magic, the Rowdies, Southern Ways, and Goot Ways (i.e., Good Ways).

Some impromptu, quickly formed teams may choose a colorful name for a single tournament. Table 4 includes a sample of western Oklahoma handgame team names with their primary family, tribal affiliations, and home areas.

Some names have a colorful origin. In 1988 Phil "Joe Fish" Dupoint and nine other men decided to enter a tournament at Carnegie, Oklahoma, but needed a team name. His nephew Mike Daugomah, who had been listening to the radio inside the house, came out and said, "Hey, Sègî (Uncle), I got a name. Bad Medicine." Phil recalled, "That's kind of catchy because we got the medicine man, and he's gonna pass out the bones, and, well, in that modern version, well, bad means good, you know. So I said, 'Okay. Well, let's go sign

260   CHAPTER 5

Table 4: Western Oklahoma Handgame Teams

Arapaho Nation	Ava Benson (Arapaho), Canton, Okla.
Bad Medicine	Phil "Joe Fish" Dupoint (Kiowa), Carnegie, Okla.
Billy Goat Hill	Thurman Kadayso (Apache), Boone, Okla.
Bone Collectors	Jeremy Shield (Crow) and Haskell Indian Nations University, Lawrence, Kans.
Boone Raiders	Gregory Haumpy Sr. (Kiowa), Carnegie, Okla.
Buzzard Creek	Jack Yellowhair family (Kiowa and Apache), Fort Cobb, Okla.
C and A Renegades	Laverne Buffalomeat family (Cheyenne-Arapaho), Geary, Okla. Later Dip City (see below).
Cache Indians	Carl Atauvich family (Comanche), Cache, Okla. Later called Camp 7.
Camp 7	Carl Atauvich family (Comanche), Cache, Okla.
Canton Indians	Jed Querdibitty family (Comanche-Arapaho), Canton, Okla.
Carnegie Eagles / Eagles	Bill Koomsa Sr. family (Kiowa), Carnegie, Okla.
Carnegie Roadrunners	Bruce Haumpy (Kiowa), Carnegie, Okla.
Challengers	Moses Starr family (Cheyenne), Clinton, Okla.
Clinton Challengers / Challengers	Roger Reynolds (Cheyenne), Clinton, Okla. Later the Prairie Chief and Hoffman families (Cheyenne), Weatherford and Hammon, Okla.
Comanche Indians	Battise family (Comanche), Lawton, Okla.
County Line	Vernon and Moon Atauvich, Orin Chasenah (Comanche), Apache, Okla.
Dip City	Laverne Buffalomeat family (Cheyenne-Arapaho), Geary, Okla.
A Dozen Excuses	Ira and Charlotte Sankey (Arapaho), El Reno and Geary, Okla.
Elgin Indians	Bill Paddyaker (Comanche), Elgin, Okla.

The Handgame Today 261

Table 4: Western Oklahoma Handgame Teams continued

The Gang	Flora "Gussie" Weryackwe and the Klinekole family (Comanche-Apache), Apache, Okla.
KCA	Ace Chalepah (Apache) and Jack Yellowhair (Kiowa) family, Fort Cobb, Okla.
Kiowa County / Kiowa County Warriors	Adam Kaulaity (Kiowa), Mountain View, Okla.
Kiowa Kickers	Helen Koomsa Chasenah and Trecil Koomsa (Kiowa), Carnegie, Okla.
Little Monkeys	Kerchee family (Comanche), Lawton, Okla.
Magic	Pete and Chee Bearshield family (Cheyenne), Clinton, Okla.
Northern Wind	Sankey family (Arapaho and African American), Geary, Okla.
North Spur Heights	Robert Oldbear and Jennie Chanate family (Comanche-Kiowa), Porter Hill, Okla.
No Shame	Ernestine Berryhill (Kiowa), Carnegie and Mountain View, Okla. Formerly Up to No Good.
Oklahoma Handgame Club	Gregory Haumpy (Kiowa), Carnegie, Okla.
Oklahoma Indians	Willie Bearshield, now Mary Bearshield Beaver (Cheyenne), Clinton, Okla.
Oklahoma Roadrunners	Bruce and Gregory Haumpy (Kiowa), Carnegie, Okla.
The Outsiders	Jack Yellowhair family (Kiowa-Apache), Fort Cobb, Okla.
Post Oak	Teehigh family (Comanche), Cache, Okla.
The Redskins	Floyd Moses, Apache, Okla.
The Roadrunners	Bruce Haumpy, Tom Kaulaity (Kiowa), Carnegie, Okla.
Rock Creek	Carl Atauvich family (Comanche), Cache, Okla. Later called Camp 7.
The Rustlers	Attocknie family (Comanche), Apache, Okla.

262   CHAPTER 5

Table 4: Western Oklahoma Handgame Teams continued

South B.C.	Jack Yellowhair (Kiowa), Fort Cobb, Okla.
Southern Thunder	Jack Yellowhair (Kiowa), Fort Cobb, Okla.
Southside	Keith and Frieda Tahchawwickah Wetselline family (Comanche-Blackfeet), Lawton, Okla.
The Thunderbirds	Buddy Pappio family (Kiowa), Carnegie, Okla.
Thunder Heights	A combination of the Red Thunder and North Spur Heights teams. Yellowhair (Kiowa-Apache) and Robert Oldbear (Comanche) families, Caddo and Comanche Counties, Okla.
The Villagers	Dee Sankey and Mary Lou Blackbear (Cheyenne-Arapaho), Geary, Okla.
The Wild Bunch	Bill Koomsa Jr. (Kiowa), Carnegie, Okla.

up.'" When he asked his nephew where he got the name, he told him about Bon Jovi singing "Bad Medicine" on the radio, a song that was released that year, and began singing it for him. Later they were asked to sing at the Red Earth Festival in Oklahoma City and, needing a name, used the same name. Later that fall, Bad Medicine was singing at the Navajo Nation Fair when a group of long-haired men came to Dupoint's drum group and began tapping on their drum. Not knowing who they were, Dupoint told them they were disrespecting the drum and to move along. Later his comrades told him that they were the band Bon Jovi. While they had planned to change the name later, it stuck, and Bad Medicine has continued as a well-known Kiowa drum group and handgame team to this day.[46]

Team names may last for a few months or for years or decades. Some teams, who associate keeping or changing names with winning or losing, may change them quickly and sometimes repeatedly if their luck has not been good. One elder player stated that when they do not have any luck for a prolonged period, they occasionally change the name of their team, and several players described changing team names to improve their luck or after some players leave and join another team. Occasionally a segment of one team will split off and form a new team. In 1999 this occurred with a segment of the Oklahoma Indians who wanted to take the team's name with them. That year at the state handgame tournament the two teams were registered as Oklahoma Indians

I and Oklahoma Indians II. Ace Yellowhair described how after losing for a period under the names of Southerners and KCA, the name Red Thunder came to him. After the Yellowhair family team changed to that name, the teams experienced an increase in winning.[47]

There are less teams today per tribe, and intertribal participation is usually needed to hold a round-robin tournament. The southern plains handgame crowd is a relatively small but highly dedicated one of individuals ranging from small children to elders. One hundred fifty people at a handgame is a pretty large turnout. This makes for a social network in which nearly everyone knows everyone and helps one another by attending each other's tournaments and benefits.

While there are sometimes junior tournaments for school-age children, most tournaments in western Oklahoma are primarily adult, although children are often on some of these teams, unless there is an age restriction such as in a tournament held at a casino. In 2023 I was in a tournament in which the Little Monkeys played. Composed of four boys and three girls from the Kerchee (Comanche) family, the oldest perhaps twelve years old, they were excellent players, started their own songs, and performed all parts of play by themselves. I was impressed by how fearless they were, never showing trepidation in their play, even when they were down or struggling in a game. In one game they were behind several points but battled back to win over an experienced adult team. The leader of the losing team smiled and remarked, "I can't believe we're getting beat by a bunch of kids."

HANDGAME SITES

Occasionally handgame sites that are repeatedly used are named. Near Boone, Oklahoma, the Apache constructed a large permanent arbor that was dubbed the Astrodome. "Holiday handgames" were held there at Christmas, Valentine's Day, Easter, and other special occasions, usually preceded by a supper. Two miles west of Apache Wye, in Caddo County, Oklahoma, was James Paddlety's house, which passed to his daughter Ina Paddlety Chalepah, the wife of Acc Chalepah. After a new home was built nearby, the family gutted the largest room in the old house, put in a wood stove to heat it, and used it for handgames. It was named Shady Front for a long row of cedar trees along the front of the house on the west side. For several years, games were held frequently from Friday through Sunday nights. Led by Ace Chalepah, the KCA team used to host the Crow regularly during their November visits to Oklahoma. As Jack Yellowhair Sr. explained, "When we was having ours, we called it Shady Front. Everybody in the world knows of Shady Front. We had free-for-alls. When you come in you sit on any side you want. Mostly

264 CHAPTER 5

the Kiowas from Carnegie played the Comanches and Apaches. They'd be sitting on one side like that, and we'd have free-for-alls. Everybody enjoyed themselves, you know, and we had a little concession stand." Games were held for approximately twelve years until a tornado destroyed the house around 1979.[48] Ace Yellowhair described the nature of the games, which were largely free-for-alls: "You know, different people would come over, and . . . when we had that old home place up here, everybody knew that we had that place, and they'll come every weekend . . . get up different side, you know, and just get a game going, and pretty soon, you know, before you know it, whole house full, lot of people."[49]

TERMINOLOGY

Like the term "barn burner," used to describe a close basketball game, southern Plains Indians have developed their own Native and English terminology for aspects of the handgame. A close game that see-saws back and forth to the end when each side is competing for the last stick is commonly known as a "crowd pleaser." A person who is easy to guess correctly is said to have "glass hands," as if one can easily see through their hands to correctly guess them. A person who continues to hide in the same hand is referred to as a "homebody," and doing this is called "staying home," while one who is prone to switch hands is known as a "grasshopper," and doing so is called "jumping."

To "put horns on him" is still commonly used by some Kiowa to describe making someone a guesser. Over the years some creative variants of putting "horns" on guessers have occasionally manifested. One year during a handgame shortly after Halloween, Phil "Joe Fish" Dupoint stuck two small Halloween horns with a sticky backing on a nephew's forehead, making him the guesser. He began guessing, and their team eventually won the game. He continued to wear them for two or three games and guessed well. Dupoint described another Halloween-inspired instance of "putting horns" on a team member during a game.

> Another time it was Halloween time, and we got this Viking [hat]. We went to Hobby Lobby or something like that, with Halloween stuff out there. It was a Viking hat . . . but it had them two horns on it. We got that, so, okay, here's the horns right here [motions with hands]. We're gonna pass them out. I said, "Uh, don't put them on me." . . . So, sure enough, one of my nephews again, he was out there, and we were guessing, and we couldn't get them. And I said, "Where's that helmet, where's that hat?" He says, "Right here." I says okay. So I went over there, and I was gonna set it on him like this, but he turned towards me like that, and I sat it, and it was like that [crooked]. "Dang, boy, you got the horns." . . . So he got up, and

The Handgame Today   265

he guessed, and he got a couple of them, and after while he missed. And then he got them all, and then he passed them on.[50]

A new player sometimes frustrates guessers because they have had no opportunity to learn the new player's habits. A new player who can "get out" and score several points, or one who does very well guessing the other side, is sometimes called "secret weapon." During one game, a girl in a family that had stopped by to look on was invited to sit on our team. She scored several points her first hide. Later she did the same on two additional hides. She left after a couple of games and we never saw her at a handgame again.

In 2003 we placed second at a round-robin tournament at the Tri-County Building in Geary, Oklahoma. Afterward, a mini-tournament was begun with fifteen-stick rounds. Our team lost on the first round. At the start of our second round, Jack Yellowhair Sr. put the horns on me and made me the guesser. On the first guess I got both hiders. Our team then scored a few sticks. On my second time to guess I got both hiders again on the first guess. We scored a few more points. On the third time I missed one hider but got the remaining hider on the next guess. We scored more points. On my fourth round of guessing I got both hiders again on the first guess. We continued to score sticks on our turn. The fifth time I again got both hiders on the first guess, and after regaining the offense we went out. The other team scored only one stick. Team members quickly congregated around me and began patting me on the back and calling me "secret weapon." Laughing, I told them, "I want you all to know just one thing. This will never, never, ever happen again." Everyone had a good laugh. In the next game I did well on the first guess, but after missing three or four points I put the horns on someone else.[51]

"Handgame hangover" is the term used to describe the physical tiredness acquired from several nights of traveling, staying up late, and playing handgames. Subsequently, some people sleep late to catch up on their rest following a long weekend of games.[52] Because guessing both hiders on the first guess is so important in the game, when a guesser is preparing to guess the other side, their teammates regularly call out statements of encouragement and support. Kiowa will occasionally holler out "*Èm qìgóp* (Hit him!) or *Chátcá bè hól* (Kill them at the door!), meaning "Guess the hiders correctly" and "Don't let them get out." Jack Yellowhair described some of the Kiowa and English exclamations made toward the opposing sides hiders: "They got slang for that too, you know. 'Doorknob 'em.' You know that's one . . . 'Doorknob 'em.' It means 'Get them right at the door' [guess correctly on first guess]. 'Hit them in the door.' . . . They used to use Kiowa words. Some of the Kiowas, they got their own words, they say it in Kiowa. 'Kill them at the door,' or something like

266   CHAPTER 5

that. *Chátcá bè hól.*[53] "Doorknob," "door pop," and "kill them at the door" are all used to encourage guessing both hiders correctly on the first guess. The glossary lists terminology associated with western Oklahoma handgames.

TABOOS

Elders have frequently cited the taboo against playing in the summer and the possible repercussions, but say they no longer believe in it. As Marie Yokesuite Haumpy remarked, "Comanches always say when you play handgame during the summer you catch the itch or snakes bite you. . . . But anymore, you know, this generation is just going so fast that we play even during the summertime. But it's really a winter game."[54] Gregory Haumpy agrees from the Kiowa perspective: "It's the season for it. They said 'Don't ever play in the summertime because you catch the itch.' Yeah, you scratch, scratch, everywhere you go, he said, you get the seven-year itch. Everybody don't go—they got scared, you know. They didn't want to catch the itch. But we play now. We play those months, summertime. But nothing ever happened."[55]

Carl Atauvich related that the Comanche used to play between Halloween and late January or February. Older people told him that not only were you supposed to not play handgame in the warmer months, you were also not to sing handgame songs or you would draw snakes around your home. When he got started in the game, he used to sing the songs to himself all the time, even in the summer, and he found snakes in his house. Upon finding a snake he was instructed not to just take it out and release it, but to kill it and burn it, and then other snakes would not come around your house. He did this and had not had a snake in his house for over ten years, he said.[56]

One time I saw the taboo come to fruition at a handgame tournament in the fair building at Apache, Oklahoma. On April 11, 1998, during a break between the handgames, an Easter egg hunt was held for the children. Late in the afternoon, a small snake, approximately twelve inches long, slithered across the floor, causing the game to suddenly stop. Darnell Atauvich caught the snake, took it outside, and let it loose. Several of the Comanche began talking about the taboo of playing in the warmer months and saying that snakes would come into your house or bite you. Everyone had a good laugh, and play resumed.[57]

GENDER ROLES

One of the biggest changes in the contemporary southern plains handgame has been with gender roles. Traditionally women could only sing, hide, and sit on the second row, which would apply only to mixed-gender games. One Kiowa elder maintained, "It is a man's game," and he said that he only allowed men to

The Handgame Today 267

sit on the front row, drum, hand out the bones, guess, and referee in games he sponsors.[58] One elder player described how this has changed in the handgames in western Oklahoma while it has continued among the Crow in Montana.

> See, we're modern here and now. You would include women to guess, which I don't care for. I think it's a man's game, the guessing part. The hiding, now that don't make that much difference. But to me, the guessing is up to the man. Also, the person that is handing out the hiding objects, it's a man's position, I think, and that's how I feel. Up north [at Crow], you don't see the ladies out in front, they're sitting back there . . . they're really traditionalists up there. The women, they stay on the back even when it comes time to eat, the men eat first and then the ladies will eat. Of course, down here, if we done that, we'd have a big war [laughs]. . . . Usually we like to put all the men in the front, right on the front row, a couple rows in front, and the ladies will sit in the back.[59]

Gender roles are much closer today. In most games women participate in nearly all roles, frequently serving as hiders, guessers, referees, scorekeepers, and, although rare, even sitting on the front row and drumming. Several women are also team captains. There have been several all-women handgame teams over the past twenty-five years. One year, Jack and Lela Yellowhair sponsored an all-women's handgame tournament in Carnegie. Each team was women-only and had to provide their own singing and drumming.[60] Bill Koomsa Jr. remarked, "Women are sometimes the best hiders for us."[61]

Today some women also sponsor and run tournaments, such as Mary Beaver, who is frequently sought in this role. As Mary recalled, "I used to always be afraid to speak in front of crowds, and when I went to leadership training they taught you how to get up and speak. So it's like, when we go to these handgames, all these men that are sitting back looking like 'who's running this thing?' I'll go there and grab that microphone and, you know, start talking [laughs]. A lot of old-time thoughts, you know, go into that. 'Cause it's, you know, it's a man's place to do it, but, you know, anybody can do it now."[62]

The age of players is also significantly changing. In the pictures on the covers of the *Handgame of the Kiowa, Kiowa Apache and Comanche* recordings made in 1968 (Indian House Records 1969, 1974), all of the players and almost everyone visible is of adult age. Whereas the game used to be more of an adult activity, today players range down to small children as young as three or four. Jack Yellowhair commented on this change: "We enjoy ourselves a lot. We like handgame. A lot of people like handgame. You know, used to you didn't have but elders come out all the time. You know, for a long time when I was playing. Now a lot of us encourage a lot of young people to go ahead and play

Genevieve Chanate (Kiowa) guessing. Red Buffalo Hall, Carnegie, Oklahoma. Author's photo, 2019.

The Handgame Today 269

handgame, come out, you know, and enjoy yourselves. And a lot of them are coming out now. I mean we've got a lot of young people in it . . . we encourage them to come out and play."[63] From 1993 to 2021, I observed a wide age range in handgame players that continues. In 2000 and 2021 consultants mentioned a noticeable number of new young people had begun to play. The presence of younger players and the formation of handgame teams in local schools with significant Indian populations suggest that the southern plains handgame is in no danger of fading away.

SEASON

The handgame used to be a largely winter event played from about November through mid-March. Today it is a year-round activity. Annual visits to the Crow in April–May and the Oklahoma State Handgame Tournament in late May expanded the season. Oklahoma teams began a state tournament, possibly around 1978 or 1979. First sponsored by Bill Koomsa Sr. for several years, it became a rotating event. For several years it was the end of the handgame season. While most western Oklahoma handgames and tournaments are still held between November and May, other games have been added during the summer months, often as part of powwows and tribal fairs. Occasional small round-robin tournaments and larger tournaments at events such as Red Earth (June), the American Indian Exposition (August), the Cheyenne-Arapaho Labor Day Powwow (September), and since 1992 the Comanche Nation Fair (September), and Kiowa and Comanche casino tournaments, have become regular annual events, and there are occasional trips to play against other Great Basin or Plateau tribes. Like powwows and society dances in western Oklahoma, the handgame has its own circuit or "handgame road" of regular events. Tournaments have become the most common form of play. As Carl Atauvich described, "Open handgames and, you know, just free-for-alls are second now. Tournament is number one. That's what they play. That's the main attraction right now . . . the tournament, the round-robins." According to Atauvich, round-robins began in Southwest Oklahoma around 1973, eventually superseding free-for-alls and match-games.[64] Beyond nearly weekly round-robin tournaments, table 5 lists the major annual handgames involving western Oklahoma tribes.

Since 1998, the entry fee for most smaller weekend round-robin tournaments in western Oklahoma averages around $50 per team, with an average of eight teams. Larger tournaments range from $75 to $250 for team entry fees. If the prize money reaches $1,000 or more, team entry fees usually increase. As one individual explained, "If you go for, like, a $1,000, [for] first place, then it's

270 CHAPTER 5

Table 5: Annual Handgame Schedule—Western Oklahoma

APRIL	Crow Junior Handgame Tournament, Crow Agency, Montana
APRIL–MAY	Crow Senior Handgame Tournament, Crow Agency, Montana
MAY	Oklahoma State Handgame Tournament
JUNE	Red Earth Festival tournament, Oklahoma City
AUGUST	American Indian Exposition (Thurs.–Fri. free-for-all; Sat. round robin tournament)
Labor Day weekend	Cheyenne-Arapaho Powwow, Colony, Okla.
SEPTEMBER	Comanche Nation Fair, Fort Sill, Okla. (Fri. evening free-for-all; Sat.–Sun. round robin tournament)
OCTOBER	Kiowa casino tournaments, Devol and Verden, Okla.
NOVEMBER	Kiowa-Crow handgames, Oklahoma (hosted by Kiowa, Comanche, Apache, Cheyenne-Arapaho, and Wichita teams)
NOVEMBER–APRIL	Miscellaneous weekend tournaments, usually in Anadarko, Apache, Cache, Carnegie, Clinton, Geary, and Lawton, Okla.

probably either $75 or $100." While the team entry fees make up much of the prize money, if the sponsors have advertised set amounts for places they must be able to provide that amount, often through fund-raising prior to the event and, if needed, through concessions sold that day. Some tournaments have additional funding allowing them to offer smaller entry fees while still being able to offer a sizeable prize. Others, like the Jacobson House tournament, have increased significantly in entry fee yet offer more substantial prizes. A few of the larger tournaments have also begun offering prizes for best singer, best hider, best guesser, and best-dressed team.

While purses have increased over time, they represent relatively small amounts when divided between the members of a team, compared with larger tournaments in the US Northwest and adjacent parts of Canada. Mary Beaver commented on the difference in scale of Oklahoma and more-western hand-games: "What makes a good handgame? People—you have to have people

The Handgame Today

271

there. The more teams, the better participation you're going to get. Money. We're not [at that level], if you look at Oklahoma versus other states, in other states their prize money is like $50,000, $40,000, you know [laughs]. It would be nice to have something like that."[65]

The following sample of team entry fees and prize money in larger Oklahoma handgame tournaments from 1984 to the present was obtained from event fliers, advertisements, and tournaments I attended. Around 1984 the Oklahoma State Tournament prizes ranged from $1,000 to $700. The 2002 Oklahoma State Tournament required a team entry fee of $180. First Place was $1,800 and a trophy, second place was $1,000 and a trophy, and third place was $400 and a trophy. Monetary awards were also given for the team with best shirts and for the individual best guesser (highest-percentage guesser in the final game), and a king and queen were crowned.[66]

On September 21–22, 2005, the Comanche National Museum and Cultural Center sponsored a tournament with $18,800 in cash prizes (first place $10,000; second place $5,000; third place $2,000; fourth place $1,000; fifth place $500, sixth place $300), and other prizes were given for best-dressed team, best singing team, best women backup singers, and best-presented banner. The tournament was restricted to ages eighteen and above and required a $275 team entry fee.

In 2016 Carlene Atauvich sponsored an independent tournament at Lawton, Oklahoma, that drew twenty-one teams with prize money of $8,000, $4,000, and $2,000 for first, second, and third place. Teams from Oklahoma, Kansas, New Mexico, and the Ute Nation played. The Oklahoma Indians won the tournament. This tournament was unusually large for western Oklahoma, in both the number of teams playing and prize money, in large part due to significant support from tribal casinos.[67]

In 2017 the Kiowa Casino Verden and Oklahoma City Pow Wow Club tournament included $4,000 for first place, $2,000 for second, and $1,000 for third place. Fourteen teams entered, with a fee of $250 per team. The 2018 Oklahoma State Handgame Tournament included $4,000 and a trophy for first place, $2,000 and a trophy for second place, and $1,000 and a trophy for third place; a plaque and $100 for best hider and best guesser; and a best-dressed team award.[68]

The 2019 Oklahoma State Handgame Tournament required a $200 entry fee per team. First place was $4,000 and a trophy, second place was $2,000 and a trophy, and third place was $1,000 and a trophy. The championship game included prizes of $100 for best guesser and best hider, $250 for best-dressed team, and $100 for best banner. Table 6 provides a sample of western Oklahoma tournaments, entry fees, and prize money.

CHAPTER 5

Table 6: Western Oklahoma Handgame Tournaments, Entry Fees, Prize Money

Tournament	Entry fee	Prize money
1997 Red Earth	?	$2,500; $1,500; $800
1998 Oklahoma State Tournament	?	$150
1999 Jacobson House Native Art Center	$75	$500; $300; $200
2002 Oklahoma State Tournament	$180	$1,800, $1,000; $400
2003 Jacobson House Native Art Center	$250	$1,500; $750; $500
2004 American Indian Exposition	$75	$1,000; additional cash for second and third
2005 Comanche Nation Museum	?	$10,000; $5,000; $2,000; $1,000; $500, $300
2009 Kiowa Casino Tournament	?	$5,000, $3,000, $2,000
2017 Red Earth Festival	$100	$1000
2017 Comanche Nation Tournament	none	$800, $400, $200, $100
2017 Kiowa Casino Tournament, Verden	$250	$4,000; $2,000; $1,000
2018 Oklahoma State Tournament	$200	$4,000; $2,000; $1,000
2019 Oklahoma State Tournament	$200	$4,000; $2,000; $1,000
2021 Summer Handgame, Comanche Nation Complex	$100	$1,500
2021 Indian Hills Handgame Tournament	$125	$2,000
2021 Cheyenne & Arapaho Tournament	$100	$2,000
2021 Bearshield Family Tournament	$200	$4,000; $2,000; $1,000
2023 Comanche Nation Fair	$200	?

While prize money ranges widely, some of the largest tournaments are in the northwestern United States. In 2010 the Tulalip Tribes hosted the three-day Battle of Nations Stick Game Tournament. The event was organized by Rusty Farmer (Colville), who organizes tournaments every year but wanted to hold a bigger event that year. The largest tournament ever held in the United States at that time, it drew nearly one thousand players from Canada and the United States, comprising 177 teams competing for a $30,000 first prize and over $100,000 in total prize money, double of what it had offered before. While other tribes were interested in hosting the event, the Tulalip Tribes, who provided the prize money, won with the highest bid (Tsong 2010).

A 2017 Coeur d'Alene tournament was held at the Coeur d'Alene Casino Resort Hotel in western Idaho to honor the tribe's veterans. Following open games on Friday evening, the main tournament on Saturday, with a $100 entry fee, offered $39,000 in prizes, including ones of $15,000, $10,000, $5,000, and 2,500, while a consolation tournament had a $1,500 prize. On Sunday, a kid's tournament, requiring no entry fee and with teams of three to five players aged seventeen or under, offered $1,000, $500, $300, and $200 prizes, while a three-on-three tournament offered a $3,000 prize.

The Pit River Tribe's first annual handgame tournament at its casino in California offered $4,000, $2,000, $1,000, and $500 prizes for its main tournament, for teams of three to five players, with a $125 entry fee. It also offered $600, $300, $150, and $80 prizes for its "bone hog" tournament (two-player teams), with a $40 entry fee. Two meals were provided on each day, and all registered players got a T-shirt.

MEDICINE

Native views about the use of medicine in the handgame continue in many Native communities. From the accounts I collected, beliefs in the use of medicine associated with the handgame fall into two categories: 1) medicine to help one win, and 2) medicine to physically harm others. Some view the use of medicine in the handgame as an unfair advantage or a form of cheating. Native views on cheating differ significantly from non-Native beliefs. Cheating can be viewed as a strategic means of increasing one's chances. Indeed, the culture heroes and tricksters of many tribes won through trickery or external assistance, whether helping the people or not. In oral history this is not viewed as negative but instead as anticipated and amusing. In some instances it is simply the way things are or came to be. In contrast, non-Native thought typically associates cheating as unfair and spoiling the character of the activity (Gabriel 1996, 150).

274   CHAPTER 5

Almost anything can be attributed to the effects of medicine. An elder described one game when the Crow were playing the KCA in Oklahoma and an unusually large amount was bet, around $4,000. A long game ensued in which few points were scored. When the Crow began missing, they began talking in Crow. As one man explained, "It's medicine. You make medicine any way you can make medicine—some way, somehow." The KCA finally won the game.[69]

Of the elder Kiowa I interviewed, individuals indicated that while some of the "old-timers" or members of their grandparents' generation had real medicine, they did not. This generation believed in the abilities of their elders' generation, whether consisting of legerdemain, real supernatural power, or some combination thereof. Gregory Haumpy noted that when he was a young man he often saw older men demonstrate the ability to hide an elk tooth in their hands, then open their hands, which were both empty. He noted that these men sometimes put their closed hands to their mouth, hid the tooth in their mouth, and later blew it into their hands. He also recalled seeing Old Man Neconie (George or "Chicken" Neconie) do this and give other demonstrations, but the elk tooth was not in his hands or mouth.[70]

Combinations of psychological techniques, including bluffing and intimidation through making one think that you have power, are an important part of the game, aimed toward confusing an opposing guesser and reducing their confidence. A hider or guesser for example might tie a handkerchief around his neck, making him look like a medicine man. A variety of hand motions and gestures, many used to suggest that one knows where the other is hiding the item, or to pantomime the deflection or casting off of another's ability or power are common.

As Greg Haumpy explained, "Well, they just do that to whoever's guessing. It's to give him something to think about. And they try harder to guess him the way he's supposed to guess him. To make it harder, yeah. See, like I've got medicine. Hey, I'm gonna use it. . . . Then when you go out there and play, it makes it hard for the guesser to think where you've got it, how you're hiding. It just goes to show you."[71] Discussing how he once foiled the repeated efforts of a guesser, a younger Kiowa player described, "I tell you, it's all a mind thing, psychological. But to me that was my favorite moment. Breaking his horns, you know. He thought he had us, you know, all that whole game."[72]

One Kiowa player related that today the Kiowa talk about making medicine only in a "more-or-less joking way." According to this individual, you might rub a stick to get a little power, or just anything that might make the opposition think you have power. Players make all kinds of motions to make the other side think they have something or can do something. As one player

The Handgame Today 275

described, "We talk about making medicine, but, more or less, I just say in a jokester way. I guess, you know, to tell somebody. Rub that stick over there, you know, it might give it a little power. Just anything, just to try to make the opposition think [you have something] . . . you see guys make all kinds of motions, you know. Boy, they do, they do everything just to make [you] think that [they] can [do something], but it comes down to just luck."

Bill Koomsa Jr. explained that when the Crow visit Oklahoma to play, he sometimes asks them to add a little more excitement and interest to the games, and he added that the more animated style of play of the north was increasing in the south. "These Crow boys, I tell 'em, 'Kinda cut up a little bit tonight. Make these people like it.' And they do, they add on a little bit more when they play. But that's really good, I think, cause that kinda, you know, makes the game more interesting. . . . That's the way them guys play up there. So it's kinda rubbing off down here. You'll see some of our boys now, they kinda got that."[73]

While these accounts suggest that colorful performance and belief in medicine make the handgame largely a game of psychology and mathematical odds, others believe differently regarding the nature and efficacy of medicine. While some attribute beliefs in medicine associated with the handgame as more for show, others believe it can be used against them, including for physical harm. As Gregory Haumpy described,

> Just like them Crows. They got ways, they make medicine, and whenever you see them, play against them, boy, they got all kind of medicine ways. But we know that they ain't got medicine, they're just putting a show on [laughs]. Yeah, when we play them, we do the same thing. We act like we know something, but we don't know nothing [about medicine] [laughs]. It's just for show, yeah. It makes it lively. It makes it interesting, you know, for the people that's watching. Some of them say, "Boy, you sure got some medicine. Boy, you guys beat them." See, make them think that we know something.[74]

One long-time player indicated that some southern plains players believe that the Crow players' more animated use of hand motions represents the use of medicine, and some allege instances of the use of medicine by the Cheyenne to do physical harm to their opponents:

> Just a few of us do that; we don't all do that. When they do see it, they kind of back off a little bit from it. All they think when somebody [uses elaborate hand motions] is medicine. But that's why they don't do the motions with their hands, just a few of us does it, very few. . . . Well, they think that whoever does it's got medicine or something like that, but we

don't use no medicine here in Oklahoma. Not that I know of. But yet, I was told the Cheyenne are bad about it, they still use it. That's why we kind of, we don't hardly, we're kind of not . . . into playing against the Cheyennes or the Arapahos, because we're afraid they, they did use it on us before. They did on my team, you know, my mother-in-law, my wife, even Tuke got hit like that. I don't know if he ever told you or not. I did too, I got hit right here in my throat, just like now, [we] went up there the other day to play, come back. Next day my throat was just burning and hurting. It still does. Kind of bothering me in my head. I'm thinking that's what happened when I was up there. That's why I kind of assume. There's some older people that plays up there, you know, they're pretty bad."[75]

In conversations and interviews in the late 1990s and early 2000s, several KCA stated that they believe the Southern Cheyenne still possess and use medicine in the handgame. As an elder Kiowa man related,

To this day, them Cheyennes, they use it every now and then. One time we went to play handgame. We went to the Cheyenne country, and there's an old lady. I forgot her name. Old Lady Starr they called her. She used that a lot, you know, when we play. She would go like this [rubs hands and palms together] around her paws, you know, her hands, make 'em kind of a circle, like. And then she looked like she was throwing [makes outward throwing motion with his hand], like that, you know, at people. Well, all the time when she was doing that, I guess, you know. And one time she was doing that and I was singing. Pretty soon I couldn't sing. Nothing was coming out, and I thought, boy. You know, after the games and everything was over, my throat was just hurting so bad, my chest, and I had blue spots all over me like that [points to places on his arms, chest, and legs], here and there. I couldn't sing, you know. You know, I couldn't ignore her, seems like.

My wife she got hit, you know, with big spots too on her like that. My mother-in-law she got hit, and she couldn't hardly walk. And Bill, he got hit some way too like that. He can tell you about it. And I couldn't sing. I mean she just done us in, boy, and then we finally got together, you know, the whole groups or clubs [handgame teams]. We told them [Cheyenne] people if she's gonna do that, we don't want her to play. We don't want her in there. We're not going to go up there to play with you all no more. We told her son and husband, 'We know she's using it, but we don't want to say nothing, you know, to her, she might turn it loose on us. But anyway, we told them, "If you want us to come up and play with you, we'd be more than glad to, but we don't want her to be doing that to us." So I guess they talked to her, and she quit for a while. She started back again later on, though. They told her to quit, don't do that.

The Handgame Today 277

So she wouldn't play; she sat way back on the side. Finally she died. But some of them, the older people still uses it [power] to this day.[76]

From this perspective, medicine can be viewed as a mental process or as a psychological strategy. That is, you can make the opposing guesser worry so much that you shake their confidence and increase the likelihood of them missing you. Sometimes it works, and after several missed guesses you have the guesser thinking so hard that you can see the increased level of confusion, a lack of confidence, frustration, and stress in a guesser's body language.

In the late 1990s, an elder Comanche commented on the use of medicine in the game by the Cheyenne:

> Oh, they still have it in the handgame. You know, I honestly believe that I've been . . . voodooed. They call it "you been shot," you know. I believe I've been shot several times . . . at a handgame. They still have it. They still have that voodoo. The Cheyenne have it, and . . . some of the Crows and different tribes probably . . . the Arapahos probably have it too. I don't know whether the Kiowas still got it or not because most of their old folks are gone, just like ours now. Comanches now, we don't have no old folks that play handgame. No old folks, they're all gone. We are the elders now.[77]

Less frequently, the Crow are believed to still use medicine in handgames. When asked if the Crow use medicine against them, a Kiowa elder stated,

> Well, they did use it for a while when they was first coming down. It's been way back. But here recently they told them people, these Crow people, the people here in Oklahoma, Okies, don't use none of that medicine stuff. If you [are] thinking of trying to use it here on my people, stop right now. Don't do that or . . . we'll never let you come back and play with them again. So, they don't use it. Not the Comanche, Apaches, Kiowa. Cheyennes is the only one that we know of so far [that] uses it. We don't know who they really are, but they haven't . . . recently used it on us here too much anymore. I think the elders died out. . . . We know they aren't using it, so we enjoy playing with them. We want to play with them. But if they start that stuff again, that's going to be it."[78]

Another elder described, "I don't know. I guess they might have, 'cause they all bunch up when we beat them. They all get up and go over in the corner somewhere and just bunch up together and talk, you know. Well, when they get through, they come back, and they're ready. I've seen them. We don't always talk about anything, [we] just go over there and get our money, and then we mess around. When we're ready to play again, we play again [laughs]."[79] One year the Kiowa team experienced a severe snowstorm on their drive to

278   CHAPTER 5

Montana. One man interpreted this as the Crow working against them and not wanting them to come.

These accounts reflect three patterns. First, the possession and use of medicine is usually associated with elders. Second, behavior perceived as unusual or different from the KCA tribes' point of view, such as bunching up to discuss something after a game or excessive hand motions, may be interpreted as using medicine. Third, unusual occurrences, especially en route to a game, may be perceived as the use of medicine by others against one.

While power was obtained by several methods in earlier times (though vision quests, dreams, apprenticing, purchase, or spontaneous reception) and used in a variety of activities, including hunting, warfare, curing, and even love, the vision quest is now virtually absent on the southern plains, and very few traditional doctors remain. Thus, gambling, in which the handgame is the most prevalent remaining traditional form, is one of the few arenas in which "power" can be demonstrated. Merriam (1955, 315) reports that expert gamblers, among then contemporary Flathead (Salish), develop special notoriety, often acquiring medicine songs through the vision quest that are reported to bestow specific powers for gaming. Even in other regions, constant success in the handgame is often attributed to the possession of personal power (Lesser 1933, 318; Jorgenson 1972, 300; Green 1979, 273) or medicine.

Harmful Medicine

Beliefs involving the use of medicine to harm others through witchcraft or sorcery also exist. A Comanche man and woman described a woman who got "shot" at a handgame and had severe hacking, coughing, flu-like symptoms for a week afterward. This man also described a time that he became sick after playing the Crow during their annual visit to Oklahoma. "I really got sick one time at the handgame. I got so sick, boy, I tell you, I had to get in bed. And the medicines just weren't helping me. Cold medicines weren't helping me. It was just bad." About the woman who got "shot," he recalled: "She said, 'Boy, I got that way.' She said when the Crows were down, she said 'I was guessing,' and she said something happened. 'Boy, I got really sick at the handgame.' She said, 'I went home, and I had to cedar myself and pray over it,' and she said 'I got better.'" This couple also recalled a Kiowa and Apache woman who became sick at the same game.[80]

One elder noted that Frank "Doc" Given, the son of Kiowa chief Sitting Bear, had medicine but not handgame medicine. One time during a game, Given was challenged to guess the other side. He told them that he could "sce" in their hands and immediately guessed the hider correctly. Although this silenced the crowd, he did not continue to play.[81]

Oklahoma handgame players I interviewed tended to believe that one is more susceptible to having medicine put on them while playing outside of their home area. Although one elder player stated that he didn't know much about people using medicine, I think he may have been holding back. He stated that maybe they did but that it depended on what you believe. He indicated that he carried red Indian paint as protection from medicine and that it was easier to get medicine put on you when you were playing in someone else's area. He also spoke of another game in which a man from an Oklahoma tribe came out and asked his daughter if she had any of the paint, because he believed the other team was putting medicine on them that evening.[82]

Gifts may be suspected of having medicine placed on them. One year at Crow Agency a Kiowa man was picked as the head guesser for the Oklahoma team. A Crow man gave him three or four small bone objects to place in his pocket and to give him medicine to help him guess and the Kiowa to win. When he told the Kiowa group leader about it, the leader told him to give them back to the man and said that if they won, they won, but they were not playing that hard to win. They were playing for fun, and if they won, it would be on their own account, with no other help (i.e., from medicine).[83]

Teams may exhibit a bit of apprehension and mistrust when playing against those they have never played before, because they are often unfamiliar with their style of play. One elder told of a group of Kiowa who went to play against a Great Basin tribe. This tribe uses large hiding items that are about 1 to 1.5 inches thick, often place a bandanna over the hider's hands as they hide them, and keep their hands there until the guess is made. Each side has five score sticks. To win, one side must get all five of the other side's sticks, then give them back to them, then get them all again. The Kiowa got all five of the other tribe's sticks, gave them back, and continued to play. The other tribe then got all five of the Kiowa sticks and then declared that they had won the game. Although the Kiowa side believed they had been cheated, no one said anything to the other side.[84]

Teams are also quick to believe that someone is using medicine if their style of play is unusual or unorthodox or if they win too often. As one elder consultant described to me an individual I knew well: "People say that [she] is using that, you know. 'Cause she'll hide in one hand. She claims her other arm is hurt or something, you know [the consultant held their left hand up and put their right hand under the bottom of their shirt]. But I've seen her carry a baby with two arms, seen her swinging him like that [motions], . . . putting him up like that [lifting him], and grabbing, anything—she's using two hands. But when we go to a handgame, she's like this [right hand under shirt]." I often saw this individual hide in this style.

280 CHAPTER 5

Unsure whether the woman had medicine under her shirt or in her purse, where she was also said to put a hand, this elder continued:

> She'll have her hand in her purse and going like this [showing left hand raised and hiding a bone]. Then the other hand is down here maybe [at waist or purse]. But . . . a lot of times she gets away, you know. She's won a lot of times, but the group, they don't say nothing. We tell [her husband], but he says, "Ah, she's hurt, you know." He makes up excuses [for her], you know. We know better, but yet—. That's why they've been winning all these years. They win tournaments, state tournaments, year after year. And that's what's getting them by, I think.

This individual stated that the woman's father and grandfather were peyote men, the latter a medicine man, and that he believed she obtained her power through them.[85] That the woman was clearly capable of playing in the normal fashion with both arms visible but claimed otherwise and continued to play with one hand concealed, combined with her and her team's frequent success, led others to suspect her of using some means, whether cheating or medicine, to play.

Most elder Kiowa today state that while some old people (generally of their grandparents' and earlier generations) had medicine, people today do not. Yet beliefs in medicine continue. At a 2017 tournament I noticed a guesser on one team who did most the guessing for his team that day. He was especially accurate throughout the day, and his team eventually won the event. This guesser often remaining seated or sometimes arose and walked to the middle of the floor, rarely looking at the opponents but rather simply looking downward and concentrating until raising his head and signaling his guess. Discussing his efficacy in guessing with others after the tournament, two individuals independently told me that the individual is known to carry a special form of medicine that he uses in the handgame.[86]

Protective Medicine

To protect themselves and counter the use of medicine, some individuals undertake a range of protective religious rituals. Players have described varied activities undertaken prior to playing handgame, including ensuring they have a proper frame of mind, prayers, cedaring, sweat lodges, and even Native American Church meetings. Individuals stated that you do not go into these types of religious events to ask for material things or to win in an upcoming handgame but rather to ask for protection for yourself and your family.

There is a strong belief by some individuals that you can be harmed by the thoughts of others and that negative mental powers can harm. One of the classical anthropological distinctions between witchcraft and sorcery is that witchcraft involves harming others through mental or psychic means, while sorcery uses actual physical objects. In some cultures, the two forms can be combined. From this stance, the concern with mental processes is clearly witchcraft. As one individual described, "The mind is a powerful thing, and if you set your mind to something you can do it, even if it means, like, harm, anger, jealousy, those things. You know [if] your mind's set on that . . . someone's gonna get hurt by it." This individual stated that they occasionally take a sweat lodge.

> [I do this] to pray for protection for my family. . . . I don't want them to be hurt from another person's bad thoughts, you know. So that's what I do. . . . I go in there and pray about the people we play with and that they won't be having hard feelings, won't be jealous, and even I won't be jealous and even I won't have hard feelings because, like I said, the mind, it's a powerful thing. . . . I pray for protection, that these things will come about, that we'll be protected, [that we] we won't be hurt, [that we] enjoy ourselves. If we win, so be it. If we don't, so be it. Like that, that's how I go in a frame of mind.[87]

Occasionally ritual purification or a blessing may be undertaken prior to playing handgame. The evening before the 1998 state handgame tournament, the Yellowhair family, who I played with, had a Kiowa Native American Church leader come and perform a cedaring and ask for luck for the team.[88] Some players continue carrying protective medicine on their person while playing. After one evening's games, an individual showed me a sample of tobacco in the form of part of a cigarette that he carried in his pocket. Comanche consultants have told me that some women may wear red paint on their body, in their rouge, or concealed on their body as protective medicine. As Kehoe (1996, xvii) notes among the Pawnee handgame, there remains "the feeling—by no means confined to American Indians—that luck in a game may be affected by prayer, spiritual exercises, and personal amulets."

Many cultures engage in rituals for luck, confidence, and protection in a variety of cultural activities, including subsistence, health care, warfare, attracting mates, procreation, sports and games, and other activities. Bronislaw Malinowski (1948) discovered that the Trobriand Islanders practiced two types of fishing—one in inner lagoons where fish were plentiful, the water calm, and there was little danger, the other on the open sea where yields were more varied and the waters more dangerous. While the men used no magic for fishing in the calmer lagoons where they relied solely on knowledge and skill, they used a great deal of magical ritual on the open seas to ensure safety and increase their yield.

282   CHAPTER 5

Games and gambling often include rituals. Widespread use of magic is documented in games and sports, including the Aztec ballgame, Zulu soccer, Maori and Tikopian dart matches, Trobriand cricket, American baseball, and southeastern American Indian stickball, softball, and baseball (Blanchard 1981, 29–52; Blanchard 1995, 108, 174–91; Gmelch 2005). James Mooney (1890), John Swanton (1946, 674–80), Raymond Fogelson (1962), Kendall Blanchard (1981, 155–66; 1995, 177–78), and Thomas Vennum (1994) all report a large body of practices, taboos, and forms involving both witchcraft and sorcery associated with stickball and lacrosse among the Cherokee, Choctaw, Creek, Iroquois, Menominee, Ojibwe, Mystic Lake Sioux, and others. These practices involve forms of medicine for protection, medicine to harm or make others lose, and actions associated with gambling. Following the end of warfare, the Trobriand Islands incorporated a wide variety of chants, dances, songs, dress, and magic, once associated with warfare, into their indigenized form of British cricket. A comparison of fifty groups in the nonprofit Human Relations Area Files found that the degree of complexity in games of strategy increases with the degree of complexity in social organization, and that games of chance appear to be associated with religious activities. As Roberts, Arth, and Bush (1959, 601) describe, "It is commonly thought by many peoples of the world that the winners of games of chance have received supernatural or magical aid." While some scholars have taken issue with their findings (cf. Blanchard 1995, 17–18), they hold true in the handgame and in other Native sports such as Cherokee and Choctaw stickball, where beliefs in the use of "medicine" and "power" are common.

These principles can also exist in games of skill. Former professional baseball player and anthropologist George Gmelch (2005) found that, similar to Trobriand subsistence fishers, many American baseball players, whose livelihood depends on how well they play, developed magic rituals in an attempt to control the element of chance. In baseball chance is highest for pitchers, then batters, and least of all for fielders. Consequently, ritual practices are highest for pitchers, then batters, and only rarely for fielders.

B. F. Skinner (1938, 1953) and Gmelch (2005) describe how animals often begin to associate specific behaviors with rewards. Baseball players often begin to associate rewards (successful performance) with prior behavior, often leading to the adoption of rituals, but they are quicker to change those rituals once they no longer work. Baseball rituals include the wearing of certain numbers, carrying a talisman, and maintaining culinary, dress, or other habits associated with success or a streak of success. An activity is associated with and correlated to success and continued in an attempt to continue that success.

The Handgame Today 283

For example, eating a certain food, leaving a certain button unbuttoned, listening to a particular style of music, wearing a certain item of clothing, using a certain bat or batting gloves, may be believed to be associated with recent success and continued in some ritual form or routine to continue that success. Developing a routine or ritual is not only comforting but also serves to reduce chance and feelings of uncertainty. Through repetition of the correlated behavior, the player uses the ritual to gain control over his performance, increase good luck, and thus improve their chances of success. Most baseball rituals are personal and unique to individual players. If the ritual begins to fail, such as a player experiencing a slump, many make a conscious decision to change to a new ritual and routine.

Similar to what Malinowski (1948) found in Trobriand fishing magic and Gmelch (2008) found among professional baseball players, the carrying of fetishes or talismans, or the practice of ritual habits, superstitions, or taboos, especially among batters and pitchers, are often beneficial because they instill confidence in a player. Gmelch compares fielding in professional baseball to lagoon fishing of the Trobriands, while pitching and batting resemble open sea fishing. While the first is relatively safe, ensured, and successful (fielders have a success rate of over 97 percent), the latter is characterized by more unpredictability and chance and thus less assurance of success. Consequently, activities with greater chance are more typically associated with magic rituals. Regardless of whether the talisman has any actual supernatural power associated with it, a confident player is more likely to perform better than one lacking confidence.

I have recorded similar practices to increase success or ensure protection from magic in the handgame. Some teams change their name if they continue to play poorly or do not win for a period. Singers may avoid singing a song if they feel it has become unlucky, usually if their team has been quickly and repeatedly guessed correctly during that song. Hiders and guessers sometimes try a new strategy in an attempt to perform better. Teams may change the bones they use to improve their success. Players may carry forms of protective medicine when playing certain teams or tribes.

Players may change the items they carry on their person for protective medicine. Fetishes, or charms in the form of material objects believed to contain supernatural power that can aid or protect the owner, are common in Native American cultures and the handgame, both for success and as personal protection. A variety of medicines for protection and to ensure success in play continue to be used. Some Kiowa and Comanche handgame players stated they still carry protective medicine, most commonly small buckskin bundles of red paint worn on their person whenever going around people from another tribe. One elder Kiowa player related that he wore a protective bundle under his shirt. Another had a small leather medicine bag inside of his hand drum with two mescal beans tied to it. I have seen players pick a piece of sage prior to a game to carry in their pocket, or carry tobacco, cedar, feathers, and bear root on their person prior to playing handgame. Others have reported that they carry paint or small medicine bundles on their person during play. Some players report that they undertake prayer prior to handgames. As one player related, "It's all individual. . . . I don't know what other people, how they go about it . . . [but] for my own family I use prayers for protection for them, so they won't be hurt and like that." I have participated in sweats with Crow in Montana and in cedaring ceremonies with Kiowa in Oklahoma prior to playing in tournaments.

One day when I came to visit Jack Yellowhair at his house, I discovered that he had bought a small rubber figure of Daffy Duck at a store. This Daffy's clenched fists extended upward, and he had a look of consternation. Jack had drilled holes through his fists and inserted small carved sticks as handgame bones. When I saw it I began laughing so hard that Mr. Yellowhair gave me the figure as a gift and told me it could be my handgame *dáui* (medicine). I turned it into a necklace and have worn it in some games, producing many laughs and sometimes some luck. "The Duck" has produced a myriad of family jokes that we all enjoy.

ANGER AND JEALOUSY

Sometimes anger and jealousy arise in the handgame community, most often when someone loses or feels they did not get to hide or guess as much as they should have. As in any social setting, I became privy to grumblings, in this case about some individual players and teams. What animosities I heard or witnessed during or shortly after tournaments largely consisted of gossip or heated words and venting that was soon checked. Sometimes disagreements were quickly put aside, and individuals assumed a friendlier mood as free-for-alls began to be played, often mixing members of several teams together. One long-time player explained that tempers sometimes flare but are usually quickly smoothed over. "Sometimes words do get exchanged, you know, feelings get hurt, but then it comes back around next week, or, you know, the next time you see them . . . it's all smoothed over. Just back to normal again, but, yeah, I've witnessed that before. Tempers fly and stuff." Players may refer to opponents during a game as their "enemy" and play hard against one another but are most always friendly afterward.

The Handgame Today 285

Teams in the past had one or only a few guessers. Today many are given a chance to guess, which, as one team captain stated, "results in less griping." I have only seen one physical fight at a handgame. In 1998 two women playing on opposite sides had been taunting one another all night. The fight erupted after the last game concluded and was quickly broken up, with the women being forcibly pulled apart and taken out of opposite sides of the building while making colorful parting verbal statements. Individuals stated that the two had been fighting for some time prior to that day. Several individuals left the game. After one more free-for-all, with relatively few people, the evening ended at 9:50 p.m., early for a handgame.

As one older player described, "They say don't get mad, it's just a hand-game, you know, just a game. But a lot of them takes it real serious, too serious. Some people, you know, get mad 'cause they get beat, or they get mad at you 'cause you kept guessing right."[89] One night I saw a woman wearing a T-shirt that said "Don't Get Mad. It's Just a Game" Below this was a picture of a set of score sticks in their holder and, below that, "Hand Game!"

If a team frequently or consistently wins tournaments, it is not unusual to hear grumblings about their success. One woman described what she perceived as overt jealousy toward their team:

> Sometimes, if you get up in the finals—well, I know our team . . . we've never done anything to anyone, but [we're] the most, how do you say it, challenging team, to where they hate to see us win [laughs]. . . . If we should start getting up there towards the finals . . . if we get beat or if we should start getting down on the sticks, the other side winning, everybody claps for the other side. It's really, you know, it kind of hurts you a little bit in here [points to her heart]. But I think that's what they want you to feel so that you can go down emotionally, psychologically, and get beat. And I've seen that at so many tournaments. . . . If we should start getting beat, I don't care how many teams there is, they all be one another against us you know [laughs], and they'll be clapping."[90]

Some players describe what they perceive as increased seriousness and competition in play despite fluctuations in the size of prize money. As one man described in 1998,

> It's a lot of fun but not like it used to be. Today they take the competition very serious. Back then it was no problem to get beat, you know—you laughed it off. You enjoyed it, and if you get beat, well, you still laugh about it. Today they don't laugh about it. It's gotten pretty serious now. But me, I still enjoy it. . . . The handgame world has . . . made a terrific turn, and it's getting pretty serious now. Man, they got to win at any cost. In

the last few years I think it's gotten that way since we . . . [have] gotten so strong and we've won tournament after tournament, weekend after weekend. . . . Okay, it's gotten so bad they've said, "We've got to break their spell someway."[91]

This individual stated that some teams have videotaped them to find a way to beat them, which could provide them with the ability to determine frequencies in hiding. However, even in videotaping games one is not always able to see every hide and guess.

What makes these statements interesting is that long-time players from other teams described this individual as one of the most competitive and easily-angered individuals on the circuit. Occasionally someone may become miffed and not shake hands with the winning side, but overall these transgressions appear short-lived and do not seem to have any detrimental impacts on the game. Jealousy is likely behind some of the allegations regarding cheating and the use of medicine.

GAMBLING AND LEGAL STATUS

Many non-Indians misunderstand the handgame, both in organization and purpose. Often viewing it as simply a form of gambling among people with a higher level of unemployment and poverty than the national average, they fail to understand the importance of tradition, community, competition, and performance associated with the game. Because the money bet is quite small on a per capita basis and only involves a double-or-nothing principle, it is neither costly to play nor able to make someone wealthy nor associated with larger-stakes gaming. Non-Indians are also often unaware of the legal right of Indians to play handgame, related gaming traditions, and their associated legal and political implications.

Since the early 1980s, gaming has become a significant economic activity in many Indian communities. Awareness of a rising number of tribal gaming enterprises, conflict over state and federal laws and jurisdiction, and the decision in *California v. Cabazon Band of Mission Indians* prompted passage of the Indian Gaming Regulatory Act (IGRA) in 1988. Although tribal gaming was encouraged by the Reagan administration and signed into law by him in 1988, considerable non-Indian resistance existed. This act was created to provide a legislative basis for the operation and regulation of gaming by Indian tribes, establish a federal agency (National Indian Gaming Commission), address congressional concerns, protect gaming as a means of producing tribal revenue, strengthen self-sufficient tribal government, promote economic development, protect tribes from organized crime, and assure fairness to operators and players (Utter 1993, 134).

The IGRA established three classes of gaming. Class I includes social and traditional games associated with tribal ceremonies, celebrations, and powwows that fall under the exclusive jurisdiction of each tribe. Class II includes bingo and related gaming, banking and non-banking card games, and grandfathered card games (those specifically included and not precluded in state laws). This includes lotto, pull tabs, and punch boards. Class III includes all forms of gaming not covered in Classes I and II, such as the casino games of baccarat, blackjack, roulette, and craps, as well as slot machines, video poker, horse racing, and dog racing (CWAG 1998, 345–76; Utter 1993, 133–35).

As described by CWAG (1998, 349), Class I gaming is defined as "social games solely for prizes of minimal value or traditional forms of Indian gaming engaged in by individuals as part of, or in connection with, tribal ceremonies or celebrations" (25 U.S.C. 2730[6]). "The Senate [Select Committee on Indian Affairs] was hesitant to attempt to define traditional or ceremonial gaming as it is clearly an area of tribal self-government."[92] Included in this class of gaming are "traditional gaming activities such as the 'stick' or 'bone' games that are played by tribes in conjunction with ceremonies, powwows, celebrations" and "rodeos, horse races, or other kinds of gaming with purses or prizes . . . traditionally . . . held in conjunction with such activities for members and guests, including invited guests." The defining criteria in Class I gaming is the absence of the possibility for significant monetary gain or loss.[93] In handgames, typically bets can only be doubled or lost with no higher odds. In Class I gaming, provisions associated with the handgame are left to individual tribal regulation.

Some Oklahoma Indians do not speak favorably of the handgame, typically those who do not play and view it as gambling. One Kiowa man explained that some Christians talk against the handgame mostly because they disapprove of the betting—which they view as gambling. While it is a form of gambling, the scale involved is so small that it merits context to understand it with a degree of cultural relativism. One way to compare the Oklahoma handgame is simply from the cost of entertainment. For a team of ten players, and many teams are larger than this, a small tournament with an entry fee of $50 costs only $5 a person, while larger tournaments with entry fees that rarely exceed $250 would cost only $25 per person. A tournament can often last from six to ten hours, and dinner is usually provided by the host. Few other public events of this duration are so inexpensive. Going to the movies, the theater, or attending a concert or sporting event are all shorter in duration and costlier. Betting is arguably smaller than in the pre-reservation era. For example, no one today usually bets cash amounts equivalent to the value of a horse, saddle, or even the cost of a new Pendleton wool blanket. Individual bets during free-for-alls

288 CHAPTER 5

rarely exceed $25 per game and thus remain rather small. As described earlier, the total bets placed per game may only amount to $300 to $350 dollars per side, per game. Usually made up from numerous betters on each side, the individual amounts are rarely large.

Essentially a form of gambling, raffles are held at many types of Indian activities including handgames, powwows, and benefit dances. However most people do not view raffles as gambling as much as they do a way to support the event or cause at hand, with the chance that they might win something. Some individuals have described buying chances on a raffle as simply a donation, as the chance of winning is small. Gambling associated with the handgame in Oklahoma is modest and, unlike casino gaming, is limited to weekend events and to some degree can be viewed as chipping in for a shared social activity.

GUESSING AND HIDING STRATEGIES

The Plains handgame has long been classified solely as a game of pure chance (Dorsey 1901a, 363; Culin 1907, 31; J. Roberts, Arth, and Bush 1959, 597–98; Cheska 1979, 229), and even today some players maintain this view. One Comanche women indicated that she only guessed when she felt like it: "It's just luck. It's not that you're good. It's just luck. It's just like bingo. Sometimes you're lucky at bingo, sometimes you hardly win." But another Comanche woman described the handgame as "a game of skill."

One of the theoretical purposes of this study is to reexamine this classification. The observation and memorization of other players' habits to gain an edge in play is a common part of sports and games.[94] My fieldwork and interviews revealed that some players approach the game in relation to skill and strategy in observation and memorization of hiding and guessing patterns and body language. As Alfred Chalepah described, "Sometimes it shows in your hand. There's a way, like if you don't have a poker face, you know. If you don't have that, well, you give yourself up."[95]

An individual who frequently guesses for his team spoke candidly and at length about guessing techniques:

> Yeah, the body movement or the eye movement or the hand, you know. To me, I work—if I tell you my secret, somebody else might hear it and then see [laughs]. No, I'll go ahead. I go by the speed of the hand; one hand is always slower than the other. Somebody else, they got different ways, you know, but mine is . . . you concentrate on that black [marked], one and it will get heavy [i.e., it gets heavy in the hider's hand because of their concentration], slows down like that. I don't know what you'd call it, psychology or something like that, you know. But that marked bone in your hand

The Handgame Today   289

and the plain [one] is on the other, well, you're gonna concentrate on that one with the mark. Well, it slows you down. And . . . you get fooled a lot of times, you know. Some of them get tricky. They're gonna say, "Well, I'm gonna go this one slow" [move the hand with the unmarked bone slower than the other], and I'm gonna think he's gonna go that way, which . . . happened to me several times. It'll open, you know, and it ain't there. And then you can get the eyes. I can look at you and just go like that [makes a hand motion toward the hider]. See, you just looked at my finger, and one eye is going to squinch on you, just a very little. Then that's the side you got it on. Same way with anybody, you know. I use that. I used to use that a lot, but I don't hardly use it anymore you know. The movement of your foot here, that's the side you got that mark (marked bone) on. Or the body movement, one side kind of down like this, you know, a little lower, then that's the side too, you know. Or . . . when you're playing, you keep looking a certain way, you know. Well, that's the way looking, that's where it's at. See, them things you look for in the handgame."[96]

This guesser continued:

Some of them don't look. I've seen a lot of them, you know, they just [signal]—they'll think way back before they get up, you know. They'll think of their use, you put it in your mind, which side it is on, then you get up, and you just guess right quick that way, and a lot of times it works. You don't even have to stand there and look at them . . . because by the time you get up you already concentrated on [them]. Some of them used to go like this, you know, put their hand in front of their eyes [he demonstrates], close your eyes [and] you can see it, where that marked bone is, and then that's the way they'd guess, and it's there then a lot of times. So that's the way we people guess. . . . [It's a] skill game, you know. People try to figure things out.[97]

The hider can also apply these principles to the guesser, by studying their patterns and tendencies. As one player explained,

You can do what I just got through saying about the mind—you can look at a person. Most of them don't do that now. They look at you, and they're gonna figure you out, which way you're gonna guess. And a lot of them, it works. I've seen it done. You come out like that all of the time. I'm knowing your gonna [guess] that way. So now I'll put that plain bone over here. And when you guess that way, well, the plain bone is there 'cause I'm concentrating on you. Like I always tell my [team), concentrate on that guesser. Outdo him, you know. And that's the way it works. But a lot of them, well, you can go like me—I can go so far, and then I forget, then you just come out, and they got me all the time. Yeah, it's a thinking game, you know.[98]

290   CHAPTER 5

Some of the more experienced players even pay attention to what the other hiders and guessers on their team have been doing to figure the odds of their selections in hiding and guessing.

Another individual elaborated on how they study the habits of hiders:

> A lot of them has got habits. And that's what you have to really remember and go by. And the guesser also has got habits, most of the time, you know. They, a lot of them, most of the guessers, . . . will be [gestures in direction of guess], and a lot of them will be . . . just going outside and the middle, outside and the middle. You hardly find a guesser that will go this way [left], outside, in the middle, this way [right], you know, whatever. Those kind are real unpredictable. But a lot of them will get up there outside, or a lot of them will go this way [inside], or some of them will go, let me see, to the right or this way [to the left]. A lot of them, you know, just their habit. And you've got to remember that as a hider. And as a guesser, you've got to remember the habits that a hider's got. If you can remember all these things, you'll be a darn good guesser or a good hider.[99]

Carl Atauvich, the leader of Camp 7, described the importance of becoming familiar with the habits of other players and the difficulty of guessing new players:

> For some of the new beginners, I would call it luck. You know some that aren't that experienced, you know, you don't know their habits. If they're new hiders and haven't been playing that much, then they're new to you, they're strange to you. You don't know what they're going to do. Like the old ones, you almost know what they're gonna do. The new ones you don't, and I think that's luck. But the old experienced handgame players that did a lot of guessing and hiding, I call it skill because they know. They know what you're gonna do. And they have to use their skill to get you, and the same way they do when they're hiding, when they're guessing a new hider, you've got to use that skill to get them because you don't know what they're gonna do. But the older handgame players, you know their habits, and you know exactly what they're gonna do. Same way as a guesser, you know what they're going to do . . . you know how they guess, and you got to try to outwit them. Hiding and seeking, you're seeking that bone, and the other one's hiding [laughs]. That's a lot of fun, that's competitive. I really enjoy it.[100]

One team leader described the advantage of having many new players on their team whose habits the guessers have not become familiar with: "They all went up there to Red Earth with us. They played with us. We got them all involved in it, that's the reason why we were so strong at that tournament. Because they were new at it, and . . . the guessers at the handgame and the hiders, if you're new, you don't know, you don't know them. You don't know what they're gonna do. You don't know just how a hider is gonna hide, the habits they got."[101]

Some team guessers also emphasized that guessing requires consistency in focus and practice. In discussing consistency in guessing, one elder guesser described, "I kind of turned it over to my boys. You know, my boys are fresh at it, in the guessing department, and I turned it over to them. Well, I kind of lost a little bit. Because, see, when you're in the habit of guessing and hiding, you get to know everybody [i.e., their habits] and . . . it stays on your mind all the time because you're staying with it, you know. You don't give it up or sit down or quit for a while. If you do, you're gonna lose a little bit."[102] As an example, this individual commented on how he often used to be able to door-pop the Crow, correctly guess both hiders on the first guess, several times in a row but cannot do it as often anymore.

During my research I encountered other observations indicating the studying of hiders and guessers in the game. One such observation was that brothers, sisters, and husbands and wives tend to hide beside one another. During a game in which two Comanche brothers were hiding, an elder Kiowa man leaned over and said "I'd go up the middle." The guesser guessed inside and, just as he predicted, guessed both hiders correctly. Although there are only four possible hiding combinations, I have also noticed that married couples sometimes tend to hide on the side closest to their spouse. While I have not been able to gather statistics on the prevalence of this trait, players frequently comment about its prevalence, and it does seem to have an observable frequency.[103]

These accounts demonstrate that some individuals do not approach the game merely as a game of chance but rather one of skill in observing and remembering patterns in human behavior and strategy in weighing their implications within a limited number of possible hiding and guessing combinations. Players are consciously trying to outdo their opponent by studying their body behavior and by memorizing their previous hides or guesses as far back as they can remember, to learn their tendencies. This in turn allows them to make a more informed choice based on mathematical frequencies and possibilities. Although numerically smaller in possibilities, this aspect of the handgame resembles chess in that often the strongest player is the one that can see ahead the farthest numbers of moves in the most possible scenarios. Therefore, the handgame should not be characterized as simply a game of chance but instead as one involving both chance and skill.

Guessers also study the physical characteristics of the bones used in play, but sometimes there is no distinguishing the bones. As one guesser said, "That's how I was killing them . . . I was going by their habits. Because I couldn't tell the difference in the bones. They had a good set of bones, and, man, I was knocking them out because I was going by their habits. See I was door-poppin' them."[104] There is a widespread concern about cheating, especially involving the alteration of the hiding bones. As I interviewed more team leaders, I encountered more references to the studying of the bones, looking for observable chips, cracks, or blemishes in the ends to identify them in a hider's hands. I also recorded allegations of opponents using a third unmarked bone, switching the markings on bones during play, and switching entire sets of bones during a tournament.

The use of an additional unmarked bone would only work if one were showing the guessed hand and not both hands. Ensuring that the hider opens both hands simultaneously negates this tactic. It seems that the only reason one would switch the markings on a set of bones or switch an entire set of bones would be if one were observing physical differences in the end of the bones, such as color or physical characteristics, and basing their guesses on that factor. As one individual described,

> It's been that way, you know, in the handgame world. It's getting bad. It's not going out there to have fun, boy, they're going out there for blood. They want to win at any cost. And I've seen it done. I've seen them take the tape off and switch it on the other side. You see, you go to a handgame nowadays, you cannot find a perfect set of bones. There's some kind of discrepancies on it. Somewhere along the way you just have to look for it. If you're a guesser, you've got to look for it. You've got to watch for it. And then you find it—okay, you're going to be getting them. . . . But pretty soon that same set of bones is going to change. You know why? Because they switch the tapes. They do that a lot. That's what happened this weekend. In fact every time they play. The medicine man has got all four bones, that's when they do it, and then they hand them out."[105]

One possible reason for switching the markings on a set of bones is to change them quickly, if needed, after one is guessed. One woman commented that one team always uses hiders far in the back, thus making it easy to change the tapes. She also stated that when the players on this team are guessed, they do not come up or show the bones in their hands immediately, allowing them time to switch the markings. This tactic can be negated if the referees ensure that hiders keep their hands separated, visible at all times, and open them immediately after a guess.

Claims of individuals switching sets of bones during play are rare but do occur. One man spoke of a handgame at Apache in which the sponsor was using two sets of real bones in the free-for-alls and two sets of plastic bones in the round-robin tournament. Becoming suspicious at a certain point in the tournament, the man's team checked the bones being used and discovered that another set of bones had entered play. They ended up with one set of real bones and two sets of plastic bones. The MC announced the violation over the public address system, but it was unclear who was responsible.

Although tampering with the bones is considered grounds to disqualify a team, I have never heard of a disqualification based on this rule breach occurring. One team captain showed me how he attempts to prevent this in his team's bones by fixing them with tape and thread wrappings on the marked bones that are then coated with layers of glue to prevent the markings from being pulled off and switched. A team captain described playing at a place where the marked bones contained beaded portions around the middle that were so thick that they were apparent in your hands while trying to hide them, especially for women with smaller hands. He related that hiders and guessers look for such differences.

Another change was a shift from a single hiding object to a pair of hiding objects for each hider. Even in the original form of the game, once a hider had made their hide and brought their hands forward, they were not supposed to switch the object. In the old style of play, the presence of a single, small hiding item, such as a bead, bean, animal tooth, or small bone cube, combined with the dexterity of some players, nevertheless resulted in some individuals cheating. To prevent hiders from throwing the single hiding object from hand to hand, teams have adopted the use of two larger hiding implements, today typically two bone or plastic hair pipes. Matched pairs of hair pipes or "bones" are now the most common form of hiding implement now used in the southern plains handgame.

Carl Atauvich described:

> It's gotten so bad that people got pretty fast with their hands. I've seen some old folks that could throw them bones into the other hand that you can't even see them do it. . . . They've gotten away from that, and they've gotten bigger [hiding items]—they use bones, plastic bones. They used to use real bones like these plastic bones we got. In fact, we used some not too long ago, Oris [Chasenah] had some real bones, but they fade too easy, and they get scratched too easy, and it just shows a difference real easy, so we don't use bones no more, we use plastic, plastic imitation of bones. And we use bigger ones, the bigger the better because they won't be able to throw them.[106]

294 CHAPTER 5

Noticing discoloration or abrasions on the hiding implements suggests that guessers use this as one method of determining how to guess. However, this only works if part of the bones were exposed and the hider's hands were moving slowly enough to see the bones. Some hiders conceal the bones in their hands so that no part is visible to the guesser and some teams use smaller-sized three-inch hair pipes that inhibit seeing any part of them in a hider's hands. Another tactic is to use hiders sitting farther back in the crowd, away from the referees and the guesser.

Even then, players must be vigilant. As one individual described, when some hiders are guessed they "go down" or lower their hands to see which way they were guessed before opening their hands and showing how they hid the bones. If the judges are not near them when they are guessed, some people become suspicious of the bones being changed after a guess. In such cases some referees will make a conscious effort to go where the hider is before the guess is made. Another individual described a game he was judging where a hider switched the bones after being guessed by laying them on the floor but crossing his hands over one another in doing so.

Although teams are not supposed to discuss guesses during play, this occasionally occurs. In the winter of 1997–1998 there were two teams that I witnessed, and others pointed out in interviews, that often consulted among themselves before making a guess. Some tournament rules specify that no advising or consulting is allowed in play. One year at Red Earth, Carl Atauvich told me that after missing several guesses his son jokingly called out, "Dad, wipe your glasses. You can't see." A member on the opposing team stated that Atauvich was seeking advice and demanded a stick (point) be awarded as a penalty.[107] This individual frequently pointed out any possible mistake or violation of play by others and called for a penalty stick, but I rarely saw one awarded.

During a game in 2017, I watched an individual pass the position of guesser to another player after missing a guess. Before he sat down, and while still standing in front of the newly appointed guesser with his back to the opposition, he signaled where one of the hiders had the marked bone by concealing his hand on his abdomen. Although the second hider re-hid, the one that the former guesser signaled about did not, and the new guesser guessed the hider correctly. I have seen this occur several times over the years.

When a guesser starts missing and gets rattled, they often pass the position to another to try to stop the opponent's scoring run. If the new hider stops the opposition, it calms their team, and they begin to sing and prepare to hide. If the new guesser starts missing, it often feeds the energy of the team hiding.

The Handgame Today 295

In some instances, a team will go through multiple guessers, each unable to correctly guess the opposition, and the spirit and intensity of the offense increases and is easily observed. In such instances the defense becomes almost frantic, seeking to find a guesser that can stop the run, and some people may look away and try to avoid being chosen as the next guesser.

SOCIAL FUNCTIONS

The handgame community is one of several cultural arenas in the life of contemporary Native Americans in Southwest Oklahoma and elsewhere. As with powwows, Gourd Dances, men's and women society dances, the Native American Church, Christian churches, and softball leagues, it has its own regular crowd, some of whom also regularly participate in other cultural events. It is associated with longstanding social networks through tribal identity, intertribal participation, friendships, marriages, intratribal and intertribal adoptions, and competition, and it provides many social functions for those involved.

Following the establishment of reservations and the increased proximity of many tribes, more frequent play has facilitated the development of an intertribal, multigenerational community. As Jackie Yellowhair described, "It's like a big extended family. We're not all related by blood, but we all know one another. Over the years we know everyone and now their kids, and their grandkids."[108] The structure of the game makes it a group effort.

Plains Indian societies are well-known for their practice of "taking one another as relatives" or adopting one another, even as adults. While adoptions occurred as part of the Calumet Ceremony, and with both other Native and non-Native individuals, they occur in a wide range of relationships to the present. Although people involved in such adoptions are referred to in anthropology as "fictive kin" to differentiate from blood relations, Natives often view these relations as strong or even stronger than blood relations. While several members of varied tribes have adopted one another in the handgame community, there is also a general sense of a "handgame family" that applies to the frequent interaction between players.

Mary Beaver (Cheyenne) described the nature of the extended family and their mutual support of one another's events that forms the handgame community in Southwest Oklahoma:

> We have tournaments throughout the year here in Oklahoma, and like
> every weekend we get together. We throw in an entry fee of fifty bucks,
> say, per team. You can have anywhere from four to eight teams, that's four
> hundred bucks, and we just basically want to have fun and . . . enjoy the

time with all the other teams because we call each other our handgame family. We see, whether it be Comanches or Kiowas, we see each other weekend after weekend. And a lot of friendships have really developed from that, and you always know that if there is a fund-raiser for a specific person, people are going to show up. That's our family; that's our way. We go help where we can. So that's the way we do here in Oklahoma.[109]

Players have stated that the handgame is a team effort and should be approached as such. When one's side wins, everyone on that side wins. As Lydia Meat Yellowhair described, "It's all teamwork in handgame, we work together as one people."[110]

Mary Beaver described the importance of teamwork and establishing momentum in playing, and the feeling when one's team wins a tournament:

It's a good feeling when you win a handgame and you walk away knowing you did the best you could. You did perhaps some good hiding to help your team get to the top. Maybe you did some good guessing to help your team get up to the top. Everybody plays a part in a team. Whether you sit there and sing for your team. We have some shakers, whether you shake your shakers in time with the music. You just have to have that rhythm going, and once you get it, I mean, that's probably how people win. Everything is going your way. Everything—your guessing, your hiding, the singing is good, and it's just like nobody can stop you. And then when they announce that winner, you know, announce your team, it's just a really good feeling.[111]

Ace Yellowhair similarly described the importance of the singing and being in sync or "rhythm" while hiding, "That's when it's hard to make sticks, you know. My point of view on handgame [is] that it's hard to make sticks when you can't get your music together. Like, it's my own theory on it, you know, [if you] can't get in gear, in other words. I think a lot of it has to do with the singing too."[112] When a team loses a song while playing or has trouble remaining in tempo together, they often perform poorly in hiding.

The Wild Bunch was an all-male team formed by Bill Koomsa Jr. that was well known for both their success in playing and their singing. One elder described the popularity of their singing. "The Wild Bunch went for a long time. . . . They sound real good. When the Wild Bunch came around, everybody got in the mood. They want them to sing." Carla Atauvich also remembered the Wild Bunch as a difficult team to beat. "They were real tough, woo, they were tough, boy. You'd be afraid to play them, at one time they were good. They had a lot of players that are gone now."[113]

The handgame is an important component of social significance in terms of strengthening family, intra-tribal, and intertribal ties and cooperation in competition and sponsoring of events. It is one of several arenas that help maintain traditional values associated with drumming, singing, gambling, wit and humor, mental concentration and strategy, competition, skill in observation, and teamwork. It also reinforces traditional values of reciprocity and redistribution through widespread economic cooperation and support. The game involves its own unique form of aesthetics, in the kinesics involved in play (hiders, guessers, medicine men), singing, and organizing a well-run event. The handgame is one contemporary cultural activity in which individuals and groups express a sense of pride on several levels (individual, family, tribal, and intertribal).

Medicinal and Therapeutic Qualities

Another important social aspect of the handgame is the medicinal and therapeutic qualities obtained from the game. As a long-established cultural tradition, singing is an effective and therapeutic means of release for many Indian people. The handgame holds important therapeutic functions for participants, and a key part of the release that handgame provides involves the accompanying music. The healing qualities Native participants and spectators describe from hearing drumming and singing at powwows and society dances (Meadows 2010, 93, 193–94, 211–12) are also attributed to handgame music. For many it serves as a reprieve, even if only temporary, from the mental, physical, financial, and other stresses of everyday life. As Jack Yellowhair described:

> To me, when I play I forget everything. I forget about my bills, my sickness, and all that stuff. I forget about them. That's the way I do. I don't know how the other people feel. I owe somebody over here a lot of money, and I'm worrying about it, you know, and when I get in a handgame he's away from me. I don't even worry about it. It makes me feel good, you know, until the next day, then that same thought would come back to me. I owe this guy over here [laughs]. So that's sort of a—make you forget your sickness. That's why they got a saying, "I'm sick, I don't think I'll go to the handgame today." And they say, "Nah, go to the handgame, and your sickness will go away. It will make you forget." Which is really true, you know. There's a lot of people say they're sick, and then they get all right when they get them bones and they start hiding like that. That rhythm of the drumbeat makes you forget. Sometimes you forget you had a wife, you know [laughs]."[114]

Later Mr. Yellowhair continued, "So all of that goes with the handgame. So scream as loud as you want, holler and whistle [laughs]. Everybody has fun, and they'll say it'll make you forget your sickness. You're ailing somewhere,

298   CHAPTER 5

and you go to handgame—well, it's gone. But it comes right back when it's over [laughs]."[115]

Mary Beaver described how she enjoys the people, the competition, and the release that playing handgame brings. "Just the people. You know, I say I know a lot of people. The competition, the friendly competition, the playing, you know, the guessing. It's just something recreational that to me . . . takes a lot of stress [away], because I do a lot of things, you know, during the week."[116]

The relaxing effect that handgame provides involves the accompanying music. Throughout my fieldwork, members of many tribes and participants in many kinds of activities have described the power of song to serve as a release from physical ailments, stress, and the problems of everyday life. As Gregory Haumpy explained,

> It takes a lot of worry off of my mind. I don't know if it does [for] the other guys, but it does for me. See, I stay home and think about a lot of these deals that's wrong with me [at this time Mr. Haumpy was a double amputee], what kind of trouble I'm having here at home. When I go sing, well, it takes everything off of my mind, just that singing. Concentrate on singing, you know. And that's what I like about it. And you meet a lot of friends, you meet friends, you make friends. Some guys get jealous —[but] you don't pay no attention to them. Yeah, that singing is something good. It expands your lungs, you know, and beating that drum. . . . Nothing is in my mind except in singing when I get in that powwow or a handgame.[117]

Ace Yellowhair commented on how handgames provide a release from physical pains and psychological stress:

> Oh, yes, lots of times, you know—like, "Oh, I don't want to go." Well, I'm going to have to go. Maybe I might have to drive for Dad or something like that . . . and I don't feel like going, but once I get over there and you could hear them singing in the building, then I'm, like, "All right, yeah." Go back, go right in there, get in the game, you know, and feel good about it. And you don't have to worry about what's bothering me or, you know, what's on my mind, just kinda push it to the side and enjoy the day and games. It goes game by game, day by day to me. That's the way I look at it. Every game is different. Every place you go is different. You hear the same songs or whatever, but it'll be something about it is different. That's what I like about it too. . . . Cause the singing, you hear that drumming and singing like that it'll make you forget about your aches and your pains. I used to tell my grandma, "Let's go handgame and get rid of your pains over there, and that way you won't have to think about it." It just makes you feel better, handgame, or I guess any other kind of music. Native American music, you know, gets that . . . good feeling on there. But that's what it is for me, the singing part.[118]

Kiowa singer Phil "Joe Fish" Dupoint described the importance of music in the handgame to spirit, team size, momentum, and its medicinal properties,

> Music plays a big part of it. So at least sitting on the front row I want ten guys with me. Ten guys with me that can all sing and they can all guess . . . [and] the same amount of women. . . . If your women, if they can sing along with you, chime in along with you, sing along with you, that just makes everything more powerful. It just makes it. Because you go to these lively handgames, well, the whole side there, all them menfolks sitting on the front, and all them women sitting in the back, chiming in together, they're making a raucous . . . noise over there, same way over here. So it's just kind of there's a spirit there that's coming out of that music, and everybody's just kind of more or less forget your ailments and forget your problems and things like that because you're having a good time. You're all just kind of chiming in, and it just makes you want to try harder.[119]

Several elder players with increasing medical problems and limited mobility told me that the handgame provided an important social opportunity for them to get out and meet, visit, and even flirt with people. Because the game can be played from a stationary position, it offers elders with limited mobility an important and lively outlet for social activity. Gregory Haumpy and Roland Tsatoke frequently sang and played together in handgames, even after both became amputees. Handgame can also serve as a release for younger players. Jackie Yellowhair described that, "The handgame is . . . my main [activity], how I relieve stress, you know. I go over there and sing my heart out. Sing till I'm dripping sweat. Give it all, you know, and I get satisfaction out of that."[120]

Individuals in other regions also describe therapeutic aspects of playing handgame. As Derek Knows His Gun (Northern Cheyenne) described, "When I'm singing, I'm letting go of a lot of things built up inside. It relieves a lot of stress" (Tsong 2010). Randy Farmer (Colville) described the game as a way to connect tribes with their oral culture, while providing an alcohol-free and drug-free zone for adults and children that feels safe (Tsong 2010). Blanchard (1984, 191) notes, "Play is a mechanism which human beings employ to remove themselves from the angst of reflecting on the realities of existence. Play is symbolic distancing that relieves or at least limits that tension." While games and sports are not the only activities to provide an escape from the realities of daily life, the handgame serves as an excellent example of this principle.

Players have also commented on the enjoyment they get by sponsoring a tournament in realizing what it provides for the participants. Randy Farmer (Colville), who runs the Battle of Nations Handgame Tournament in Tulalip, Washington, explained (Hughes 2017):

300 CHAPTER 5

As I was doing the tournaments over the years I got to see and understand and learn that for one weekend I get to take everybody's heart aches, sorrows, away for that one weekend. Because when people are playing handgame or stickgame or slahal, you know, you don't think about anything that's going on in your life . . . Someone may have went through a loss, someone maybe lost a job, or going through a financial hardship. But for that one weekend alone I get to take all of that sorrow and heartbreak away from them and introduce laughter, and love, and friendship . . . Stickgame is a true extended family. We all are extended family. We all help out one another."

Handgames and Prison

Handgames also provide an important social and cultural activity for incarcerated Native Americans in some states. As Elizabeth Grobsmith (1994) describes for incarcerated Natives in Nebraska, the handgame became one form of cultural and ethnic maintenance as well as a subject of legal contention. In addition to educational opportunities, inmates have access to "self-betterment" clubs designed to provide inmates with help in increasing "their business connections with the outside community, enhancing adjustment, facilitating successful interaction with the non-incarcerated world, and promoting interest in prison programs and affairs" (Grobsmith 1994, 33–34). At the Nebraska State Penitentiary eight such clubs existed in the 1990s, including the Native American Spiritual and Cultural Awareness Group (NASCA). Each club was allowed a weekly meeting and, like other self-betterment groups, two special events per year, normally one symposium and one banquet per year. Native American inmates used NASCA to sponsor various Indian activities, including handgames, powwows, visits by medicine men, classes, speakers, Indian mental health counselors, and other beneficial services (Grobsmith 1994, 33–34, 58). Among the Omaha, the handgame was originally a ceremony associated with mourning. More recently, the game is considered as a social event and occasionally used as an opportunity to invite outside guests to visit (1994, 57).

In time, problems arose concerning prison definitions of NASCA as a "self-betterment club" or a "religious" group, as prison regulations prohibit any organization classified as both and as each category is entitled to a different range and number of activities. Although inmates regard NASCA, still active, as a religious, cultural, and spiritual group (hence the name Native American Spiritual and Cultural Awareness group), prison officials classified the organization as a "self-betterment" club, which directly conflicts with the goals of NASCA. If classified as a religious group, NASCA would lose its privileges to hold weekly meetings, symposia, and banquets. Legal conflict began in the mid-1980s as requests to approve Indian activities (powwows, handgames, Native American Church services, Yuwipi meetings, etc.) led to the question of whether NASCA was a club or a religious group. Requests to cook Indian foods and hold handgames met with increased resistance (Grobsmith 1994, 57, 85). Many requests were denied on the basis that the prison categorizes NASCA as a club, and thus it is not allowed to sponsor events requiring longer periods of time, like religious events. The prison maintained that such requests would provide differential privileges to one self-betterment club over others. In the end, cancellation and rescheduling occurred due to increased penal system resistance toward the holding of Indian activities. Often these deterrents were based on a lack of agreement on Native requests regarding length of activities, guest lists, kitchen availability, Native food preparation, and other issues (Grobsmith 1994, 178).

A reduction of permitted annual club events, from four to two, and a reduction in the allowed length of activities produced resentment and lawsuits concerning the denial of religious freedom. The denial of requests to hold a handgame and other activities resulted in a lawsuit in 1989, *Thomas v. Hopkins et al.*, that was never heard in court (Grobsmith 1994, 57, 80). Because NASCA is classified as a club, and family members are not permitted to attend self-betterment club activities, Indian inmates were unable to invite family members or anyone on their visiting lists to their special cultural and religious events (Grobsmith 1994, 178–79). Cultural events without family and community support are unheard of from the Native perspective.

Nebraska prison inmates thus faced a catch-22 based primarily on two items. First, those running state prisons, as directed by the state courts, believe they must treat all inmates equally, although Native inmates perceive themselves and are legally classified on a federal level as distinct cultural, religious, and sovereign groups. Even with some accommodations concerning the use of religious items (sacred objects, sweat lodges, traditional foods, and plants) in prison, the location and use of these is limited. They are sometimes not allowed at all, and this often negates individual and group religious and legal rights (Grobsmith 1994, 180). Second, there is a cultural difference of classification—the Anglo secular (cultural) versus sacred (religious) categorization of Native events (and associated rights for each type of activity) that contain both cultural and religious elements. A review of NASCA's website suggests that handgames are no longer held in prison.

Today most rights directly related to Native Americans in prison involve protections of spiritual and religious rights (MSP 2012; NARF 2014). For

302   CHAPTER 5

many years Native American prisoners have sought religious rights while incarcerated. Most often the sweat lodge, pipe, tobacco, smudging, powwows, drum groups, talking circles, and certain plant, animal, and bird parts have been sought. Oklahoma prisons also allow cultural traditions for Native inmates such as powwow and the sweat lodge. The Confined Intertribal Group have held a Gourd Dance and powwow inside the Joseph Harp Correctional Center since the late 1980s. The center is a medium-security facility in Lexington, Oklahoma. As one Oklahoma inmate remarked, "The system wasn't designed to think about providing cultural needs, but the warden did it at that time to try to ease our pain, if you will, or help us become enveloped in our culture."[121] These cultural activities allow them to stay connected or to reconnect with their cultural traditions and to give Native inmates a sense of pride, self-worth, and dignity in a place where those components can be hard to acquire and maintain."

Probably because they are viewed as secular rather than sacred, handgames do not appear in the lists of permitted Native American cultural activities for most state prison systems. My consultants were not aware of any handgames in Oklahoma prisons and had never been asked to hold any in these institutions for inmates. Based on the importance of drumming and singing, and the game's potential to provide another link to cultural traditions, handgames could provide a beneficial social event for incarcerated Native Americans. While betting with any kind of money would not be allowed, an older style game in which teams compete for a basket of food, which is then shared equally by the winners with the losers, could provide a format for the game.

Holidays and Special Events

Handgame people like to make their events fun. One way of achieving this is by incorporating elements of US national holidays into their own events. These include events such as choosing a king and queen for Valentine's Day, an egg hunt for children around Easter, and treats around Halloween. On April 12, 1998, the family of Jack Yellowhair sponsored a tournament at the Anadarko Fair Building. Close to Easter, an egg hunt was held in the afternoon for the children. In addition, a "King and Queen Bunny" contest was held in which three men were lined up in front of the crowd. Edmond Tate Nevaquaya and Pete Bearshield sang a Forty-nine song while people voted for their choice by throwing down money in front of them. The same was held for three women, while a Round Dance song was sung. The winners were Allen Sutton and Mary Beaver, who each received a basket of gifts. Money raised during the voting was donated to help the host with costs. Jack Yellowhair, the

The Handgame Today 303

host of the event, explained that this is how you do something special to add some fun to the event while making back a little money to help cover the costs of sponsoring the event.[122] Like high school homecomings, special statuses are sometimes awarded at handgames such as king and queen, a tradition that came with trophies at the Oklahoma State Handgame Tournament for several years. At one tournament, a Mr. and Mrs. Universe were selected and given money, a rose, and a red carpet to walk on. On November 25, 2023, a Thanksgiving handgame tournament was held at the Comanche Nation Complex.

Families sometimes sponsor a handgame tournament for a family member's birthday at any age. In 1998 a birthday round-robin tournament was held in the Oklahoma Fair Building in Apache for Orin Chasenah by his team County Line. The building was decorated with streamers, balloons, and a large birthday card for everyone to sign. During a special for Chasenah, three men sang a Forty-nine song with English words in it that included "Happy birthday." People placed money on a blanket for him and after the song came up and shook hands and hugged him.[123] In 2002 a birthday tournament and meal were held for William Laverne Dale Geionety at the Kiowa Tribal Complex for his seventh birthday.[124] A tournament in 1998 was held as a baby shower for two families. One of the babies was the great-grandson of an elder on the sponsoring team.[125]

Jackie Yellowhair explained the nature of birthday handgames: "Like on a birthday handgame, the handgame itself is a show, a showing to that person, you know, that everybody cares for them, and they respect them, you know, and they're gonna come out." Yellowhair once sponsored his own birthday handgame. "That's how I wanted to celebrate, you know. I fed everybody. . . . Usually people give someone gifts, you know, and things like that. Me, I turn it around. I wanted to give to everybody you know, feed them . . . tried to have a little giveaway . . . got the building and had a handgame, and everybody enjoys themselves. So that made me feel good that I got to do that."[126]

Youth Handgames

Children's handgames are also held, sometimes before an adult tournament. Some adult teams will have their kids play in a children's tournament under a variation of their team's name, such as Little Red Thunder or Little Oklahoma Indians. These tournaments are often for ages fifteen and under or eighteen and under. On November 24, 2017, the Yellowhair Family sponsored a junior tournament, with no entry fee, for players up to eighteen years old at Apache, Oklahoma. With a small entry fee put up by the parents and the rules slightly relaxed, such events emphasize learning and having a good time. The children

304   CHAPTER 5

perform all of the normal roles, sing their own songs, and learn to divide the prize money when they win. Typical of how most Indian culture is handed down, these events provide an opportunity to pass culture on through firsthand direct involvement. As Jackie Yellowhair explained, "They'll have to sing their own songs and do everything themselves, you know. That's how we teach them, you know . . . to be in there, get in there and, you know, hands on."[127]

School teams from Anadarko, Apache, Fort Cobb, and other towns, and from the Riverside Indian School, bring teams to tournaments that are played exactly like the adult version, with one to three adults singing for each team. In some instances, adults provide the singing and let the children do the rest of the playing. Some of the children have shown themselves to be excellent players.[128] Handgame is also spreading to urban school programs in central Oklahoma. Children's handgames have become a regular activity between many local schools and at summer tribal culture camps. Involving drumming, singing, teamwork, and one of the most traditional remaining forms of entertainment, the handgame provides an important way to pass on several elements of traditional Indian culture for many Native communities. Ace and Jackie Yellowhair, Phil "Joe Fish" Dupoint, Alan Yeahquo, Mary Beaver, and others have conducted handgames for several years in Kiowa tribal culture programs and Apache culture camps, and at the University of Oklahoma, Cameron University, and public schools across Southwest Oklahoma.[129]

For several years Mary Beaver has taught handgame in the Oklahoma City, Moore, Norman, and Edmond public schools.

> They all have your handgame tournaments, and they all participate. And I have helped and actually went to teach the kids how to play handgame. I've taken the sticks, I've taken a drummer and a singer, you know, somebody to watch the sticks, the rattles—you know, take the rattles and show the girls how to do a handgame and actually let everyone participate. So now the team from Moore is going to participate in all of the kids' tournaments that they have down around Apache and Lawton. Yeah. They're bringing teams. They're starting to branch out. They want to know more and learn.

These events are held as a part of the schools' cultural activities, and the four schools have their own state tournament each year.[130]

Minority groups frequently encounter mainstream sports in public schools such as baseball, football, basketball, wrestling, and cross country, and Oklahoma Indians participate heavily in these activities. Sports anthropologist Kendall Blanchard (1995, 226–29) describes how recreation programs and sports programs in schools can significantly affect cultural attitudes and multicultural education, noting that "teaching young people to play games that are characteristic of a minority culture or ethnic group can increase understanding and sensitivity." In multicultural societies, sports programs can also provide "social maintenance." By highlighting and reinforcing the meanings and values of tradition for minority participants, such programs serve as a statement about individual identity, ethnic identity, and cultural survival (Blanchard 1995, 229). Whether one supports maintaining traditional sports or values assimilation into the larger society, today some youth participate in both school sports and handgames. The growth of handgames in rural and urban public schools in Oklahoma with significant Indian membership, between Indian colleges and universities, and participation by non-Indians can be seen to be positive for all involved.

Handgames are increasing in tribal culture programs. At the request of their tribes, Cheyenne and Arapaho in Oklahoma have formed a handgame committee. In the fall and winter of 2016, they traveled to several towns to teach the handgame to children, culminating with three mini-tournaments between the towns. As Mary Beaver described, "All the kids from the different towns came and participated, played against each other. They got to meet each other, and again making new friends, learning how . . . the different songs are for the different communities. So that's how we're teaching our young people that handgame is a part of our culture."[131] Handgames also occur on the collegiate level, usually among Indian colleges, but do not allow any betting. Jeremy Shield (Crow) has taken teams from Haskell Indian Nations University to play teams at Bacone College, Comanche Nation College (no longer operating), Little Priest Tribal College, Nebraska Indian Community College, the University of Oklahoma, the Red Earth Festival, and the American Indian Higher Education Consortium of Tribal Colleges and Universities (AIHEC) conferences. Each year AIHEC holds a series of intercollegiate competitions between its thirty-one members at its annual conference. These include archery, art, a science bowl, and a handgame tournament (Garcia 1996, 230).[132]

Occasionally someone may create a new style of play just for fun. In 2017 Jackie Yellowhair created a new variety that his family frequently plays at home. It involves three hiding implements (two sets of bones and one elk tooth, or two elk teeth and one set of bones), a set of sticks starting on the ground between the two teams (usually six or nine), and competition for the first point (winning one stick and the offense). Guessers can choose to guess one, two, or all three hiders, but once a number is chosen, they must be finished (guessed correctly) before moving to the remaining hiders. When correctly guessed, the hiding implements are thrown over to the other side. Play continues until one side has all the sticks. Like the Crow handgame, because the score sticks are on the floor in the center, the game is played while seated. Played simply for fun, with no betting, they named the style for the creek near their home and the three hiding implements—Buzzard Creek Three.[133]

Death and Memorials

As with powwows and society dances, some individuals or entire teams will cease participation and sit out for a time following the death of a close relative or team member. The amount of time may vary from a few months to a year or more depending on the family and individual. Upon returning to the arena and public participation, the family of the deceased commonly asks for a "special" at an event. These events are generally similar to those held at dances except that at handgames there is often no dancing, hand drums are used to accompany singing of the songs, and the giveaways are typically smaller. During breaks in the program, the MC will announce that a special is being held. The family requesting the time will come forward into the arena and give a short speech explaining who they are and why they are asking for the time, and then songs, a dance (especially at a powwow or dance), and a giveaway are held to mark the end of their mourning and their reentry into the event.

At a tournament in Apache in 1999, a woman whose father had died some time back asked for a special. After recounting her father's passing and why she had been sitting out, she asked for a memorial song. Three singers came to the announcer's stand, sat down, and sang. She then proceeded with a giveaway, calling individuals up to receive gifts, then thanked everyone.[134] Just like regular tournaments, memorial handgames put on by a family often include special prizes. A year after the passing of longtime handgame player LaVerne Buffalomeat (Cheyenne), his family had a memorial handgame in his honor in 2004. A special prize provided by the family was a jacket and fifty dollars for best guesser. Ace Yellowhair won the jacket, which was embroidered with "Laverne Buffalomeat Memorial Handgame," "Best Guesser," and the year of the memorial on the back, and eventually the winner's name on the front. In 2021 Mary Beaver sponsored a tournament in memory of her brother Pete Bearshield.[135]

WHAT MAKES A GOOD HANDGAME?

I often asked players what makes a good handgame. While individuals have given different responses and opinions, some of the most common responses included: 1) people enjoying themselves, 2) a close finish, 3) beating an opponent who has beaten you for a long time, 4) out-hiding a guesser until you

The Handgame Today

"break his horns" and force him to give up the position to another, and 5) making a run to put a team out. As Jack Yellowhair described,

> People enjoying themselves, you know. You look around, and you see everybody . . . enjoying themselves. They really . . . like to hear the songs, you know, and a good [game], like we played the other night [a game in which I played on his team]. We had a real contest, you know. Boy, everybody was excited, you know. They were standing up all around, wanting to see who's gonna win it, you know. That's a good handgame, one stick to one, you know, fighting for that [last] one. That's what I call a good handgame. If you play one side like we played that bunch, you know we kept going [our team scored fourteen straight points]. We didn't even give them a chance to hide—just one song, and that was it, you know. Yeah, that was a terrible deal to me . . . but that team is always beating us. Every time we go play, you know, the Gang, and this time we put it on them, boy, . . . we tore them up, and I started teasing some of them women, you know, on that. That's a good handgame.[136]

When a team gets down to only one stick, whether in the old or new style of play, the urgency of the game sets in. The team that is hiding realizes that they are only one point from winning, while the team that is guessing is in a do-or-die situation and must rise to the occasion or be eliminated. Like in other sports, competition can sometimes be unpredictable and change suddenly, as when the momentum of a game is reversed and a team makes a run. As Adam Kaulaity recalled of a game, "They played the old style. Well, they put four sticks out there [in the middle], and they can go either way, back and forth. It takes a long time going back and forth like that sometimes. I remember one time those Comanches come down there at Bruce's [Bruce Haumpy]. We got down to one stick there, and they guessed us [laughs], and then they start going the other way, and they went all the way, and they took them all."[137]

Even in the modern tournament form, with up to nineteen sticks on each side, a team may occasionally run (hide) all the way through, winning the game in a single round. One team captain described a time when they went all the way through the sticks against a team from a neighboring tribe. When he offered his hand to the captain of the opposing side and said "I'm sorry, my friend," the captain of the losing team responded: "My friend, hell!"[138]

Close games seem to have the most intensity because everyone is visibly involved and trying so hard to win. Although lopsided victories occur, they are clearly more enjoyable for the winner than the looser. While a blowout is truly enjoyed by the winner, a close game that goes down to the last stick clearly involves everyone on a near-equal level of participation and emotion. Often a team that is down will make a comeback, resulting in a close finish.

Occasionally a series of correct double guesses occurs, which adds to the excitement, drama, and competitiveness of the game. Adam Kaulaity recalled one such exchange of correct guesses in a game against the Apache. "I remember one time we went down to Steve Mopope's. He's there northeast of Fort Cobb, up there on a hill. He had a big hill. We played those Apaches one time. Boy, we started playing the old-style game. Boy, me and that woman from Apache, we had it out. Boy, we'd door-pop each other a bunch of times. Finally she got the best of me. She wound up putting me down [laughs]."[139]

As with any sport, a shift in momentum is easily noticed and is one of the most exciting parts of handgames. As in a basketball game when a team makes a run and starts repeatedly rebounding or stealing the ball and scoring, the opposing team seems unable to stop it. In handgame a team may make a run through the sticks, or a team may continue to score sets of sticks while their opponent gets door-popped (correctly double guessed) every time they gain the offense. When the other team makes a run and scores a large number of consecutive points to win the game, their side is celebratory and nearly ecstatic, while the losing side, having the wind taken out of them, is often visibly dejected and frustrated. When a run is made, the increased drumming and singing, celebratory cheering, and often jeering only increases the stress for the other side. It is the unpredictability of the game and the ways in which it may suddenly shift and change that makes the handgame, like any sport, so dynamic, suspenseful, and enjoyable.

Phil "Joe Fish" Dupoint described the importance of music in gaining momentum during play. "We have a rhythm, and I mean that rhythm can get you going . . . and most people like to sing so they can get into it. . . . So we'll start a song, and then everybody gets in that beat and everything, and that's why—there we go—and after a while we pass them up, and then maybe we win that game. But music has a lot to do with it." He noted that especially during the last point a team should sing a high-energy song and let the group get into it before the hider comes forward with their hide.[140]

In a 2017 tournament I witnessed, Team A was coming out of the winner's bracket and was well ahead in the final game, and both they and the crowd seemed confident that they would win. Team B, from the loser's bracket, then went on a run and won the game. In the tiebreaker, Team B scored large sets of sticks while repeatedly correctly guessing Team A, which soon appeared deflated. Team B beat them twice to win the tournament.

Like many sports, the spontaneous and unpredictable nature of the handgame creates an atmosphere in which any circumstance may suddenly occur—a blowout, a comeback, something humorous, or even someone briefly

The Handgame Today   309

losing their temper out of frustration. Mary Beaver described how something memorable occurs every weekend at a handgame and the importance of keeping the perspective that, after all, it is just a game.

> Oh, there's always . . . something that happens, like every tournament, you know. Something funny, or . . . somebody might get mad, you know. "We'll talk about it later." "Did you see how mad he got [laughs] because they didn't find so and so?" Just different things like that, but, you know, it's just a game, and that's what I tell my team. It's just a game. Don't get mad. Do not get mad. I mean, if you get found, you get found. I've been in that situation where I couldn't even get a stick. . . . Yeah, and you talk about frustration, you know that's frustrating. So, it's like I said, it's just a game. If it's your day, it's your day. You know, if you can guess good, you're gonna guess good. If you're gonna hide good, you're gonna hide good.[141]

One significant change has been the increase in fancier hand motions. Elder KCA players report that in the past the southern style of handgame involved less kinesics. Guessers mainly rubbed their hand together, kneaded their fingers together, then clapped and signaled their guess. Around the 1980s, more elaborate hand motions began to be used that most elders attribute as coming from the Crow.[142] While the Kiowa used to blow in their hands, clasp them together, rub them together, then signal a guess, the Crow used motions such as shaking their hands, hitting their stomachs, and making motions toward their opponent with a closed fist. In using a rapidly moving closed fist, the Crow attempt to fake the hider out by making them believe they have signaled a guess and thereby making them open their hands and show the location of their bones. Often this resulted in the referees directing the hider to hide the bones again, but by seeing the initial location of the bones, the guesser had already gained an advantage toward understanding the hider's strategy.[143]

In the handgame, increased body movement and actions generally produce increased intensity in play and spirit. Although some individuals make slight or no hand motions, such as freezing and simply staring down the opposing guesser, and some players put their head down while hiding, women more so than men, hand motions are one of the liveliest parts of the game. As Gregory Haumpy noted, "The hand motions make it lively. . . . Hollering and whistling and all of that, well, that's what makes it go, you know."[144] While some players show little emotion, others are very active, often employing dramatic motions in guessing and hiding and showing emotion when they or their teammates are missed or when they or their teammates correctly guess. Some players enjoy using exaggerated movements, especially when the opposition misses guessing them. These movements serve to taunt the opposition and get players in the mood by stirring up the emotional atmosphere of the game.

Myriad hand motions and spontaneous acts are part of what makes hand-games so fun. While our team was hiding in a tournament in 2021, a Kiowa friend on the other side made the motion of circling a lasso over his head, then throwing it toward us and pulling it back—inferring they would take back the offense. The next time he made that motion, I responded by making the motions of reaching out, catching it, cutting it with a knife, and throwing it down. Everyone laughed. Apparently it worked, as we won the tournament.

When the opposition missed guessing him, Jack Yellowhair used to raise one arm upward and with the other hand made a ratcheting movement at his elbow while shaking his upraised wrist and hand, then repeated the movements in reverse with his other arm.

> Fancy work, you know. I like to put on the dog. I like everybody to get in the mood. That's the way I play. Everybody get in the rhythm of it, you know. That's the way I do. But a lot of them can sit there and go like that [expressionless, no movement in hiding]. Nothing, you know, nothing to it. Just dead players, I call them. But you get those guys that move around [and it's exciting]. . . . Some people have fancy styles, you know. Like me, when he missed [guessing] me, well, I look like I'm screwing my elbows together. I'm making it shake. That's what they don't like, you know. Boy, when they see that, they know they missed me. I hadn't used that in a long time.[145]

Just as spirit comes to individuals in Gourd Dances, church services, and other activities, it is also found in the handgame and can ebb and flow throughout a tournament. Spirit is most evident in close games when both sides are fighting for the last point to win. In these situations, the increased tempo of the music, cheering, and physical movement builds and builds until it reaches a fever pitch. Similar developments are found in the Turn Around Dance of the Black Legs Ceremony and the end of the Kiowa Gourd Clan Ceremonials (Meadows 1999, 2010).

Flannery and Cooper's (1946, 403) description of spirit in the Gros Ventre handgame closely resembles that of the southern plains:

> The atmosphere of the hand game was a holiday one. Raillery was a little rough at times. But for players and spectators, the game was a major source of enjoyment, relaxation, and pleasurable excitement. What with the singing, the drumming, the twitting, the shouting, the often loud and uproarious cheering, the hand game—in rather sharp contrast to the quiet, grave wheel game—was apt to be decidedly noisy, not to say boisterous. Not the least appreciated feature of the hand game was the showmanship,

The Handgame Today 311

the grace and virtuosity of the players, who played to an appreciative and discriminating house. The victors gloated conspicuously over the losers and bantered them unmercifully, but the losers were expected to keep their tempers, an expectation, however, not always realized.

Players have noted that people come to play for different reasons and that everyone has some strength—some in singing, some in hiding, some in guessing. Ideally teammates should learn their strengths and maximize them in play to win. One elder man admitted that his strength was singing and that he wasn't a very good hider or guesser. He rarely guesses because others expect to. However, individual personality and desires do emerge in relation to satisfaction. People come to handgames to do what they enjoy the most: whether singing, hiding, guessing, or just watching. As in Gourd Dances, powwows, and other cultural activities, some individuals attend as spectators or participate more for the music than any other aspect. Bill Koomsa Jr. described how some individuals are drawn to particular aspects of the game and the importance of music:

> There's people that come to the game to guess. There's people that come to the game to do a lot of hiding. There's some people that come to watch and some people that like to sing. So I'm a person that likes to sing. So that's where I get my enthrallment. . . . Some guys are lucky, some guys can hide, are good hiders. And then they're some that aren't good. Like I can't hide worth a damn. The only reason I enjoy the game, I like to sing. And there's a lot of singing involved. And my theory, me and my dad's theory, was that the better the music is, the more you feel like playing. And my sisters, when they're all together, you know, we can really get some music going. The northern Crow people really like it when we get together. When we are all together, man, they think we are gonna have some music.[146]

Jack Yellowhair Sr. described the tendency of looking forward to singing. "I got to where I'd rather sing. . . . I like to go, just to sing. Maybe I write a new song. I want them to hear it, and I want them to learn it. A lot of times I can't hardly wait to go to a handgame because I want to sing. That's the way it is. . . . I could go singing and enjoy it . . . I just want to get in there and sing."[147]

Carla Atauvich also described her enjoyment of the singing, the faster pace of northern handgame songs, and how when her son-in-law begins singing certain songs it provides a psychological boost in playing.

> The most enjoyable part of it, I think, is the singing. . . . I can't hardly sing the old-timey ones. They're too slow for me. And the modern ones, I guess there's a lot of old people who gripe, because they say "You're not singing Comanche songs," you know. But they're slow, and they're kind of boring

312 CHAPTER 5

to me [laughs] . . . [Today's songs,] most of them, I guess, are songs from
up north, but they're more jivey to me. And when [my husband] sings
them, it just really, it just seems like you could just feel it, when he starts
singing that. . . . You just get this good feeling, and you know that. I don't
know what it is, but you could just feel it when he sings certain songs.
I noticed my daughter too. Certain jivey songs that he sings, they can
really hide good. It just builds them up, I guess, to where they want to
play.[148]

Ace Yellowhair described why he likes playing handgame and the importance of the singing for him and his family:

I've been around and played the game, and I enjoy it a lot, you know. I like
it a lot because I feel at ease when I get in there. It's like seeing everybody,
big family again, you know. You feel good. And sing, that's my part right
there. I like to sing a lot, you know. I guess overall, if I was to hide, or
guess, or something, I'd rather sing. . . . It's the feeling that it gives me,
into myself. It makes me feel, like I said, at ease. [When] I'm singing, I
can look up and see other people tapping their feet or singing along, and
it's just that spirit. To me I get chills, I can just feel that, like adrenaline
and stuff like that, you know, that's what I get from that singing part. . . .
Certain songs I can remember from way back, when my folks used to sing
them songs. I could remember, and I could hear my mom sing, and she
was always there for me, you know. When I first started singing, she always tell me, "Son, go ahead, start a song, and I'll be right there. I'll back
you up." Because I was kind of scared. I didn't know, 'cause older people
that sung and all that, they would kind of look at me, like a young guy
trying to sing, and I was scared. But my mom, she really pushed me, like,
"Go ahead, sing. It's all right. I'll back you up right there." Sure enough,
she went right there, soon as I started a song she knew it and jumped and
helped me out on it. And then, that's what I get out of that, that spirit, that
chills and joy and the feeling of it, you know, 'cause it gets going, you can
feel that good, when everybody's . . . got their hands tapping or their feet
moving. That's what I like, that singing part, you know, making people
feel better, feel good.[149]

Others are drawn to the guessing. One elder player said, "I enjoy guessing now. Sometimes you get unlucky, well, people get mad at you, you know
[and say] 'Damn, he can't guess worth, well, you know' [laughs]. That's the
way it goes sometimes."[150] Some individuals like all parts of the game. As
Carl Atauvich explained, "I really don't have no favorite part. I like the whole
thing . . . we just like the whole shebang. We like the competitiveness. We
like the singing and, you know, the drumming. . . . And we like the hiding

The Handgame Today   313

and guessing. It's all there in a nutshell. We enjoy the whole thing." His wife Carla added, "We just love to play. We go there to have fun."[151]

One elder said that how they perceived the game has changed:

> The elder people that played the handgame. A lot of them went just to enjoy the game. They're not like today. Today they bet money . . . they play for blood almost. Back there they played for fun, even if they bet a nickel, even if they didn't bet, they still, you know, the singing and the drum beating, and they challenge another team, you know, it was enjoyable. They really enjoyed singing, you know, the men, singing and beating the drum. It was a lot of fun, and they act silly. And back there they didn't get mad, they teased each other."[152]

For most people, money is not the driving force behind playing handgame. As Jack Yellowhair commented,

> Yeah, it's the love of the game. I love it. Everybody else loves it. You know, I think they like to meet people too. Things like that. Maybe you got a girlfriend over there, you want to go see her or something like that. But there's an old saying I heard many years ago that you lose your wife at a handgame. That's why a lot of them don't come out, they're afraid they might lose their wives or their husbands. . . . There's a lot of people that know handgame, they can come out if they want. But they're afraid—"I'm gonna lose my wife; somebody's gonna take my wife away"—you know. That's just talk, you know [laughs].[153]

Many players mentioned this, having your wife or husband stolen at a handgame, but pointed out that it happens at powwows, church, or any social activity. Mr. Yellowhair continued:

> A lot of them like to play handgame. I mean, they enjoy themselves. They like, I guess—whatever there is on their minds of something they're worried about, and this here is like I said, this is where I'll go to make you forget. And then that certain group is having a benefit or something for somebody, a birthday. Well, hey, it's my cousin's birthday, I gotta go, and just like that. And it draws. . . . Mostly you just like to play and want to play, you know. That's the way I feel. I like to play and I go.[154]

For the Cheyenne handgame, Mary Beaver described: "It's changed a lot in history. In the 1860s it was considered a ceremonial game . . . and anybody who wanted to play handgame would have to fast three days and night. . . . But [now] it's a fun game. It's like a family game. Kids like this game as much as adults do."[155] For any cultural tradition to continue it must be carried forward.

314   CHAPTER 5

The handgame of western Oklahoma has maintained a sizeable following with more and more younger people becoming regular players.

UNIVERSITY CLASSES

For many years I have incorporated handgames into my university classes. At Colorado State I held modified handgames in my Native American classes from 1995 to 1997. Lacking singers, I used a cassette tape of handgame music, allowing the students to focus on the hiding and guessing. In 2004 at Missouri State, I began hosting the Yellowhair family each November to hold an evening of handgames for my classes and the campus as part of our Native American Heritage Month programs. Recently we have been joined annually by a team from Haskell Indian Nations University led by Jeremy Shield. I am including a brief section summarizing those experiences to demonstrate how the western Oklahoma handgame is experienced by non-Indians, to show how quickly many become drawn to it, and to share with Native people some of the lessons non-Indians have gained from the experience.

Each year I explained the history and rules of the game to my students in class, showing them the equipment, images of games, and a video clip of a game prior to our handgame. I have offered the activity as a class assignment and sometimes as an extra credit opportunity to conduct ethnographic fieldwork by attending to observe, participate, take notes, and make a sketch map of the event. Afterward they typed up a report on the event, describing the rules and content of the game, answering several questions about the experience, and reflecting on the experience, and they turned the report in with their field notes. The exercise is valuable for anthropology students in two ways. First, they gain experience in learning how to observe and record as much detail as possible of a cultural event they are attending, trying to figure out the context associated with the activity. Second, it requires them to try to identify patterns of behavior in another culture while reflecting on their own.

The Yellowhair family and the Haskell group provided a referee and the singing for the evening and also played. The students were divided into two sides and played against one another, with some taking turns at drumming. Typically, we played Oklahoma tournament style, with the standard scoring rack, and a game or two of Crow or Flathead style, starting with sticks in the middle. Most years we played five or six games over a three-hour period.

In American universities it is often difficult to get students to attend out-of-class events unless required or unless extra credit is offered. Many tend to view anything that is not recent, let along not involving electronics, as passé, outdated, or useless and often fail to recognize the value of long-standing cultural traditions. Some come, observe one game, and leave within the first hour, thinking they have grasped the event. However, their write-ups often demonstrate that they grasped little. The core of cultural anthropology, fieldwork, involves immersing oneself in an activity or culture. Rarely can anyone come close to grasping the cultural patterns of any event from one observation.

Most come away with a very positive view, usually with a direct correlation between the length of time they stay, the quality of their observations, and their overall experience. Those who stay the longest tend to learn and experience the most. One year, students from a class who came and stayed for the entire evening of games realized this. One of the girls in this group wrote, "I was really surprised how we had so many people starting out playing the handgame then after the first hour 80% of the people left! If I had left when they all did I would not have the full understanding of the game that I now have since I stayed the entire [evening]. . . . Overall this was a super fun experience . . . We had a blast with this game and we continue to talk about it." One male wrote, "I really enjoyed myself that night. I had no idea that playing a game that was played so long ago would be fun and interesting to play."

Many are shy and reluctant to participate at the beginning, with some preferring to stand rather than take a seat. Even then, some individuals decline to hide the bones. Some students described feeling nervous at the start of the event. One student wrote, "After I relaxed and got more comfortable, I ended up having a lot of fun." One female student wrote, "Overall this was a fun event and a unique opportunity. I wish that there had been more Native Americans there because they were so lovely and excited about playing. Many of the college students were rather timid and shy about participating, but we all had a good time and learned quite a bit. I do think it would be really interesting to see actual Native American teams compete against one another because of how competitive the Yellowhairs seemed to get." Another girl described how she "became more comfortable with the style over time."

A student from Africa reported how he "wasn't too interested in the Indian game" and that he had been wondering "if it was going to be fun or boring" or think it was "completely a waste of time" when he showed up to play. He continued, "After we started playing the game, I started really having fun and got the hang of what was going on. Moments later . . . everybody was enjoying the game." A western Asian student wrote, "When we first started playing the game, I thought it was childish and would not be competitive. I was completely wrong with that assumption because within ten minutes of playing the game, I was very competitive and was having a lot of fun. . . . When we first started the game, I thought a lot of people would leave early, yet, much to my surprise everyone including myself had a lot of fun with the game."

In what I jokingly describe as "handgame possession," students quickly get the bug, becoming absorbed and competitive. Several years I have videotaped the games, and you can observe many passive and complacent individuals soon changing. Tapping their feet, intense in following the play, beginning to pick up arm and hand motions, or improvising on their own, they become eager, often asking to hide or guess. In their write-ups, students described the play as "exciting," "very intense," "an upbeat environment that almost felt like a sporting event at times," and "quicker and more competitive the longer we played." Others stated that they quickly got into the game and were "shocked at how many people were actually engaged and excited to play." A male student described, "When I arrived to the event, I was consumed by the game as soon as I had stepped into the building. . . . At first I was in shock because I had no clue what was happening. The game was moving fast, and the music was loud. . . . I was really becoming interested in the game and was getting anxious to play after getting the hang of it and knowing what to do." Another male student who served as a captain for one side observed, "Some people were very excited to play and would ask ahead of time to be either a hider or guesser. One man would always ask to be the hider."

Students are attracted to different styles of play. Most preferred playing the southern tournament style, which has fewer hiders and is often faster, over the Crow style. Several described the southern style as "simpler." As one male student wrote, "I preferred the short version because my attention span with this game lasted longer with the short version." One girl enjoyed the Crow style of play the most, stating, "I personally found this type more exciting and fun because you could never be sure if your team was going to win."

Students commonly experience a bit of culture shock, both in attempting the ethnographic assignment and in letting themselves relax and join in what is to them an unfamiliar cultural activity of another culture. Some described it as having "many rules" and having trouble understanding how to guess and how points were scored. Some described how hard it was to "look natural," "move fluidly," or move both arms identically while trying to hide. One girl described, "I also failed to guess correctly every single time it was my turn. It is much more difficult to be successful in this game than I thought." Another girl observed, "I really enjoyed participating in this game that may seem simple, but under the surface can be rather complex." Not fully grasping the subtleties in studying people's body language and limited to only one evening's play, one individual described the game as "easy if you know someone's style" yet still attributed the game to "pure luck." In 2015 one girl picked up the deeper patterns involved in playing beyond mathematical chance: "Originally I thought this was a pure chance and luck game, with the persons just taking a wild guess as to where the sticks would be, but as the game progressed, along with some insight from the Kiowas, I realized that a lot of decision making is based on other things such as body language or other indications like past tendencies."

A male student who picked up on studying the hiders' habits described, "One thing that I noticed when I actually played was that it seemed like everyone was using a lot of psychology to try and determine which hand the marked bone was in . . . I tried to do some tricking things like not switching the hand it was in and just trying to keep a straight face. I got by two whole rounds and they didn't guess me. So one of the Native Americans came over to try and guess me. I noticed that he was very serious about guessing it and when he came up, he was really looking for signs in my face and any kind of body language that I was giving off. He ended up guessing the hand on his first try, so I was very impressed. It was evident that it wasn't just a guessing game."

Students commonly note how their initial lack of interest in taking part changed once they began doing so. One male student summed up his experiences:

> Usually when you have extra credit opportunities, they are unbearable and not very entertaining, but this was one that did not fall into this stereotype. Everyone that I saw was interested and paying attention to what was going on and which team was winning. . . . The game was very much hands on and there were many ways to be involved in it. Whether you were guessing which hand the marked stick was in, or you were playing along on the drums with the Indians, there were many ways to stay involved in this. I really enjoyed that they passed out the drums for everyone to play on. It was a good time because some of the students really got into it and had a great time with it . . . people were smiling and having a good time and I think this is due to the environment that Dr. Meadows had. He made it a very relaxed, laid-back vibe where everyone felt comfortable to have fun and enjoy the game. I myself actually enjoyed the game and once I played it for the first time, I was hooked on it and wanted to play more.

One year our event was co-hosted by the Student Activities Council (SAC). When a player held up a dollar then laid it down on the floor as a challenge and bet to someone on the other side, the SAC representative jumped up, grabbed the dollar, apologized for stopping the game, and announced, "I am sorry, but SAC events do not allow any tipping of the cultural performers." The student didn't realize that the dollar was a bet and not a tip. As the dollar was returned to its owner all of the Native people and I were laughing heartily.

As reflected in their write-ups, many of the students realized important aspects of what the handgame represented, both as an attempt to conduct

318   CHAPTER 5

participant-observation in an ethnographic observation and in terms of cultural themes and patterns in the Kiowa and their own culture. In terms of ethnographic fieldwork, they realized how difficult it is to observe and record in detail a new cultural practice. Many came to realize the emphasis on family, fellowship, friendly competition, tradition, cultural sharing, and the complexities of what they thought was a simple game.

Unaccustomed to observing something in another culture and attempting to describe it while taking notes, many students said the hardest part of the assignment was figuring out the unspoken rules. Making an especially valuable observation for a cultural anthropologist, one noted, "I also learned that you need to be willing to throw yourself into something you do not understand." Another noted, "This activity taught me that in order to fully understand cultural anthropology, you must put your own views aside." One student wrote, "It was more fun than I really thought it would be. I would like to play it again just to watch the psychological aspect of it. It is really interesting that a game that is so fun can teach you about observing your opponent [i.e., subject] and studying them, which is what Anthropology is all about."

Noticing the group aspects of the game, one female student wrote, "I believe handgame is an amazing family practice. In my culture, there is nothing quite like it in regards to whole family participation in a game consistently." Another young woman observed, "I was glad I came out to experience this as it gave me a taste of Native American culture and a sense of community that American culture can sometimes lack." Yet another reflected, "Being a part of the Native American Handgame showed me the respect and importance these people place on togetherness, music, tolerance, and friendly competition. It was great to learn something from them."

One student noted,

> To be perfectly honest I was a bit unenthusiastic to attend this gathering, and skeptical that I would enjoy myself. The experience seemed very foreign to any other game commonly played amongst any people I've ever known. And I was nervous to participate or even be involved in something like this. . . . For me, once the drums started up, I was 150% positive. I made a great decision in giving this idea a chance. I think I gained a great deal not so much from learning the game but largely from the warmth of the environment that was created when we all sat together to just relax, play, and have a good time.

She then explained how she was glad to have done poorly on her earlier quizzes in the class, otherwise she would not have needed to take part in the extra credit opportunity!

CHAPTER

6

Conclusions

SINCE I FIRST observed western Oklahoma handgames in 1993 and started playing in 1997, both minor and major changes have occurred. Overall, variation in the range of rules (team size, registration deadline, starting time, range of guessing motions) does not differ a great deal, and thus anyone can easily learn and play another's style. An emphasis is placed on transparency and fairness regardless of what set of rules are used. The game still contains skill, luck, mathematical odds, and magico-religious and psychological aspects. In contrast to earlier ethnographic accounts classifying the game as only a game of chance, players maintain that the game contains elements of luck (with mathematically limited percentages in guessing) but also—in accord with anthropological studies (Densmore 1943, 65; Helm, Lurie, and Kurath 1966, 77–78; Maranda 1984, 44–46)—skill in studying and memorizing the body language and hiding and guessing patterns of players.

Beliefs in supernatural power by some players remain one of the few ways to demonstrate individual "power." There are also elements of social power through prestige. In addition to financial capability, sponsoring handgames largely determines the set of rules for how the game will be played on that day. Some individuals state that they prefer attending other's events to sponsoring them, due to the cost and time involved.

Many players know one another, joking and teasing remains frequent during play, and singers may sing to help another team when their own team

320   CHAPTER 6

is not playing. Fellowship, handshakes, and hugs are ubiquitous, reflecting the continuation of a tight-knit intertribal community. Several elements of the new style of handgame are said to have diffused from the Crow. These include fancy hand motions, larger betting, and the use of rattles, hair pipes, judges, and many Crow songs. Fewer players use a pronounced "Ho!" when signaling their guess.

Over the past ten years, fewer Crow come to Oklahoma for the annual November handgames, producing a concern that this tradition is fading. Many of the elder players that came for decades have passed on. In 2017 the first night of the Oklahoma games was canceled because no Crow were present to play. That year only five Crow attended the Oklahoma handgames. Because several Crow were competing in a major rodeo in Las Vegas, many Crow went there to support them. Several times during the week, Kiowa, Cheyenne, and Crow spoke of the need to maintain the tradition. On November 10 that year, Phil "Joe Fish" Dupoint, the MC for the handgame that night at Red Buffalo Hall, spoke at length about the decline of Crow attendance, encouraging everyone to carry the tradition forward as far as possible and expressing the hope that more Crow would attend in the future. Jeremy Shield (Crow) stated that when he returned home he would speak to other Crow and encourage the younger men to continue the annual November visits.[1]

Few Crow came in 2021, but the play was spirited. Most of the Crow were young and no longer dressed like the Crow men and women who came in years past. Discussing the passing of many older players, Shield observed, "I sure miss those guys, you know. Just like this year it was kind of a different setting. A lot of people are gone."[2] Around thirty younger Crow came in 2022. In 2023 members of two Crow families made it. Time will tell.

TECHNOLOGY AND MEDIA

One of the most obvious changes is the presence of cell phones. As in other Indian and non-Indian events, many spectators and even some players repeatedly use them to film, photograph, and post handgames on social media and to visit and check their messages during tournaments. While media is a major factor associated with professional and amateur sports in many cultures, its role in the handgame of western Oklahoma has long been relatively small but is increasing. For many years, aside from newspaper announcements such as the "Powwows and Handgames" column in the *Anadarko News* and brief articles on the winners of the annual state tournament in the Cheyenne and Arapaho tribal newspaper, most communication involved xeroxed flyers, announcements at handgames, and phone calls. More recently email, texts,

Conclusions 321

and the listing of larger tournaments and tournaments associated with larger tribal fairs on the internet and social media have emerged. Handgames posts on platforms such as Facebook and film clips placed on YouTube are also increasing. Overall, less media exposure is needed in western Oklahoma since the handgame community and tournaments are smaller than in the Northwest.

COVID-19

The most recent major change in the handgame has been due to the Covid-19 pandemic. When the pandemic began in the United States in March 2020, many social events were canceled, including handgames in Oklahoma. While most events stopped, and the 2020 Oklahoma State Handgame Tournament was canceled, some family games and tournaments continued. As one played described, "Played a whole tournament, you know. Hand sanitizer, you know, after we get done playing, everybody sanitize up. Get the bones and sanitize those. Replay and get done and sanitize and put them back. Then we all had our mask, you know, ready in case they said we could do it." Trying to sing while wearing a face mask is difficult. As one individual described, "They called down to the tribe [tribal office], and they said, 'Yeah, you all can do it as long as you all social-distance and follow the CDC guidelines for social distance, mask up, and sanitize.' 'You got to wear your mask' is what they said. You can't sing with a mask on. I tried it. It's like singing like this [places hand over mouth]. You can't. First of all you can't breathe, and you take a deep breath and then the mask is pulled in? It's crazy, you can't sing. I tried it, you know." In two instances individuals from out of state came and played and then, after returning home, came down with Covid. Local teams were checked, but no one tested positive. One played reflected, "We went and played. Even though, you know, we probably shouldn't have . . . but we did anyways."[3]

Slightly before the pandemic began, individuals in several tribes had begun holding singing, Round Dance, and other contests virtually or online. When the pandemic was announced and isolation accelerated, virtual handgames began to be held. They increased rapidly with the development of handgame websites. Where people once had to check weekly newspaper announcements for handgames, many people tagged friends on Facebook to announce upcoming virtual handgames. Increased postings of cultural events are also available on many tribal websites. Many games are run through laptop computers using Zoom meetings with a live link address and a designated start time. Teams generally set their laptop across the room so that all players are visible. Any style can be played, usually that of the sponsor. Flathead style is popular in the northern plains, while groups in Southwest Oklahoma play their local style. After team size, entry fees, and regulations are agreed upon, play begins. Some modifications were made for the virtual play. Guessers must point one way and hold their guess. Hiders must keep their hands visible at all times and may be counted out if they move below the range of the screen. Disputes commonly arise when a hider moves their hands out of sight. Often a clicking sound is heard, which opponents interpret as switching the bones. With no referees, an honor system is relied on. Payments are made through applications like PayPal that send the money to a designated bank account, some requiring a small transfer fee.[4]

Virtual handgames allow teams to contact and play other teams from a wider geographic span than usual. As one individual explained, "I would like to play someone that I probably wouldn't ever play, from maybe Canada or Idaho or Blackfoot, or, you know, some family or some tribe or somebody that I wouldn't have the opportunity to play unless I go to where they're located at. So I think it's kind of cool to be able to play someone like that."[5] Jackie Yellowhair said, "Social media is a benefit to bring people, you know—to let people know. Most are gonna be on Facebook. Most everybody is on Facebook. So you let people know, you want them to come around, you want to share it, share that good feeling of blessing with them."[6] By enabling players to reach beyond physical isolation and social distancing, social media has helped the handgame and other traditions continue during this period, especially among the younger, more tech-savvy generation. While many elders do not use such technology, their younger family members can quickly inform them of current events and set them up. Some people have continued to play virtual handgame matches even after Covid declined and live matches resumed in 2022. This form will likely continue. The First Americans Museum, which opened in September 2021 in Oklahoma City, includes a virtual handgame exhibit that explains some of the basics of the game and allows one to attempt guessing two hiders.

ECONOMICS AND COMPETITION

In American Indian societies the redistribution of wealth occurs through both merit (giveaways) and chance (gambling). The handgame was one traditional form of commerce. Because bets can be placed by both players and spectators, both could win or lose wealth. Today the economic role of the handgame in western Oklahoma is relatively small. Compared to other recreational activities, it is one of the most affordable in relation to cost and the length of the event. Entrance fees are fairly small, usually pooled by several members, and

Conclusions 323

groups of people commonly carpool to the events. Little material culture is required compared to the cost of powwow regalia. Most money exchanged at handgames (through concession stands, bets, and prize money) remains in Native families and communities, at least in its initial redistribution. The game serves as a center of redistributing food, money, and goods through giveaways and betting, while providing a valued social activity. Today bets almost exclusively involve money, but as Jackie Yellowhair described, "It wasn't always all for money. It was all material things that we used to bet. That was one of our first forms of commerce, was this handgame."[7] Tournament prizes garner a few hundred to a few thousand dollars shared among a team's members, and the economic rewards are valued even if somewhat limited.

Games and sports do not have to be competitive. There are several examples of cultures desiring ties (draws) and thus no winners or losers exists (MacClancy 1996, 8). But the handgame is competitive. Plains Indian cultures have long prized athletic competition ranging from social pastimes to activities that enhanced skills for warfare and the social rank derived therefrom. The relatively small stakes involved in the southern plains handgame, small-scale individual contributions to support it, its role in redistributing economic resources in communities, and the widespread presence of sharing and extended kin support make its social and communal aspects arguably worthwhile and more valuable than any concern for the amount spent or lost.

NATIONAL AND ETHNIC IDENTITY

Sports and games frequently contribute to a sense of ethnic identity in many human communities. MacClancy (1996, 12) discusses how sport can assist in the creation of identity, "at the level of the nation-state, particularly perhaps for subject countries within imperial regimes and for newly independent states within the developing world eager to transcend traditional ethnic affiliations." For Native Americans, the handgame contributes to maintaining Native identity on several levels. It serves as a marker of ethnic identity between tribes through differences in songs and style of play. Surviving cultural forms like the handgame continue to distinguish Native communities from the larger encapsulating non-Indian culture. As tribal sovereignty increases, the handgame and its relatively small-stakes betting, protected under Class I of the Indian Gaming Regulatory Act of 1988, contribute to cultural, legal, and fiscal distinctions between Indian nations and the US government. Lastly, whether intended or not, the game's continuation through the reservation and pre–Indian Reorganization Act (1934) era served as cultural resistance to the Bureau of Indian Affairs, missionary policies, and forced assimilation.

324   CHAPTER 6

As the most traditional remaining game among western Oklahoma tribes, the handgame sets Natives apart from non-Indians. In the same way that stickball serves as a "cultural maintenance device" among southeastern tribes (Blanchard 1981, 66), the handgame contributes to the retention of ethnic identity as Natives and members of specific tribes. Although a few non-Indians play handgame, the handgame community is overwhelmingly Native, forming the basis of teams, directing the events, leading the singing, and so on. In contrast, Native people participate in virtually all mainstream non-Indian sports found in public school systems and summer leagues (football, baseball, basketball, volleyball, horseshoes, etc.). As anthropologists have found in the sports and games of other cultures (Blanchard 1981, 65), sports reiterate and specify the "integral features and expressions of cultural patterns."

Ethnic awareness and revival can foster the revitalization of varied traditions, including sport. Blanchard (1981, 42–43, 64), Vennum (1994) and Zogry (2010) have described revivals of Native American lacrosse and Mississippi Choctaw and Eastern Band Cherokee stickball. Fisher (2002) and Downey (2018) have provided similar works for lacrosse, and Bassett (2024) for Haudenosaunee women's lacrosse, while Jarvie (1991) has focused on the Highland Games of Scotland, and MacClancy (1996, vi, 181–200) has documented the revitalization of traditional Basque sports. Elder handgame consultants describe a reinvigoration of handgames in the 1960s that coincided with the larger civil rights, ethnic awareness, and sovereignty movements by Native Americans during this period when powwows increased and numerous men's societies and Sun Dances were revived (Meadows 1999, 2010; Archambault 2001). While handgames became more frequent and named teams formed, the game retained many traditional aspects while also taking on several distinctly modern innovations such as the nineteen-point tournament style, sitting on benches and folding chairs, using permanent community buildings and public address systems, betting in cash, using handgames to celebrate birthdays and American holidays such as Easter and Valentine's Day, and using the internet and social media to promote and hold events. Like Basque football as discussed by MacClancy (1996, 10, 181–200), the western Oklahoma handgame allows groups to demonstrate continuity with both traditional cultural forms and modernization. The handgame thus contains elements that are deeply rooted and distinctive to tribal cultures as well as innovations and adaptations reflecting the larger American culture. The new technologies and forms of material culture adopted and adapted into the game have been quickly indigenized into Native patterns that are easily observable in seating arrangements, matched bets with no additional odds, and syncretism with

Conclusions

Camp 7 (Comanche) scoring two points. Watchetaker Hall, Comanche Nation Complex, Lawton, Oklahoma, November 8, 2017. Author's photo.

previously non-Indian holidays. Like powwows, men's societies, giveaways, naming ceremonies, and other cultural and religious traditions, the handgame represents an ongoing component of Plains Indian life aimed at maintaining traditional activities.

The handgame remains an important native "arena of enculturation" in western Oklahoma Indian communities (Meadows 1999) for maintaining valued cultural ethos and forms. The game provides an important public forum in which social and cultural prominence may be obtained through community face, socializing, generosity and sharing, reciprocity in supporting one another's events and families during challenging times (e.g., illnesses and funerals), and redistribution (giveaways). Handgames reinforce other Native values such as hospitality, sharing of food, respect for traditions and elders, social honoring, competition and good sportsmanship, communal harmony, non-drinking at public cultural events, and maintaining sovereign rights to play and bet on the game. Individuals and teams may also gain prominence as singers, hiders, guessers, team captains, organizers, sponsors, concession stand operators, or cooks. For some spectators and youth, the opportunity for socialization takes precedent over playing.

326   CHAPTER 6

SOCIAL IDENTITY

The handgame and stickgame remain the most widespread, popular traditional Native American game. Among the KCA, the handgame continues to be played almost year-round. Handgame manifests a frequent form of focused interaction for them and neighboring tribes that unites a cross section of Indian communities that differs in membership from that focused on other Native activities (powwows and participation in military societies, Native American Church, Indian Christian churches, etc.). In the handgame, social interaction and maintenance of "social face" and multilevel identity plays a major part. It also transcends sex, gender, age, ethnicity, social position, geographical location, and political and religious affiliation. Among Plains Indians, handgame remains one of the most frequent traditional guessing games fostering group identity, commonly played by family or tribal teams (Cheska 1979, 233; Culin 1907, 321). Although the handgame is not heavily entwined with tribal politics, there are said to be parallels with sports in the Soviet Union: "It has proved to be of utility by reason of its inherent qualities of being easily understood and enjoyed, being capable of generating mass enthusiasm" (Riordan 1977, 8).

Of traditional Plains Indian sports and games that reflect pre-reservation cultures, the handgame is the most intact and frequently held event. As such, it continues to contribute to a sense of ethnicity for several tribes and to a sense of community on both tribal and intertribal levels. This is perhaps best reflected by the term "handgame people" to describe those individuals and families active in the game in contrast to labels such as "powwow people," "ceremonial people," "church people," or "Sun Dance people." "Handgame people" is only one of several social identities among the Native American communities of western Oklahoma. From my observations, although there are handgame participants who participate in other focused activity areas, the handgame crowd tends to be made up of individuals who value participating in traditional activities. Identity as a handgame person may be the primary social identity for some individuals and for others only one of several identities that exist simultaneously, seasonally, or consecutively over time. The range of participation and identities one holds depends on which cultural activities an individual chooses to participate in (MacClancy 1996, 4–5), of which sports are only one.

As consultants describe, some "powwow people" shift their emphasis to becoming handgame people while other participate in almost all tribal activities, and still others have only recently taken up handgame to create or add a new social identity in the community. Like other areas of focused activity, another social identity of handgame participants stems from the adoptive

Conclusions 327

kin relations between individuals in several tribes. With little overall cost or required material culture, virtually anyone can participate, even if only hiding during a free-for-all. Blanchard (1995, 232) notes, "Peoples in tribal and nonstate societies are more spontaneous and egalitarian in their sporting so that individuals are just as likely to be participants as spectators."

Some handgame families have played for several generations and continue to carry on the tradition. In the early to mid-1990s the Oklahoma City Red Earth Festival hosted handgame tournaments organized by Mary Beaver and Barbara Pappio Poe, who were both on the festival board. The tournament started when several non-Indians on the board wanted to have a handgame and asked Poe to organize it. She received funding from the festival and asked Mary Beaver to run the tournament. After Poe's term as a board member ended, board member John Parrish helped obtain funding. After his term ended, the tournament become intermittent after around 1997, with one held in 2003.[8]

With Barbara Poe's passing in 2013, bringing back the game to the festival became a way for her son Joe Poe Jr. to honor the memory of his mother. In 2017 Poe asked the board to sponsor the tournament, and one was held that year at the Red Earth Festival, sponsored in part by the Oklahoma City Pow Wow Club. First place was $1,000. As Joe Poe Jr. explained, "I became involved in it when I was a little kid when I used to go with my mother to these things around the state. I'm involved in all of this out of memory of my mom and my Indian heritage."[9] Continuing the traditions of one's parents or other close relatives by maintaining handgame teams or sponsoring handgame tournaments or powwows is common in Southwest Oklahoma.

Youth continue to take up the handgame. In 1998 Jack Yellowhair stated, "We've got more younger people than there ever was in the handgame world. We encourage a lot of these younger people to come in and play. A lot of them did, and they liked it. Now they're in. We would like to get more, just like them Crows, [they have] big teams."[10] Later in 2003 he noted, "Where the elders are really glad is that the young people coming out. Then we'll go and try to teach them how to play. And that's what we like. That's an old tradition you know, way, way, way back, before my days. And that's how they try to get everybody to keep that tradition up. Go on with it. It's a lot of fun, you know."[11] I meet new players every time I attend handgames.

Singing remains central to most Plains Indian cultural events. Despite the passing of elders and the effects of the recent pandemic, the western Oklahoma handgame is thriving. Jackie Yellowhair commented on the resiliency of the event and new players in 2021,

328   CHAPTER 6

> Yeah, it's gonna find a way to move forward in this day. . . . I went to a handgame here last couple weekends ago, and I was looking around. And there was a whole bunch of different young people there. I didn't know who they were. Wow, this is going to go on. These young people, they want to play, and they're here for a reason, you know. A few of the old ones I recognized . . . you know, the older ones what I knew as being the elders when I was there, that is the thing, now I am [one of] the elders, now they are coming up to me. Yeah, it's gonna find a way. This game has got its own spirit about it; it's going to find a way to keep going. It's like our medicine. It is going to find a way to keep moving forward in the future. It is up to us to take care of it just long enough for someone to pick it up.[12]

Yellowhair described youth learning the key component to the game's survival, singing. "Them little guys you all seen singing every night. They're singing—they've got all kind of big volume of songs. Songs I don't even know, that I don't sing. I sing the older songs. But they know several newer songs that I don't know. . . . They know them, they sing them. They're catchy, they got their own tunes to them, you know. I like it. I like the way that they keep it going."[13]

GENDER ROLES

In terms of gender, the handgame has long been a male-dominated activity, while the awl game has long been considered a female game. However, ethnographic and historical accounts dating to the mid-1800s indicate that women have long played handgames among themselves or with men primarily as hiders and singing in support. Over the last thirty years, women's roles have become closer to men's in terms of overall participation in handgames.

Noting the increase of Choctaw women's power and status in athletics, Blanchard (1995, 178, 218–19) has suggested that the increased role of women in sports may correlate with Ernestine Friedl's (1978) model regarding social status and gender, in particular with how much women contribute to the subsistence strategy and control economic exchange in a society. As Blanchard (1995, 218) explains, "From an evolutionary perspective it is likely that the role played by women in a society's sport activities is a product of the role women play in the broader worlds of technology, subsistence, and economy. The greater the perceived importance of women's contributions to the economy, the greater the esteem accorded to their sporting activities." Today many Indian women in Oklahoma have sought higher education and professions, and in some households they are the primary income earner.

While there is still clear deference given to men in many Plains Indian groups, including some teams who do not allow women to sit on the front row

Little Monkeys (Comanche), Watchetaker Hall, Comanche Nation Complex, July 2023. Author's photo.

or drum in the handgames, and the Crow, who do not allow women to drum, guess, and sit in front, today nearly all roles—hiders, guessers, referees, scorekeepers, team captains, medicine men, and even tournament organizers—are held by southern plains women who are quite successful. As one Kiowa man remarked, "Some women, they're pretty salty at guessing." Although I have seen a couple of instances of women leading songs and drumming, these are the two areas that remain primarily led by men. Overall, women's roles have clearly expanded in the handgame, as they have in many other areas such as powwows and tribal government. For some, ability and efficacy in organizing and directing a team or event is clearly more important than gender. The existence of female team captains, and tournament directors such as Mary Beaver, reflect these developments. Although I have only occasionally seen a transgender person participating in handgames, they participated fully with no differential treatment.

CONFLICT

As MacClancy (1996, 11) described, "Sport can divide as much as it may unite." Sports may result in conflict, and thus the potential for discord and conflict in sporting competition is not uncommon. Blanchard (1995, 57) maintains that "sport is by definition a type of activity that entails aggressive behavior

330 CHAPTER 6

and some form of competition, and in any given cultural setting it can be viewed as having social conflict dimensions." While varied forms of factionalism are well documented in Native American cultures, and some handgame teams have fissioned, it does not seem to seriously affect the handgame. During my fieldwork, several individuals named and voiced things they did not like about other individuals or handgame teams. Most related to the style that individuals sang and drummed (too hard, fast, or slow), nonstandard hiding methods, using extensive hand motions in guessing (considered "power" or "trick" motions), how tournaments were run (the enforcement of certain rules or lack thereof), or of certain teams winning repeatedly. Some complaints were based largely on tribal and individual difference in personality and style of play. In most instances they simply constituted venting. Individuals or teams who become angry at others may simply sit out certain events, however, as most tournaments involve most of the same teams from western Oklahoma, one cannot sit out too long if they want to play. Failure to support other tournaments through prolonged nonattendance could potentially weaken the degree of reciprocal support one receives when sponsoring an event.

POPULARITY

With a long history and distinct music, why is handgame, a distinct subculture, so popular among its proponents? As a wintertime activity it originally provided a group-oriented and socially dynamic form of entertainment that helped pass the long, cold, dark nights. A large part of the game involved spirited competition with good-natured joking and taunting often associated with close games. Betting on the games and beliefs in medicine or power provided other aspects to the game, whether playing or watching. The unpredictability of the game, along with the opportunity to bring home additional goods and eventually money also added to the suspense of play and winning. The drumming and singing provided a strong appeal for many individuals. Whether playing or watching, all could sing along or just bask in the excitement, artistry, and power of the songs. It also remained a distinctly traditional Indian activity. As Stuart (1972, 112) found among the Coast Salish, the ethnic basis of the game stands out: "[It] is an Indian game, played by Indians, and which stands for Indianness." On tribal or intertribal levels, the game has provided a team-oriented opportunity for recreation that, with some skill and luck, can produce a sense of achievement, monetary winnings, and social status (Stuart 1972, 112).

For the KCA, who retain linguistic and cultural differences but have shared a long and overall related cultural and historical experience since the early

Conclusions 331

1800s, the handgame can entail competition against one another or cooperation when playing together against the Northern Cheyenne or Crow. Less extensive than among Plateau and some Northwest Coast tribes, handgame play remains an important cultural activity among the southern plains tribes in Oklahoma. While the handgame "crowd" is relatively small, it is a close-knit network of individuals and families with social and kinship ties who enjoy the game and one another's company. By supporting one another's tournaments, they have maintained the game and expanded its seasonality of play. For southern plains handgame people, the game remains an important, culturally specific, and positive expression of Indian identity.

If the handgame were used to reflect on the tribes that play it, I would maintain that the primary message it sends is an emphasis on community sociocultural interaction. That is, while it serves as a form of enculturation and ethnic maintenance, it is the social enjoyment derived from the game, demonstrating fellowship, support of one another's event, sharing and generosity, and seeing friends, relatives, and even opponents, that outweighs any won or lost column, which isn't kept anyway, or how much money is made. Everyone likes to win, but winning is clearly not the reason for playing handgame, as teams continue to play regardless of winning or losing. The psychological and medicinal effects obtained from the associated socialization and music of handgames offer other valued benefits.

The development of the Indian handgame in western Oklahoma correlates with most of Blanchard's (1995, 195–202) eight areas of observations regarding the evolution of sports with levels of political organization. The handgame has become more secular, although some magico-religious aspects still exist. It has developed greater structure, formal organization, complexity, and rules. In terms of social identity, most teams are composed of relatives, although some involve a wider array of members. Concerning social distance, intra-tribal play is sometimes observably less intense than play between some intertribal teams or long-term rivals. While little specialization exists overall and most players perform varied roles, some individuals focus on certain aspects of the game such as singing, hiding, or guessing. The technology and equipment associated with the handgame has increased in complexity as evident in the use of public address systems and online advertising. Although redistribution is still an important aspect of the handgame, its direct ecological meaning has become less immediately evident as the game has become more complex and individual bets are relatively small. Finally, while permanent recordkeeping is not practiced, other forms of quantification have developed, including titles, trophies, jackets, T-shirts, and cash and special prizes.

332 CHAPTER 6

More than anything, the social relationships, visiting, fun in playing, and continuation of tradition are what Oklahoma Natives emphasize as the most important aspects of the handgame. Carl Atauvich commented on why he likes the handgame, acknowledging how the game was handed down from their elders and the importance of respecting and continuing the tradition:

> It's really how you outdo, outwit the guesser . . . if you're hiding, how you outwit the guesser, and, if you're guessing, you really got to try to outdo the hider. It's just really competitive. It's a lot of fun. That's the reason why I enjoy it. I don't go, you know, trying to carry myself disrespect-fully. I try to respect it because it's one of our traditional handgames that we should all enjoy and, you know, take care of it. Because . . . there's no other game in the world that's like it. And it's our game, and we should take care of it. I really enjoy it, and there's a lot of people especially back there, way back there, the elders, the elder people that played handgame.[14]

Jackie Yellowhair offered his view on what is most important about playing handgame, the importance of continuing tradition, and how certain traditions are carried forward by core families:

> To me the most important thing about handgame is enjoying yourself. That would be the first thing. Most importantly would be not to get mad. To go with an open mind to where you cannot be mad when you lose, and be a good sport about winning, not rubbing it in, you know, or things like that. I think that's the most important thing of it and also preservation—preservation comes in. It's gonna go on when I'm gone, you know. Like this one right here [points to his young niece] will carry it on too. These guys watch, them little guys, and then they'll carry it on. It's just certain people, certain families that do these different things, like Gourd Clan, . . . they got just certain families that just do that, you know. Certain families that just do the meetings in the Native American Church. Certain families that just do the handgame. And I think that's the way the Creator made it. It's not just everybody. There's people that come and go, but he blessed these, he made these certain ones to take care of these certain things, different aspects of the culture and language, and things like that. And I think we've been blessed to take care of this handgame, to carry it on. Other people will know about it, how to be respectable and to do things right.[15]

Many Native people believe that things always happen for a reason, that traditions like handgame were given to them as a people by the Creator and were meant to develop in a certain way. With this belief comes a responsibility to pass the traditions on to future generations. As Jackie Yellowhair stated, "I want to keep this drumbeat alive through this handgame and through this

Native American Church." His grandmother, Ina Paddlety Chalepah, perhaps summed up the most important aspect of the southern plains Indian hand-game. As she told me in 1998, "This is about our last traditional recreation, our last surviving game. We come to play to have a good time, above all else. And as long as we have a good time and everyone gets to play, that's all that really matters."[16] Ho!

GLOSSARY

Western Oklahoma Handgame Terminology

bone hog tournaments. Tournaments played with two-person teams (both players on a single team normally hiding each time).

break their horns. To make the other side's guesser consistently miss guessing you, often resulting in a change of guessers. This references the old Kiowa tradition of a guesser wearing a horned headdress when guessing and the sign language sign for putting horns on, denoting a chief or leader. *See also* **put horns on**.

bull snake. To be lying, deceiving. The term is sometimes heard in reference to a hider faking in attempt to make the guesser guess incorrectly.

come out. To hide the bones in a game and then bring one's hands forward to be guessed.

door knob. To guess both hiders on the first guess (i.e., to not let them out of the door or get started). The term reportedly originated with the Cheyenne. *See also* **door pop** and **kill them at the door.**

door pop. To guess both hiders on the first guess (i.e. to not let them out of the door, or to get started. *See also* **door knob** and **kill them at the door**.

free-for-all. An informal style of handgame in which members may sit on either side, in any combination or number, to play. Although matched collective bets for each team and individual bets may be placed, there is no entry fee, thus participation is free for all.

get away. To not be correctly guessed while hiding, thereby scoring a point and enabling another chance to hide. Often used in past tense to describe a series of successful hides, resulting in a streak of scoring several points.

GLOSSARY

glass hands. Being easy to guess when hiding (as if your hands were made of glass and the opposing guesser can see through them to tell where you are hiding the marked bone).

go down. To lower one's hands or secret them behind something at the start of a hide.

go down again. Attempt to lower one's hands out of sight to hide, and potentially switch, the hiding objects again after being guessed but before opening one's hands.

grasshopper. Someone who tends to switch hands or "jump" frequently in their hiding practices. *See also* **jump**.

handgame babes. A joking term for single women who frequent handgames.

handgame fix. A term used by individuals who miss playing handgame and seek to remedy their desire to play.

handgame hangover. Tiredness the day after playing handgame late into the night.

homebody. Someone who frequently tends to hide the marked bone repeatedly in the same hand. *See also* **stay home**.

jump. To frequently switch the location of the bones in your hands from your last hide. The opposite of **stay home**. *See also* **grasshopper**.

kill them at the door. To guess both hiders on the first guess (i.e., to not let them score a point or get out of the door). Often said in Kiowa: *chátcá bè hól*. *See also* **door knob** and **door pop**.

medicine man. The individual man or woman who chooses the hiders and guessers for their team. Often viewed as the team captain.

put horns on. Selecting someone to serve as the guesser, associated with the sign language sign for putting horns on, denoting a chief or leader.

round robin. A modern form of tournament, modeled after softball and other athletic tournaments. In the handgame this usually means a double elimination tournament with a winner's bracket and a loser's bracket, not a tournament in which every team meets each of the others, round-robin style.

secret weapon. A joking term sometimes used to refer to a new player who does especially well, in reference to successful hiding or guessing.

side bet. A bet between two individuals in the crowd or between two players, generally after the game begins and placed on the floor between the two teams.

stay home. To continue hiding the bones in the same position as one's last hide. The opposite of **jump**. *See also* **homebody**.

NOTES

INTRODUCTION

1. While both "hand game" and "handgame" appear in the literature and are still used today by Native groups, I have chosen to use "handgame" for convenience and consistency.

CHAPTER 1

1. Lesser (1933, 324) reported, "My own experience among the Wichita shows that the ceremonial hand game still follows early Ghost Dance forms." Blaine (1982, 126) reported, "For some time, . . . the hand game has been an integral part of the Wichita and Pawnee visitation cycle, and is usually given at night in a large arbor." Today the Wichita and Pawnee alternate extended annual visits to one another's communities for ceremonials, including handgames. During these visits, the Wichita and Pawnee still play a highly ceremonially related form of handgame that is reportedly not open to attendance or participation by other tribes or the public. Author's field notes, Wichita and Affiliated Tribes, Anadarko, Oklahoma, March 4, 1998. For a more detailed discussion of the reciprocal Pawnee-Wichita tribal visits, including handgame play, see Blaine (1982).

2. Author's field notes, Plains Apache and Ponca; John Williams (Ponca) to the author, December 8, 1997. The Oglala Lakota generally played the moccasin game (Walker 1982, 64, 67) but also knew how to play the handgame. Ruxton (1951, 101) reports Lakota playing the handgame against various Plains tribes in 1847.

3. Helm, Lurie, and Kurath (1966, 75, 88) describe most of these factors for the Dogrib.

4. Sets of wooden hand- and stickgame sticks commonly differ in number and painted design. The "center" or "kick" stick is normally differentiated from the remainder of scoring sticks in size and or design in past and contemporary Plateau (Brunton 1998) and Plains populations.

5. Seattle Times (2012); AAANA (2012). The artifacts are now in the Washington State History Museum in Tacoma.

6. AAANA (2012).

338   NOTES TO PAGES 26–47

7. According to Katherine Maker, the Osage learned the handgame from a party of visiting Cheyenne who taught the game to some Osage in the early 1920s. Katherine Maker (Osage) to Leonard Maker, November 29, 1968, DD, T-341-A, 1–3. According to Mrs. Maker, she was given this account by her aunt Mary Morrel Russell. The Cheyenne camped on the allotment of Mr. and Mrs. John Abbot, west of Hominy, Oklahoma. However, compared with Tixier's reports of the game among the Osage in 1839–40 (McDermott 1868, 181), Mrs. Maker's account may refer to the introduction of a new form of the game or to the revival of a gaming form that had lapsed among the Osage by the 1920s.

8. Howard (1965, 129) notes, "Parrish Williams stated that these warriors were playing the moccasin game rather than the hand game, and that the hand game had developed from the older moccasin game. If so this 'original legend' is an interesting example of syncretism."

9. Brackets in original. See Clark (1885, 71) for a variation of this story as the origin of scalping among the Blackfeet.

10. Known among the Blackfeet as "the stick game," handgames continue at the annual North American Indian Days celebration at Browning, Montana, and local games are held throughout the winter in communities throughout the Blackfeet Reservation (McFee 1972, 78–80).

11. Culin (1907, 824–25, 832) reports neither the handgame nor the moccasin game among the Mandan. However, Catlin's firsthand observations suggests that the moccasin game was present during his travels in the 1830s.

12. Charley Apekaum and Frizzlehead II (Kiowa) to Donald Collier July 25, 1935, SFN, 118.

13. During my fieldwork, members of various tribes reported attending and participating in contemporary handgames among the Wind River Arapaho, Fort Hall Shoshone, Ute Mountain Ute, Uintah and Ouray Paiute, Blackfeet, Northern Cheyenne, Rocky Boy Cree, Crow, Ponca, Osage, Iowa, Oto, Wichita, Pawnee, and other tribes. Bill Koomsa Jr., John Williams, Allen Little Light, Melissa Jacoby to the author, 1997–1998. The Blackfeet continued to play a secular form of handgame with gambling as late as 1903–6 (Wissler 1911:59) and the 1970s (McFee 1972, 78–80). See also Fowler (1982, 1987) concerning brief mention of Arapaho, Gros Ventre, and Assiniboine handgames.

14. Some accounts claim that the extra stick or "kick stick" was introduced by the Paiute Prophet Wovoka when he traveled to the northwest teaching the Ghost Dance (Wikipedia 2017). While Wovoka did not travel beyond his home area in Nevada (Bailey 1957, 79–83), the Ghost Dance diffused northward and westward to other regions.

15. AAANA (2012).

16. Ibid.

17. Charley Apekaum and Frizzlehead II to Donald Collier, July 25, 1935, SFN, 118. See also Brant (1969, 115); Lesser (1933, 152); and Parsons (1929, 121).

18. Author's fieldnotes, 1993.

19. See Dodge (1989, 281) for a nearly identical statement.

20. Cecil and Jenny Horse to Julia Jordan, October 19, 1969, DD, T-141, 21–22.

21. See, for example, Fletcher (1983, 34, 1915, 80–83); Mooney (1896, 1008–9); Kroeber (1907, 368–82); Densmore (1936, 68–78); and Driver (1961, 201).

22. Introduced by Alice Beck Kehoe, Lesser's work was reprinted in 1996.

NOTES TO PAGES 51–63

23. While the basic thesis of Boyd's 1979 article is included, several problems appear, including a sketchy and brief treatment of the stickgames and handgames involved, minimal tribal distinctions, unqualified and potentially biased statements about specific tribes by other tribes and non-Indians, and awkward terminology such as "purest sector" and "purest portion of tribal identity" (1979, 219).

24. Thomas Green analogizes the micro and macro levels of conflict to Clifford Geertz's model of "deep play." Although his sample was limited to six individuals and four games played in their homes, the potential difference in use of the game is worth further investigation.

25. In these works, Gelo (1986, 6) conducted five months of fieldwork over three summer seasons (1982–1984), while Lasko (1997) performed three months of summer fieldwork in 1995. As most handgames are from late October through May, they may not have attended many. More recently, handgames in the summer months have been increasing.

CHAPTER 2

1. Hamilton (1984). Interviews with elder Kiowa and Comanche handgame players produced few stories. The eldest Apache tribal member and my consultant knew and related only portions of the two stories (Alfred Chalepah Sr. to the author, January 23, 1998) that I found in McAllister (1949) and present later in this chapter.

2. Sherman Chaddlesone to the author, July 21, 2004.

3. Frank Given and Ioleta McElhaney to Alice Marriott, VII, 20–22, August 14, 1935, AMFN. The water monster is the Zémáutqūné of Kiowa mythology. This account closely resembles a Kiowa-Apache story. Given's father, the noted chief Setagai (Sitting Bear), was half Kiowa and half Plains Apache and periodically camped with both the Kiowa and Apache during Sun Dances; JMKFN 6, pt. 2, 199. This account may have originated from or have a strong influence from the Apache.

4. Gregory Haumpy Sr. to the author, March 24, 1998.

5. Solomon Katchin, narrator; Alvin Shaman, translator. In Apache mythology, Nistcre is a supernatural being that resembles a human but is made of stone. "Nistcre," which may be used as either singular or plural, is translated as "Stone Monster" and "Stone Monsters" (McAllister 1949, 18). While Nistcre is referred to in singular form in the first story, singular and plural references are found in the second story.

6. Ray Blackbear to William Bittle, April 19, 1956, WBFN-WHC; Schweinfurth (2002, 81).

7. Mooney (1898, 399); Parker McKenzie to the author, October 24, 1993, and January 29, 1998; Bill Koomsa Jr. to the author, December 3, 1993; Cecil Horse to Julia Jordan, DD, T-141, 15, October 19, 1969.

8. HLS-FSA 3, 22–23. The Kiowa name of the game is *jò-áu-gà* (tipi game), not *jò-áu-gà* (moccasin game). Today the southern plains game is popularly called handgame. No tradition of the Kiowa playing the game with the use of moccasins, as found in the northeastern plains and Great Lakes region is known. Scott's designation "Moccasin Game" may stem from two factors. First, the game is known as moccasin game in parts of the northern plains where he worked for thirteen years before coming to the southern

340 NOTES TO PAGES 63–69

plains. Second, the Kiowa name for tipi and moccasin is the same, whether single, dual, or triplural: *jǒ-hį* (McKenzie 1991, column 20, page 5).

9. A Comanche elder reported the same sign language sign for the handgame and demonstrated it for me. Vernon Atauvich to the author, February 1, 1998. Clark (1885, 185) contains no entry for the handgame, only this: "Game. Specify whatever kind it may be."

10. Bill Koomsa Jr. to the author, December 3, 1993, and March 27, 1998.

11. George Hunt and Biatonma or Mrs. Horse to Alice Marriott, July 17, 1935, AMFN. Mrs. Horse, one of two wives of Tsa-toke, popularly known as Hunting Horse, was enrolled as Po-e-to-mah (or Fíjómā [Food Keeper]). Biatonma is a variant spelling of the name.

12. Ibid.

13. If in a Pawnee encampment, it could have been held inside a tipi as well. Because the Pawnee practiced a dual mode of subsistence alternately focusing on bison and horticulture, their extended summer and winter hunts out onto the plains, like the Wichita and other semi-sedentary horticulturalists, entailed the use of tipis while away from their permanent sedentary earth lodges.

14. Cecil Horse to Julia Jordan, DD, T-141, 7, October 19, 1969.

15. KCA versus the Crow, videotaped game, November 12, 1993; author's field notes.

16. Charley Apekaum and Frizzlehead II to Donald Collier July 25, 1935, SFN, 118.

17. Cecil Horse to Julia Jordan, DD, T-141, 6–8, October 19, 1969.

18. Densmore (1936, 71) infers that, among many other items, beans were sometimes used in Cheyenne and Arapaho games.

19. George Hunt and Biatonma or Mrs. Horse to Alice Marriott, July 17, 1935, AMFN.

20. Sherman Chaddlesone to the author, July 21, 2004. Phil "Joe Fish" Dupoint also pointed out this mural, noting that the Kiowa had the game while still in the northern plains, possibly from a dream or another tribe. Phil "Joe Fish" Dupoint to the author, June 22, 2018. Other images of Plains Indian handgames include a ledger drawing by Making Medicine (Cheyenne) titled "A little game" (Viola 1998, 30–31); a painting by Victor Pepion (Blackfoot) titled "The Hand Game," depicting a northern plains stick game (Wycoff 1996, 109); and a painting of a Pawnee handgame by Gerald Osborne (Pawnee), circa 1950, now in the Philbrook Art Museum in Tulsa.

21. Large rawhide bass drums were developed during the late 1800s when marching band bass drums were introduced through military and school bands.

22. Charley Apekaum and Frizzlehead II to Donald Collier, July 25, 1935, SFN, 118; Bill Koomsa Jr. to the author, December 3. 1993; Isaacs (1969).

23. Cecil Horse to Julia Jordan, October 19, 1969, DD, T-141, 2–5, 7.

24. Gregory Haumpy was told this exact form of starting a game by his grandfather, except that one stick from the middle was awarded upon winning the first point. He was also told that in his grandfather's time the Kiowa sometimes used to arm wrestle to determine who hid first. Gregory Haumpy Sr. to the author, May 23, 1998. This may have been a recreational variation and not a standard practice. Bill Koomsa Jr. to the author, December 3, 1993. Cecil Horse reported a variation in which each side alternated taking turns guessing the other four times in succession, but the context was not specified as to whether this was to start a game or the normal form of play. Cecil Horse to Julia Jordan, October 19, 1969, DD, T-141, 2–3.

NOTES TO PAGES 69–77   341

25. Charley Apekaum and Frizzlehead II to Donald Collier, July 25, 1935, SFN, 118–19; Isaacs (1969).

26. Cecil and Jenny Horse to Julia Jordan, October 19, 1969, DD T-141, 2–3.

27. George Hunt and Biatonma or Mrs. Horse to Alice Marriott, July 17, 1935, AMFN.

28. Cecil and Jenny Horse to Julia Jordan, October 19, 1969, DD, T-141, 5.

29. Ibid., 3–4.

30. Ibid., 4–5.

31. Ibid., 5, 17.

32. Ibid., 5–6.

33. Ibid.

34. Ibid., 16.

35. Ibid., 16–17.

36. Bill Koomsa Jr. and Jack Yellowhair to the author, 1998; Mary Beaver to the author July 9, 2018. See also Densmore (1936, 70).

37. George Hunt and Biatonma or Mrs. Horse to Alice Marriott, July 17, 1935, AMFN.

38. Ibid.

39. Ibid.

40. Gregory Haumpy Sr. to the author, March 24, 1998.

41. Hamilton (1984).

42. Bill Koomsa Jr. to the author, 2/1/1998.

43. Gregory Haumpy Sr. to the author, 3/24/1998.

44. Author's field notes, 1998.

45. There appears to have been both single-hider (Mooney 1898, 348; Parsons 1929, 121) and double-hider (Isaacs 1969) versions among Kiowa games, as was common among most tribes. In the Santa Fe Laboratory of Anthropology School Notes, a different scoring method is recorded from Frizzlehead II and Charley Apekaum. According to this account, if a guesser missed both hiders of the opposing team, one counter (instead of two) was taken from the neutral pile and placed on the side of the hiders. "[When] all the counters have been moved from the neutral pile to one side, that side began taking counters (score sticks) from the opposing side (normally only one score stick is taken [and] then the counters are returned to the middle and play resumes). If a guesser correctly guesses one of two hiders, then the leader of the hiding team placed one of the neutral counter sticks at right angles 'to indicate that half a point had been won.' The man who was guessed passes his elk teeth to the captain who then hides along with the other remaining hider (but only one hider remains and should be allowed to hide). If the captain is guessed by the other side, they take the counter and the teeth to hide. If the captain is missed the counter is placed in its original position and his team gets the other counter, and it is their turn to hide." Whether this is an incompletely recorded but separate set of rules or contains mistakes in the translation of the interview and subsequent recorded account is uncertain. However, the presence of major discrepancies in hiding and scoring rules compared to accounts from current elders who played the older form well into their forties suggests that something was lost in the translation. Charley Apekaum and Frizzlehead II to Donald Collier, July 25, 1935, SFN, 119.

46. According to Lesser (1933, 129) a one-out-of-two chance is typically found in the stick game, while a one-out-of-four chance is generally associated with the moccasin and reed games and the four stick games, which reflects the number of hiding items used.

342   NOTES TO PAGES 77–87

47. Lesser (1933, 129–30) elaborates on possible relationships between the various chance principles and the various North American guessing games.

48. Author's field notes.

49. Charley Apekaum and Frizzlehead II to Donald Collier, July 25, 1935, SFN, 118.

50. This tradition does not appear to have continued, as one song is often sung the entire time a team is on offense.

51. Charley Apekaum and Frizzlehead II to Donald Collier, July 25, 1935, SFN, 118.

52. Ibid., 119.

53. Guy Quoetone to Julia Jordan, DD, T-150, 29–30, September 19, 1967.

54. George Hunt and Biatonma or Mrs. Horse to Alice Marriott, July 17, 1935, AMFN.

55. Gregory Haumpy Sr. to the author, March 24, 1998.

56. Cecil and Jenny Horse to Julia Jordan, DD, T-141, 22, October 19, 1969.

57. Herman Asenap, June 30, 1933, and July 1, 1933 (Kavanagh 2008, 40, 338–39); Carl Atauvich to the author, March 2, 1998.

58. My thanks to Dr. Daniel Gelo, University of Texas, San Antonio, for linguistic insights into this term and related sources. Daniel Gelo to the author, February 19, 2018. Wick Miller (1972, 120, 162) gives the related Shoshoni term *naaiyawi* ("to play the handgame").

59. Herman Asenap June 30, 1933, and July 1, 1933 (Kavanagh 2008, 40). Vernon Atauvich gave the name *poe-kway* (gambling) as a name for the handgame, but this likely refers to gambling in general. Vernon Atauvich to the author, February 1, 1998.

60. Howard White Wolf, August 3, 1933 (Kavanagh 2008, 338).

61. Frank Chekovi, August 4, 1933 (Kavanagh 2008, 339).

62. Carl Atauvich to the author, March 2, 1998.

63. Ibid.; Lanny Asepermy to the author, June 30, 2023.

64. Marie Looking Glass Haumpy to the author, March 24, 1998.

65. Alfred Chalepah to the author, January 23, 1998.

66. Bittle (1964, 8) suggested that while this story is probably similar to that of pre-contact times, the narrator may have attempted to "bring it up to date" in equating the monsters with dinosaurs. Beatty (1999) provides a basically similar account, relating to the Apachean tendency to construct metaphors along behavioral lines rather than physical appearance. The neighboring Kiowa call dinosaurs *chóicàultǫ̀sègàu* (singular), *chóicàultǫ̀sè* (dual and triplural), literally "liquid-animal-bones," from their prevalence of being found near swampy areas. Parker McKenzie to the author, December 12, 1993; Meadows (2008, 81–82). I also recorded other versions of this account. Alfred Chalepah to the author, January 23,1998; Jackie Ray Yellowhair to the author, November 16, 2017.

67. Louise Saddleblanket to William Bittle, July 14, 1964, box 2, folder 31, Recreation, WBFN-WHC.

68. Ray Blackbear to William Bittle, June 29, 1964, box 1, folder 49. Ethnobotany, WBFN-WHC.

69. Ray Blackbear to William Bittle, June 9, 1961, box 2, folder 31, Recreation, WBFN-WHC.

70. Rose Chalepah to William Bittle June 14, 1963, box 2, folder 31, Recreation, WBFN-WHC.

71. Ray Blackbear to William Bittle June 9, 1961, box 2, folder 31, Recreation, WBFN-WHC.

NOTES TO PAGES 88–101   343

72. Alfred Chalepah to the author, July 21, 1995, and January 23, 1998. Incidentally, this was also the Apache name of Claude Jay (Plains Apache): Elk Teeth, from *dah-say-sah* (elk) and *bee-gwoo* (teeth).

73. Alfred Chalepah to the author, July 21, 1995, and January 23, 1998.

74. Belah was Old Man Archilta's sister and Alfred Chalepah's mother's aunt, and thus a classificatory grandmother to Alfred. Alfred Chalepah to the author, January 23, 1998.

75. Ibid.

76. Ibid.

77. Ibid.

78. Ibid.

79. Alfred Chalepah to the author, July 21, 1995, and January 23, 1998.

80. Instances of Native Americans disturbing Native burials for power are known. As Gabriel (1996, 43; see also Fowler 1989, 239) writes of the Northern Paiute in western Nevada, "The bones of women who have been dead for thirty or forty years were considered to be powerful gambling medicine. Gamblers would disinter their graves and remove their middle or upper finger bones. They would wash the bone while talking to it about their planned use of it. While they slept with the bone, it might say, "Keep me for two years and you'll always win, but if you don't return me to the grave after two years, you will die." Flannery and Cooper (1946, 405–6) reported the acquisition and use of power in the Gros Ventre handgame by men (never women), who might obtain it unsought or seek it from fasting and dreaming on hilltops. Such power, which was used only in handgames and not in other gambling games or sports, was often obtained from prairie chickens and less commonly from "good natured ghosts." Different forms of power for the handgame or wheel game were often sought by an individual who had lost heavily in prior games and wished to recoup losses and begin a gambling career anew. However, such power was strongly advised against as it was said to cost a heavy penalty in terms of physical ailments, and the acquisition of any type of power was said to result in a premature death.

81. Author's field notes.

82. Hampi [Haumpy] to William Bascom, XVIII-6, August 9, 1935, SFN, 999.

83. Desmond (1952, 51) reports elevated social status for those individuals known as "professional gamblers," similar to that afforded to rich and outstanding athletes, while bone game contest supervisors and criers or masters of ceremonies were accorded the same recognition as that given to political headmen, shamans, sweat lodge leaders, and hunting party and salmon fishing group leaders.

84. Charley Apekaum, Frizzlehead to Donald Collier July 25, 1935, SFN, 119. As Frizzlehead II was born in 1860, this event would have occurred around 1870.

85. Keeps His Name a Long Time (Jáudèkāu) was a young man who announced early in 1882 that he had had a vision in which he received the mission to bring back the buffalo. He subsequently began to make medicine and changed his name to Páujépjè (Bison Bull Coming Out), in relation to his new powers (Mooney 1898, 349–50).

86. Alfred Chalepah to the author, January 23, 1998. The identity of the Comanche individual named in this account is unknown.

87. The Kiowa won the preliminary hiding round and the right to hide first.

88. Hwmpi [Haumpy] to William Bascom, XVIII-6; August 9, 1935, SFN, 1001–2.

344   NOTES TO PAGES 101–108

89. McAllister (1949) developed pseudonyms for his consultants. "Alvin Shaman" was the name McAllister used for Alonzo Chalepah. Compare this account with his other accounts of this game (McAllister 1970, 54–55).

90. McAllister (1970, 55) stated, "[The Comanche] continually lost until they refused to play. And so the game ended." There are slight differences in the two versions of this game as provided by McAllister (1949, 10; 1970, 54–55). Alonzo's son Alfred Chalepah did not attend the game but remembered the event well. He stated that he believed his dad was just an ordinary man and was lucky. He believed that concentration was the key to guessing in handgames. He also reported that Sam Klinkole was a good hider. Alfred Chalepah to the author, July 21, 1995, and January 23, 1998.

91. Alfred Chalepah to the author, January 23, 1998. Ace Yellowhair was told a version of the game by Leon Redbone, who attended the game. Redbone reported that it occurred south of Gawkey Creek, possibly at the home of Bitsiddy. Ace Yellowhair to the author July 28, 2004.

92. Alonzo Chalepah to the author, June 17, 2023.

93. Alfred Chalepah to the author, January 23, 1998.

94. Ibid.

95. Gambling on the arrow game was primarily a man's affair, while shinny was a woman's game. The stick game, a game focusing on bouncing a set of four decorated sticks off a flat rock and moving an awl around a square hide or canvas game board based on the score of the dropped sticks and often known as the awl game, is considered as a women's game among the Kiowa and was played primarily by women. However, both Quoetone and Cecil Horse report that men occasionally played it (Guy Quoetone to Julia Jordan DD, T-150, 25–28; Cecil Horse to Julia Jordan DD, T-141, 6). Alfred Chalepah reported that he also sometimes played the game with groups of Apache women, sitting in if they were short of players. Alfred Chalepah to the author, January 23, 1998.

96. Cecil Horse to Julia Jordan, DD, T-141, 2–8.

97. School Superintendent Harvey, September 1, 1902, ARCIA, 1901–2. See also Lesser (1933, 324).

98. Agent Woolsey, August 15, 1894, ARCIA, 1893–94.

99. ARCIA, 1865, 253.

100. Hoxie (1995, 213–18) reports on the efforts of Crow Indian agents and local priests against the Beaver Dances, Tobacco Society, handgame, and other traditional dances. In addition, a lengthy discussion of the evils of the handgame is found in Sam Lapointe to C. H. Asbury, March 1, 1922, item 15, box 83, file 13, 1, RCIA-FRC; Farmer's Weekly Report, November 20–25, 1922, item 15, box 86, folder 139, RCIA-FRC.

101. Kracht (1989, 820–75; 1992; 1994); Meadows (1999, 113–22); DD, T-64, 3–5.

102. Guy Quoetone to Julia Jordan, April 30, 1968, DD, T-643, 3–5, 14.

103. Cecil Horse to Julia Jordan, October 19, 1967, DD, T-141, 16.

104. Guy Quoetone to Julia Jordan, June 14, 1967, DD., T-28, 26–28.

105. According to Wayland, Wayland, and Freg (2004), the game of monte was originally introduced to Indians by Spanish explorers who brought forty-card monte packs containing numeral cards from one (ace) through seven and court cards of rey (king), caballo (horseman or knight), and sota (page) in the suits of coins, cups, swords, and clubs. It became popular in the United States, especially in Texas, after being brought back by troops returning from the Mexican-American War in 1848.

NOTES TO PAGES 108–115   345

106. Louise SaddleBlanket to William Bittle, July 11, 1967; and Louise SaddleBlanket to William Bittle, July 11, 1967, DD, T-79, 20–25.

107. Parker McKenzie to the author, April 18, 1993.

108. Cecil and Jenny Horse to Julia Jordan, October 19, 1967, DD, T-141, 22–24. Jenny's father was enrolled as Haun-py, but the family name is now often given as Haumpy. Cecil and Jenny Horse noted allegations of cheating in the late 1800s and early 1900s by Anglos and by a Wichita man named Jim who allegedly marked the cards by mashing them and making impressions with fingernails. They stated in 1967 that few people still gambled at cards, though they noted that some Apache still gambled at cards and dominoes with "colored people" west of Apache, Oklahoma. Ibid., 31–32. Alfred Chalepah recalled that few Apaches gambled in cards but that most liked handgames. The number of Apache gambling at cards likely ebbed and flowed at different periods and may have varied in different social circles.

109. Cecil and Jenny Horse to Julia Jordan, October 19, 1967, DD, T-141, 24–25.

110. Guy Quoetone to Julia Jordan, September 19, 1967, DD, T-150, 24.

111. The Indiana statute may refer to the Delaware, Kickapoo, Potawatomi, or other groups inhabiting that state.

112. Guy Quoetone to Julia Jordan, April 30, 1968, DD, T-148, 20.

113. Parker McKenzie to the author March 5, 1994; L-Troop membership roster, Seventh Cavalry, Kiowa Misc. File, FSA.

114. Guy Quoetone to Julia Jordan, September 19, 1967, DD, T-150, 24–30; September 26, 1967, DD, T-148, 20–24; April 30, 1968, DD, T-643, 3–5.

115. Guy Quoetone to Julia Jordan, September 19, 1967, DD, T-150, 24–30; September 26, 1967, DD, T-148, 20–24; April 30, 1968, DD, T-643, 3–5, 14.

116. Ibid., T-643, 3–5. Quoetone later stated that he often loaned money to Indians who were hard up for cash.

117. J. Lee Hall, 1886, ARCIA, ser. 2467, 348. Blanchard (1981, 41–42) describes the suppression and state laws against gambling at Mississippi Choctaw stickball games beginning in the 1890s.

118. Guy Quoetone to Julia Jordan, September 19, 1967, DD, T-150, 25–28.

119. Ibid., 29.

120. Ibid., 29–30. Horse participates briefly in this interview with Guy Quoetone.

121. Guy Quoetone to Julia Jordan, September 26, 1967, DD, T-148, 24.

122. Cecil and Jenny Horse to Julia Jordan, October 19, 1967, DD T-141, 21.

123. Ibid., 6, 16.

124. Parker McKenzie to the author, August 15, 1994.

125. Parker McKenzie to the author, October 24, 1993.

126. Alfred Chalepah to the author, July 21, 1995.

127. Ernestine Kauahquo Kauley to the author, March 25, 2005.

128. Delores Toyebo Harragarra to the author, March 19, 2003.

129. Mrs. Horse (Po-e-to-mah or Fíjómà [Food Keeper]), to Alice Marriott, July 15, 1935, AMFN.

130. "Kiowa Giveaway and Dance," July 14–18, 1937, AMFN.

131. Bill Koomsa Jr. to the author, December 3, 1993; Parker McKenzie to the author, January 29, 1998.

132. Author's field notes, Bruce Haumpy (September 10, 1922–October 9, 1991).

346 NOTES TO PAGES 115–130

133. Jackie Ray Yellowhair to the author, July 16, 2004.

134. Ina Paddlety Chalepah to the author, June 30, 2004.

135. Marie Yokesuite Haumpy to the author, March 24, 1998.

136. Gregory Haumpy Sr. to the author, April 2, 1998.

137. Bill Koomsa Jr. to the author, February 1, 1998; Gregory Haumpy Sr. to the author, April 2, 1998.

138. Gregory Haumpy Sr. to the author, April 2, 1998.

139. Mary Beaver to the author, July 9, 2018.

140. Sam Dicke to Boyce Timmons, March 3,1968, DD, T-200, 1:18–22.

141. Gregory Haumpy Sr. to the author, March 24, 1998.

142. Myrtle Lincoln to Julia Jordan, December 15, 1969, DD, T-586, 11.

143. Mary Beaver to the author, July 31, 2004.

144. Mary Beaver to the author, July 9, 2018.

145. Author's field notes, Colony, Oklahoma, September 5, 1993.

146. Mary Beaver to the author, July 9, 2018.

147. Ibid.

148. Myrtle Lincoln to Julia Jordan, December 15, 1969, DD, T-586.

149. Author's field notes, 1998.

CHAPTER 3

1. Author's field notes, September 18, 1993. Blanchard (1981, 42–43, 63–73) describes the revival of Mississippi Choctaw stickball with the rise of Indian awareness, identity, and self-determination in the 1950s and 1960s.

2. Bill Koomsa Jr. to the author, December 3, 1993, and February 1, 1998.

3. Bill Koomsa Jr. to the author, December 3, 1998.

4. Cecil and Jenny Horse to Julia Jordan, October 19, 1967, DD, T-141, 22–24.

5. Gregory Haumpy to the author, March 24, 1998.

6. Bill Koomsa Jr. to the author, December 3, 1993.

7. Ibid.; Phil "Joe Fish" Dupoint to the author, June 22, 2018.

8. Bill Koomsa Jr. to the author, December 3, 1993.

9. Ibid.; Phil "Joe Fish" Dupoint to the author, June 22, 2018.

10. Hamilton (1984).

11. Jack Yellowhair to the author, February 9, 1998.

12. Hamilton (1984).

13. Mary Beaver to the author, July 9, 2018.

14. Jack Yellowhair to the author, 2/9/1998.

15. Adam Kaulaity to the author, March 20, 2003.

16. Carl Atauvich to the author, March 2, 1998.

17. Ibid.

18. Bill Koomsa Jr. to the author, December 3, 1993.

19. Bill Koomsa Jr. to the author, 1998; Ina Paddlety Chalepah to the author, 1998.

20. Author's field notes, 1997. Stuart (1972, 102–16) found many of these same characteristics in her study of Coast Salish Slahal (handgame).

21. Jack Yellowhair to the author, March 18, 2003.

22. Charley Apekaum and Frizzlehead II to Donald Collier, July 25, 1935, SFN, 118–19.

NOTES TO PAGES 131–141

23. Hamilton (1984).

24. The use of songs for power and aid in playing handgame is recorded for other tribes. Mooney (1896, 1009) states, "Among some other tribes, particularly the Navajo, as described by Dr. Washington Mathews, the songs have meaning, being prayers to different animal or elemental gods to assist the player." Densmore (1936, 70) reports that Elk Woman (Cheyenne) "used to fast and get lots of new songs to sing at hand games."

25. Bill Koomsa Jr. to the author, November 8, 1997.

26. Ina Paddlety Chalepah to the author, June 30, 2004.

27. Gregory Haumpy to the author, March 24, 1998. Although translated as "knee," *bél-tó* is the dual and triplural form for "jaws" and "chins," likely intending jaws.

28. Phil "Joe Fish" Dupoint to the author, June 22, 2018. Dupoint stated that these are the only Kiowa handgame songs with English lyrics he knew of.

29. Jack Yellowhair to the author, May 11, 1998.

30. Rose Chalepah to William Bittle, July 26, 1961, box 2, folder 31, Recreation, WBFN-WHC.

31. Carla Atauvich to author, March 2, 1998.

32. AFN (1998).

33. Gregory and Marie Haumpy to the author, March 23, 1998; Vernon Atauvich to the author, February 1, 1998.

34. Jackie Ray and Ace Yellowhair to the author, October 28, 2012; Alonzo Chalepah to the author, June 17, 2023.

35. Alfred Chalepah Sr. to the author, January 23, 1998.

36. Gregory Haumpy to the author, March 24, 1998.

37. Bill Koomsa Jr. to the author, November 8, 1997.

38. Bill Koomsa Jr. to the author, December 3, 1993; Gregory Haumpy to the author, April 2, 1998; Ace Yellowhair to the author, December 21, 2021. Among the Lakota, Powers (1973, 186) notes the similar use of songs following handgames to taunt the opposition. "A war song was often sung at the conclusion of the game by the victorious players, inserting an opponent's name in the song in place of the enemy's."

39. Bill Koomsa Jr. to the author, December 3, 1993.

40. Mary Beaver to the author, July 9, 2018. Anonymous initials used in place of names she mentioned.

41. Gregory Haumpy to the author, March 24, 1998.

42. Jack Yellowhair to the author, May 11, 1998.

43. Ace Yellowhair to the author, July 23, 2004.

44. Ibid.

45. Author's field notes, February 2, 1998.

46. Bill Koomsa Jr. to the author, December 3, 1993.

47. Alfred Chalepah Sr. to the author, January 23, 1998.

48. Author's field notes, February 7, 1998.

49. Author's field notes, 1997–2021. Densmore (1936, 70, 73) reports of an Arapaho handgame song belonging to a woman and of possession of handgame sets by Cheyenne and Arapaho women.

50. Hamilton (1984).

51. Jack Yellowhair to the author, March 18, 2003.

52. Jackie Ray Yellowhair to the author July 16, 2004.

348   NOTES TO PAGES 142–163

53. Jack Yellowhair to the author, February 9, 1998.

54. Gregory Haumpy to the author, April 2, 1998.

55. Adam Kaulaity to the author, March 20, 2003.

56. Jack Yellowhair to the author, February 9, 1998, May 11, 1998; Carl Atauvich to the author, March 2, 1998.

57. Mary Beaver to the author, July 9, 2018.

58. Bill Koomsa Jr. to the author, November 8, 1997.

59. Author's field notes, February 6, 1998.

60. Bill Koomsa Jr. to the author, November 8, 1997.

61. Author's field notes, February 28, 1998.

62. Jack Yellowhair to the author, February 9, 1998.

63. Author's field notes, 1998.

64. Jack Yellowhair to the author, May 11, 1998; Gregory Haumpy to the author, March 24,1998.

65. Gregory Haumpy to the author, April 2, 1998.

66. Adam Kaulaity to the author, March 20, 2003.

67. Author's field notes, February 28, 1998.

68. Author's field notes, 1998.

69. Mary Beaver to the author, July 9, 2018.

70. Ibid.

71. Jack Yellowhair to the author, February 9, 1998.

72. Gregory Haumpy to the author, April 2, 1998.

73. Jack Yellowhair to the author, May 11, 1998.

74. Bill Koomsa Jr. to the author, December 3, 1993.

75. Ace Yellowhair to the author, July 28, 2004.

76. Jackie Ray Yellowhair to the author, August 6, 2023.

77. Copy courtesy of Mary Beaver, 2018.

78. Bill Koomsa Jr. to the author, April 25, 1998.

79. Author's field notes, April 25, 1998.

80. Author's field notes, Crow Agency, Montana, April–May, 1998.

81. Author's field notes, 1998.

82. Carl Atauvich to the author, March 2, 1998.

83. Ibid.

84. Jack Yellowhair to the author, February 9, 1998.

85. Alfred Chalepah to the author, January 23, 1998.

86. Author's field notes, November 13, 1997.

87. Jack Yellowhair to the author, July 16, 2004.

88. Gregory Haumpy to the author, April 2, 1998.

89. Alfred Chalepah Sr. to the author, January 23, 1998; Gregory and Marie Yokesuite Haumpy to the author March 24, 1998, Gregory Haumpy to the author, April 2, 1998; Phil "Joe Fish" Dupoint to the author, June 22, 2018.

90. Alfred Chalepah Sr. to the author, January 23, 1998.

91. Marie Yokesuite Haumpy to the author, March 24, 1998.

92. Jack Yellowhair to the author, February 9, 1998; Jackie Yellowhair to the author, November 25, 2023.

NOTES TO PAGES 163–179

93. Author's field notes, 1997–1998; Phil "Joe Fish" Dupoint to the author, June 22, 2018.

94. Bill Koomsa Jr. to the author December 3, 1993; Ina Paddlety Chalepah to the author, June 30/, 2004.

95. Mary Beaver (Hughes 2017). Mary told me this man was Lonnie Tsotaddle.

96. Author's field notes, November 13, 1997.

97. Bill Koomsa Jr. to the author, March 27, 1998.

98. Author's field notes, February 7, 1998. Regarding strategy in studying the body language of hiders, there is a correlation in the game Rock, Paper, Scissors. In a 2003 article on a contest involving 120 players and a $1,000 prize sponsored in California by the Toronto-based World Rock Paper Scissors Association, co-president Doug Walker described the use of studying kinesics in play. "It's really about the mind games. There is a lot of trash talking and mental intimidation." As one player described, "Whenever you see a tense muscle, they're going rock. If they look relaxed, it's going to be paper." Contestants emphasized that the game was all about subtle strategy. "Rock, Scissors, Paper Contest Set," ADN, March 18, 2003.

99. Ace Yellowhair to the author, July 28, 2004.

100. Author's field notes, 1998–2004.

101. Author's field notes, 1998.

102. Author's field notes, November 12, 1993.

103. Author's field notes, March 7, 1998.

104. Author's field notes, 2004.

105. Author's field notes, May 9, 1998.

106. Author's field notes, 1998.

107. Ibid.

108. Ibid.

109. Author's field notes, February 1, 1998.

110. Eddie Longhat to the author, February 1, 1998.

111. Jack Yellowhair to the author, May 9, 1998.

112. Gregory Haumpy to the author, April 2, 1998.

113. Ibid.

114. Ibid.

115. Mary Beaver (Hughes 2017).

116. Author's field notes, 2004.

117. Ibid.

118. Author's field notes, 2018.

119. Author's field notes, 2004.

120. Cecil Horse to Julia Jordan, October 19, 1969, DD, T-141, 16–17.

121. Ina Paddlety Chalepah to the author, June 30, 2004.

122. Gregory Haumpy to the author, March 24, 1998.

123. Ibid.

124. Hamilton (1984).

125. Bill Koomsa Jr. to the author, November 8, 1997.

126. Gregory Haumpy to the author, March 24, 1998.

127. Marie Yokesuite Haumpy to the author, March 24, 1998.

128. Author's field notes, February 9, 1998.

350 NOTES TO PAGES 180–196

129. Author's field notes, 1998.

130. Adam Kaulaity to the author, March 20, 2003.

131. Gregory Haumpy to the author, April 2, 1998.

132. Author's field notes, 1998.

133. Ibid.

134. Marie Yokesuite Haumpy to the author, March 24, 1998.

135. Author's field notes, November 14, 1997.

136. Author's field notes, March 7, 1998.

CHAPTER 4

1. Bill Koomsa Jr. to the author, September 11, 1993, December 3, 1993, November 8, 1997, January 1, 1998; Bob Little Light to the author, November 12, 1993; Ed Little Light to the author, November 12, 1997.

2. Bill Koomsa Jr. to the author, December 3, 1993.

3. Bill Koomsa Jr. to the author, September 11, 1993, December 3, 1993, November 8, 1997, January 1, 1998; Ed Little Light to the author, November 12, 1997.

4. Adam Kaulaity to the author, March 20, 2003.

5. Author's field notes, November 12, 1993, November 1997, November 7–11, 2017.

6. Author's field notes, November 12, 1993.

7. Bob Little Light to the author, November 12, 1993.

8. Marie Yokesuite Haumpy to the author, March 24, 1998.

9. Ed Little Light to the author, November 12, 1997.

10. Mary Beaver to the author, July 9, 2018.

11. Author's field notes, 1997–1998.

12. Marie Yokesuite Haumpy to the author, March 24, 1998.

13. Bill Koomsa Jr. to the author, September 18, 1993.

14. Author's field notes, November 12, 1997.

15. Author's field notes, November 13, 1997.

16. Author's field notes, November 12, 1997.

17. Gregory Haumpy to the author, March 24, 1998.

18. Jack Yellowhair to the author, February 9, 1998.

19. Bill Koomsa Jr. to the author, December 3, 1998.

20. Author's field notes, 1998.

21. Author's field notes, 1993–1998.

22. Author's field notes, 1998–2018. Some occasional players do very well, whereas others are guessed quickly when hiding or miss in guessing.

23. Author's field notes, 1998.

24. Author's field notes, 2004.

25. Author's field notes, 1998.

26. Author's field notes, November 11, 1997, February 9, 1998.

27. Ina Paddlety Chalepah to the author, June 30, 2004.

28. Alfred Chalepah to the author, January 23, 1998.

29. Jack Yellowhair to the author, February 9, 1998.

30. Ibid.

31. Ace Yellowhair to the author, July 28, 2004.

NOTES TO PAGES 196–223 351

32. Bill Koomsa Jr. to the author, November 12, 1993; Phil "Joe Fish" Dupoint to the author, June 22, 2018.

33. Bill Koomsa Jr. to the author, February 7, 1998.

34. Carl Atauvich to the author, March 2, 1998.

35. Author's field notes, 1998.

36. Author's field notes, April–May, 1998.

37. LLBHC (2022a).

38. Jeremy Shield to the author, December 2, 2021.

39. Ibid.

40. Jeremy Shield to the author, October 18, 2023.

41. Jeremy Shield to the author, December 2, 2021; October 18, 2023.

42. Ibid.

43. Bill Koomsa Jr. to the author, November 8, 1997.

44. Jeremy Shield to the author, December 2, 2021.

45. Ibid.

46. Author's field notes, Crow Agency, Montana, May 1998.

47. Jeremy Shield to the author, December 2, 2021.

48. Author's field notes, Crow Agency, Montana, April 1998.

49. Author's field notes, 1993–2022.

50. Jeremy Shield to the author, December 2, 2021.

51. This individual explained that he had a special magpie feather that he kept until it was borrowed by a nephew and stolen from him by someone.

52. Ed Little Light to the author, Crow Agency, Montana, May 1998.

53. Kemmick (2017).

54. Author's field notes, 1993–2022.

55. Author's field notes, Crow Agency, Montana, April–May 1998.

56. Ibid.

57. Author's field notes, 1993–2022.

58. Jackie Yellowhair to the author, July 21, 2021; Jeremy Shield to the author, December 2, 2021.

59. Bill Koomsa Jr. to the author, December 3, 1993.

60. Kemmick (2017).

61. Author's field notes, Crow Agency, Montana, May 1998.

62. Bill Koomsa Jr. to the author, February 1, 1998, and April 11, 1998.

63. Phil "Joe Fish" Dupoint to the author, June 22, 2018; Bill Koomsa Jr. to the author, February 1, 1998, and April 11, 1998.

64. Jeremy Shield to the author, October 18, 2023.

65. Author's field notes, 1998.

66. Bill Koomsa Jr. to the author, April 25, 1998.

67. Bill Koomsa Jr. to the author, November 8, 1997, and January 1, 1998; Jeremy Shield to the author, January 20, 2022. See also Kemmick (2017). The 2021 Crow Senior Handgame Tournament flyer advertised it as the "54th Annual," which may have been the result of two years the tournament was canceled.

68. Kemmick (2017); Phil "Joe Fish" Dupoint to the author, June 22, 2018.

352   NOTES TO PAGES 224–244

69. Bill Koomsa Jr. to the author, November 8, 1997, January 1, 1998, and April 25, 1998; Phil "Joe Fish" Dupoint to the author, June 22, 2018; Mary Beaver to the author, February 3, 2022.

70. Bill Koomsa Jr. to the author, November 8, 1997, January 1, 1998.

71. Author's field notes, Crow Agency, Montana, April 1998.

72. Jeremy Shield to the author, December 2, 2021, and January 20, 2022. Calcutta auctions are named for practices first seen by the British in Calcutta, India. Western rodeos may have influenced this practice.

73. Bill Koomsa Jr. to the author, November 8, 1997.

74. 1998 Crow Senior Handgame Tournament rules and regulations, April 1998.

75. Jeremy Shield to the author, October 18, 2023.

76. Author's field notes, 1993–1998.

77. Bill Koomsa Jr. to the author December 3, 1993; author's field notes, Crow Agency, Montana, April–May 1998.

78. Author's field notes, 1993–2018. Claims of losing one's singing voice, losing the ability to ululate, the appearance of spots, or sudden illness attributed to witchcraft also occur at powwows.

79. In a championship game for $5,600 in prize money and fourteen sticks in a game, each stick would be worth $400.

80. Author's field notes, Crow Agency, Montana, April 1998.

81. Ibid.

82. Ace Yellowhair to the author, July 1, 2005; Jeremy Shield to the author, January 20, 2022.

83. LLBHC (2022b).

84. Bill Koomsa Jr. to the author, February 3, 1993; Phil "Joe Fish" Dupoint to the author, June 22, 2018; Mary Beaver to the author, July 9, 2018. Some Kiowa and Comanche dancers still wear paint around their eyes or on other areas of the body to thwart witchcraft at powwows.

85. Bill Koomsa Jr. to the author, September 18, 1993.

86. Jeremy Shield to the author, January 20, 2022.

87. Ibid.

88. Honoring the memory of Edmund Old Crow, Crow Style Handgame Invitational, https://rdb075.wixsite.com/eocht.

89. Handgame flyers, author's collection. The neighboring Northern Cheyenne also hold several handgame tournaments throughout the year.

90. Mary Beaver to the author, July 9, 2018.

91. Jeremy Shield to the author, January 20, 2022.

92. Ibid.

CHAPTER 5

1. Jackie Ray Yellowhair to the author, July 16, 2004.

2. Jack Yellowhair to the author, May 11, 1998.

3. Author's field notes, November 18, 2004.

4. Jack Yellowhair to the author, May 11, 1998.

5. Mary Beaver to the author, July 31, 2018; Mary Beaver (Hughes 2017).

NOTES TO PAGES 244–257

6. Jack Yellowhair to the author, 1998; Gregory Haumpy to the author, March 24, 1998, and April 2, 1998.

7. Author's field notes, 2018.

8. Author's field notes, 1998–2021.

9. Mary Beaver to the author, July 9, 2018.

10. Author's field notes, 2018.

11. Author's field notes, 2018.

12. Author's field notes, 1998.

13. ADN "Powwows and Handgames" column, 1997–2021.

14. Ibid., September 29, 2000, and December 8, 2000; Jackie Ray Yellowhair to the author, July 16, 2004.

15. Jack Yellowhair to the author, February 7, 1998.

16. Gregory and Marie Yokesuite Haumpy to the author, March 24, 1998.

17. Author's field notes, 1998.

18. CATT (2017).

19. Adam Kaulaity to the author, March 20, 2003.

20. Gregory Haumpy to the author, March 24, 1998.

21. Jed Querdibitty to the author, April 12, 1998.

22. Gregory Haumpy to the author, March 24, 1998.

23. Author's field notes, 2018.

24. Author's field notes, May 17, 1998.

25. Author's field notes, 1998.

26. Adam Kaulaity to the author, March 20, 2003.

27. Jack Yellowhair to the author, May 11, 1998.

28. Gregory and Marie Yokesuite Haumpy to the author, March 24, 1998.

29. Author's field notes, 1998.

30. Author's field notes, May 11, 1998.

31. Author's field notes, 1998, 2018.

32. Ace Yellowhair to the author, July 28, 2004.

33. Phil "Joe Fish" Dupoint to the author, June, 22, 2018.

34. Author's field notes, July 31, 2004.

35. Jackie Ray Yellowhair to the author, July 16, 2004.

36. Ace Yellowhair to the author, July 28, 2004.

37. Mary Beaver to the author, July 9, 2018.

38. Author's field notes, 2004.

39. Author's field notes, 1998.

40. Ibid.

41. In the late 1800s a Gros Ventre handgame team "would commonly be composed chiefly of members who were kin to one another, but non-relatives could also be on the team; the opposing team would likewise be commonly composed chiefly of another kinship group." Among the Gros Ventre, blood relatives could not gamble against one another on any amount and were required to back their own kinsman or kinsmen in bets against other fellow tribesmen or unrelated non-tribal members (Flannery and Cooper 1946, 409).

42. Bill Koomsa Jr. to the author, December 3, 1993.

NOTES TO PAGES 257–278

43. Mary Beaver to the author, July 9, 2018.

44. DD, T-521, 1. "The tournament was played according to Cheyenne rules, which somehow make the games shorter than playing by the southern rules."

45. Eleanor Atauvich McDaniels to the author, July 21, 2023.

46. Phil "Joe Fish" Dupoint to the author, June 22, 2018.

47. Ace Yellowhair to the author, July 28, 2004.

48. Jack Yellowhair to the author, February 9, 1998, April 11, 1998, May 12, 1998; Ace Yellowhair to the author July 28, 2004.

49. Ace Yellowhair to the author, July 28, 2004.

50. Phil "Joe Fish" Dupoint to the author, June 22, 2018.

51. Author's field notes, March 16, 2003.

52. Author's field notes, November 23, 1999.

53. Jack Yellowhair to the author, February 9, 1998.

54. Marie Looking Glass Haumpy to the author, March 24, 1998.

55. Gregory Haumpy to the author, March 24, 1998.

56. Carl Atauvich to the author, March 2, 1998.

57. Author's field notes, April 11, 1998.

58. Author's field notes, 1993–2018.

59. Ibid.

60. Ace Yellowhair to the author, July 28, 2004.

61. Bill Koomsa Jr, to the author, December 3, 2018.

62. Mary Beaver to the author, July 9, 2018.

63. Jack Yellowhair to the author, February 9, 1998.

64. Carl Atauvich to the author, March 2, 1998.

65. Mary Beaver to the author, July 9, 2018.

66. Hamilton (1984); "Powwows and Handgames," ADN, May 18–19, 2002.

67. Author's field notes, November 11, 2017; CATT (2017, 2018).

68. Author's field notes, 2017.

69. Author's field notes, 1998.

70. Gregory Haumpy to the author, April 2, 1998.

71. Ibid.

72. Author's field notes, 2004.

73. Bill Koomsa Jr. to the author, December 3, 1993.

74. Gregory Haumpy to the author, April 2, 1998.

75. Author's field notes, 1998.

76. Ibid.

77. Author's field notes, 1998. This woman reported that the medicine used against her was not at a handgame but occurred after her son and his Cheyenne wife divorced. Her father, a Native American Church member, took her to an Indian doctor who used a sucking method to doctor her four times, the last time getting her to spit up a black substance—that she was ostensibly shot with. Afterward he cedared her, and she had no more pain.

78. Author's field notes, 1998.

79. Ibid.

80. Ibid.

81. Ibid.

NOTES TO PAGES 279–299

82. Ibid.

83. Ibid.

84. Ibid.

85. Ibid.

86. Author's field notes, 2017. To protect this individual's identity, the date of the tournament and type of object he reportedly carries are omitted.

87. Author's field notes, 2004.

88. Author's field notes, May 22, 1998.

89. Author's field notes, 1998.

90. Ibid.

91. Ibid.

92. S. Rep. No. 446, supra note 18, at 8, reprinted in 1988 U.S.C.C.A.N. 3078.

93. S. Rep. No. 446, supra note 18, at 11, reprinted in 1988 U.S.C.C.A.N. 3081. For a discussion of potential contradictions concerning "traditional forms of Indian gaming" and the definition of Class I gaming, see CWAG (1998, 349).

94. Blanchard (1981, 51) describes how Choctaw baseball players developed "an encyclopedic knowledge of . . . each of their regular opponents."

95. Alfred Chalepah to the author, January 23, 1998.

96. Ibid.

97. Author's field notes, 1998.

98. Ibid.

99. Ibid.

100. Carl Atauvich to the author, March 2, 1998.

101. Author's field notes, 1998.

102. Ibid.

103. Author's field notes, February 28, 1998.

104. Author's field notes, 1998.

105. Ibid.

106. Carl Atauvich to the author, March 2, 1998.

107. Ibid.

108. Jackie Ray Yellowhair to the author, November 18, 2004.

109. Mary Beaver (Hughes 2017).

110. Lydia Meat Yellowhair to author, November 19, 2004.

111. Mary Beaver (Hughes 2017).

112. Ace Yellowhair to the author, July 28, 2004.

113. Carla Atauvich to the author, March 2, 1998.

114. Jack Yellowhair to the author, February 9, 1998.

115. Jack Yellowhair to the author, March 18, 2003.

116. Having retired after thirty years with the federal government, Mary undertakes many church activities, watches children, visits and prays with the sick, and works with the Oklahoma City Pow Wow Club.

117. Gregory Haumpy to the author, April 2, 1998.

118. Ace Yellowhair to the author, July 28, 2004.

119. Phil "Joe Fish" Dupoint to the author, June 22, 2018.

356   NOTES TO PAGES 299–313

120. Jackie Ray Yellowhair to the author, July 16, 2004. In my fieldwork in Japan, many Japanese have related how they similarly use karaoke singing as a means to release stress.

121. Brewer (2016).

122. Author's field notes, April 12, 1998.

123. Author's field notes, Apache, Oklahoma, February 7, 1998.

124. "Powwows and Handgames," ADN, October 25, 2002.

125. "Powwows and Handgames," ADN January 23, 1998.

126. Jackie Ray Yellowhair to the author, July 16, 2004.

127. Jackie Ray Yellowhair to the author, July 16, 2004; Ace and Jackie Ray Yellowhair to the author, November 10, 2017; Phil "Joe Fish" Dupoint to the author, June 22, 2018.

128. Author's field notes, February 2, 1998; Phil Dupoint to the author, June 22, 2018.

129. Ace and Jackie Ray Yellowhair to the author, November 10, 2017; Phil "Joe Fish" Dupoint to the author, June 22, 2018. The Apache Tribe of Oklahoma announced their first annual Apache Day, that included handgames, to be held on September 29, 2001. ADN, September 27, 2001.

130. Mary Beaver to the author, July 9, 2018. The 2018 tournament was canceled due to a teacher strike in Oklahoma.

131. Mary Beaver (Hughes 2017).

132. Jeremy Shield to the author, December 2, 2021.

133. Ace and Jackie Ray Yellowhair to the author, November 10, 2017.

134. Author's field notes, February 7, 1998.

135. Ace Yellowhair to the author, July 28, 2004; author's field notes, November 11, 2021.

136. Jack Yellowhair to the author, February 9, 1998.

137. Adam Kaulaity to the author, March 20, 2003.

138. Author's field notes, 1998.

139. Adam Kaulaity to the author March 20, 2003.

140. Phil "Joe Fish" Dupoint to the author, June 22, 2018.

141. Mary Beaver to the author, July 9, 2018.

142. Jack Yellowhair to the author, May 11, 1998.

143. Gregory Haumpy to the author, April 2, 1998.

144. Ibid.

145. Jack Yellowhair to the author, February 9, 1998.

146. Jack Yellowhair to the author, May 11, 1998.

147. Bill Koomsa to the author, December 3, 1993.

148. Carla Atauvich to the author, March 2, 1998.

149. Ace Yellowhair to the author, July 28, 2004.

150. Author's field notes, 1998.

151. Carl and Carla Atauvich to the author, March 2, 1998.

152. Author's field notes, 1998.

153. Jack Yellowhair Sr. to the author, March 18, 2003.

154. Ibid.

155. McDonnell (2017).

CHAPTER 6

1. Author's field notes, November 2017.
2. Jeremy Shield to the author, December 2, 2021.
3. Author's field notes, 2021.
4. Jackie Yellowhair to the author, June 25, 2021.
5. Author's field notes, 2021.
6. Jackie Yellowhair to the author, June 25, 2021.
7. Ibid.
8. McDonnell (2017).
9. Ibid.; Mary Beaver to the author, July 9, 2018.
10. Jack Yellowhair to the author, May 11, 1998.
11. Jack Yellowhair to the author, March 18, 2003.
12. Jackie Ray Yellowhair to the author, June 25, 2021.
13. Ibid.
14. Carl Atauvich to the author, March 2, 1998.
15. Jackie Ray Yellowhair to the author, July 16, 2004.
16. Ina Paddlety Chalepah to the author, May 23, 1998.

REFERENCE LIST

ARCHIVAL AND PRIMARY SOURCES

ADN—*Anadarko Daily News*. Anadarko, Oklahoma.

AMFN—Alice Marriott Fieldnotes. Western History Collections. University of Oklahoma, Norman.

ARCIA—*Annual Report of the Commissioner of Indian Affairs.*

DD—Doris Duke Indian Oral History Collection, University of Oklahoma Libraries, Western History Collections, Norman.

FSA—Fort Sill Archives. Fort Sill National Historic Landmark and Museum, Fort Sill, Oklahoma.

HLS–FSA—Captain Hugh L. Scott Ledgers, Fort Sill Archives, Fort Sill National Historic Landmark and Museum, Fort Sill, Oklahoma.

JMKFN—James Mooney Kiowa Field Notes, MS 2531, vol. 6, National Anthropological Archives, Suitland, Maryland.

RCIA-FRC—Records of the Crow Indian Agency, Federal Records Center, Seattle.

SFN—1935 Santa Fe Laboratory of Anthropology Field Notes—Kiowa. Weston La Barre, William Bascom, Donald Collier, Bernard Mishkin, and Jane Richardson under the direction of Alexander Lesser. Weston La Barre Papers, National Anthropological Archives, Smithsonian Institution, Washington, DC.

WBFN-WHC—William Bittle Papers. Apache Ethnographic Fieldnotes. Western History Collection, University of Oklahoma, Norman.

SECONDARY SOURCES

AAANA (AAA Native Arts) 2012. "Ancient Sla-hal Bones Identified, Also Known as the Bone Game or Stick Game." https://www.ativearts.com/ancient -sla-hal-bones-identified-also-known-as-the-bone-game-or-stick-game.

Aikens, C. Melvin, and David B. Madsen. 1986. "Prehistory of the Eastern Area. " In *Handbook of North American Indians*, vol. 11, *Great B*asin, edited by Warren L. D'azevedo, 149–60. Washington, DC: Smithsonian Institution.

REFERENCE LIST

Albers, Patricia C. 1993. "Symbiosis, Merger, and War: Contrasting Forms of Intertribal Relationship among Historic Plains Indians." In *The Political Economy of North American Indians,* edited by John H. Moore, 94–132. Norman: University of Oklahoma Press.

Archambault, JoAllyn. 2001. "Sun Dance." In *Handbook of North American I ndians,* vol. 13, *Plains,* edited by Raymond J. DeMallie, 983–95. Washington, DC: Smithsonian Institution.

Bailey, Paul. 1957. *Wovoka: The Indian Messiah.* Los Angeles: Westernlore Press.

Baldwin, Gordon C. 1969. *Games of the American Indian.* New York: Grosset and Dunlap.

Bancroft, Hubert H. 1886. *The Native Races.* 5 vols. San Francisco: A. L. Bancroft.

Barnett, Homer G. 1955. *The Coast Salish of British Columbia.* University of Oregon Monographs, Studies in Anthropology 4. Eugene: University of Oregon.

Bassett, Sharity L. 2024. *Haudenosaunee Women Lacrosse Players: Making Meaning Through Rematriation.* East Lansing: Michigan State University Press.

Battey, Thomas C. 1968. *The Life and Adventures of a Quaker among the Indians.* Williamstown, MA: Corner House Publications. Originally published 1876.

Bauerle, Phenocia. 2003. *Way of the Warrior: Stories of the Crow People.* Compiled and translated by Henry Old Coyote and Barney Old Coyote Jr. Lincoln: University of Nebraska Press.

Beatty, John. 1999. "Naishan Dene Creativity with Monsters." *Plains Anthropologist* 44, no. 167: 74–77.

Beauchamp, W. M. 1896. "Iroquois Games." *Journal of American Folklore* 9:269–77.

Berlandier, Jean Louis. 1969. *The Indians of Texas in 1830.* Edited by J. C. Ewers. Washington, DC: Smithsonian Institution Press.

Bittle, William E. 1964. "Six Kiowa Apache Tales." *University of Oklahoma Papers in Anthropology* 5, no. 1, 8–12.

Blaine, Martha Royce. 1982. "The Pawnee-Wichita Visitation Cycle: Historic Manifestations of an Ancient Friendship." In *Pathways to Plains Prehistory: Anthropological Perspectives of Plains Natives and Their Pasts*, edited by Don G. Wyckoff and Jack L. Hofman, 115–34. Duncan, OK: Oklahoma Anthropological Society Memoir 3. Cross Timbers Press.

Blanchard, Kendall. 1979. "Stick Ball and the American Southeast." In *Forms of Play of Native North Americans*, edited by Edward Norbeck and Claire R. Farrer, 189–208. Proceedings of the American Ethnological Society, 1977. St. Paul: West Publishing.

———. 1981. *The Mississippi Choctaws at Play: The Serious Side of Leisure.* Urbana: University of Illinois Press.

———. 1995. *The Anthropology of Sport: An Introduction.* Rev. ed. Westport, CT: Bergin and Garvey.

REFERENCE LIST 361

Boller, Henry A. 1868. *Among the Indians: Eight Years in the Far West, 1858–1866*. Philadelphia.

Boyd, Susan H. 1979. "Stick Games/Hand Games: The Great Divide." In *Forms of Play of Native North American*, edited by Edward Norbeck and Claire R. Farrer, 209–26. Proceedings of the American Ethnological Society, 1977. St. Paul: West Publishing.

Brant, Charles S. 1969. *Jim Whitewolf: The Life of a Kiowa Apache Indian*. New York: Dover Publications.

Brewer, Graham Lee. 2016. "In Oklahoma's Prison System, Native American Inmates Carry on Tradition." *Oklahoman*, December 25, 2016.

Brunton, Bill B. 1974. "The Stick Game in Kutenai Culture." PhD diss., Washington State University.

———. 1998. "The Stick Game." In *Handbook of North American Indians*, vol. 12, *Plateau*, edited by Deward E. Walker Jr., 573–83. Washington, DC: Smithsonian Institution.

Bryan, William L., Jr. 1996. *Montana's Indians: Yesterday and Today*. 2nd ed. Helena, MT: American and World Geographic Publishing.

Catlin, George. 1973. *Letters and Notes on the Manners, Customs, and Conditions of North American Indians, Written during Eight Years' Travel (1832–1839) amongst the Wildest Tribes of Indian in North America*. 2 vols. New York: Dover Publications.

CATT (*Cheyenne and Arapaho Tribal Tribune*). 2017. "2017 State Hand Game Tournament." *Cheyenne and Arapaho Tribal Tribune* 13, no. 11 (June 1, 2017), 5.

———. 2018. "2018 Hand Game Tournament—First Place Winner 'Magic.'" *Cheyenne and Arapaho Tribal Tribune* 14, no. 11, 9.

Chartkoff, Joseph L. 1998. "Gaming Pieces (California)." In *Archaeology of Prehistoric Native America: An Encyclopedia*, edited by Guy Gibbon, 310–11. New York: Garland.

Cheska, Alyce T. 1974. "Ball Game Participation of North American Indian Women." In *Proceedings from the Third Canadian Symposium on the History of Sport and Physical Education*. Halifax: Sport Nova Scotia.

———. 1979. "Native American Games as Strategies of Social Maintenance." In *Forms of Play of Native North Americans*, edited by Edward Norbeck and Claire R. Farrer, 227–47. Proceedings of the American Ethnological Society, 1977. St. Paul: West Publishing.

———. 1982. "Ball Game Participation of North American Indian Women." In *Her Story in Sport: A Historical Anthology of Women in Sports*, edited by Reet Howell, 19–34. West Point, NY: Leisure Press.

Clark, William Philo. 1885. *The Indian Sign Language*. Philadelphia: L. R. Hammersley.

CLCPC (Comanche Language and Culture Preservation Committee). 2010. *Revised Comanche Dictionary*. Lawton, OK: Comanche Nation.

362   REFERENCE LIST

Commons, Rachel S. 1938. "Diversions." In *The Sinkaietk or Southern Okanangon of Washington*, edited by Leslie Spier, 183–94. General Series in Anthropology 6. Menasha, WI: George Banta.

Coues, Elliott. ed. 1893. *History of the Expedition under the Command of Lewis and Clark*. 4 vols. New York: Francis P. Harper, New York.

Crawford, Isabel Alice Hartley. 1998. *Kiowa: A Woman Missionary in Indian Territory*. Lincoln: University of Nebraska Press, Lincoln. Originally published 1915 as *Kiowa: The History of a Blanket Indian Mission*.

Culin, Stewart. 1903. "American Indian Games." *American Anthropologist 5*, 58–64.

———. 1907. *Games of the North American Indians: Twenty-fourth Annual Report of the Bureau of American Ethnology to the Smithsonian Institution, 1902–1903*. Washington, DC: Government Printing Office.

CWAG (Conference of Western Attorneys General). 1998. *American Indian Law Deskbook*. 2nd ed. Julie Wrend and Clay Smith, chief editors. Niwot: University Press of Colorado.

Daniel, Z. T. 1892. "Kansu: A Sioux Game." *American Anthropologist 5*, no. 3, 215.

Denig, Edwin T. 1930. *Indian Tribes of the Upper Missouri*. Edited by J. N. B. Hewitt. 46th Annual Report of the Bureau of American Ethnology, 1928–29.

Densmore, Frances. 1918. *Teton Sioux Music*. Bureau of American Ethnology Bulletin 61. Washington, DC: Smithsonian Institution.

———. 1929. *Pawnee Music*. Bureau of American Ethnology Bulletin 93. Washington, DC: Smithsonian Institution.

———. 1936. *Cheyenne and Arapaho Music*. Southwest Museum Papers 10. Los Angeles: Southwest Museum.

———. 1943. *Music of the Indians of British Columbia*. Bureau of American Ethnology Bulletin 136, Anthropological Papers 27. Washington, DC: Government Printing Office.

Denton, Joan Frederick, and Sanford L. Maudlin Jr. 1987. "Kiowa Murals: Behold I Stand in Good Relation to All Things." *Southwest Art*, July 1987, 68–75.

Desmond, Gerald R. 1952. *Gambling among the Yakima*. Anthropological Series 14. Washington, DC: Catholic University of America Press.

Dockstader, Frederick J. 1957. *The American Indian in Graduate Studies: A Bibliography of Theses and Dissertations*. New York: Museum of the American Indian, Heye Foundation.

Dodge, Richard Irving. 1882. *Our Wild Indians: Thirty-three Years' Personal Experience among the Red Men of the Great West*. Hartford, CT: A. D. Worthington.

———. 1989. *The Plains of North America and Their Inhabitants*. Edited by Wayne R. Kline. Newark: University of Delaware Press. Originally published 1876.

Dorsey, George A. 1901a. "Hand or Guessing Game among the Wichitas." *American Antiquarian* 23:363–70.

REFERENCE LIST

———. 1901b. "Certain Gambling Games of the Klamath Indians." *American Anthropologist*, 3:14–27.

———. 1995. *The Mythology of the Wichita*. Norman: University of Oklahoma Press. Originally published 1904.

Dorsey, George A., and A. L. Kroeber. 1903. *Traditions of the Arapaho*. Field Columbian Museum Anthropological Series 5. Chicago: Field Columbian Museum.

Downey, Allan. 2018. *The Creator's Game: Lacrosse, Identity, and Indigenous Nationhood*. Vancouver: University of British Columbia Press.

Driver, Harold E. 1961. *Indians of North America*. Chicago: University of Chicago Press.

Duff, Wilson. 1952. *The Upper Stalo Indians of the Fraser Valley, British Columbia*. Anthropology in British Columbia, Memoir 1. Victoria, BC: British Columbia Provincial Museum.

Elmendorf, William W. 1960. *The Structure of Twana Culture*. Research Studies, Monograph Supplement 2. Pullman: Washington State University.

Eubank, L. 1945. "Legends of Three Navajo Games." *El Palacio* 52, no. 7 (July 1945): 138–40.

Ewers, John C. 1958. *The Blackfeet: Raiders of the Northwestern Plains*. Norman: University of Oklahoma Press.

Fisher, Donald A. 2002. *Lacrosse: A History of the Game*. Baltimore: Johns Hopkins University Press.

Flannery, Regina, and John M. Cooper. 1946. "Social Mechanisms in Gros Ventre Gambling." *Southwest Journal of Anthropology* 2:391–419.

Flaskerd, G. A. 1961. "The Chippewa or Ojibway Moccasin Game." *Minnesota Archaeologist*, 23, no. 4, 86–94.

Fletcher, Alice C. 1915. *Indian Games and Dances with Native Songs, Arranged from American Indian Ceremonials and Sports*. Boston: C. C. Birchard.

Fletcher, Alice C., and Francis La Flesche. 1893. *A Study of Omaha Indian Music*. Archaeological and Ethnological Papers of the Peabody Museum vol. 1, no. 5. Cambridge, MA: Peabody Museum.

Fogelson, Raymond. 1962. "The Cherokee Ball Game: A Study in Southeastern Ethnology." PhD diss., University of Pennsylvania.

Ford, James. 1979. "Inter-Indian Exchange in the Southwest." In *Handbook of North American Indians*, vol 10., edited by Alfonso Ortiz, 711–22. Washington, DC: Smithsonian Institution.

Foster, Morris W. 1991. *Being Comanche*. Tucson: University of Arizona Press.

Fowler, Don D., and John F. Matley. 1979. *Material Culture of the Numa: The John Wesley Powell Collection, 1867–1880*. Smithsonian Institution of Anthropology 26. Washington, DC: Smithsonian Institution Press.

Fowler, Loretta. 1982. *Arapaho Politics, 1851–1978*. Lincoln: University of Nebraska Press.

———. 1987. *Shared Symbols, Contested Meanings: Gros Ventre Culture and History, 1778–1984*. Ithaca, NY: Cornell University Press.

364   REFERENCE LIST

Fox, Stephen J. 1977. "A Paleoanthropological Approach to Recreation and Sporting Behaviors." In *Studies in the Anthropology of Play*, edited by Phillips Stevens Jr., 65–70. West Point, NY: Leisure Press.

Frey, Rodney. 1987. *The World of the Crow Indians: As Driftwood Lodges.* Norman: University of Oklahoma Press.

———. 2001. "Hand Game: The Native North American Game of Power and Chance" (review). *Wicazo Sa Review* 16, no. 2, 149–53.

Friedl, Ernestine. 1978. "Society and Sex Roles." *Human Nature* 1, no. 4, 68–75.

Gabriel, Kathryn. 1996. *Gambler Way. Indian Gaming in Mythology, History, and Archaeology in North America.* Boulder, CO: Johnson Books.

Gage, Justin. 2020. *We Do Not Want the Gates Closed between Us: Native Networks and the Spread of the Ghost Dance.* Norman: University of Oklahoma Press.

Garcia, Louis. 1996. "Hand Game." In *Encyclopedia of North American Indians*, edited by Frederick E. Hoxie, 228–30. Boston: Houghton Mifflin.

Gelo, Daniel. 1986. "Comanche Belief and Ritual." PhD diss., Rutgers University.

Gmelch, George. 2005. "Baseball Magic." In *Annual Editions in Anthropology, 2005/2006*, edited by Elvio Angeloni, 170–75. New York: McGraw-Hill.

Green, Thomas A. 1979. "Activism in an Agonistic Frame: A Study of Hand Game Symbolism." In *Forms of Play of Native North Americans*, edited by Edward Norbeck and Claire R. Farrer, 267–78. Proceedings of the American Ethnological Society, 1977. St. Paul: West Publishing.

Grinnell, George Bird. 1908. *The Story of the Indian.* New York: D. Appleton.

———. 1923. *The Cheyenne Indians: Their History and Ways of Life.* 2 vols. New Haven, CT: Yale University Press.

Grobsmith, Elizabeth S. 1994. *Indians in Prison: Incarcerated Native Americans in Nebraska.* Lincoln: University of Nebraska.

Hamilton, Angie. 1984. "Indian Handgames Survive Test of Time as Popular Winter Recreation." *Oklahoman*, November 11, 1984. Accessed August 20, 2024. https://www.oklahoman.com/story/news/1984/11/11/indian-handgames -survive-test-of-time-as-popular-winter-recreation/62784191007.

Hanson, Lee K. 1966. *The Hardin Village Site.* Studies in Anthropology 4. Lexington: University of Kentucky Press.

Hargreaves, John. 1982. "Sport, Culture, and Identity." In Sport, Culture, and Identity, Jennifer Hargreaves ed. Rutledge & Kegan Paul, London, England.

Harner, Michael. 1982. *The Way of the Shaman.* New York: Bantam Books.

Hayden, F. V. 1863. "Contributions to the Ethnography and Philology of the Indian Tribes of the Missouri Valley." Transactions of the American Philosophical Society 12:274–320.

Helm, June, Nancy Oestreich Lurie, and Gertrude Prokosch Kurath. 1966. *The Dogrib Hand Game.* Bulletin 205, Anthropological Series 71. Ottawa: National Museum of Canada.

Herzog, George. 1935. "Special Song Types in North American Indian Music." *Zeitschriffur vergleichende Musikwissenschaft* 3, nos. 1–2, 1–11.

REFERENCE LIST

Hough, W. 1888. "Games of Seneca Indians." *American Anthropologist* 1:132–41.

Howard, James H. 1950. "The Omaha Hand Game and Gourd Dance." *Plains Archaeological Conference News Letter* 3:39–42.

———. 1965. *The Ponca Tribe*. Bureau of American Ethnology Bulletin 195. Washington, DC: Government Printing Office.

Hoxie, Frederick E. 1995. *Parading through History: The Making of the Crow Nation in America, 1805–1935*. Cambridge: Cambridge University Press.

Hughes, Art. 2017. "Hand Games." *Native America Calling*, April 14, 2017. Accessed February 28, 2018. https://www.nativeamericacalling.com/friday-april-14-2017-hand-games.

Huizinga, Johan. 1949. *Homo Ludens*. Translated by R. F. C. Hull. London: Routledge and Keegan Paul.

Irving, Washington. 1961. *The Adventures of Captain Bonneville U.S.A., in the Rocky Mountains and the Far West, Digested from His Journal by Washington Irving*. Edited and with an introduction by Edgeley W. Todd. Norman: University of Oklahoma Press. First published 1837.

———. 1964. *Astoria, or Anecdotes of an Enterprise beyond the Rocky Mountains*. Edited by Edgeley W. Todd. Norman: University of Oklahoma Press. First published 1836.

Isaacs, Tony. 1969. Jacket sleeve to *Hand Game of the Kiowa, Kiowa Apache and Comanche*, vol. 1. Indian House Records IH-2501.

Jarvie, Grant. 1991. *Highland Games: The Making of a Myth*. Edinburgh Education and Society Series. Edinburgh: Edinburgh University Press.

Jennings, Jesse D. 1957. *Danger Cave*. University of Utah Anthropological Papers 27. Salt Lake City: University of Utah Press.

———. 1974. *Prehistory of North America*. New York: McGraw-Hill. 2nd ed.

Kavanagh, Thomas W., ed. 2008. *Comanche Ethnography: Field Notes of E. Adamson Hoebel, Waldo R. Wedel, Gustav G. Carlson, and Robert H. Lowie*. Lincoln: University of Nebraska Press.

Kehoe, Alice Beck. 1996. Introduction *to The Pawnee Ghost Dance Hand Game: Ghost Dance Revival and Ethnic Identity*, by Alexander Lesser, ix–xix. Lincoln: University of Nebraska Press.

Kemmick, Ed. 2017. "At Crow Hand-Game Tourney, the Spectacle Rules the Night." *Missoula Current*, April 23, 2017. Accessed January 1, 2018. https://missoulacurrent.com/montana-crow-reservation-hand-games.

Kracht, Benjamin R. 1989. "Kiowa Religion: An Ethnohistorical Analysis of Ritual Symbolism, 1832–1987." PhD diss., Southern Methodist University.

———. 1992. "The Kiowa Ghost Dance, 1894-1916: An Unheralded Revitalization Movement." Ethnohistory 39(4):452-477.

———. 1994. "Kiowa Powwows: Continuity in Ritual Practice." American Indian Quarterly 18(3):321-348.

Kroeber, A. L. 1907. *The Arapaho*, pt. 4, *Religion*. Bulletin of the American Museum of Natural History, vol. 18, pt. 4. New York: American Museum of Natural History.

366 REFERENCE LIST

Lasko, Steven B. 1997. "A Strong and Humble People: An Ethnicity Study of the Apache Tribe of Oklahoma." Master's thesis, University of Oklahoma,.

La Vere, David. 1998. *Life among the Texas Indians*. WPA Narratives. College Station: Texas A&M University Press.

Lesser, Alexander. 1933. *The Pawnee Ghost Dance Hand Game: Ghost Dance Revival and Ethnic Identity*. Columbia University Contributions to Anthropology 16. New York: Columbia University Press.

———. 1996. *The Pawnee Ghost Dance Hand Game: Ghost Dance Revival and Ethnic Identity*. Introduction by Alice Beck Kehoe. Lincoln: University of Nebraska Press.

LLBHC (Library@Little Big Horn College). 2022a. "Aashkaatbaaaaxuahiluua [Hand Game Creek]." Apsáalooke Place Names Database. Accessed January 22, 2022. https://web.archive.org/web/20210921224658/http://lib.lbhc.edu/index.php?q=node/200&a=A.

———. 2022b. "Apsaalooka Clans." Accessed January 22, 2022. https://web.archive.org/web/20210921223340/http://lib.lbhc.edu/index.php?q=node/106.

Lowie, Robert H. 1922. *The Material Culture of the Crow Indians*. Anthropological Papers of the American Museum of Natural History, vol. 1, pt. 3. New York: American Museum of Natural History.

———. 1954. *Indians of the Plains*. Published for the American Museum of Natural History. New York: McGraw-Hill.

———. 1983. *The Crow Indians*. Lincoln: University of Nebraska Press. Originally published 1935.

———. 1993. *Myths and Traditions of the Crow Indians*. Lincoln: University of Nebraska Press. Originally published 1918.

Lucas, J. 1983. "Deerfront in Britain: An Amazing American Long Distance Runner. 1861–1863." *Journal of American Culture*, Fall 1983, 13–19.

MacClancy, Jeremy ed. 1996. *Sport, Identity and Ethnicity*. Oxford, England: Berg Press.

MacFarlan, Allan A. 1958. *Book of American Indian Games*. New York: Association Press.

MacFarlan, Allan and Paulette. 1985. *Handbook of American Indian Games*. Mineola, NY: Dover Publications.

Malinowski, Bronislaw. 1948. *Magic, Science and Religion and Other Essays*. Boston: Beacon Press.

Malotki, Ekkehart. 1978. *Hopitutuwutsi/Hopi Tales: A Bilingual Collection of Hopi Indian Stories*. Flagstaff: Museum of Northern Arizona Press.

Maranda, Lynn. 1984. *Coast Salish Gambling Games*. Mercury Series 93. Ottawa: National Museums of Canada.

Marriott, Alice. 1945. *The Ten Grandmothers*. Norman: University of Oklahoma Press.

Maximilian, Prince of Wied. 1843. *Travels in the Interior of North America, 1832–1834*. Translated from the German, by H. Evans Lloyd. 2 vols. London: Ackerman.

REFERENCE LIST

McAllister, J. Gilbert. 1949. "Kiowa-Apache Tales." In *The Sky Is My Tipi*, edited by Mody C. Boatright, 1–141. Publications of the Texas Folklore Society 22. Dallas: Southern Methodist University Press.

———. 1970. *Dävéko: Kiowa-Apache Medicine Man*. Bulletin of the Texas Memorial Museum, no. 7. Austin: University of Texas.

McDermott, John Francis, ed. 1968. *Tixier's Travels on the Osage Prairies*. Translated by and Albert J. Salvan. Norman: University of Oklahoma Press.

McDonnell, Brandy. 2017. "Native Games: Red Earth Festival Adds Hand Game Tournament." *Oklahoman*, June 4, 2017. Accessed August 20, 2024. https:// www.oklahoman.com/story/entertainment/columns/brandy-mcdonnell /2017/06/04/native-games-red-earth-festival-adds-hand-game-tourna- ment/60595787007.

McFee, Malcolm. 1972. *Modern Montanans: Blackfeet on a Reservation*. New York: Holt, Rinehart, and Winston.

McKenzie, Parker P. 1991. *Kiowa Disyllables*. Mountain View, Okla.: Privately published. Author's copy.

Meadows, William C. 1999. *Kiowa, Apache, and Comanche Military Societies*. Austin: University of Texas Press.

———. 2008. *Kiowa Ethnogeography*. Austin: University of Texas Press.

———. 2010. *Kiowa Military Societies: Ethnohistory and Ritual*. Norman: University of Oklahoma Press.

———. 2015. *Through Indian Sign Language: The Fort Sill Ledgers of Hugh Lennox Scott and Iseeo, 1889–1897*. Norman: University of Oklahoma Press.

Medicine Horse, Mary Helen. 1987. *A Dictionary of Everyday Crow*. Crow Agency, MT: Bilingual Materials Development Center.

Merriam, Alan P. 1955. "The Hand Game of the Flathead Indians." *Journal of American Folklore* 68, no. 269: 313–24.

Miller, Robert J. 2021. "Establishing Economies on Indian Reservations." *Regula- tory Review*, April 8, 2021. Accessed October 20, 2021. https://www.theregre- view.org/2021/04/08/miller-establishing-economies-indian-reservations.

Miller, Wick R. 1972. *Newe Natekwinappeh: Shoshoni Stories and Dictionary*. Anthropological Papers 94. Salt Lake City: University of Utah Press.

Monthly Labor Review. 2019. "American Indians and Alaska Natives in the U.S. Labor Force." November. Accessed October 20, 2021. https://www.bls.gov /opub/mlr/2019/article/american-indians-and-alaska-natives-in-the-u-s-labor -force.htm.

Mooney, James. 1890. "The Cherokee Ball Play." *American Anthropologist* 3:105–32.

———. 1896. "The Ghost Dance Religion and the Sioux Outbreak of 1890." In *Fourteenth Annual Report of the Bureau of American Ethnology, 1892–93*, 641–1110. Washington, DC: Smithsonian Institution Press.

———. 1898. *Calendar History of the Kiowa Indians*. Bureau of American Ethnology Annual Report 17. Washington, DC: Government Printing Office.

368 REFERENCE LIST

———. 1911. "In Kiowa Camps." *Proceedings of the Mississippi Valley Historical Association* 3:43–57.

Moore, John Hartwell. 1996. *The Cheyenne*. Cambridge, MA: Blackwell.

Moulton, Gary E, ed. 1991. *The Journals of the Lewis and Clark Expedition*. 8 vols. Lincoln: University of Nebraska Press.

MSP (Montana State Prison). 2012. "Native American Religious Programming Guidelines." As revised June 8, 2102. Accessed November 25, 2023. https://leg .mt.gov/content/Committees/Interim/2019–2020/State-Tribal-Relations/Meetings/November-2019/STRC-Nov11–2019-Ex2.pdf.

Nabokov, Peter. 1981. *Indian Running*. Santa Barbara, CA: Capra Press.

———. 2007. "Guest Opinion: History Lessons: Requiem for a Round Hall." *Billings Gazette*, June 1, 2010.

NARF (Native American Rights Fund). 2014. "Protections for Native Spiritual Practices in Prison." March. Accessed November 19, 2023. https://www.narf. org/wordpress/wp-content/uploads/2014/12/2014-03-xx-FINAL-Prison-Guide-00041641x9D7F5.pdf.

Neighbors, Robert S. 1852. "The Nauni, or Comanches of Texas." In *Historical and Statistical Information respecting the History, Condition and Prospects of the Indian Tribes of the United States*, edited by Henry H. Schoolcraft, 2:125–34. Philadelphia: Lippincott, Grambo.

Nettl, Bruno. 1967. "Studies in Blackfoot Indian Musical Culture, Part I, Traditional Uses and Functions." *Ethnomusicology* 11, no. 2, 141–60.

Nettl, Bruno, with Stephen Blum. 1968. "Studies in Blackfoot Indian Musical Culture, Part III, Three Genres of Song." *Ethnomusicology* 12, no. 1, 11–48.

Nye, Wilbur S. 1962. *Bad Medicine and Good: Tales of the Kiowas*. Norman: University of Oklahoma Press.

Oxendine, Joseph B. 1988. *American Indian Sports Heritage*. Champaign, IL: Human Kinetics Books.

Parker, Samuel. 1838. *Journal of an Exploring Tour beyond the Rocky Mountains*. Ithaca, NY: S. Parker.

Parsons, Elsie Clews. 1929. *Kiowa Tales*. Memoirs of the American Folk-Lore Society 22. New York: American Folk-lore Society/G. E. Stechert.

Peavy, Linda, and Ursula Smith. 2014. *Full Court Quest: The Girls from Fort Shaw, Indian School Basketball Champions of the World*. New York: Oxford University Press.

Powers, William K. 1973. *Indians of the Northern Plains*. New York: Capricorn Books. Originally published 1969.

Randle, Martha C. 1953. "A Shoshone Hand Game Gambling Song." *Journal of American Folklore* 66, no. 260, 155–59.

Rathbun, Bill. 1992. *Handgame!* Berkeley: Yerba Buena Press.

———. 2000. *Whatever Happened to Professor Coyote? A Journey to the Heart of the Handgame*. Berkeley: Yerba Buena Press.

REFERENCE LIST

Richardson, Rupert N. 1996. *The Comanche Barrier to South Plains Settlement.* Austin, TX: Eakin Press, Austin, TX. Originally published 1933.

Riordan, James. 1977. *Sport in Soviet Society: Development of Sport and Physical Education in Russia and the USSR.* Cambridge: Cambridge University Press.

Ritzenthaler, Robert E., and Pat Ritzenthaler. 1991. *The Woodland Indians of the Western Great Lakes.* Prospect Heights, IL: Waveland Press.

Roberts, Chris. 1992. *Powwow Country.* Helena, MT: American & World Geographic Publishing.

Roberts, John M., Malcolm J. Arth, and Robert R. Bush. 1959. "Games in Culture." *American Anthropologist* 61, no. 4, 597–605.

Robinson, Lila Wistrand, and James Armagost. 1990. *Comanche Dictionary and Grammar.* Publications in Linguistics Publication 92. Arlington: Summer Institute of Linguistics and the University of Texas at Arlington.

Ruxton, George Frederick. 1951. *Life in the Far West.* Edited by Leroy R. Hafen. Norman: University of Oklahoma Press. First published 1848.

Sack, Allen. 1977. "Sport: Work or Play?" In *Studies in the Anthropology of Play*, edited by Phillips Stevens Jr., 186–95. West Point, NY: Leisure Press.

Salamone, Frank A. 2012. *The Native American Identity in Sports.* Lanham, MD: Scarecrow Press.

Saum, Lewis O. 1965. *The Fur Trader and the Indian.* Seattle: University of Washington Press.

Schweinfurth, Kay Parker. 2002. *Prayer on Top of the Earth: The Spiritual Universe of the Plains Apache.* Boulder: University Press of Colorado.

Seattle Times. 2012. "Tribal Gathering Celebrates Unifying Culture of an Ancient Game." May 5, 2012.

Shimkin, Demitri B. 1986. "Eastern Shoshone." In *Handbook of North American Indians*, vol. 11, *Great Basin*, edited by Warren L. d'Azevedo, 308–35. Washington, DC: Smithsonian Institution.

Skinner, B. F. 1938. *Behavior of Organisms: An Experimental Analysis.* New York: D. Appleton-Century.

———. 1953. *Science and Human Behavior.* New York: Macmillan.

Slotkin, James S. 1975. *The Peyote Religion: A Study in Indian-White Relations.* New York: Octagon Books. Originally published 1956.

Southwell, Kristina L., and John R. Lovett. 2010. *Life at the Kiowa, Comanche, and Wichita Agency: The Photographs of Annette Ross Hume.* Norman: University of Oklahoma Press.

Stevenson, M. C. 1903. "Zuni Games." *American Anthropologist* 5:691–702.

Stuart, Wendy Boss. 1972. *Gambling Music of the Coast Salish Indians.* Mercury Series 3. Ottawa: Ethnology Division, National Museum of Man, National Museums of Canada.

Suttles, Wayne. 1955. *Katzie Ethnographic Notes.* Anthropology in British Columbia, Memoir 2. Victoria, BC: British Columbia Provincial Museum.

Swanton, John R. 1946. *The Indians of the Southeastern United States*. Smithsonian Institution, Bureau of American Ethnology Bulletin 137. Washington, DC: Government Printing Office.

Thompson, David. 1916. *David Thompson's Narrative of His Explorations in Western America, 1784–1812*. Edited by J. B. Tyrrell. Champlain Society Publications, 12. Toronto: Champlain Society.

Thwaites, Reuben Gold, ed. 1966. *Early Western Travels, 1748–1846*. 32 vols. New York: AMS Press.

Todd, Edgeley W. 1982. "Benjamin L. E. Bonneville." In Mountain Men and Fur Traders of the Far West, edited by Leroy R. Hafen, 272–90. Lincoln: University of Nebraska Press.

Tsong, Nicole. 2010. "Traditional Game Unites Tribes." *Seattle Times*, August 21, 2010. Accessed August 20, 2024. https://www.seattletimes.com/seattle-news/traditional-game-unites-tribes.

Utter, Jack. 1993. *American Indians: Answers to Today's Questions*. Lake Ann, MI: National Woodlands Publishing.

Van de Logt, Mark. 2010. *War Party in Blue: Pawnee Scouts in the U.S. Army*. Norman: University of Oklahoma Press.

Vennum, Thomas, Jr. 1994. *American Indian Lacrosse: Little Brother of War*. Washington, DC: Smithsonian Institution Press.

———. 2007. *Lacrosse Legends of the First Americans*. Baltimore: Johns Hopkins University Press.

Vibert, Elizabeth. 1997. *Trader's Tales: Narratives of Cultural Encounters in the Columbian Plateau, 1807–1846*. Norman: University of Oklahoma Press.

Voget, Fred W. 2001. "Crow." In *Handbook of North American Indians*, vol. 13, pt. 2, *Plains*, edited by Raymond J. DeMallie, 695–717. Washington, DC: Smithsonian Institution.

Walker, James R. 1982. *Lakota Society*. Edited by Raymond J. DeMallie. Lincoln: University of Nebraska Press.

Wallace, Ernest, and E. Adamson Hoebel. 1952. *The Comanches: Lords of the South Plains*. Norman: University of Oklahoma Press.

Wayland, Virginia, Harold Wayland, and Alan Ferg. 2004. "'The Indians Also Have a Game Somewhat Similar to Cards': Native American Cards of French and English Derivation." *American Indian Art* 29, no. 3, 54–63.

Weltfish, Gene. 1965. *The Lost Universe: Pawnee Life and Culture*. Lincoln: University of Nebraska Press.

Wheeler, R. W. 1979. *Jim Thorpe: World's Greatest Athlete*. Norman: University of Oklahoma Press.

Wikipedia. 2017. "Handgame." Accessed 11/27/2017. http://en.wikipedia.org/wiki/Handgame.

Winters, Howard D. 1969. *The Riverton Culture: A Second Millennium Occupation in the Central Wabash Valley*. Reports of Investigations 13. Springfield: Illinois State Museum.

REFERENCE LIST

Wislizenus, Frederick A. 1912. *A Journey to the Rocky Mountains in the Year 1839*. St. Louis: Missouri Historical Society. Originally published as *Ein Ausflug nach den Felsen-Gebirgen in Jahre* 1839 (St. Louis, 1840).

Wissler, Clark. 1911. *The Social Life of the Blackfoot Indians*. Anthropological Papers of the American Museum of Natural History 7, pt. 1. New York: The Trustees.

———. 1913. *Societies and Dance Associations of the Blackfoot Indians*. Anthropological Papers of the American Museum of Natural History 11, pt. 4. New York: The Trustees.

———. 1955. *The Horse in Blackfoot Indian Culture*. Bureau of American Ethnology Bulletin 159. Washington, DC: Smithsonian Institution.

Wissler, Clark, and D. C. Duvall. 1908. *Mythology of the Blackfoot Indians*. Anthropological Papers of the American Museum of Natural History vol. 2, pt. 1. New York: The Trustees.

Wycoff, Lydia, ed. 1996. *Visions and Voices: Native American Painting from the Philbrook Museum of Art*. Tulsa: Philbrook Museum of Art.

Wyeth, Nathaniel J. 1899. *The Correspondence and Journals of Captain Nathaniel J. Wyeth, 1831–6*. Edited by F. G. Young. Sources of the History of Oregon, vol. 1. Eugene: University Press.

Young, Gloria A., and Eric D. Gooding. 2001. "Celebrations and Giveaways." In *Handbook of North American Indians*, vol. 13, pt. 2, *Plains*, edited by Raymond J. DeMallie, 1011–25. Washington, DC: Smithsonian Institution.

Zogry, Michael J. 2010. *Anetso, the Cherokee Ball Game: At the Center of Ceremony and Identity*. Chapel Hill: University of North Carolina Press.

Zo-Tom. 1969. *1877: Plains Indian Sketch Books of Zo-Tom and Howling Wolf*. With an introduction by Dorothy Dunn. Flagstaff, AZ: Northland Press.

VIDEOS

Johnson, Lawrence. 2001. *Hand Game: The Native North American Game of Power and Chance*. Portland, OR: Lawrence Johnson Productions.

Kernan, Sean. 2016. *Crow Stories: Time on the Reservation*. Accessed August 27, 2023. https://www.youtube.com/watch?v=_UqT8CdH0iE.

AUDIO RECORDINGS

Collections of several tribal handgame and stickgame songs are available on commercial cassettes from Canyon Records in Phoenix and Indian House Records in Taos, New Mexico. Other sources are available on the internet.

Canyon Records

Antiste, Mary. *Flathead Stick Game Songs*. CR-8017.
Big Spring and Runner. *Blackfeet Hand Game Songs*. CR-6188.
Trejo, Judy. *Stick Games of the Paiute*. CR-6284.
Washington, Joe. *Lummi Stick Game Songs*. CR-6124.

INDEX

sticks, 117; Crow handgame, 239, 254; enjoyment, 176, 295, 298; Kiowa guesser, 168; memorial handgame, 306; new style of play, 123; philosophy, 309; programs, 304–305; singing styles, 135–136; sportsmanship, 309; teamwork, 296; therapeutic qualities, 298; tournaments, 147, 327, 329; types handgame, 143

Beaver, Myron (Kiowa/Caddo), 147

betting. *See* handgame

Big Bow (Kiowa), 31

Big Shoulder Blade, Jim (Crow), 223, 230

Billy Goat Hill, (handgame site of Thurman Kadayso, Apache, near Boone, OK), 124, 149, 257, 259–60

Bison Bull Coming Out (Pá ujépjè, Kiowa). *See* Keeps His Name a Long Time (Já udèka͞u).

Bittle, William, (anthropologist): Apache handgame, 84–87, origin accounts, 84–85, 87; rules, 86–87; songs, 133

Blackbear, Ray (Plains Apache): handgame, 85–86, 87

Bon Jovi, musical group, 262

bone game. *See* stickgame

Bone Hog, 273, 335

Botone, Moses (Kiowa), 185

Boyiddle, Parker (Kiowa): mural painting, 65

Breaks Something (Comanche), 40–41

Buffalomeat, LaVerne (Cheyenne), 306

Buzzard Creek Three, 305–306

Calumet Ceremony: adoption, 295

Camp 7: Comanche community of, 259; handgame team, 83, 160, 260–61, 290, 325

Captain Kosope (Plains Apache), 89; Arapaho, 39; card games, 36, 344n105; 345n108; Comanche, 52;

gambling on, 39, 105–111, 113–114, gaming classification of, 287; Yakama, 36. *See also* Monte

Carnegie Roadrunners (handgame team), 124, 257, 260–61

Chaddlesone, Sherman (Kiowa): handgame painting, 58; handgame origin account, 54; Parker Boyiddle mural painting, 65

Chalepah, Ace (Plains Apache), 136, 261, 263; handgame song, 134

Chalepah, Alfred (Plains Apache), Apache handgame 88–90; arrests for gambling, 113; awl (stick) game, 344n95; cards, 345n108; enjoyment, 157–58; father's play, 101, 344n90; handgame medicine, 103; hand motions, 157–58; hiding, 288; Sam Klinekole, 100; locations, 88–89; origin accounts, 339n1, 342n66; Plains Apache handgame, 88, participation, 88, 113; social gatherings, 104; sense of humor, 158; singing, 134, 138, 195–96; spirit 157–58; taboos, 88; taunting, 157–58; tells, 288; tongue pointing, 162

Chalepah, Alonzo I (Plains Apache): handgame medicine, 101–103; handgame song, 134, 344n89

Chalepah, Alonzo II (Plains Apache), 103

Chalepah, Ina Paddlety (Kiowa): Crow influences, 195; family participation, 242; first handgame, 115; location, 263; medicine and sleight of hand, 177–78; philosophy, 333; rattles, 127; songs, 131–32

Chaletsin, Apache Ben (Plains Apache), 60

Chaletsin, Rose Chalepah (Plains Apache), 86–87, 133

Challengers (handgame team), 257, 259–60

Chasenah, Ken (Comanche), 154

INDEX

Chekovi, Frank (Comanche), 83

Cheyenne Indians handgame, 116–18; changes, 313; Cheyenne and Arapaho Handgame Committee, 304;; locations, 118; name, 116; pointing sticks, 117–18; religious association, 117; split finger guessing, 117; Sun Dance, 118, women, 347n49

Christian missionaries: accounts of, 46; cultural suppression of, 104, 108, 111–13

Clovis points: and possible stickgame set, 24

Coast Salish handgame, 32–35, 36, 50, ethnicity, 330; songs, 33, 127

Comanche Indians handgame: 79–84; betting, 79–84; cedaring, 278, 354n77; Christmas encampment, 84; counters, 80–82; dice, 40–41; early accounts, 79–81; gender roles, 83; locations, 115–16; medicine, 94; name, 79; popularity, 81; reservation era, 103–104; rules, 80–82; songs, 133; term for medicine, 94; terminology, 91–92. *See also* Kiowa handgame; Plains Apache handgame

community: sense of among handgame players and teams, 7, 139, 255, 284, 295, 321, 324

Coeur d'Alene Indians: stickgame, 25

Covid-19: impacts of, 256, 321–22

Crawford, Isabel (missionary), 108

Crow handgame, 105, 143, 185–240; adoption, 189, 201–202; bets, 203; box socials, 203; changes, 237–40; cheating in, 218; clans, 189–90, 202, 203, 207–209, 221–23, 227, 236–37; clan games, 236–37; competitiveness, 205, 240; Crow versus Lakota, 27–28; counting coups, 201; districts, 187, 201–205, 222, 223–24, 232; dress, 320; entry fee, 225–26; ethnic maintenance, 240; first point, 214–15; ghosts, 199, 204, 212, 225,

240; guessing, 206, 218–22; 234–36; hand motions, 211–15, 219–22, 233; junior handgame tournament, 203–204, 222–25; hiding, 215–18, 232–34; joking clans, 22; match games, 194, 203, 209, 214, 218, 222, 237; medicine, 200, 206–12, 232–34; medicine men, 212–214; modern handgame, 201–202; Oklahoma team, 231–32; original game 198–201; "outfitting them," 201–202; pipes, 200; prizes, 225–26; protective medicine, 210; purchase, 208–209; recent changes, 237–40; relationship with Kiowa, 185–98, 320; roundhouse, 203, 224, 225, 237; ; rules, 226–31; senior handgame tournament, 203–204, 222–25, 228–30, 238–39; singing, 206, sponsorship, 244–46; sportsmanship, 199, 238, 240; style of play, 205–206; tells in hiding, 216; tournament rules, 228–30, 238–39; tournaments, 204, 228–30, 238–39; types of handgames, 202–204; women's roles, 191, 200, 205–206, 210, 212–15, 217, 220, 221, 223, 227–28, 233

Culin, Stewart: classifications of Native games, 11, 12, 18; ethnography, 5–6, 19, 45–47; sign language in handgame, 22

culture areas: North American, 20

Danger Cave, Utah, 23

Daveko (Plains Apache): 95–101; Kiowa name of, 95; power of, 95; versus Cheyenne, 97–99; versus Kiowa, 95

dice, 14, 18, 49, 51; archaeological finds, 23; Cherokee and Choctaw, 106; Comanche, 40–41; game of chance, 11–12; Piegan, 23

Dicke, Sam (Cheyenne), 117

Dodge, Col. Richard I.: accounts of handgames, 37, 39, 42, 80, 106–108

Dogrib stickgame, 17, 32–34; betting, 45, 106; study of, 50

Domebo, Bertha (Sànémằ or Snake Woman, Kiowa), 168

Dupoint, Phil R. "Joe Fish" (Kiowa), 253; Bad Medicine Team, 259–60, 262; Bon Jovi, 262; Halloween handgame, 264; handgame music, 299, 308, 347n28; handgame origins, 340n20; handgame programs, 304; hosting Crow, 197; playing the Crow, 219, 320; putting horns on, 264–65; trading songs, 138, 196

enjoyment / favorite part of handgame. *See* individuals by name

ethnic identity / maintenance. *See* handgame; Kiowa handgame

Evarts, Mark (Pawnee), 78

Farmer, Randy (Colville): tournament sponsor, 273, 299–300; therapeutic qualities, 300

First Americans Museum: virtual handgame, 322

Flathead handgame, 31, 36, 51–53; noted gamblers, 278; style, 314, 321–22; versus Gros Ventre, 105

free-for-alls, 3, 135, 248–252, 256–257, 270; betting in 252, 255, 287–88; benefit, 153; characteristics, 142–45, 168; cheating, 178; Crow, 236; decline in 144–45, 149, 178, 246–47, 269; definition of 243, 335; hiding and guessing in, 162–64, 168–69, 248, 293; Shady Front, 263–64; strategy, 173

fictive kinship, 295. *See also* adoptions

Flathead handgame, 31, 36, 52–53, 105, 278, 314, 321–22

Fort Ancient Culture, 24

Frizzlehead II (E-mau-ta—Èmáuthââ̰ or Arising Crying, Kiowa): birth, 343n84; hiding, 69; songs, 78;

Tape-deah, 94–95; teams and leaders, 65

gambling, Native American: addiction, 36–41, 106; archaeological evidence, 23–24; card games, 39, 106, 107–11, 344n105, 345n108; grass lease payments, 52, 107–109; controlled wagering, 42–45; horse racing, 30, 35, 52, 93, 104, 106, 287, monte, 52, 101, 104, 107–10, 344n105; role of, 37–42; Native and Euro views, 3, 40, 42

Gang (handgame team), 261, 307

Ghost Dance handgame: Arapaho, 119; ethnography, 5, 20–21; new cultural form, 22, 94; Otoe, 105; Pawnee, 47–50; traditional activity, 113; Wichita, 337n1, Wovoka, 338n14

Gourd Dance: 114, 240, 247; bandoliers, 208; benefit dances, 153; crowd, 295, 332; Kiowa Gourd Can, 120; prisons, 302; rattles, 126; songs, 130, 136, 139, 141, 311; spirit, 310

Gros Ventre handgame, 16, 31, 353n41; decline of gambling, 106; gambling, 30, 37, 50, 51, 105; gambling power, 93, 252–53, 343n80; identity 7; songs, 131; spirit, 310–11; team composition, 353n41

Given, Frank (Kiowa—Plains Apache): family descent, 339n3; guessing, 278; medicine, 278; water monster story, 57

handgame, Native American: aboriginal distribution of, 13, 19–21; archaeological evidence of, 23–24; betting, 37–46; categorization of, 6, 11–13, 288; changes in music, 136–39; cheating in, 34, 271, 279–80, 286, 292–94, 345n108; conflict, 329–30; culture camps,

305; distribution of, 19–21; early accounts of, 28–32, 38–45; enjoyment, 38; ethnic identity, 34, 250–51, 323–25; ethnographic studies of, 5–8, 45–53; family and kinship, 44, 125, 139, 182–86, 193, 197, 201, 209, 212, 232, 237 240, 244–45, 252, 254, 256–63, 280–81, 284, 292, 295–97, 300–303, 306, 312–13, 318, 326; films, 52–53; gambling on, 27, 28, 37–45; guessing and hiding strategies, 288–95; guessing styles, 17–19; hand drums, 1, 18, 32, 36, 67–68, 77; "handgame fix," 256, 336; hiding,14–18; hiding implements, 16–17; historical accounts of, 28–32; ghosts, 26–27, 46, 47, 103, 199, 204, 212, 225, 240; kick stick, 24, 32, 337n4; mathematical odds in, 1, 177, 275, 290, 319; match games, 142–43, 145–46, 149, 178, 190, 194, 203, 209, 214, 218, 222, 237, 246, 251, 254, 256–57; medicine in, 6, 7, 10, 29, 33; medicine man, 29, 33, 51, 74, 93; memorials,139, 306; memorization, 33–34, 155, 174–75, 288, 291, 319; military societies, 30; music of, 50–51, 127–39, mythological accounts, 23–28, 38–39, 43, 48–49, 54–62, 198, 339n3, 339n5; names of, 14; new players, 290–91; non-Indians playing, 314–19; object in play, 17–18; oral traditions of, 24–28; origins and longevity of, 23–24; outside Influences, 106–10; overview of, 14–19; paintings, 340n20; popularity, 14, 41, 111, 330–33; prisons, 300–302; prizes, 148; programs, 304–05; public school programs, 304–305; round robin tournaments, 9, 36–37, 145–53, 269–73; rules in, 1–2; scalps as bets, Blackfoot, 27; scalps as bets, Crow, 28; scoring sticks, 12, 16–18,

24–26, 28, 32, 50–51; seasonality of, 14–16; sex and gender, 16; sign language, 21–22; spirit, 1–2, 77, 105, 134, 154, 157–58, 211, 213, 295, 299, 309–11, 328; sportsmanship, 39, 49; strategy in, 13, 33, 35; taboos associated with, 14–16, 266; technology and media, 320–321; tells in hiding, 173, 216; terminology associated with, 335–36; therapeutic qualities, 297–300; types of, 14–19; uses of, 14; warfare analogies, 31, 48, 49, 78, 90–94, 108, 200–201, 216, 278, 281–82, 323; women's roles, 16, 31, 37–38, 328–29. *See also* stickgame; Crow handgame; Kiowa handgame; Comanche handgame; Plains Apache handgame

Harragarra, Delores Toyebo (Kiowa), 114

Haskell Indian Nations University: collegiate handgames, 305; Missouri State University handgames, 314

Haumpy (Haun-py, Kiowa): doctoring and power, 94; gambling, 109; location, 115

Haumpy, Bruce (Kiowa), 115, 122, 142, 243–244, 307; influence on game, 125, 145; team of 253, 259–60; trip to play Crows, 186, 193

Haumpy, Gregory (Kiowa), 58; Bull Durham story, 116; cheating stories, 178–79; childhood games, 179; Crow handgames, 192, 275; drinking, 182; entry fees, 148; favorite part, 271; hand motions, 309; hiding, 162–63; match games, 142; medicine man, 75, 94, 274; new style of play, 248; old style of play, 116, 122; picking a guesser, 76; round robin tournaments, 145; shift to handgame, 244; singing, 134, 136; skill, 175–76; song, 132; sponsorship, 244, 251–52; taboos, 266; teams, 259–61;

INDEX

therapeutic qualities of handgame, 298; tobacco, 115–16

Haumpy, Marie Lookingglass (Comanche): alcohol, 183; betting, 190; Christmas handgames, 84, 115; Comanche games, 115; Crow visits, 188–90; enjoyment, 188–89; handgame hangover 189; hiding, 179; powwows, 247; taboos, 266; tongue pointing, 163; tournament sponsors, 251–52

HeapoBirds, Alfrich (Cheyenne), 118

Horse, Cecil (Kiowa): betting, 40, 104, 107, 111–12; cards, 109; cheating, 70–71; disputes, 177; gambling, 109; guessing 69; horse racing, 109; inter-community play, 65; lodges, 64; teams, 68

Horse, Jenny Haumpy (Kiowa), 40, 70, 121; betting, 79, 104, 113; cards, 109; cheating in handgame, 72, 345n108; missionaries, 113

Hunt, George (Kiowa): cheating, 70; rules, 73–74; songs, 70

Indian Gaming Regulatory Act of 1988 (IGRA), 53, 323; classes of, 287; history of, 286–88

Indian police, 108–11, 113

"Indian time," 225–226, 249

Isaacs, Tony: handgame recordings, 123–24, 137; handgame teams, 257

Iseeo (Kiowa): horse racing medicine, 109

Jennings, Vanessa (Kiowa / Plains Apache), xiii, 121

Kadayso, Thurman (Plains Apache), 257, team, 259–60

Kaulaity, Adam (Kiowa): bets, 251; bingo, 139; match games, 142; old style of play, 125, 145, 248, 307; strategy, 180–81; team, 261;

tournaments,145; versus Apaches, 308; versus Crows, 186–87

Kauley, Ernestine Kauahquo (Kiowa): missionaries, 113

Kaulaity, Tom (Kiowa), 261; guessing four hiders, 219

KCA (Kiowa-Comanche-Apache): acronym, xi, 5–6; handgame team, 136; song, 136–37

Keeps His Name a Long Time (Já udèkáu, Kiowa), also Known as Bison Bull Coming Out (Pá ujépjè), 95–96, 343n85

Keres Pueblo, 31

Kiowa Indians: Armistice Day encampments, 114, 120, 185, 197; awl/stickgame, 106, 344n95; cedaring, 278, 280–81; Christians and traditionalists, 104, 112–13; Christmas encampment, 108; Fourth of July, 108–109, 114; Kiowa Gourd Can, 120; horseracing medicine, 109; Séndé, 54–55; Underwater Monster, 58

Kiowa handgame: anger and jealousy, 284–86; awards, 148, 150, 245, 272, 306, 331; benefit handgames, 153–54; betting, 251–56; 277–78; betting types, 143, 155–59; breaking their horns, 274, 307, 335; calendar entry, 95–96; chance principle, 77; changes, 88, 90, 123–24, 136–39, 162–64, 184, 248–50, 266–70; 309, 319–23; cheating, 68–72, 92, 162, 177–81, 292–95; 345n108; classification, 13; coin guessing, 152, 163; conflict 329–30; costs, 139, 148, 322–23; Covid-19, 321–22; crowd composition, 247; diagram, 66; economic shifts, 93–94, 105–106, 322–23; equipment, 65–67; ethnic identity and maintenance, 250–51, 323–25; facilities 139–40; fights, 285; first point, 68–69; floor bets,

INDEX 379

157–58; Fort Sill, 105; free-for-alls, 143–45; gambling medicine, 94; gambling term, 4; gender roles, 266–69, 328–29; guesser, 75–76; guessing, 72–75, 162–63, 168–72; hand drums and drumsticks, 67–68, 125–26; handgame people, 326; hand motions, 70, 75, 145, 169–70, 249, 274, 275–76, 309–10; harmful medicine, 278–80; hiding, 69, 169–70; hiding implements, 161–62; historic accounts, 62–63; holidays and special events, 114, 246, 263, 302–303, 310, 324–25; humor, 116, 130, 133, 136–37, 147, 158, 297, 310; Indian agency suppression, 104–11; Kiowa-Crow association, 185–240; locations, 115–18, 245–47, 263–64; master of ceremonies, 160–61; match games, 142–43; meals and concessions, 141; medicine, 90–103, 271–78; medicine man, 75, 165, 168; music and singing, 77–78, 128–39, 158, 311–12; name of, 4, 62; new cultural forms, 94; new style of play, 6, 122–23; newspaper column, 320; observation skills, 172–77; officials, 68, 159–60; old style of play (4-4-4), 66–69, 73, 116, 121–25, 149, 159, 195, 248, 293, 307; origins, 23, 54–58; paintings, 58, 65–67, 340n20; popularity, 330–33; "Powwows and Handgames" news column, 320; protective medicine, 103, 280–84; public contests, 94–101; public school teams, 304–305; putting horns on, 75–76, 87, 264, 265, 336; rattles, 126–27; reservation era, 103–104; round robin tournaments, 145–48; scoring, 76–77, 331; scoring examples, 165–67; scoring racks, 122, 156, 163–67; scoring sticks, 65–69, 73, 77; season, 269–70; seating arrangement, 66, 125; social

functions, 295–97; social identity, 326–28; Southern / Oklahoma Style handgame, 6,122–23; sponsorship, 139–42, 244–46, 299–300, 319, 327, 330; sportsmanship, 165, 222, 285, 325, 332; starting song, 68–69, 77, 78, 129; strategy, 169–70, 288–95; success (factors of), 141, 306–14; summer play, 114; supplemental income, 251–56; suppression of 104–14; table bets, 155–57; team formation and composition, 64–65, 154–55, 256–59; taboos, 266; team names, 259–63; teamwork, 295–97; technology and media, 320–321; tells in hiding, 173; term for medicine, 94; terminology, 91–92; therapeutic qualities, 297–300, 313; tongue pointing, 145, 146, 162–63, 170, 206; tournament entry fees, 158–59; tournaments, 3, 9, 137, 139, 142, 145, 146–54, 158–84, 246–56; two-finger guessing (Lazy-V), 163, 229; types of handgames, 142–48, 153–54; vision quest, 90, 93; witchcraft and sorcery, beliefs in, 70, 103, 109, 278, 352n78, n.84; women's roles, 248, 266–69, 271, 285, 299, 302, 307, 309, 329, 344n95; youth participation, 241–42, 303–305, 327. *See also* Comanche handgame; Crow handgame; Plains Apache handgame

Kiowa Casino-Devel, Oklahoma, handgame tournament of, 58, 247, 251, 270

Kiowa Casino-Verden, Oklahoma, handgame tournament of, 247, 270–72

Kiowa-Apache. *See* Plains Apache handgame

Kipp, Woody (Blackfeet), 131

Klinekole, Sam (Plains Apache), 89, hiding of, 100; 344n90

380 INDEX

Knows His Gun, Derek (Northern Cheyenne), 299

Koomsa, Bill Jr. (Kiowa), 236; adoption, 189; cheating, 178; Crow influences, 138; Crow style, 216; enjoyment, 311; favorite aspects, 311; fundraising, 154; giveaway, 193; guesser, 76; handgame decline and revival, 114–15; handgame origins, 54; hand motions, 170–71; hosting Crows, 193, 197, 275; match games, 142; Montana trips, 186; new style of play, 121–23; Oklahoma State Handgame Tournament, 149; old style of play, 121–23; putting horns on, 76; rattles, 127; seasonal play, 54; singing of, 232; songs, 129–31, 135, 196, 311; structures, 120–21; tournaments, 145, 147; Wild Bunch, 257, 262, 296; winning songs, 135; women hiders, 267

Koomsa, Bill Sr. (Kiowa), 8, 121, 142, 243; Carnegie Eagles, 257, 259–60; Oklahoma / Southern Style of play, 122, 145; origins of Kiowa handgame, 54; Oklahoma State Handgame Tournament, 149, 269

Koomsa, Bob (Kiowa), 121; racehorse, 109

lacrosse, 23; ethnography on, 45–46, 282; ethnic maintenance, 324; witchcraft and sorcery in, 278

Lefthand, Ira, (Crow), 223, 230

legerdemain. See sleight of hand; handgame; Kiowa handgame; Plains Apache handgame

Lesser, Alexander (anthropologist): betting, 37–38; chance principal, 77, 341n46, 342n47; ethnography 5, 46–50, 64; handgame, 11, 14; Pawnee, 31; Pawnee Ghost Dance handgame, 47–50, 94; Pawnee-Kiowa game 64, 78; reclassification 46; variations,

18–19, 22–23, 46; warfare analogy, 48; Wichita handgame, 337n1

Lincoln, Myrtle (Arapaho), 118–19

Little Light, Ed "Buck Day" (Crow), 9, 154, 158, 189, 193, 224; Crow senior tournament, 223, 230; gambling, 226; handgame medicine, 208; playing, 211, 218, strategy, 219

Little Monkeys (handgame team), 263, 329

Longhat, Eddie (Delaware): coin guessing, 163; guesser, 154; humor, 144; tongue pointing, 163; two-finger guessing, 163; strategy, 175

Magic (handgame team), 257–59, 261

Mah-kah-nas-sy (Comanche), 115

Maker, Katherine (Osage): handgame, 338n7

match games, 145, 155; characteristics, 142–43; Crow, 203, 214, 218, 222; decline, 146, 184

McAllister, Dr. Gilbert J. (anthropologist): Apache handgame, 56–62, 65, 84, 96–97, 101, 344n89–90

McKenzie, Parker P. (Kiowa): early 1900s, 113; Kiowa gambling term, 4; mid-twentieth century, 114

medicine / power. See handgame; Kiowa handgame

Missouri State University handgames: student experiences, 314–18

moccasin game: age, 23, 338n8; classification, 11–14; comparison of, 80; distribution of, 13, 19, 21, 29, 31, 338n11; gambling on, 110; gender, 32; misidentification for handgame, 63, 339n8; Navajo, 16, 26; oral traditions, 24

Mooney, James, (ethnologist), 18; Arapaho handgame, 20; Kiowa handgame, 16, 30–31, 78–79, 90–92; handgame songs, 77, 347n24; Kiowa Underwater Monster, 58;

INDEX

Kiowa-Plains Apache match, 95–96, 343n45

Mopope, Jeanette Berry (Plains Apache—Kiowa), 121

Mopope, Stephen (Kiowa): handgames at home, 115, 121, 308; handgame set of, 121

Monetatchi, Edgar (Comanche), 163

Monte (card game), 52, 101, 104, 107–10, 344n105. *See also* card games

Native American Church, 7, 22, 52; Apache meetings, 90; handgame 115, 185, 280–81; Kiowa meetings, 115; prison, 300–301; rattles in, 126; traditional culture, 104, 295, 326, 332–33

Native American games: classifications of, 3–5, 11–13, 288; sacred association with gambling, 23, 25; studies of, 5–8, 45–53

Navajo Indians: gambling, 36, 43; moccasin game, 26; songs and prayer, 347n24; taboos, 14–16

Neconie, George "Chicken" (Kiowa): hiding ability, 273

Nestell, Sadie (Kiowa), 115

Northern Cheyenne: 237, 331; songs, 138; Crow intermarriage, 203; Crow tournament 224, 232, 235; dress, 227; lengthy game, 207; therapeutics, 299; versus Kiowa, 236

Okanagan/Oakinacken Indians: handgame and gambling, 26, 41

Old Bear, Robert (Comanche/Cheyenne), 261

Old Bear, Jenny Chanate (Kiowa), 261, 268

Old Coyote, Barney Jr. (Crow), 200

Old Coyote, Henry (Crow), 200

Old Horn, Henry "Sargie" (Crow): handgame medicine, 209

Oklahoma oil boom (1980s), 251–52

Oklahoma City Pow Wow Club, 147, 327

Oklahoma Indians (handgame team), 261–63, 271

Oklahoma State Handgame Tournament, 142, 149–53, 184, 247, 251, 272, 280; origin, 149, 269; other tribes, 31; prizes and fees, 271; public school tournament, 304; winners, 320

Omaha Indians handgame, 300; War Dance, 22, 94

Osage handgame, 29, 31; 1937 visit to Kiowa, 114; origins, 338n7; style, 241

Otoe handgame, 105

Oyebi, Collier (Kiowa), 161

Paiute handgame, 14, 15, medicine and power, 343n80

Pappio, Buddy, 263

Pappio, Nell (Kiowa), 123

Pawnee handgame, 253; betting, 38, 41; Comanche, 82; ethnic maintenance, 50; fight with Arapaho, 90, 93; gambling, 42; Ghost Dance handgame of, 20–21, 46–50, 78, 105; Indian agent, 105; painting, 340n20; religious components, 281; scouts, 110; sports of, 30; tipis, 340n13; versus Cheyenne, 71; versus Kiowa, 64, 78; versus southwest Oklahoma teams, 241; visit to Kiowa, 114; warfare analogy, 48–49; Wichita-Pawnee visit, 337n1

Pewenofkit, Major (Plains Apache), 89, 116

Piegan/Blackfoot handgame: account of, 27; betting, 38; Crow clan, 236; games, 28, 30; lengthy games, 41; military societies, 30, 39

Plains Apache handgame: 84–90; animals, 84–85; box suppers, 90; changes, 88, 90; cheating in, 85–88;

Daveko, 95–101; hand motions, 158; locations 88–89; medicine, 94; medicine bundles and taboos, 85–86; midwinter encampments, 104; name of, 84–85; *Nistcre* / Rock Monster stories, 58–61, 85, 239n.5; old style of play (4-4-4), 86–87, 98; origins, 26, 58–62; public contests, 94–101; reservation era, 103–104; rules, 86–87; songs, 133–34; term for medicine, 94; terminology, 91–92. *See also* Kiowa handgame; Comanche handgame

Plateau Culture Area: handgame, 32–37

Poe, Barbara (Kiowa), 327

Poe, Joe (Kiowa), 327

Ponca Indians handgame: 21, 24, 31, 114, 248, historical account of 26–27; style of, 241

power. *See* handgame; Kiowa handgame

powwows, 2, 6, 36, 90, 244–45; circuit, 269; class I gaming, 287; concessions,141, 153; deaths, 202; drinking, 182; giveaways, 193; identity, 326; increase, 120, 324; newspaper column, 320; participation, 311; prisons, 300–302, 306; protective medicine, 210; social network, 295; songs, 136; suppression, 106, 113; therapeutic qualities, 287; traditional activity, 326–27; women's roles, 329; witchcraft, 352n84; youth, 241

Pueblo Bonito Site: archaeological finds, 24

Querdebitty, Jed (Plains Apache/Comanche), 248, 257, 260

Quoetone, Guy (Kiowa), 78, 107, 344n95; agency policeman, 109–11; bets, 104; collecting debts, 112; gambling, 104, 109–12; grass payments,107; police raids, 110–11

Red Bone Dance Ground (Plains Apache), 89

Red Earth Festival, Oklahoma City: handgame tournament, 146–48, 154, 247, 252, 262, 269–70, 272, 290, 294, 305, 327

Riverton Culture, 24

rock-paper-scissors strategy, 349n98

round robin tournaments, 145–48

Saddleblanket, Louise (Plains Apache), 85, 108

Salish. *See* Coast Salish

Sankadota, Jasper (Kiowa): Oklahoma/Southern style of play, 122; two-finger guess, 163

Satepauhoodle, Edgar (Kiowa), 115

Scott, Captain Hugh L. (cavalry officer), 63, 339n8

Shady Front (Yellowhair family handgame site), 149, 197, 263–64

Shield, Jeremy (Crow/Lakota), 320; collegiate play, 305; Crow style dress, 201, 237; Crow tournaments, 237; family and kinship, 237; favorite aspects, 237; ghosts/spirits, 199, 240; hiding, 221; Missouri State University, 314; philosophy of play, 240; team, 260

shinny, 49, 104, 106, 110, 344n95

slahal (stickgame),14; archaeological interpretation, 24; music, 33, 127; studies of 32, 50, 346n20; therapeutic qualities, 300. *See also* bone game; stickgame

sleight of hand (legerdemain), 1, 6, 29, 69–72, 94–101, 274; ability of doctors and shaman, 92; Dogrib, 33; Kiowa, 69–70, 94–95, 94–101, 177–78; Plains Apache, 95–101; Yakama 35. *See also* handgame; Kiowa handgame; Plains Apache handgame

Smokey, Enoch (Kiowa), 111

INDEX

Southern/Oklahoma Style handgame. *See* Kiowa handgame

spirit, in handgame. *See* handgame

sports: academic studies, 2–5; ethnic maintenance, 50, 323–25; films, 4–5; Native participation, 304, 324, 355n95; political organization, 327, 331; rituals and magic, 278, 281–82

Spotted Horse and Red Bear (Crow): pipes and medicine, 200

Starr, Moses (Cheyenne), 257, 260

Stecker, Ernest (Kiowa Indian agency), 111

Stewart, Willie (Crow), 205; clan representation, 223

stickball: 45–46, 282; Cherokee, 214, 282, 324; Choctaw, 282, 324; ethnic maintenance, 323–24; medicine and power, 282; suppression of, 345n117

Stinchecum, C.V., (Kiowa Indian agency), 111

stickgame: western style of handgame, 14, 32–37. *See also slahal*; bone game

Tape-de-ah (Tépdéà̀ or Standing Sweat Lodge, Kiowa): aka. Jòáudà̀ udà̀ u or Handgame Medicine [Man], 94–95; noted handgame player, 94–95

Tofpi, Rogers (Kiowa), 115

Ton-au-kaut (Tónàuqàut or Rough Tailed, ie. Snapping Turtle, Kiowa), 100–101

Trobriand Islanders: cricket songs, 131; cricket and magic, 282; fishing and magic, 281

Troop L (7th Cavalry, Fort Sill), 110

Tsatoke, Roland (Kiowa), 299

Tsoodle, George (Kiowa), 114

Tsotaddle, Ed (Kiowa): as noted guesser, 168, 349n95

victory songs, 78, 86, 135, 201, 235

virtual handgame (online), 322

Walks Over Ice, Lewis (Crow): alcohol, 223; ethnic maintenance, 221, 240; excessive play, 200; hiding, 217; medicine man, 210; tells, 216

Watchetaker, George "Woogie" (Comanche), 255

Wermy, Del (Comanche): as guesser, 154

Weryackwe, Flora "Gussie" (Ft. Sill Apache-Comanche): team, 138, 257, 261; all-female team, 138

White Fox (Kiowa): Armistice Day encampments, 114, 120

White Wolf, Howard (Comanche), 81

Wichita Indians handgame: 9, 26, 51, 94, 101, 114, 124, 140, 186–187, 241, 270, 337n1, 340n13, 345n108; ethnography, 20–21; Wichita-Pawnee visit, 337n1

Wild Bunch (Bill Koomsa Jr's team): good singers, 296; hard to beat, 296; song of, 132; team, 257, 262

Williamson, Virgil (Crow), 147

winning songs. *See* victory songs

witchcraft and sorcery: definition, 280–81

Yakama handgame: betting, 37, 38, 445; cards, 106; contemporary play, 53; encampments, 35–36; Fourth of July games, 16; imprisonment for gambling, 105–106; intertribal play, 31, 36; power, 93; songs, 38; study of, 50

Yeahquo, Alan (Kiowa), 8, 304

Yellowhair, Anthony Ace (Kiowa/Plains Apache), 243, 306, 344n91; Crow songs, 197; enjoyment, 312; familiarity of teams, 253; guessing,

171; handgame programs, 304; head guesser, 224; singing, 137, 296, 312; SpongeBob drum, 126; supplemental income, 254; Shady Front, 264; team names, 263; therapeutic qualities, 296; tournaments, 149

Yellowhair, Jack Asau (Kiowa), 8; bets, 251; changes in play, 145, 149, 155, 196, 251, 267; Crow songs, 196; Daffy Duck figure, 284; economic support, 142; drum making, 125–26; enjoyment, 142, 145, 196, 264, 267–69, 307, 311; facility rental, 140; floor bet story, 158; gambling, 149, 155, 158; handgame set, 122; handgame terminology, 265–66; hosting the Crows, 193, 197; introduction to handgame, 242–43; hand motions, 310; new style of play, 123, 125; old style of play, 125; powwows, 244; 247; Shady Front, 263–64; singing, 130, 243, 311; social aspects, 313, 327; song composition, 132–33, 136–37; sportsmanship, 332; strategy, 175; success, 306–14; teams, 257, 260–62; therapeutic qualities, 297–98; tournament sponsorship, 302–303; youth involvement, 267, 327; zebra drum, 126

Yellowhair, Jackie Ray (Kiowa/Plains Apache): 2021 tournament, 253; betting, 254; 323; birthday handgame, 303; Buzzard Creek Three, 305–306; changes, 323; enjoyment, 303, 332; extended kinship, 295; generosity, 141; "handgame immersion," 241–42; handgame longevity, 327–28; handgame programs, 304; Missouri State University, 314; money, 254; Native American Church, 115, 332; Plains Apache song, 134; preservation, 328, 332; raffles, 141; singing, 299; social media, 322; songs, 304, 328; supplemental income, 254; therapeutic qualities, 299; virtual handgames, 322; youth participation, 241–42, 304, 328; youth tournaments, 303–304

Yellowhair, Jeremy (Kiowa/Plains Apache), 253

Yellowhair, Lela "Doll," (Kiowa/Plains Apache), 242, 312

Yellowhair, Leland (Kiowa/Plains Apache), 243

Yellowhair, Lydia Meat (Comanche-Kiowa), 253, 296

Zo-Tam (Kiowa): ledger art, 58